The Law of Reputation and Brands in the Asia Pacific

Efforts to expand the scope of legal protection given to reputation and brands in the Asia Pacific region have led to considerable controversy. Written by a variety of experts, the chapters in this book consider the developing law of reputation and brands in a fraught area.

ANDREW T. KENYON is a professor of law and Deputy Dean at the Melbourne Law School, University of Melbourne, where he is also Joint Director of the Centre for Media and Communications Law.

NG-LOY WEE LOON is a professor at the National University of Singapore Law Faculty and the Director of its LLM (IP and Technology) programme.

MEGAN RICHARDSON is a professor of law at the Melbourne Law School, University of Melbourne, where she is also Joint Director of the Centre for Media and Communications Law, and Associate Director – Law of the Intellectual Property Research Institute of Australia.

Cambridge Intellectual Property and Information Law

As its economic potential has rapidly expanded, intellectual property has become a subject of front-rank legal importance. *Cambridge Intellectual Property and Information Law* is a series of monograph studies of major current issues in intellectual property. Each volume contains a mix of international, European, comparative and national law, making this a highly significant series for practitioners, judges and academic researchers in many countries.

A list of books in the series can be found at the end of this volume.

The Law of Reputation and Brands in the Asia Pacific

Edited by

Andrew T. Kenyon, Ng-Loy Wee Loon and Megan Richardson

CAMBRIDGE
UNIVERSITY PRESS

CAMBRIDGE UNIVERSITY PRESS
Cambridge, New York, Melbourne, Madrid, Cape Town,
Singapore, São Paulo, Delhi, Mexico City

Cambridge University Press
The Edinburgh Building, Cambridge CB2 8RU, UK

Published in the United States of America by Cambridge University Press, New York

www.cambridge.org
Information on this title: www.cambridge.org/9781107017726

First published 2012

Printed in the United Kingdom at the University Press, Cambridge

A catalogue record for this publication is available from the British Library

Library of Congress Cataloguing in Publication data
The law of reputation and brands in the Asia Pacific / edited by Andrew T. Kenyon, Ng-Loy Wee Loon and Megan Richardson.
p. cm.
Includes bibliographical references and index.
ISBN 978-1-107-01772-6
1. Brand name products – Law and legislation – Asia. 2. Brand name products – Law and legislation – Pacific Area. 3. Reputation (Law) 4. Libel and slander. 5. Names, Personal – Law and legislation. I. Kenyon, Andrew T. II. Ng-Loy, Wee Loon. III. Richardson, Megan.
K1559.L39 2012
346.04′8 – dc23 2011049111

ISBN 978-1-107-01772-6 Hardback

Contents

Notes on the contributors

ELIZABETH ADENEY is an associate professor of law at Deakin University, Melbourne and has published widely on copyright and moral rights law – in Australia, Canada, the UK and Germany. She is the author of a treatise *The Moral Rights of Authors and Performers* (2006) and of the Australian chapter in Gillian Davies and Kevin Garnett (eds.), *Moral Rights* (2010).

CHRISTOPH ANTONS holds a chair in law at Deakin University, Melbourne. He is a chief investigator in the Australian Research Council Centre of Excellence for Creative Industries and Innovation (CCI) and an Adjunct Research Fellow at the Max Planck Institute for Intellectual Property and Competition Law in Munich. His recent book publications include the edited collections *Traditional Knowledge, Traditional Cultural Expressions and Intellectual Property Law in the Asia-Pacific Region* (2009); *The Enforcement of Intellectual Property Rights: Comparative Perspectives from the Asia-Pacific Region* (2011).

GRAEME AUSTIN holds the Chair in Private Law at Victoria University of Wellington, and is also a professor of law at the Melbourne Law School, University of Melbourne. His most recent book is *Human Rights and Intellectual Property: Mapping the Global Interface* (with Laurence Helfer, Cambridge University Press, 2011). He is an elected member of the American Law Institute.

MELISSA DE ZWART is an associate professor at the Adelaide Law School, the University of Adelaide and a Member of the Commonwealth Attorney-General's Classification Review Board. Prior to joining academia, she was Legal Manager at CSIRO, advising on protection and commercialisation of intellectual property. Her key areas of research interests include copyright, technology and contractual communities.

SUSY FRANKEL is a professor of law at Victoria University of Wellington, New Zealand and Co-Director of the New Zealand Centre of International Economic Law. Her main research and teaching interests are in intellectual property law, traditional knowledge and international trade law. She is a member of the Editorial Board of the *Journal of World Intellectual Property Law* and *Queen Mary Journal of Intellectual Property*. She has also held the position of an Assistant Commissioner of Trade Marks, Patents and Designs for the Intellectual Property Office of New Zealand. Susy was consultant expert to the Waitangi Tribunal on the WAI 262 flora, fauna and cultural intellectual property claim.

CHRISTINE GREENHALGH is Emeritus Professor of Applied Economics, University of Oxford, and Emeritus Fellow of St Peter's College, Oxford. She continues to be active in IP research and is the Economics Research Director of the Oxford Intellectual Property Research Centre, and a Research Associate of IPRIA. Her textbook with Mark Rogers entitled *Innovation, Intellectual Property and Economic Growth* (2010) appeals to students of economics, business and law. She has recently contributed to several research reports for the UK IP Office, including studies of IP use and enforcement in small and medium firms, of trade marks and firm performance, and of IP and market structure.

VICKI HUANG is currently a lecturer at the Deakin Law School. Prior to joining the Deakin Law School, Vicki was a research associate to Justice Finkelstein at the Federal Court of Australia and has had several years of practice in intellectual property law in Australia and the US. Her research focus is on interdisciplinary research into all aspects of intellectual property.

ANDREW T. KENYON is a professor of law and Deputy Dean at the Melbourne Law School, Joint Director of the CMCL and an editor of the *Media and Arts Law Review*. His publications include *New Dimensions in Privacy Law* (co-edited with Megan Richardson, 2006) and *Landmarks in Australian Intellectual Property Law* (co-edited with Megan Richardson and Sam Ricketson, Cambridge University Press, 2009).

KHAW LAKE TEE is a professor at the Faculty of Law of the University of Malaya. She is the author of the book *Copyright Law in Malaysia* (3rd edn, 2008). Her teaching and research interests and experience are in intellectual property, land and information technology.

KWANGHUI LIM is an associate professor at Melbourne Business School and Associate Director of IPRIA. Kwanghui's research explores the strategies used by firms to manage intellectual property and the commercialisation process. Recent papers include a study on the use of 'knowledge brokering' by biotechnology start-ups (with David Hsu, Wharton) and the impact of corporate acquisitions on the productivity of inventors (with Rahul Kapoor, INSEAD). Prior to joining Melbourne Business School, Kwanghui was an assistant professor at the National University of Singapore.

JANICE LUCK is a senior lecturer at Melbourne Law School, University of Melbourne, and has taught trade marks and designs law on the Melbourne law master's for many years. She was until recently a special counsel at DLA Phillips Fox and has been a member of the Intellectual Property Committee of the Law Council of Australia since 1985.

NG-LOY WEE LOON is a professor at the National University of Singapore Law Faculty and Director of its LLM (IP and Technology) programme. Her publications on intellectual property law include *Intellectual Property Law of Singapore* (2008); 'An Interdisciplinary Perspective on the Likelihood of Confusion: Consumer Psychology and Trademark Infringement in an Asian Society' (2008) in *Trademark Reporter*; and 'Trademark Protection for Personalities and Characters', in Grosheide and Brinkhof (eds.), *Intellectual Property Law: Articles on Crossing Borders between Traditional and Actual* (2005). Wee Loon is a member of the Board of Governors of the IP Academy, Singapore.

DON O'SULLIVAN joined the Melbourne Business School in 2008 from University College Cork, Ireland. Don's principal academic interest is in the impact of marketing activities on company performance. His research has been published in the *European Journal of Marketing*, and the *Journal of Marketing* among others, and his case studies on technology marketing are taught in business schools across Europe. Previously, Don was Client Services Director at a marketing services agency targeting the European technology sector. In this role he was responsible for a range of blue-chip clients. His team developed numerous international award-winning campaigns including a global ECHO award and two Icon Awards from *BusinessWeek*.

MEGAN RICHARDSON is a professor at the Melbourne Law School, and is currently a Director of the CMCL and Associate Director of IPRIA. Primarily an intellectual property and privacy lawyer, she is a co-author (with Sam Ricketson and Mark Davison) of an Australian casebook on intellectual property and has previously co-edited collections of essays including (with Andrew Kenyon) *New Dimensions in Privacy Law* (Cambridge University Press, 2006) and (with Andrew Kenyon and Sam Ricketson), *Landmarks in Australian Intellectual Property Law* (Cambridge University Press, 2009).

SAM RICKETSON is a professor of law at the Melbourne Law School and also practises part-time as a barrister at the Victorian Bar, principally in the area of intellectual property. He is a Fellow of the Academy of Social Sciences of Australia. Sam has written, taught and advised widely across all areas of intellectual property law, both nationally and internationally, and is currently a panel member of the World Intellectual Property Organization's dispute resolution body in relation to domain names.

DAVID TAN is currently an assistant professor at the National University of Singapore Law Faculty. He is also an accomplished fine-art fashion photographer, having published a coffee-table book *Visions of Beauty* (2000) in association with Versace, and *Tainted Perfection* (2003) in collaboration with Cartier in Singapore. David was formerly with the Singapore Administrative Service, serving as Director of Sports at MCYS and Director of International Talent at MOM. In the area of law, he has published in a diverse range of journals including the *Cardozo Arts and Entertainment Law Journal*, *Yale Journal of International Law*, *Harvard Human Rights Journal* and *Media and Arts Law Review*.

TAY PEK SAN is an associate professor at the Faculty of Law of the University of Malaya. She is the author of the book *Protection of Well-Known Trade Marks in Malaysia* (2007) and several articles on intellectual property. Her teaching and research interests are in trade mark law, IP law and contract law.

KIMBERLEE WEATHERALL is an associate professor at the Sydney Law School of the University of Sydney. She specialises in intellectual property law with particular focus on interdisciplinary empirical research into intellectual property law court and administrative proceedings, and the interaction between intellectual property and international law. Her recent publications include 'Patent infringement in Australia: Results from a survey', in the *Federal Law Review* (with Beth Webster); 'ACTA as a New Kind of International Lawmaking', in the *American University Journal of International Law* and 'Of Copyright Bureaucracies and Incoherence: Stepping Back from Australia's Recent Copyright Reforms', in the *Melbourne University Law Review*.

BETH WEBSTER, an economist, is the Director of IPRIA and a professorial research fellow at the Melbourne Institute of Applied Economic and Social Research (University of Melbourne). Her recent publications include 'Patent Infringement in Australia: Results from a Survey', in *Federal Law Review* (with Kimberlee Weatherall); 'Do Patents Matter for Commercialization?', in *Journal of Law and Economics* (with Paul Jensen); 'Misclassification in Patent Offices', in *Review of Economics and Statistics* (with Alfons Palangkaraya and Paul Jensen).

PETER K. YU holds the Kern Family Chair in Intellectual Property Law and is the founding director of the Intellectual Property Law Center at Drake University Law School, USA. He is also a Wenlan Scholar Chair Professor at Zhongnan University of Economics and Law in Wuhan, China. In the summer, he has served as a visiting professor of law at the University of Hong Kong Faculty of Law. Born and raised in Hong Kong, Professor Yu is a leading expert in international intellectual property and communications law, a prolific scholar and an award-winning teacher.

Foreword

Because they interfere with creativity in the name of promoting creativity, intellectual property rights are perennially puzzling. But no law is as mystifying as the legal doctrines that recognise exclusive rights in brand names and celebrity reputations. Copyrights and patents protect finite advances – a book, a song, an invention – that are directly attributable to a particular innovator or team. The rights endure for limited periods of time. They can be critical to protecting those who invest in innovation from free riders. Trade mark law is somewhat more problematic. Protection lasts indefinitely. The audience can play as important a role as the producer in vesting marks with meaning and value. But classically, trade mark law has a benchmark: it is triggered when unauthorised use creates a likelihood of consumer confusion. Furthermore, recognising trade mark protection serves clear public purposes: the exclusive right to a mark lowers consumer search costs and gives producers incentives to maintain quality.

The protection of brands and reputations is quite different. It is fraught with all of the problems of trade mark law – value resides partly in the eyes of the beholder and the right can endure forever. Here, however, the nature and boundaries of the advance are unclear and the social value of the protection is ambiguous. The underlying rationale appears, as in trade marks, to depend on a search–cost idea – the notion that if the consumer likes the way that X does A, then she will be equally pleased with the way it does B. But why should Calvin Klein's underwear be as nice as its outerwear? What does Ashton Kutcher really know about cameras? Is George Clooney genuinely a specialist in watches and cars; coffee and liquor? Isn't it misleading to imply that the competence of a company or a celebrity transcends the core business in which that company or celebrity is engaged? Instead of dispelling consumer confusion, these rights appear aimed at fomenting it.

There are other problems as well. Celebrities do not need incentives to invest in their own reputations. Brand protection can stifle competition, for the stronger the carry-over value of an old mark in a new market, the harder it is for other enterprises to enter that market and compete. More disturbingly, the criminal docket suggests that when some people say they'd 'kill' to own a particular brand, they come close to really meaning it. Nor do rights over brands and reputation have obvious jurisprudential roots. They borrow from the theories that animate the laws of trade mark, unfair competition, privacy, defamation and copyright. Or, as suggested in this volume, perhaps the impulse to protect derives from morality, religion, romance or magic.

Yet, clearly, branding is of growing significance to business enterprises. It has given birth to its own industry, bred a cadre of specialists, and convinced many a court. The strategy is spreading to all parts of the globe; it's been taken up by those who wish to protect the images of foodstuffs, artisanal products and traditional knowledge. Hence, the importance of this book. Since reputations transcend national boundaries, global harmonisation is highly desirable. But before international rules can be developed, the scope of the right needs more precise delineation. Its justifications need to be identified and examined critically. The costs and benefits of protecting brands and celebrity reputations must be compared in earnest and the contours of the right must be tailored to balance the needs of commerce against the social costs of privatising new swaths of the knowledge ecosystem.

This book takes an interdisciplinary approach to these questions, collecting the knowledge of experts in business, economics, law and cultural studies; professors and practitioners; doctrinalists, theoreticians, historians and empiricists. Most intriguingly, it focuses on the Asia Pacific, a region of increasing commercial importance, but whose law is largely unknown elsewhere; a region where legal doctrine is influenced by the United States and Europe, but leavened by such diverse sources as Islam, Confucius and traditional practice. These materials examine branding and reputation law in places where it is emerging (Indonesia, Malaysia, Hong Kong, Singapore) in light of the experience of countries where it is of longer standing while still evolving (the United States, Australia, New Zealand). The book illuminates the range of policy choices available. As such, it is sure to influence the shape of the ultimate transnational regime.

ROCHELLE COOPER DREYFUSS
Pauline Newman Professor of Law
New York University School of Law
New York, June 2011

Editors' preface

Trade marks – or brands as they are popularly known – can be extremely valuable intangible assets, not just in the Asia Pacific. The rights conferred by trade mark law together with other forms of legal protection are considerable, and firms have sought to exploit these to bolster their creative strategies designed to build and foster relationships with consumers and other audiences. Not surprisingly, they look to law to protect against attack by others when self-help measures seem inadequate for the purpose. At the same time, individuals who trade on their reputation have sought to establish allied forms of legal protection – extending the trope of the 'personality' of a brand to their own personal attributes which they may treat more or less as brands in their professional lives. In addition, individuals may draw on the powerful metaphor of privacy as a further rhetorical device to demand legal protection of their personalities against a diverse range of personal attacks by others in situations when the language of brands seems less appropriate or persuasive. This of course is not to deny that for many if not most people, privacy and personality have significant human dimensions, taking their functions beyond the commercial. Sometimes we even see 'analogous' reasoning extended to commercial brands, with traders now arguing that not merely commercial but more 'personal' features of their brands are under threat if law does not intervene to provide yet further protection against, for instance, dilution by blurring or tarnishment of the brand, or taking advantage of the brand's distinctiveness or reputation. These arguments further challenge existing efforts to measure the value of a brand and the impact on a brand of competitive and other conduct, leading us to wonder about the use of scientific measures in the increasingly non-positivistic field of trade mark law. Most recently (in this part of the world) a range of other groups have begun to insist that their rights over their signs and symbols should be recognised by law, arguing that these have distinct cultural significance, serving as markers of the group's personality as well as commercial value. On the other hand, all these extended forms of behaviour and attempts to enlarge the scope of legal protection have attracted considerable controversy, due to the severe limits these behaviours and laws may impose on competition and free speech and more specifically on the creativities and personalities of others.

What then makes the Asia Pacific distinctive in its response to these issues and controversies? For one thing it is more commercially and culturally diverse than other parts of the world, even if there is a common interest and history in engaging in international trade (especially among countries of the former British Empire). And the trade mark and other intellectual property laws that we are talking about are often newer there. Therefore rights may be less entrenched and more able perhaps to be contested. As the French sociologist Alexis de Tocqueville wrote in relation to his America field study in the 1830s:

> Generally men become attached to a right or feel respect for it because of either its importance or the long period over which it has been in force. Such individual rights as are found in democracies are usually unimportant or of very recent date or impermanent. As a result they are often given up without trouble and almost always violated without remorse.[1]

De Tocqueville spoke as a former European coloniser staring at a part of the new world that was growing in power and authority, was not like Europe or Britain in important ways, and was showing its independence. Now Europe (including the United Kingdom) and the United States are staring at the 'new world' of the South. Moreover, in the same way as France and Britain's relations with America were reshaped in the nineteenth century by the previous century's wars so relations between the United States and other parts of the Asia Pacific are now being rewritten by the conflicts of the current and immediate past century, in ways that are not yet completely clear and with the future even more fluid and unpredictable.

This lack of clarity and predictability is also relevant to our project. There is a substantial and growing body of high-quality writing around the law of reputation and brands in the United Kingdom and more broadly Europe as well as the United States, including in other books in the Cambridge Intellectual Property and Information Law Series. In contrast, far less is known – certainly of a scholarly reflective character – about the equivalent law of the Southern Asia Pacific. There is an important gap in knowledge here which this book seeks to address (or at least begin to address) with a range of linked essays written by scholars working

[1] Alexis de Tocqueville, *Democracy in America* (George Lawrence trans., JP Mayer (ed.), Anchor Books, Garden City, New York, 1969) 699 [trans. of: *De la Démocratie en Amérique*].

in the diverse specialisations of the typical modern academy, and mostly coming from the common law world. Primarily we are legal scholars and practitioners, in keeping with the book's focus on law. But we also include experts in economics, marketing and business strategy, whose contributions are designed to enlarge legal understandings.

The essays in this book have grown out of workshops held at the University of Melbourne and the National University of Singapore in January and June 2010 respectively. We are grateful to those who participated, as their questions and comments helped the authors of the papers that have ended up as chapters in this book to extend their knowledge and refine their ideas – and we are delighted that Rochelle Dreyfuss, who participated in the Melbourne workshop and offered many useful ideas, also generously agreed to write the Foreword. We are grateful also to our editorial assistant Oscar O'Bryan and to Vicki Huang who acted as editorial consultant for much of the project, as well as staff at the Melbourne Law School and NUS Law Faculty who assisted with the workshops. We also express our appreciation to the research and professional institutes which have made financial as well as specialised in-kind contributions to this project: the interdisciplinary Intellectual Property Research Institute of Australia (IPRIA) at the University of Melbourne, the Centre for Media and Communications Law (CMCL) at the Melbourne Law School, and the IP Academy in Singapore. Finally, we are grateful to the editors of the Cambridge Intellectual Property and Information Law Series and its referees for their advice and guidance and to our Commissioning Editor Kim Hughes for her patient and helpful support.

ANDREW T. KENYON
NG-LOY WEE LOON
MEGAN RICHARDSON
Melbourne and Singapore, June 2011

Part I

Trade marks and brands

1 What is the value of a brand to a firm?

Don O'Sullivan, Kwanghui Lim and Janice Luck

A brand for a company is like a reputation for a person. You earn reputation by trying to do hard things well.

Jeff Bezos, founder and CEO of Amazon.com

I. Overview

Brands play a pivotal role in the marketing of goods and services and thus are valuable assets. For example, Interbrand, a management consultancy, estimates the value of the world's top brands in 2010 to be worth US$70 billion (Coca-Cola), US$65 billion (IBM), US$61 billion (Microsoft) and US$44 billion (Google).[1] For many leading firms, the value of its brands is a significant proportion of the firm's overall market value. Hence, brands are a tremendously important intangible asset to firms.

This chapter provides three different perspectives on the importance of brands as assets to firms – from a marketing perspective, from a strategic management perspective and from a legal perspective. The first and second perspectives focus on the value and use of brands within firms, while the third perspective focuses on the extent to which the law protects these uses and values.

II. Brands and reputation, a marketing perspective

Within marketing, a brand is viewed as a name, sign or symbol that delineates one product as being unique from others in the market.[2] Delineating a product, within the mind of the customer, as being unique is a critical precondition for firms to be able to secure channel access and support,

[1] Interbrand, *Best Global Brands Ranking for 2010* (2011), www.interbrand.com/en/best-global-brands/best-global-brands-2008/best-global-brands-2010.aspx.

[2] See, for example, American Marketing Association, *Dictionary* (2011) www.marketingpower.com/_layouts/Dictionary.aspx.

charge a premium price, build and maintain customer loyalty and ultimately enhance the profitability of the firm. In this regard, brands are clearly valuable and firms seek to build brand value (also referred to as 'brand equity') through their marketing activities.

To facilitate our discussion, it is useful to consider the process by which brands are built (hereafter, 'branding'), why brands are valuable and how firms look to utilise this value. One way of thinking about a brand is as conveying a promise that the firm makes to potential customers. The assumption underpinning this perspective on branding is that in choosing between brands, consumers seek to maximise their expected satisfaction or utility. Thus they are drawn to those brands that make the most attractive promise. In a competitive marketplace, where consumers face a myriad of brand choices in any given category, firms try to ensure that their brand makes a uniquely attractive promise of satisfaction. The attractiveness of a brand promise may extend to the market as a whole, or more commonly to a specific group, or segment of the market. For example, a brand promise may appeal particularly to young males (Axe deodorant), or price conscious families (Walmart). The brand promise may focus on functional benefits (Dyson vacuum cleaners), emotional benefits (Apple iPhones and iPads), symbolic benefits (Louis Vuitton handbags) or in many cases a combination of all three.[3]

Typically, brand builders look to establish a unique promise – or at least a promise that is uniquely believable. Uniqueness and believability become key concerns for the marketer. On the issue of uniqueness, marketers usually focus on establishing what their brands will offer in terms of points of differentiation and points of parity. Taking points of differentiation first, products/services (offerings) will typically have multiple features and benefits. Many of these will not be exclusive to any given brand. Cars, for example, have multiple common features that come readily to mind: internal combustion engine, steering wheel, electric windows, power steering, etc. Therefore, in building a car brand, it is of limited benefit to focus on features and benefits that are common to all brands of car – instead marketing focuses on emphasising the attributes where the brands have unique advantages or where they can claim unique advantages. Turning to points of parity, typically a provider will struggle to credibly claim superiority on all possible dimensions of an offering. However, firms will commonly need to be able to claim parity (with competitors) on performance dimensions that are important to the

[3] For an extended discussion, see Sicco van Gelder, *Global Brand Strategy: Unlocking Brand Potential across Countries, Cultures and Markets* (Kogan Page, London, 2005).

customer. Often these points of parity are, in turn, claimed as points of differentiation by the competition.

A typical example of the battles that brands wage in claims of parity and differentiation can be seen in the branding activities of Apple and Microsoft in the personal computing market. Since the launch of the Apple Mac in 1984 Apple has positioned its brand as being less corporate, more creative and more personal than Microsoft-powered personal computers (PCs). In parallel, Microsoft and its hardware partners have tended to position the PC as the ultimately efficient and reliable computing solution. In 2006 Apple began a sustained campaign to pointedly highlight the brand's unique points of differentiation – creativity and personality over its more corporate and sedate competitor.[4] In doing so, Apple sought to build its brand equity while simultaneously diminishing the attractiveness of the PC alternative. This enhancement of the Apple brand and simultaneous diminishment of PCs is largely unavoidable given that in this instance the consumer is limited to two broad choices – Apple or PC. In response, Microsoft on the launch of its operating system in 2009, focused on demonstrating with their 'I'm a PC' campaign how Microsoft-supported PCs appeal to 'creative' people. While the situation is in this regard extreme, it does help to draw our attention to an essential element of branding – brands exist as competing promises – because customers assess promises against one another.

The perspective that brands are about making promises is helpful in understanding the role brands play in ensuring that a product is chosen from, for example, a crowded supermarket shelf. Promise-making is, however, but one component of brands and brand building. Equally important is the notion of promise-keeping. As consumers tend to evaluate both the attractiveness and credibility of brand promises, failure to deliver on a given promise or promises may result in high levels of customer dissatisfaction, low levels of repeat purchase (or loyalty) and a lower likelihood that the customer will buy other products carrying this brand. In this respect, failure to deliver on the brand promise may be seen as an erosion of value, or, in extreme cases the creation of a brand liability, at least with respect to the firm's ability to engage with dissatisfied customers.

When brand promises are delivered, then the firm may benefit through increased customer loyalty, lower price sensitivity, higher propensity to trial new products and higher levels of product endorsement or word-of-mouth referral. Brands might then justifiably be said to have a value or

[4] To see examples of this campaign: YouTube, Buy a Mac (15 Ads in 1 Pack) HQ (14 October 2007) www.youtube.com/watch?v=C5z0Ia5jDt4.

equity attached to them. An indication of the growing interest in brand value is the emergence over the last decade of a range of providers offering brand valuation services that put a dollar amount on the equity tied up in a brand.[5] Typically, these service providers apply a valuation mode that discounts future revenues and profits based on current expectations. The emergence of these service providers is in part a response to the void left by global accounting standards, where brand values are, in most circumstances omitted from the firm's balance sheet.[6]

Firms that have successfully built brand equity are typically concerned with issues of protection and utilisation. Protection normally relates to ensuring that the promise continues to be articulated to the market or target market and the relevance of the promise is maintained in light of market changes. Utilisation is concerned with fully realising the potential value of the brand – by optimising the price charged, bringing new offerings to the market under the brand name, extending market share, building customer loyalty or introducing the brand to new markets. In sum, brand value, or reputational value, is influenced by the awareness and trust customers have in the brand's promise and the firm's success in leveraging that value.

For many firms in developed markets, brand value accounts for much if not most of the total value of the firm. The growing importance of brand and reputational value as a portion of overall value is a relatively recent phenomenon, driven in part by the shift in emphasis from industrial to service economies and in part by the trend towards outsourcing of production. Think, for example, of the value of a successful legal practice – and consider what portion of that value is likely to be bound up in the reputation of the firm, its associates and senior partners. Then consider the portion that is likely to be bound up in tangible assets such as premises, fixtures and fittings.

Some recent examples are useful to illustrate our consideration of brands and their value. First, consider the US firm Gillette. In 2005, the consumer goods company Procter & Gamble (P&G) acquired Gillette for US$57 billion. The Gillette acquisition gave P&G control over extremely valuable brands such as Gillette and Braun in the personal grooming market, and Duracell in the batteries market. It was therefore broadly welcomed by investors and P&G's share price appreciated after the acquisition. What is perhaps most interesting about the acquisition is

[5] See, for example, Brand Finance www.brandfinance.com and Interbrand www.interbrand.com.

[6] Roger Sinclair, 'The Importance of Brand Equity in Creating Firm Value', Prophet, www.prophet.com/downloads/whitepapers/sinclair-brand-equity-firm-value.pdf.

its scale. To put the US$57 billion acquisition price in context, it equates to approximately US$10 per person alive on the planet at the time. P&G justified the price of the transaction by citing the strength of the Gillette brand in particular.[7] Indeed Gillette is an excellent example of brand equity. It has high levels of brand awareness globally, high levels of channel support (Gillette is in the vast majority of retail outlets that it needs to be in) and crucially, Gillette enjoys very high levels of product loyalty coupled with low levels of price sensitivity. The portfolio of products offered under the Gillette brand ranges from disposable razors to premium-priced multi-blade shaving systems. This portfolio, which includes products for the male and the female markets, allows the firm to service a wide range of income groups in any market. For decades, the company has invested behind its brand promise. This investment is in the form of heavy expenditures on awareness-building marketing, high-profile endorsement with leading sports personalities, and continuous product innovation and upgrades. It is this latter activity – product upgrades – that has enabled Gillette to consistently deliver enhanced earnings from the brand year on year in spite of operating in a mature market that had limited ability to grow. At the time of the acquisition commentators noted that P&G could add further to the value of the brand through its distribution strength in emerging markets including China and the wider Asia Pacific region.[8]

Another notable example is Cadbury. In 2010, US food company Kraft (originally part of Philip Morris) acquired the UK chocolate manufacturer Cadbury. Again, this acquisition points to the value of brands. Cadbury, like Gillette has a brand that enjoys high levels of awareness and loyalty in many markets globally. While the deal (worth approximately US$19 billion) included the entire firm and not just the brand, the Cadbury brand was a critical – if not the most critical component of the deal. It is noticeable that in the period prior to the acquisition Cadbury had been aggressively cutting costs, closing factories and reducing the number of Cadbury employees. In other words, Cadbury was actively reducing the physical assets on its balance sheet. In the absence of these hard assets, we are left with intangible assets (mostly brands in this instance) and cash. What is perhaps most interesting about the Cadbury acquisition is the particular attributes of Cadbury's brand strength. First,

7 Nanette Byrnes, Robert Berner, Wendy Zellner and William C Symonds, 'Branding: Five New Lessons', *BusinessWeek* (online), 14 February 2005 www.businessweek.com/magazine/content/05_07/b3920042_mz011.htm.

8 See for example P&G press release at the time of the launch: 'P&G Acquires the Gillette Company' (28 January 2005) www.pginvestor.com/phoenix.zhtml?c=104574&p=irol-newsArticle&ID=871677&highlight=.

the firm's brands had a dominant position in the Asia Pacific region and in other emerging markets. While these markets tend to have lower per-capita consumption, they also tend to have higher growth and growth expectations associate(d) with them. Thus, dollars earned in these markets tend to be valued more highly by investors, as they are indicative of even greater future dollars. Second, Cadbury was a pure play confectionary company – all of Cadbury's revenues coming from chocolate, candy, gum, et cetera. These are products that enjoy higher levels of brand loyalty than, for example, ready meals and other food items where Kraft generated revenue. Reflecting this higher loyalty, Cadbury operated off a higher earnings multiple than Kraft.[9] In this respect, the Cadbury acquisition is a very telling example of the value created by brands.

A further interesting example is Glaceau. In 2007, Neville Isdell, the chief executive officer (CEO) of Coca-Cola, oversaw the acquisition of Glaceau, an eleven-year-old bottled-water company. Coca-Cola spent just over US$4 billion in cash for the purchase. The acquisition is remarkable for a number of reasons apart from the price paid. First, the Coca-Cola Company already had a portfolio of soft-drinks brands – including Coca-Cola, which is consistently rated as the most valuable brand in the world. Therefore, on the face of it, there would appear to have been little need for the company to pay such a large sum for yet another soft-drinks brand. Also, not only did the firm have widely recognised water brands of its own, it also had one of the strongest distribution operations in the market. However, in the years prior to its acquisition, Glaceau had enjoyed what analysts described as astronomical growth driven by the success of its brands Vitaminwater, Fruitwater, Smartwater and Vitaminenergy. Critically, from Coca-Cola's perspective, this growth was achieved in the enhanced-water and energy-drink categories, which were expected to grow significantly in the medium term. At the time of the acquisition, Coca-Cola justified its decision based on the firm's ability to add further to the value of the Glaceau brands by combining them with the firm's global distribution capability. In this regard it is notable to see how Glaceau has grown its global sales subsequent to the acquisition.[10]

While many high-profile brand acquisitions are used to gain access to emerging markets – including those in the Asia Pacific region, there are

[9] Earnings multiple is a measure of firm performance where the share price is expressed as multiple of current earnings.

[10] By 2009 Coca-Cola had achieved unit sales of 100 million for Glaceau. This represented a 33 per cent year-on-year volume growth. See for details: Coca-Cola Amatil, 'Annual Report: 2009' (14 May 2010) www.ccamatil.com/InvestorRelations/AnnualReports/2009/2009%20Annual%20Report.pdf.

also notable examples of regional competitors buying global brands. Perhaps most notable is the acquisition of IBM's PC operations (and related brands such as ThinkPad) by Chinese PC manufacturer Lenovo.[11] On the face of it, as a going concern, IBM's PC operations had little to recommend them as they were running at a yearly loss. However, motivated by a stated ambition to develop a global PC operation, Lenovo acquired IBM's PC operations for US$1.75 billion. It is interesting to note how Lenovo subsequently managed the IBM brand and the Lenovo brand in the PC market. In the first instance, Lenovo took great care to reassure IBM customers that little had changed and that they could be assured of continual product quality, service support and innovation. In effect, Lenovo began by investing to ensure that the IBM brand that it had acquired retained its reputation for quality PCs. Following this, in a deliberate strategy, Lenovo began to more clearly associate with the IBM and ThinkPad brand with the aim of benefiting from the brand association. Lenovo credits the IBM–ThinkPad association for much of its post-acquisition success in developing Lenovo as a global PC brand. Ultimately ThinkPad became a sub-brand of Lenovo once the transition period was completed.

A final interesting aspect of each of the acquisitions discussed above is that the acquiring firm clearly made the decision that it would be cheaper to buy the firm and its brands rather than create a competing brand. Thus, these examples help to focus attention on why brands are valuable. Channel support, customer loyalty, awareness and price premium, are difficult to achieve and difficult to imitate – thus the market for brands and brand-dominant firms.

III. Brands and reputation, strategic management

Apart from being important in marketing, brands are also important in strategic management, which refers to the overall management of a firm from the CEO's perspective. From this vantage point, a brand affects not just the firm's position in its marketplace, but also how internal resources are allocated and what signals are conveyed to competitors and collaborators.

The marketing promise that a brand makes represents part of the firm's strategic positioning in the marketplace. In the examples above,

[11] For a discussion of Lenovo's motivation, see Rhys Blakely, 'Interview: Yang Yuanqing, Lenovo chairman', *Sunday Times* (online), 28 August 2007 http://business.timesonline.co.uk/tol/business/industry_sectors/technology/article2341612.ece.

Microsoft positions itself as a software solution provider for desktop computers through its Microsoft Windows and Microsoft Office brands, while Apple positions itself as a boutique focusing on easy-to-use integrated solutions (iPhones, iPads, iMacs, etc.). Other players in the market pick different positions. Dell, for example, is a formidable low-cost competitor while Lenovo and Asus are increasingly viewed as notebook/laptop computer specialists. Positioning in the marketplace is important because it helps to avoid direct competition with other players: if every firm in the industry were to produce indistinguishable goods, this would lead to intense rivalry and it would drive prices and profits down for all firms.[12] From a strategic perspective it does not make sense for every firm to be identical to Apple or Cadbury or Coca-Cola, but that they aim to create value in unique ways, therefore enabling them to compete in ways other than through direct price competition.

Brands and internal strategic alignment

The importance of positioning goes beyond the promises conveyed to consumers by a firm's efforts at branding. It affects the internal allocation of resources within the firm because different brands imply different ways of creating value. This in turn affects the allocation of money, people, managerial attention and other resources within the firm.[13] It also means different kinds of capabilities have to be developed within each firm in order to generate the desired positional strength.

Consider for example two motorcycle companies, Honda and Ducati. Honda's strategy is to sell a large volume of motorcycles to the 'man in the street'. Honda is often credited for having created this market from scratch in the 1960s and 1970s through an aggressive marketing campaign.[14] For instance, in an early Honda advertisement, the reverend from a neighbourhood church is shown to ride enthusiastically on a Honda motorcycle.[15] In contrast to Honda, Ducati is a boutique Italian motorcycle manufacturer specialising in high-speed racing bikes.[16] Each unit is handcrafted and customised to the individual buyer's needs.

[12] See Joshua Gans, *Core Economics for Managers* (Thompson, South Melbourne, 2005).

[13] Robert E. Hoskisson, Michael A. Hitt and Duane Ireland, *Competing for Advantage* (South-Western/Thomson Learning, Mason, OH, 2004), ch. 4.

[14] Evelyn T. Christiansen and Richard Tanner Pascale, 'Honda (A)', Harvard Business School Case (23 August 1983).

[15] See YouTube, Classic Honda Commercial (26 November 2006) www.youtube.com/watch?v=Nz0L9PeGsHg.

[16] Jordan Mitchell and Bruno Cassiman, 'Ducati: in pursuit of magic (A)', Harvard Business School Case (27 October 2006).

While Honda bikes can be purchased for a couple of thousand dollars, Ducati machines are often in the US$10,000 to US$20,000 range per motorcycle.

What are the internal implications for the CEO of Honda versus Ducati? A firm such as Honda has to be organised for large-scale mass production, consistent with its goal of pursuing a large market share and a brand with broad appeal. Hence the source of Honda's competitive edge is the ability to produce a large number of motorcycles (millions of units per year), using the latest manufacturing and lean production techniques so that it can benefit from economies of scale and scope. Over the years, Honda has developed a strong capability in engine technology as well as producing bikes that are comfortable to ride; motorcycles that regular men and women can use as a basic form of transportation and that require little maintenance or skill to operate. In contrast to Honda, Ducati's approach of selling expensive racing bikes means it has to focus on a different set of internal capabilities. It produces only 30,000 to 40,000 motorcycles a year (much lower than Honda's output) and each is carefully built and tested by skilled engineers.[17] The experience of riding a Ducati is much more important than the engine itself. Ducati bikes generate a deep, throaty sound that their enthusiasts simply love. Ducati's designs are sleek and elegant. It invests heavily in research and development (R&D) to produce high-performance speed demons and as a result has won many racing championships. Ducati represents speed and Italian passion. In 2001, when it went through an important corporate turnaround, the CEO famously invested in building a Ducati museum rather than in upgrading factories.[18] When a customer buys a Ducati, he or she is buying into a heritage of racing excellence. Ducati now has an exclusive membership programme, which includes weekend racing events and factory tours for racing enthusiasts. This is expensive to operate but builds upon consumers' willingness to pay to be associated with its racing history and culture.

The link between branding and internal strategic capabilities is also apparent in other industries. As discussed above, Gillette is positioned as an innovative leader relative to most other 'unbranded' shavers. However, this means P&G must continue to invest heavily in R&D to sustain its position. Gillette's Mach3 line of razors introduced in 1998 cost the firm

[17] Ducati designs its own motorbikes, while a large amount of its manufacturing is outsourced to Italy's 'Engine Technology District', which also supplies to the like of Ferrari and Maserati.

[18] Giovanni Gavetti, 'Ducati', Harvard Business School Case (28 June 2001).

over US$750 million in R&D expenditure,[19] and future generations of shavers are likely to be at least as expensive to develop.

In the airline industry, there is an increasing distinction between full service airlines (such as Qantas and Singapore Airlines) versus low-cost airlines (such as Southwest Airlines, Jetstar and AirAsia).[20] The full-service airlines advertise themselves as premium brands and command higher ticket prices, but this also means that they are internally quite different than the low-cost carriers. Premium airlines invest heavily in hiring and training dedicated service staff and crew members. They allocate resources to create luxurious facilities and airport lounges, better meals and entertainment onboard, and they offer more generous salary packages to pilots. The branding also affects the type of aircraft they choose to utilise (for example, the new Airbus A380 with seats that recline into completely flat beds). Low-cost airlines look quite different inside, with basic staff training, functional airport facilities, simple or no meals onboard, less complex aircraft, etc.[21] Their main objective is low overheads and a quick turnaround so as to make a profit despite their low-ticket prices.

In theory, a firm could offer multiple brands to span these different positions in the market. This often works if the brands are complementary to one another. One example that is often cited is Toyota, which sells affordable brands such as the Corolla and Yaris, while also offering a luxurious high-end brand, the Lexus. However, multiple brands often lead to internal conflicts. In practice, there are very few firms that are able to develop diametrically opposing brands and be successful. One reason may be conflict in allocating resources internally. For example an airline that has both low-cost as well as premium brands will have to deal with internal tension because each of these businesses involves different sets of activities, facilities and people (as described above). Investing in different types of capabilities to support each type of business usually ends up in compromises that do not improve performance.[22] The firm would also have to deal with internal rivalry among its business units as they compete with one another for customers, for the CEO's attention, and for end-of-year bonuses. Conflicts with customers could also arise. For example, consider The Body Shop, a global cosmetics company known

19 Wikipedia, Gillette Mach 3 (10 March 2011) http://en.wikipedia.org/wiki/Gillette_Mach3.

20 For a good example, see Joan Enric Ricart and Daxue Wang, 'Now everybody can fly: AirAsia', Harvard Business School Case (26 May 2005).

21 For example, the case of Southwest Airlines is described in Michael Porter, 'What Is Strategy?' *Harvard Business Review* (November–December 1996) 61.

22 Pankaj Ghemawat and Jan W. Rivkin, 'Creating competitive advantage', Harvard Business School Case (25 January 1998).

for its social activism and policy against animal testing. Now, consider the hypothetical situation in which The Body Shop owns a brand (directly or through a subsidiary) that sells animal-tested products or that engages in poor labour practices. This would completely undermine its brand and possibly even lead to consumer protests. Less dramatically, if a firm such as Rolex or Ducati were to enter into making inexpensive mass-produced wristwatches or motorcycles respectively, this could lead to its core customers abandoning its higher-end products.

Brands and strategic signalling

Apart from their role in market positioning and focusing internal resources, brands are also used to send strategic signals to competitors, collaborators and other external parties.[23] This is because developing a brand involves costly, irreversible investments, and therefore represents a credible signal that a firm is being serious about a particular course of action. For instance, investing in a brand can be used by a firm to signal its intent to enter a particular market. For example, Apple's series of 'i-branded' products including the iPod, iPhone and iPad reflects a progression of products that map out its strategic expansion away from general computing into the consumer market for portable consumer devices. When Apple released the iPhone in particular, it gave a very clear message to firms such as Nokia and Motorola that their world would change for ever and that they would either have to accommodate its entry into the mobile communications market (maybe becoming an ally), or to fight back aggressively. In the Asia Pacific context, a number of firms are now signalling a strategic intent to broaden geographically into new markets by expanding their brands internationally, including firms such as Acer (Taiwan, electronics), Lenovo (China, computers), Jetstar (Australia, airline), Banyan Tree (Singapore, luxury resorts). In each of these cases, expanding a brand often involves significant strategic shifts and investments, both within the firm and through alliances and acquisitions.

Brands can also play a role as a credible defensive signal. By staking out a market position, the firm may be signalling to others that it intends to fight to defend that position.[24] For example the Australian airline Qantas owns a subsidiary Jetstar that serves the low-cost segment of the

[23] Tulin Erdem and Joffre Swait, 'Brand Equity as a Signalling Phenomenon' (1998) 7(2) *Journal of Consumer Psychology* 131.
[24] Nirmayla Kumar, 'Strategies to Fight Low-Cost Rivals', *Harvard Business Review* (December 2006) 104.

market. Whether Jetstar is better than other low-cost competitors such as Virgin Blue and Tiger Airways is a matter of debate among air travellers. However, one thing that is clear is that Jetstar sends a very strong signal to Qantas' rivals that it intends to defend the low-cost segment of the business. It also allows Qantas a mechanism by which to retaliate, so if other airlines begin to compete aggressively and attempt to capture customers from Qantas' premium full-service airline, Qantas can use its Jetstar operations to launch a counter-attack to keep them at bay. Singapore Airlines can employ a similar strategy because it owns Tiger Airways, another low-cost airline.

A firm's decisions to invest in certain brands (or not to invest in particular brands) also relate to its strategic intent more broadly. A good example is Google's recent decision to stop censoring internet search results for the China market.[25] By doing so, it went against the Chinese government's policy, and this led to it exiting the Chinese market for search engines. Google's concern was that it was vulnerable to hacking by perpetrators in China, and that it was not willing to act inconsistently with its corporate motto of 'do no evil'.[26] The departure of Google from China means it will forgo access to a lucrative and growing market for advertising revenue, its main area of business. However it also sends a signal to existing customers and partners in other markets, some of whom had begun to question Google's commitment to its stated corporate values. So perhaps what Google will lose in the Chinese market might be made up through increased customer loyalty elsewhere, but only time will tell. Google's actions, while surprising, are not entirely unusual. CEOs wake up each day thinking about how their brands tie in with their vision of the future, what it might mean to expose their brands to some markets and not to others, and how that would affect the firm's overall strategic direction and the kinds of investments that would be needed in order to deliver value.

Brands and partners' strategies

It should now be apparent that brands are not just important in themselves, but because the firm has to generate a coherent system of activities around the brand in order to generate value and deliver on the brand's promise. These activities can extend beyond the boundaries of the firm,

[25] David Drummond, A new approach to China (12 January 2010) Official Google Blog http://googleblog.blogspot.com/2010/01/new-approach-to-china.html.

[26] Brian Womack, Ari Levy and Mark Lee, 'Google may exit China after ending self-censorship', *Bloomberg* (online), 13 January 2010 www.bloomberg.com/apps/news?pid=newsarchive&sid=aU43JmiuDJaQ.

and in this case the brand may facilitate the firm's efforts to synchronise and motivate the efforts of external partners and collaborators. Apple's iPhone is not just a brand, but is also a development platform for an entire ecosystem of online services and an influential developer community. Apple's brand helped it to build early critical mass for the iPhone, which is important because the market for mobile devices exhibits 'network effects',[27] meaning that the larger the number of consumers using an Apple iPhone rather than some other mobile device, the more attractive it is for developers to build applications and content that make use of the Apple iPhone. This in turn makes it even more attractive for other consumers to buy an Apple iPhone, thereby creating a self-reinforcing cycle that benefits Apple. By building a community and momentum around a brand, Apple can shape the strategies of partners and other firms so that they commit to being part of the Apple ecosystem instead of joining that of Nokia, RIM (the firm that makes the BlackBerry device), Microsoft or Google. Many customers and developers are particularly loyal to Apple's brand because it has established a reputation for being innovative and creating products that are aesthetically pleasing and easy to use. This confers on Apple an important strategic benefit in trying to build up an innovation ecosystem around itself.

To conclude this section, brands are deeply intertwined with strategic management. The intangible value of a brand and the promises it makes to customers are reflected in the trade-offs made by the firm in market positioning, as well as in the way it allocates internal resources and signals strategic intent to rivals, partners and other parties. In the next section we explore how the market and strategic facets of brands relate to the legal issues faced by a firm when managing its brands.

IV. Brands and reputation: a legal perspective

Countries in the Asia Pacific region, like most countries, protect brands from unauthorised use by others, but such legal protection is not necessarily coextensive with how firms use and value their brands.

The primary legal means for protecting a brand is by registering the brand or a component of the brand as a trade mark pursuant to the trade mark registration regimes of the countries where it is intended to trade. While there does not appear to be a universally accepted definition of a brand, a brand is often said to comprise several components of which a

27 For a good explanation on network effects, see Carl Shapiro and Hal R. Varian, *Information Rules: a Strategic Guide to the Network Economy* (Harvard Business School Press, Boston, 1999).

trade mark is but one. The other components may include packaging, label design, colour, product shape, reputation or image.[28] Historically these have not necessarily been viewed as trade marks for legal purposes – even though brand owners may view them as such. However, currently a trade mark is generally broadly defined in trade mark registration legislation. Such a broad definition is required by the Agreement on Trade-Related Aspects of Intellectual Property Rights (TRIPS),[29] an international agreement to which all members of the World Trade Organization (WTO) are contracting parties. Article 15(1) of TRIPS requires contracting parties to ensure that:

> Any sign, or any combination of signs, capable of distinguishing the goods or services of one undertaking from those of other undertakings, shall be capable of constituting a trademark.[30]

A 'sign' is also generally broadly defined. For example, 'sign' is defined in s. 6 of the Australian Trade Marks Act 1995 (Cth) (TMA) as follows:

> *sign* includes the following or any combination of the following, namely, any letter, word, name, signature, numeral, device, brand, heading, label, ticket, aspect of packaging, shape, colour, sound or scent.

The reference to brand in this definition is generally regarded as referring to an older use of the word being a mark made by burning. Thus, it can be seen that many components of a brand may be registrable as trade marks, although some components may still not qualify for registration.

Many countries including in the Asia Pacific region also protect the goodwill of a business from injury caused by an unauthorised person using the well-established brand of the business in a manner which deceives consumers into believing the unauthorised user's goods or services are the goods or services of the business with which they are familiar or are associated in some way with that familiar business. Such protection is often achieved by bringing what is called a passing off action against the unauthorised user, an action created by English judges to protect the goodwill of businesses and which many countries in the Asia Pacific

[28] See further Chapter 2, in this volume. See also Tom Blackett, *Trademarks* (Interbrand, Macmillan Business, London, 1998).

[29] Opened for signature 15 April 1994, 1869 UNTS 299 (entered into force 1 January 1996).

[30] This distinctiveness requirement is a corollary of the badge of origin function generally required of a registered trade mark as discussed below. Unless laudatory, descriptive and geographical words and devices have acquired a capacity to distinguish through use, such words and devices are generally not capable of distinguishing a particular trader's goods or services and are thus not registrable as trade marks. Many colours, shapes and scents are in a similar position and some countries expressly prohibit the registration of purely functional shapes.

region (especially those of the British Commonwealth) have adopted as part of their domestic law. Actions such as the passing off action indirectly protect brands that have acquired a reputation whether or not the brand is registered or partly registered as a trade mark.[31]

Some components of a brand may be protected by other means. Material constituting original artistic works such as logo trade marks and label designs may be protected by copyright, and the shapes of goods or their packaging may be registrable as designs.[32] However, this last part of the chapter will focus on the registration system for protecting trade marks, as firms generally prefer to rely on this form of protection because the statutory nature of the rights granted provides a more certain and reliable source of protection.

The function protected by trade mark registration

While a registered trade mark is generally now regarded as a species of personal property, it largely remains a special kind of property. The owner of a registered trade mark is not granted a monopoly in the trade mark. When applying to register a trade mark the applicant seeking registration must specify in the trade mark application the goods and services for which the trade mark is sought to be registered. The exclusive rights to use the trade mark granted upon successful registration are limited to the use of the trade mark in particular ways in relation to the specified goods and services. However, particularly following recent international developments, the right to prevent others using the registered trade mark can extend beyond use of the same trade mark and beyond use in relation to the goods and services for which the trade mark is registered.

Traditionally the right granted to the owner of a registered trade mark has been the exclusive right to use the trade mark to identify the commercial origin of the goods and/or services for which the trade mark is

[31] In Australia similar protection can also be obtained by traders suing for contravention of consumer protection laws that proscribe misleading and deceptive conduct, such as ss. 18 and 29 of the Australian Consumer Law, contained in sch. 2 of the Competition and Consumer Law 2010 (Cth) and these provisions' predecessors. And see Chapter 5, in this volume.

[32] International treaties oblige most countries to grant, for varying periods of time, copyright in original artistic works and reproduction rights in sufficiently innovative designs. For example, the Berne Convention for the Protection of Literary and Artistic Works, opened for signature 9 September 1886, as last revised at Paris on 24 July 1971, 1161 UNTS 3 (entered into force 10 October 1974) (for copyright); the Paris Convention for the Protection of Industrial Property (opened for signature 20 March 1883) 828 UNTS 305 (entered into force 25 August 1972) as revised (for designs); and the TRIPS Agreement (for both copyright and designs).

registered so that the registered owner's goods and services can be distinguished from like goods and services of other traders. It was not necessary though that the actual name of the manufacturer or other commercial origin of the goods or services be known. That is, a registered trade mark has been traditionally protected as a badge or indicator of origin. This is reflected in provisions like s. 120(1) of the TMA which provides that

> [a] person infringes a registered trade mark if the person uses as a trade mark a sign that is substantially identical with, or deceptively similar to, the trade mark in relation to goods or services in respect of which the trade mark is registered.[33]

This level of protection reflects the traditional justification for protecting trade marks as signs which provide necessary information to consumers and thus reduce the time consumers spend on making satisfactory purchases. In many countries this origin function of a trade mark remains an essential characteristic of a registered trade mark. As recently as May 2010 the High Court of Australia said in *E&J Gallo Winery* v. *Lion Nathan Australia Pty Ltd*:

> Distinguishing goods of a registered owner from the goods of others and indicating a connection in the course of trade between the goods and the registered owner are essential characteristics of a trade mark.[34]

It follows from the earlier parts of this chapter that firms view a brand as conveying a promise that the firm makes to potential customers – and this may include a promise relating to the quality and the attributes of the firm's products and services. It is a matter of fact that a registered trade mark that has been in use for some time will inevitably inform consumers about the quality and attributes of the products and services bearing the trade mark. Such a trade mark thus also acts as a badge or guarantee of the quality of the goods and services.

In the first part of this chapter reference is made to the growing trend for firms to outsource production of their goods and franchise their services. Thus information about the quality and attributes of products and services is often more important to consumers than the commercial origin of the goods and services. After some early hesitation, countries have increasingly relaxed the limitations on the licensing and assignment of registered trade marks. Some limits generally remain in relation to licensing, largely because of the continuing insistence that the origin function of the registered trade mark remains important. Allowing the

[33] Pursuant to the TRIPS obligations referred to later in the chapter, the TMA grants owners of registered trade marks additional rights to sue for infringement.

[34] (2010) 241 CLR 144, 162–3 [42] (citations omitted).

licensing of registered trade marks despite this continuing insistence is largely achieved by requiring owners of registered trade marks to exercise some control over the use of their trade marks by their licensees. By this means, the owner of the registered trade mark maintains, in the words of the High Court of Australia quoted above, a connection in the course of trade with his or her licensee's goods or services. What constitutes sufficient control by the owner of the registered trade mark in this context is not always clear, but prudent trade mark owners will ensure that quality standards are mandated in their licence agreements and are enforced.

Given the importance of the guarantee function of a trade mark, it is surprising that there is generally nothing in trade mark registration legislation preventing trade mark owners from changing the quality and other attributes of the products and services sold under their registered trade marks. Consumers must rely on the economic interest of trade mark owners to maintain consistent quality and attributes, a reliance which, as the first part of this chapter indicates, in most cases is likely not misplaced.

TRIPS and the extent of protection granted to registered trade marks

The rights of an owner of a registered trade mark to prevent unauthorised third parties from using the registered trade mark have been extended in many countries following the coming into effect of TRIPS. Article 16(1) of TRIPS in effect requires all contracting parties to provide in their domestic law that the owner of a registered trade mark has the exclusive right to prevent third parties from using in the course of trade:

- signs identical to the registered trade mark for goods or services identical to those in respect of which the trade mark is registered;
- signs identical to the registered trade mark for goods or services similar to the goods and services in respect of which the trade mark is registered where the third parties' use would result in a likelihood of confusion; and
- signs similar to the registered trade mark for goods or services identical or similar to the goods and services in respect of which the trade mark is registered where the third parties' use would result in a likelihood of confusion.

While the legislative provisions in their domestic laws may differ, countries have generally granted owners of registered trade marks these rights of action in order to protect their registered trade marks. It can be seen that the rights of action granted are designed to protect the registered trade mark's ability to function as a badge or indicator of origin.

Extended protection for well-known trade marks

The value of a brand to a firm is linked to the level of awareness of the brand among the firm's customers and potential customers. Successful brands develop a reputation which is generally associated with an image based on the firm's strategic positioning in the marketplace. As is evident from the earlier parts of this chapter, from a marketing and strategic perspective, the reputation and image of the brand is of critical importance to the firm whether that image be one of luxury or low cost, of youth, adventure or of some other attribute. The reputation of a brand including its image is generally created by the firm's significant investment in advertising and marketing. If a high level of recognition of the brand is achieved, the brand is asserted to have a commercial value in itself separate from the goods and services in relation to which the brand has been used.

The capacity of a well-known brand to function beyond a badge or indicator of origin or quality and itself attract custom is often referred to in trade mark terms as the advertising function.[35] It is argued that this aspect of the well-known brand can suffer 'dilution' damage by the unauthorised use of the brand by third parties. This is asserted to be so even when the unauthorised use is in relation to goods and services quite different to the goods and services for which the well-known brand has been used and even if the unauthorised use creates no likelihood of confusion. Dilution damage is the lessening of the capacity of the well-known brand to distinguish its owner's goods and services (known as 'blurring') or the harming of the reputation of the well-known brand (known as 'tarnishment'). Blurring can occur if the well-known brand also comes to be associated with the different goods or services of the unauthorised user, and tarnishment will occur when the unauthorised user's goods or services are inconsistent with the image or reputation of the well-known brand or have some kind of stigma. If a well-known brand is not granted some form of protection against dilution damage, it will often be difficult for firms to use their well-established brands to extend the range of goods and services in which they trade.

The rights granted to the owner of a registered trade mark to prevent unauthorised uses of the trade mark as set out above will often not extend to protect the image or reputation of the trade mark from dilution damage. These rights of action do not extend to prevent unauthorised uses in relation to goods and services that are *not similar* to the goods and services for which the trade mark is registered. These rights of action only extend

[35] The capacity may also be called the communication or investment function.

to prevent unauthorised uses in relation to goods and services that are similar to (as distinct from the same as) the goods and services for which the trade mark is registered when the unauthorised use will result in a likelihood of confusion. Likewise, the action of passing off and equivalent actions do not generally provide protection from dilution damage in the absence of any likelihood of deception or at least confusion. However, art. 16(3) of TRIPS requires contracting parties to grant additional protection to registered trade marks that are well known in their own territory. Essentially such additional protection extends to prohibiting certain unauthorised uses of the well-known trade mark in relation to goods or services which are not similar to those in respect of which the well-known trade mark is registered.[36]

Article 16(3) of TRIPS in effect requires each contracting party to also prohibit the unauthorised use of a trade mark which constitutes a reproduction, an imitation or a translation, liable to create confusion, of a trade mark well known in the contracting party's territory when the unauthorised use is in relation to goods or services which are not similar to those in respect of which the well-known trade mark is registered, provided that

- the unauthorised use would indicate a connection between the unauthorised user's goods and services and the owner of the well-known registered trade mark, and
- the interests of the owner of the well-known registered trade mark are likely to be damaged.[37]

The ambit of art. 16(3) of TRIPS and the legislative provisions of those contracting parties who have used the language of art. 16(3) in their respective domestic laws is unclear and is the subject of debate. The critical issue is whether art. 16(3) requires protection only when the unauthorised use of the offending mark gives rise to a likelihood of confusion. If so, art. 16(3) does not protect well-known trade marks against dilution damage.[38]

[36] The Joint Recommendation Concerning Provisions on the Protection of Well-Known Marks adopted by the Assembly of the Paris Union for the Protection of Industrial Property and the General Assembly of the World Intellectual Property Organization (WIPO) in 1999 provides for more extensive protection for well-known trade marks. However, this Joint Recommendation does not itself set out mandatory standards but rather contains recommended guidelines for the protection of well-known trade marks.

[37] This summary of art. 16(3) incorporates the language of art. 6*bis* (1) of the Paris Convention 1967 on the basis that such an incorporation is required by art. 16(3).

[38] This issue was the subject of detailed analysis by the Singapore Court of Appeal in *Novelty Pte Ltd* v. *Amanresorts Ltd & Ano* [2009] 3 SLR(R) 216 where the court concluded, *obiter*, that art. 16(3) and the provision in the Singapore Trade Marks Act 1998

Some countries in the Asia Pacific region including Singapore and the United States have amended their trade mark law to expressly protect well-known trade marks against dilution damage, sometimes even if the well-known trade mark is not registered.[39] The breadth of these provisions may still be debated. For instance, it is not always clear what is necessary to prove the requisite damage by blurring. Nor is it necessarily clear what level of recognition a trade mark must have to be regarded as well known and thus qualify for the additional protection, although it may not be necessary for the trade mark to be well known among the general public. Also, some countries have granted a further level of still broader protection to well-known trade marks, protecting such marks from unauthorised persons taking unfair advantage of the mark's reputation even where there is no blurring or tarnishment of the registered trade mark.[40] Other countries including some in the Asia Pacific region, however, have not amended their trade marks law to grant well-known trade marks protection beyond the scope of protection required by art. 16(3) of TRIPS.[41] These countries presumably have not been persuaded that such an extension of protection is justified.[42]

V. Concluding remarks

This chapter has looked at the value of brands to firms from the perspectives of marketing, strategic management and the law. The chapter shows that there is much in common among the different perspectives. However, the scope of legal protection available is not necessarily coextensive with all the ways in which firms use and value their brands.

(Singapore Cap 332, 2005 Rev Ed) based on this article required the unauthorised use of the offending mark to give rise to a likelihood of confusion.

39 For example: Singapore, Trade Marks Act 1998 (Singapore, Cap 332, 2005 Rev Ed) s. 55(3)(b)(i); United States of America, Trademark Dilution Revision Act of 2006 15 USC § 1125(c)(2)(C)(2006); and see also the New Zealand Trade Marks Act 2002 (NZ) s. 89(1)(d) (although the latter provision is restricted to registered trade marks). See also Chapters 6 and 7, in this volume, for a fuller discussion of the Singapore and US provisions and current debates as to how these should be construed.

40 For example: Singapore, Trade Marks Act 1998 (Singapore, Cap 332, 2005 Rev Ed) s. 55(3)(b)(ii); and New Zealand, Trade Marks Act 2002 (NZ) s. 89(1)(d).

41 For example Australia, and also Malaysia discussed (and contrasted with Singapore) in Chapter 6 of this volume.

42 For a very recent critical discussion on protecting trade marks from dilution damage and the taking of unfair advantage, see Jason Bosland and Megan Richardson, 'Competing Discourses of "Rights" and "Harms" in Trade Mark Law', in Kathy Bowrey, Diane Nichol and Michael Handler (eds.), *Emerging Issues in Intellectual Property Law* (Oxford University Press, South Melbourne, 2011), 103.

2 The social benefits and costs of trade marks and brands

Christine Greenhalgh

I. Introduction

In many countries there is widespread use of trade marks by firms in all types of industry and services. The breadth and depth of use of this type of intellectual property (IP) right greatly exceeds that of patents, designs or copyright. As shown in Table 2.1, Australian firms apply for seven times as many trade marks as patents and on average they keep these rights for much longer (the years of trade mark rights per company are twenty-five times that of their patents). This ordering of use of these three IP rights occurs across all industries and services, despite some variation across sectors in their general propensity to use IP rights. Trade mark use even extends beyond the private sector, with many trade marks being registered by government departments and other public bodies.[1]

The reasons why firms are so willing and able to acquire and preserve their stocks of trade marks are discussed elsewhere in this volume, and reflect the desire of the firm to build successful well-known brands. The issue to be investigated here is whether or not this behaviour is good for the economy.

We can distinguish the broader concept of social value (good for society as a whole) from the narrower one of private value (good for particular economic actors such as firms). In some instances the workings of the free market align private and social value, so that the unfettered pursuit of private interest by companies provides the best outcome for society. In other situations private and social value diverge and government legislation enacts policy to try to correct the distortion.

Thus the economic motivation for IP rights is that society offers firms the opportunity to gain such rights in order to improve the workings of

[1] Similar figures to those in Table 2.1 can be seen for other advanced countries, such as the UK, for which see Christine Greenhalgh and Mark Rogers 'Intellectual Property Activity by Service Sector and Manufacturing Firms in the UK, 1996–2000', in Harry Scarbrough (ed.), *The Evolution of Business Knowledge* (Oxford University Press, New York, 2008), 295.

Table 2.1 *The prevalence of different types of IP rights in firms*

IP rights in Australian companies 1998–2003	Patents	Trade marks	Designs
IP applications (number) per company	0.030	0.219	0.013
IP stock (years of rights) per company	0.93	24.07	1.73

Source: Hielke Buddelmeyer, Paul Jensen and Elizabeth Webster, 'Innovation and Determinants of Company Survival' (2010) 63(2) *Oxford Economic Papers* 261, 271

the market, particularly in areas related to innovation. With any IP right there is a tension in that there can be both negative and positive social impacts of the right. The public bodies that design and enact the rights, and then monitor and regulate the use of these rights, need to be sure that the positives outweigh the negatives. In this chapter the aim is to investigate whether we have evidence to make this judgement in relation to trade marks and, if so, whether the audit suggests a social profit or loss from the use of these rights.

II. Law and economics of trade marks and brands

We begin here with a few points summarising the economic dimensions of the law of trade marks. Despite being regularly grouped together in economic discussions, the basic features of the various types of IP rights are very different in their economic impact. A patent offers its holder the monopoly control of production of a specified item, or use of a method, in the country where it has been awarded. In contrast, a trade mark is registered in one or more defined fields of production or service, but is not held as a monopoly across all areas of production. In this respect it could be judged to be a narrower and less powerful IP right.

Even so, whereas a patent can only be renewed for a fixed period, ownership of a given trade mark can be held as an indefinite right, so long as the firm continues to trade and use this trade mark. So while having a narrower scope, the trade mark wins hands down over a patent on the duration of monopoly ownership that it engenders. Also, acquiring a trade mark is generally less onerous and thus less costly for the firm than undertaking the formal procedures to gain a patent.

Even if the firm does not want to register its mark, it has the option of waiting to acquire a reputation for its trade under a given name or logo, at which point it is deemed to have an unregistered (or 'common law') trade mark. It can then use the common law tort of 'passing off' to prevent other firms from using unfair competition via 'lookalikes' (products using similar product design and packaging) and to defend its share of the market. In Australia there is also a further law to deny firms the ability to engage in 'misleading and deceptive conduct', which covers any deliberate attempts to confuse the customer.[2] The fact that legislation defends unregistered marks as well as registered ones again adds power to the trade mark.

Our aim here is not to explain why firms see trade marks as attractive, but to examine whether they offer a good deal for society. As already noted, for economists, any interventionist policy such as IP rights must be justified by an improvement in some aspect of market functioning. IP rights are linked with the desire of society to achieve a significant rate of innovation in goods and services, coupled with the fear that there will be too little of this activity if creators are not adequately rewarded. Without IP rights any new knowledge embodied in innovative products could be instantly copied, so that imitators would then gain most of the reward due to the innovator. For this reason the introduction of IP rights is seen as restoring the balance to ensure adequate investment in R&D takes place. In the case of trade marks, the economic analysis struggles to provide the justification for the award of these monopoly rights.

One of the early studies discussing the economic value of trade marks is that by Landes and Posner.[3] Their argument hinges on the idea that trade marks improve market efficiency by signalling the quality of the supplier's product to potential customers, who would otherwise have to expend scarce time and effort searching for this information. Thus trade marks help to solve what economists call an 'information asymmetry' between the seller, who knows his or her product quality, and a buyer who does not. Of course the firm may take a little extra profit in the form of a slightly higher product price, but the customer also gains a degree of certainty that he will be satisfied with his purchase. In the introduction to their wide-ranging text on US trade marks and unfair competition law, Dinwoodie and Janis acknowledge the influence of this economic theory of trade marks in the evolution of US judicial decisions.[4]

A second strand in the economics literature is the argument of Mendonca *et al.* that new trade marks are a signal of innovative activity.[5]

[2] See Competition and Consumer Act 2010 (Cth) Sch. 2, s. 18 (formerly s. 52 of the Trade Practices Act 1974 (Cth)).

[3] William M. Landes and Richard A. Posner 'Trademark Law: An Economic Perspective' (1987) 30(2) *Journal of Law and Economics* 265.

[4] Graeme Dinwoodie and Mark Janis, *Trademarks and Unfair Competition* (3rd edn, Aspen Publishers, New York, 2010), 15–17.

[5] Sandro Mendonca, Tiago S. Pereira and Manuel M. Godinho, 'Trademarks as an Indicator of Innovation and Industrial Change' (2004) 33 *Research Policy* 1385.

These authors present evidence of a positive correlation between innovation and trade mark activity across a number of European countries. This can be seen as a natural extension to the signalling model above, as firms need to inform their customers and investors about their innovative activity, yet many firms perform incremental innovation of a kind that is not patentable. Before embarking on a programme of advertising and marketing of their innovative product, firms need to lay claim to a unique product name for their new variety or improved quality of product.

This idea of trade marks acting as signals of innovation has been extensively developed in a recent paper by Greenhalgh and Rogers.[6] These authors draw on the Lancaster economic model of product differentiation[7] and relate this model to the much earlier Schumpeterian model of creative destruction, which posits that firms compete via product innovation.[8] The Lancaster approach formalises an economic model of firms competing to satisfy a range of varying tastes among consumers by introducing new and better varieties of products. Only those items that deliver a wide range of product characteristics at a reasonable price will survive in the marketplace. Following this line of argument it can be shown that the social value of the trade mark comes partly from the successful commercialisation of the signalled innovation, which increases customer choice and satisfaction. Added to this the market for investment funds will operate more efficiently where stock markets have information about which firms are innovating and which are not, as the former are more likely to yield higher profitability and to survive in competitive markets.

While the above models emphasise the social benefits of trade marks, there is a third view that focuses on their possible negative impact. Much of the economics of industrial organisation literature concerns itself with the ways that firms that are already well established in a market seek to create and buttress monopoly positions by making it difficult for new firms to enter the same market. Here we are beginning to talk about trade marks as if they are the basis of brands to be used by firms as weapons to retain market power. Legal texts, such as that by Dinwoodie and Janis for

[6] Christine Greenhalgh and Mark Rogers, 'Trade Marks and Performance in Services and Manufacturing Firms: Evidence of Schumpeterian Competition through Innovation' (April 2010), in evidence submitted by Christine Greenhalgh to the Hargreaves Review of Intellectual Property and Growth (2011) available at www.ipo.gov.uk/ipreview-c4e-sub-greenhalgh.pdf.

[7] Kelvin J. Lancaster, 'A New Approach to Consumer Theory' (1966) 74 *Journal of Political Economy* 132.

[8] See Joseph A. Schumpeter, *Capitalism, Socialism and Democracy* (Harper & Row, New York, 1942).

the US, are generally rather slower to acknowledge and confront the two conflicting faces of trade marks.[9] Having devoted most of their text to the examination of the routes by which trade marks act as an effective weapon for the promotion of competition, they eventually consider briefly how they might be used as part of anti-competitive behaviour.

To use the jargon of economics, incumbent firms construct barriers to entry using a combination of strategies, one of which is the building of a portfolio of brands backed by heavy advertising. This increases the costs of entry for any firms seeking to enter the same product field, as they start from a disadvantage that customers are already very familiar with existing brands and take a lot of convincing to try products from a new source. In addition incumbent firms can adopt other strategies to exclude new entrants, for example by temporarily lowering the price of their well-known product just as the new firm tries to launch its offering, so that the entrant finds that its advertised price is too high to attract customers. Once the potential entrant is beaten off, the incumbent can return to its original price and continue to enjoy monopoly profits.

Certainly Ramello and Silva stress that trade marks have moved well beyond the realm of signalling 'source distinctiveness' to that of offering 'differential distinctiveness', leading to a metamorphosis of trade marks into brands.[10] So what is the relationship between trade marks and brands? A useful starting point is that of the International Trademark Association quoted in Davis and Maniatis:

> A brand is a trade mark (or combination of trade marks) that, through promotion and use, has acquired a significance over and above its functional use by a company to distinguish its goods and services from those of other traders.[11]

In the introductory paper to a recent conference initiated by the UK government, brands are described as the promise of an experience and as an invitation to a lifestyle to which the consumer aspires.[12] This paper

[9] Dinwoodie and Janis, *Trademarks*. Thus their book leaves the thorny issue of the relationship between trade marks, unfair competition law and antitrust law to the last section of their last chapter (25 pages in a text of more than 900 pages).

[10] Giovanni B. Ramello and Francesco Silva 'Appropriating Signs and Meaning: The Elusive Economics of Trademarks' (2006) 15(6) *Industrial and Corporate Change* 937, 946–7.

[11] Jennifer Davis and Spryos Maniatis, 'Trademarks, Brands and Competition', in Teresa da Silva Lopes and Paul Duguid (eds.), *Trademarks, Brands and Competitiveness* (Routledge, New York, 2010), 119, 120.

[12] Intellectual Property Office (UK), 'Branding in a modern economy: introductory paper' (paper distributed at Branding in a Modern Economy, London, 11 November 2009), 1.

quotes John Murphy, the founder of Interbrand, who has said that the components of a brand are:

> the product itself, the packaging, the brand name, the promotion, the advertising and the overall presentation. The brand is therefore the synthesis of all these elements, physical, aesthetic, rational and emotional.[13]

Most brand analysts would also emphasise another key property of a brand, which is its ability to transfer consumer loyalty from the original product range to new goods and services.[14] This permits the brand owner to achieve a successful product launch and acquire customer loyalty more quickly and with less expense whenever it enters a new field of production. A classic example is that of the UK-based company, Virgin, that began as a music retailer and now runs an international airline.

But are strong brands good or bad for the economy? Certainly there was little fear in the minds of the UK government when stating the aim of its conference:

> [We] will explore the contribution that brands make to our prosperity, and will consider what the Government is doing and should do to provide the conditions which will allow Britain to be a country of choice in which to create, nurture and protect brands.[15]

Similarly Casson and Wadeson argue for an active role of government in promoting domestic brands internationally, seeing this as a way to enhance international trade performance.[16] Thus while in the domestic market there can be fear of large, powerful firms with strong brands making life hard for start-ups and small enterprises, simultaneously in the global market there is a conflicting need to have powerful brands to strut on the world stage.

Another possible conflict arises in the area of innovation. Due to the market power of brands, it has been argued by Litman that persuasive brand advertising then begins to divert firms' expenditure from product innovation.[17] With sufficient customer loyalty the producer can relax about their need to innovate continually and focus on repeating their message, with only minor adjustments being made to the product. Following this interpretation we are beginning to cross the line between

[13] *Ibid.*
[14] See David Haigh, *Brand Valuation: Understanding, Exploiting and Communicating Brand Values* (Financial Times Retail and Consumer, London, 1998).
[15] Intellectual Property Office (UK), 'Branding in a modern economy', 1.
[16] Mark Casson and Nigel Wadeson, 'Export Performance and Reputation', in da Silva Lopes and Duguid, *Trademarks*, 31.
[17] Jessica Litman, 'Breakfast with Batman: The Public Interest in the Advertising Age' (1999) 108(7) *Yale Law Journal* 1717.

trade marks as an aid to competition (in a market with well-informed customers) and brands as an impediment to it. Davis and Maniatis also cite another strategy frequently pursued by brand owners that they claim could reduce innovation. This is the feature of market share acquisition by buying existing brands, which could be a substitute for innovative activity to develop new products under their own brand name. They offer several examples from the US and EU that they claim illustrate this strategy, but of course with each of these particular cases the counterfactual situation about what amount of innovation the firm would have achieved in the absence of the takeover is unknown.[18]

In the following sections we shall outline what we know (and what we do not know) about the social value of trade marks and brands. The difficulty just noted of the absence of information about counterfactual situations permeates many studies of the performance of firms that are using trade marks and developing brands within the competitive process. Economic studies often involve the analysis of large datasets observing broad cross-sections of firms over several years. This is to allow for comparisons between the experiences of many different firms and to allow us to examine what happens when significant changes, such as innovation and the acquisition of IP rights, occur in some of these firms. With the use of multivariate statistical analysis such studies attempt to control for many other factors, in order to pinpoint the particular marginal contribution of the key variable of interest – for example, trade mark activity. Even with such large amounts of data, it is not possible to be sure that all relevant factors have been included in the study and that the correct attribution of causal effects has been made.

The legal and management disciplines are more often concerned with outlining particular illustrations, drawn from court cases in legal studies, and from business histories in management studies. These two types of cases shed light on the details of developments in law and management practice, but cannot be seen as representative of the whole population of similar legal judgments or firms at a given time. Nevertheless in many legal systems there is use of precedent, such that key judgments can determine the direction of future cases. In management systems there are leading firms and processes of learning and imitation in business practice, so again key examples can influence the wider population of firms. In the next sections we draw on economic studies and on legal and management cases to examine what these may tell us about the value to society of the trade mark system.

[18] Davis and Maniatis, 'Trademarks, Brands and Competition', 124–5.

III. Economic evidence on the social value of trade marks and brands

Until quite recently the empirical economic analysis of innovation has focused very largely on R&D and patents, with very few studies of trade mark activity. Even the few studies that have emerged have been concerned to demonstrate the private returns to trade marks rather than exploring social value of this activity. For example in their analysis of nearly 2,700 Australian firms observed from 1989–2002, Griffiths *et al.* found that the stock of trade marks was a significant determinant of profits, but with a smaller impact than either patents or registered designs, although the value of a trade mark was rising over this period.[19] Using data for 237 US firms from selected industries in 1993–7, Seethamraju also analysed the value of trade marks, finding a positive impact of trade mark activity on firm sales and also on the stock market value of the firm.[20]

In order to explore the social value of trade marks a shift is needed to a metric that reflects social rather than private benefit. It can be argued that company survival correlates with social welfare as when companies go bankrupt the society bears many direct costs of unemployed workers, as well as hidden costs of the destruction of productive resources, such as human skills. Some important new evidence is contained in a study by Buddlemeyer, Jensen and Webster (BJW), who have examined the relationship between innovation and company survival using a very large panel of Australian companies.[21]

In setting out the framework for their analysis of firm survival, BJW remind us that investment in R&D is a risky activity that widens the variance of outcomes. Thus, bringing a novel innovation to market raises both the probability of exceptional performance and of bankruptcy for the firm. In their empirical work these authors make an important distinction between radical innovation, something 'new-to-the-world' proxied by patents, and incremental innovation, 'new-to-the-company' proxied by registered trade marks and designs.[22] They quote 36.9 per cent as the share of patent applications that led to some sort of mass production, according to the Australian Inventor Survey for the period 1986–2006,

19 William Griffiths, Paul Jensen and Elizabeth Webster, 'What Creates Abnormal Profits?' (2011) 58(3) *Scottish Journal of Political Economy* 397.

20 Chandrakanth Seethamraju, 'The Value Relevance of Trademarks', in John Hand and Baruch Lev (eds.), *Intangible Assets: Values, Measures, and Risks* (Oxford University Press, Oxford and New York, 2003), 228.

21 Hielke Buddelmeyer, Paul Jensen and Elizabeth Webster, 'Innovation and Determinants of Company Survival' (2010) 62(2) *Oxford Economic Papers* 261.

22 *Ibid.* 263–4.

so more than 60 per cent of radical innovations were unsuccessful in reaching a large customer base.[23]

In their analysis of firm survival (as monitored by company deregistration) these authors used an extensive dataset of almost 300,000 Australian firms observed during the years 1997–2003. The database covers all sectors of the economy and for most sectors the predominant firm size is an SME, with mining and utilities the exceptions as in these two sectors production is dominated by large firms. By matching records of intellectual property for registered IP rights (patents, trade marks and designs) at the firm level, the authors construct both stock measures of the firms' achieved intangible assets and flow measures of their recent innovation investments.

The findings of the BJW study support the idea that incremental innovation is risk reducing, whereas radical innovation is risk increasing in the short term. Thus empirically, investment in incremental innovations (as monitored by trade marks) increased survival rates, but investment in radical innovations (proxied by patent applications) was associated with an immediate decrease in median survival time. However the study also revealed benefits of achieving a higher stock of both patents and trade marks, with benefits persisting strongly for at least five years and with a continuing positive impact (but smaller incremental value) for a further five years.[24] The authors conclude that, in regard to radical innovation, firms are more financially vulnerable in the first one to two years following this innovation. In contrast the firm's survival is enhanced both in the short and medium term by their trade mark activity.[25] This evidence suggests that the use of trade marks to signal new varieties of products is good for business survival, but even here we are not entirely confident that we can separate out what is a private and what is the social benefit as these authors do not examine the interactions between firms.

One study that includes such analysis for a country not in the Pacific Rim is that of Greenhalgh and Rogers, whose database is 1,600 large UK firms observed in the years 1996–2000.[26] These authors examine how the trade mark activities of different firms in the same product group play out in terms of firm performance. As may be expected, in the short run a greater amount of trade mark activity by other firms in their product group is seen to reduce the market value of any single firm. Even so there is also evidence that firms respond to such product competition by achieving greater productivity and profitability, efforts that are revealed in higher productivity growth and greater stock market value. These

[23] Buddelmeyer *et al.*, 'Innovation', 262. [24] *Ibid.* 278.
[25] *Ibid.* 281. [26] Greenhalgh and Rogers, 'Trade Marks'.

findings are consistent with the Schumpeterian process of competition through innovation, which acts to restrain profit margins in the short term while increasing product quality and variety in the medium term, thus transferring benefits to consumers and the wider society.

IV. Evidence from contested cases

When a firm gains evidence that its trade mark is being infringed, it can take a variety of routes to enforce its intellectual property. These range from simple communications between the managements of the companies to cases in court. As social scientists interested in how the enforcement of IP rights is achieved and how disputes are resolved, we lack wide-ranging statistics. How many firms have sent 'cease and desist' letters to another company? How many recipients of such letters have done so without putting up a fight? Of those firms that acceded to pressure, how many were in fact infringing and how many were simply intimidated, for example by a larger company? What proportions of trade mark disputes are taken as far as the courts in various countries? How many judicial findings were in favour of the registered trade mark owner? We have very few studies of such issues.

In a recent survey of small UK firms Greenhalgh *et al.* found that by far the most common route to achieving settlement was for the firm to issue a 'cease and desist' letter to the other firm that was either causing confusion by use of a similar mark or was deliberately passing off their goods as the plaintiff's.[27] In a large majority of instances the warning indicated by such a letter, that the owner of the mark was prepared to take further action if need be, had the desired effect and the firms were satisfied with the outcome of their dispute. Where this was not the case then there is of course the option of initiating legal proceedings to defend the mark via the courts, but for many, especially smaller firms, this can be a daunting undertaking requiring a relatively high input of scarce managerial resources as well as expensive lawyers' fees. In the Greenhalgh *et al.* study very few disputes were taken either to arbitration or to the courts and a significant minority of disputes remained unresolved. Where legal proceedings were used the respondents indicated that this was a very costly process, undertaken when the failure to enforce the trade mark would have been extremely detrimental to their business. Essentially the

[27] Christine Greenhalgh, Jeremy J. Phillips, Robert Pitkethly, Mark Rogers and Joshua Tomalin (2010) 'Intellectual Property Enforcement by Smaller UK Firms: A Report for the Strategic Advisory Board for Intellectual Property' (Research Report, Intellectual Property Office, October 2010), 17 www.ipo.gov.uk/ipresearch-ipenforcement-201010.pdf.

management was forced to 'bet the firm' by following an unpredictable process through the courts.

We can get some idea of judges' attitudes and the legal arguments used in adjudications for cases that have been contested, but these remain the tip of the iceberg in terms of the actual number of disputes. However, these cases certainly send out signals to possible future litigants about how they might fare in the courts. We cite below a number of cases that have been publicly discussed in Pacific Rim countries, some of which have yet to be resolved.

Case 1: Coca-Cola's claim over 'World Famous in New Zealand'

In New Zealand there is an ongoing dispute involving Coca-Cola Amatil, who applied in 2004 to register a trade mark for their L&P soft drink containing the phrase 'World Famous in New Zealand', with the registration being accepted in 2007.[28] This phrase is described on Wikipedia as being commonly in use to describe products that are widely known in the country, but unheard of elsewhere.[29] It is seen as conveying both pride in the country's products, but also as being slightly self-deprecating in a humorous fashion.

The trade mark registration by Coca-Cola was later opposed by a local tradesman, Tony Coombe. He owns a non-trading company of this title, but also claims that the phrase is a 'Kiwi-ism' and belongs to all New Zealanders. His opposition has recently suffered a setback when a commissioner of the Intellectual Property Office decided that there is no reason why the trade mark cannot remain registered. This seems surprising given that words and phrases commonly in use are not allowable as trade marks. Mr Coombe has (as of May 2010) lodged papers with the High Court in Wellington to continue to prosecute his objection.[30]

Case 2: The US–Australian Ugh boots dispute

A famous Australian example is the ugh, or ugg, boots dispute.[31] This is a long-running dispute about the ownership and use of the terms

[28] *Coca-Cola Amatil (NZ) Ltd* v. *Coombe* [2010] NZIPOTM 2 (12 April 2010).

[29] See Wikipedia, World Famous in New Zealand (accessed 01 April 2011) http://en.wikipedia.org/wiki/World_famous_in_New_Zealand.

[30] See '"World Famous" soft drink battle to have day in court', *New Zealand Herald* (online), 14 May 2010 www.nzherald.co.nz/business/news/article.cfm?c_id=3&objectid=10644761.

[31] *Deckers Outdoor Corporation Inc.* v. *Farley* (2009) 176 FCR 33.

'ugg', 'ugh', 'ug' and even 'ugly' to describe sheepskin boots. Despite opinions being voiced that these words were in general use for many decades, with the boots being worn by pilots as early as the First World War, an Australian businessman Shane Stedman succeeded in registering the trade mark 'UGH-BOOT' in 1971 and the term 'UGH' in 1982. These two marks were subsequently sold to the US company UGG Holdings Ltd, a subsidiary of Deckers Outdoor Corporation, which later also registered a logo containing the terms UGG, Australia, and a stylised sun picture in 1999.

All three trade marks were subsequently challenged via applications for removal being made by Australian businesses, but in each case there was opposition from Deckers. The decisions of the Australian Trade Marks Office were as follows: in January 2006 UGH-BOOTS was removed due to non-use in a three-year period;[32] in April 2006 UGH was removed similarly for non-use,[33] but in August 2006 the composite mark containing the word UGG was deemed valid as it had been in use in its composite form as a trade mark.[34] The issue of whether or not the terms were generic was not a live issue in the Trade Marks Office decisions.

In recent years Deckers has continued to maintain its trade mark in Australia and also to trade using related marks registered in the US and the EU. The company has also been active within Australia in prosecuting any firm that seeks to ignore its ownership of the UGG composite logo.

To summarise, in 2003 Deckers became aware that Hepbourne Pty Ltd was making UGG branded boots in its Melbourne factory and applied for urgent interlocutory relief, later obtaining a permanent injunction to prevent Hepbourne from making or selling this product. Despite consenting to these orders, the Australian firm continued its operations throughout 2004 to 2007, at which point Deckers again became aware of its activities. Deckers then applied for summary judgment on claims of trade mark infringement, copyright infringement, passing off, and misleading and deceptive conduct, although they eventually had to go to trial on all except the first item, as the judge was only willing to offer summary judgment on the first claim, which was in favour of Deckers that its trade mark had been infringed.[35]

[32] *Deckers Outdoor Corporation* v. *B&B McDougal* [2006] ATMO 5 (16 January 2006).

[33] Deckers' opposition to the application for removal was withdrawn on 13 April 2006. See Trade Mark Details for Trade Mark: 373173 at IP Australia, Australian Trade Mark On-Line Search System (2011) http://pericles.ipaustralia.gov.au/atmoss/falcon.application_start.

[34] *Deckers Outdoor Corporation* v. *Luda Productions Pty Ltd* [2006] ATMO 74 (11 August 2006).

[35] See *Deckers Outdoor Corporation Inc.* v. *Farley* (2009) 176 FCR 33.

At the trial Tracey J. found against Hepbourne on all claims and ordered that it should pay Deckers $3 million in compensation for lost sales, plus $3.5 million additional damages for failing to adhere to the earlier court order (and subsequent permanent injunction) restraining it from making and selling UGG branded footwear.[36] These fines reflected the judge's view that Hepbourne had persistently and flagrantly infringed Deckers' rights and shown disregard for its legal obligations following the earlier court order.

Case 3: The Cadbury 'purple' debate in Australia

A further Australian case is the long-running saga relating to Cadbury's attempt to register a trade mark over the colour purple for chocolate.[37] As early as 1998 Cadbury Schweppes Pty Ltd had applied to register purple packaging for its chocolate as a trade mark (colours have been allowable items for registration since 1995). Following approval of the application in 2003 after lengthy deliberations by the Australian Trade Marks Office, Darrell Lea Pty Ltd opposed the registration as it used similar colours for its own chocolate products. An eventual decision by a delegate of the Registrar of Trade Marks in 2006 was that Cadbury could register a specific shade of purple for two of its products (block chocolate and boxed chocolates).[38]

At various junctures both parties appealed to the Federal Court, which considered the matter afresh allowing both sides to introduce new evidence beyond that seen by the Australian Trade Marks Office. During this dispute the Cadbury lawyers referred to trade mark law as well as the common law doctrine of passing off, and also alleged that Darrell Lea was guilty of misleading/deceptive conduct under s. 52 of the Trade Practices Act 1974 (Cth).[39] In the first hearing the judge of the Federal Court ruled that expert opinions were inadmissible as evidence and in 2006 the judgment went against Cadbury, with the judge concluding that 'Cadbury does not own the colour purple and does not have an

[36] See Tracey J.'s assessment of damages in *Deckers Outdoor Corporation Inc.* v. *Farley (No. 5)* (2009) 262 ALR 53, 71ff.

[37] *Cadbury Schweppes Pty Ltd* v. *Darrell Lea Chocolate Shops Pty Ltd (No. 8)* (2008) 75 IPR 557. For an expansive discussion of the *Cadbury* litigation, see Chapter 11, in this volume.

[38] *Re: Opposition by Darrell Lea Chocolate Shops Pty Limited to registration of trade mark application 779336(30)* (Unreported, Australian Trade Marks Office, Ian Thompson (Delegate), 27 April 2006) available on the IP Australia website at www.ipaustralia.gov.au/pdfs/trademarks/hearings/779336_0406.pdf.

[39] This provision is now incorporated in s. 18 of the Australian Consumer Law, Competition and Consumer Act 2010, sch. 2.

exclusive reputation in purple in connection with chocolate'.[40] Next Cadbury appealed to the Full Federal Court, which ruled that expert evidence concerning whether Darrell Lea's products could be deemed to confuse the customer should not have been excluded, and directed the judge to reconsider all the evidence including that of experts.[41]

On further hearing in March 2008, with expert evidence now included, the judge still found against Cadbury as follows:

> Having considered the evidence of the Cadbury experts, and reconsidered the evidence at the earlier hearing, I am not persuaded that Darrell Lea, in using the colour purple, has passed off its business or products as those of Cadbury or contravened the Trade Practices Act. I am not satisfied that such usage has resulted, or would result, in a hypothetical ordinary and reasonable member of the class constituted by prospective purchasers of chocolate being misled or deceived, contrary to ss 52 or 53(c) and (d).[42]

However, this was not the end of the story as Cadbury and Darrell Lea settled out of court in 2009 (the details of this private settlement were of course not disclosed). Cadbury was ultimately able to use the universally recognised Pantone colour-coding system as the basis for registering its shades of purple as trade marks. Cadbury now owns five colours in the purple range while Darrell Lea can use other similar but not identical colours in its stores. This outcome suggests that in every dispute there is a price at which the less financially well-endowed party will settle!

Case 4: McDonald's versus MacTea in Singapore

In Singapore, McDonald's failed in its attempt to stop a local firm, Future Enterprises (FE), from registering marks for food and beverages using the prefix 'Mac'.[43] Thus in 1995 FE had applied to register three marks in class 30, for instant tea and chocolate drinks and instant food (noodles), all prefixed with 'Mac', for example 'MacTea', and using visual marks containing an eagle. McDonald's objected to these trade marks and, after its opposition was rejected both by the Principal Assistant Registrar of Trade Marks and by the High Court, it took the matter to the Court of Appeal. The two arguments made by McDonald's in bringing this case were (i) that FE had not registered these marks in good faith but had

[40] *Cadbury Schweppes Pty Ltd* v. *Darrell Lea Chocolate Shops Pty Ltd (No. 4)* (2006) 229 ALR 136, 157 [121].
[41] *Cadbury Schweppes Pty Ltd* v. *Darrell Lea Chocolate Shops Pty Ltd* (2007) 159 FCR 397.
[42] (2008) 75 IPR 557, 579 [89].
[43] *McDonald's Corp.* v. *Future Enterprises Pte Ltd* [2005] 1 SLR(R) 177.

copied the common prefix of their family of marks and (ii) that they were likely to confuse or deceive the public.

In dismissing the appeal Chao Hick Tin JA, delivering the judgment of the Court, made a number of observations. These included:

(a) the marks were 'neither visually nor aurally similar', as McDonald's marks were usually displayed with golden arches;
(b) the existence of a pre-existing series of marks was only one factor to be considered in the inquiry for confusion;
(c) the products of FE were to be sold through supermarkets, whereas McDonald's products were menu items sold for immediate consumption in its restaurants;
(d) the educated public was not likely to be easily deceived or hoodwinked, given the very success of the appellant, which was inseparable from its use of the golden arches logo;
(e) McDonald's had failed to show that FE's application marks were deceptive or confusing vis-à-vis its own marks;
(f) an allegation of bad faith should not be lightly inferred and FE had given two explanations of its choice of the 'Mac' mark that reflected its desire to project a Western image.[44]

At one point his Honour commented that:

> [McDonald's] wanted in the present proceeding to monopolise the prefix 'Mc' as far as food and beverages were concerned, irrespective of the state in which the relevant items were being sold and the manner in which they were sold.[45]

Also: 'It was pure speculation to say that [McDonalds] may one day have its products retailed in supermarkets'.[46]

Thus, far from FE trying to piggy-back on the large established firm, the view taken was that the world-famous brand was attempting to quash reasonable and essentially non-competing local enterprise.

Despite the success of the local firm in this case, the situation concerning the protection of well-known marks has not remained static, either in Singapore or worldwide. In 1999 WIPO had issued its Joint Recommendations on the Provisions of the Protection of Well-Known Marks, which called for a higher level of protection that does not depend on confusion or deception. Both the US and the UK had earlier introduced protection (in the mid-1990s) designed to prevent the dilution of well-known marks through the exploitation of their reputation. Singapore has amended its Trade Marks Act 1998 (Singapore Cap 332, 2007 Rev Ed)

[44] *Ibid.* 178–9. [45] *Ibid.* 192. [46] *Ibid.*

so that an application for a trade mark made after 1 July 2004 can be objected to by the owner of a well-known brand, on the grounds that it would 'cause dilution in an unfair manner of the distinctive character' or 'take unfair advantage of the distinctive character' of the owner's mark.[47] This provision obtains regardless of whether or not there is likely to be any confusion for the customer and refers rather to the loss of distinctiveness of the original mark. Thus the outcome for FE might have been different if this legislation had been in force for earlier trade mark applications.

Case 5: McDonald's versus 'McCurry' in Malaysia

McDonald's has continued its fight to stop the registration or use of 'Mc' and 'Mac' in relation to food and beverages.[48] In 2009 a Malaysian case also went to their Court of Appeal, where McDonald's again lost its fight against a local firm, in this case selling curry using the name Restoran McCurry ('McCurry Restaurant'). However in this instance the judgment on appeal overturned an earlier ruling in favour of McDonald's, where the trial judge had considered the use of McCurry to be a passing off of the plaintiff's trade name to which goodwill was attached.

In the Malaysian Court of Appeal, Gopal Sri Ram JCA stated four facts that led to his support of the appeal by McCurry that the use of this name was not infringing. First, the style and 'get-up' of the restaurant was very different; second, none of the individual dishes were labelled 'Mc-', while all were at a McDonald's outlet; third, the restaurant served no Western-style instant foods but only Indian and local food; and, fourth, the types of people that frequented the restaurant were very different from those going to McDonald's.[49]

So what can we learn from these cases? There are many common threads in these examples, several of which have a 'David and Goliath' character, with a small firm taking on a giant firm that has developed a well-known brand over many years and seeks to buttress this brand using aggressive tactics against smaller local firms. The media like to report such instances because the giant is presumed to be the 'bad guy' and David the 'good guy', regardless of the facts of the particular case. Big headlines appear whenever David takes on and slays the giant, so that

[47] See Trade Marks Act 1998 (Singapore Cap 332, 2007 Rev Ed) s. 55.

[48] *McCurry Restaurant SDN BHD* v. *McDonald's Corp.* [2009] 3 CLJ 540. This case is further discussed in Chapter 6, in this volume.

[49] *Ibid.* 550.

public sympathies are satisfied. Even where the giant actually keeps some power, there is often a degree of misreporting attributing all the gains to the small guy, as for example in the case of Ugg boots, where the initial successes of the local firms were not the end of the story. Equally we can see that there are many twists and turns and even reversals of fortune along the way, with at one time the courts finding in favour of the giant and at another in favour of David.

Another common feature of the cases reported here is that the judgments rely entirely on the law of trade marks and passing off, without reference to the size or resources of the litigants – seemingly an entirely appropriate and unbiased exercise of the law. Yet at the same time we also see persistence in the behaviour of those firms with deep pockets in pursuing their objectives across geographical boundaries and through time. This suggests there may be a need to consider whether the final outcomes are always fair and appropriate when adjudicated as now on a 'size-blind' basis.

V. Future research and policy

Key research need – improving public knowledge about trade mark enforcement

As highlighted in section IV, we currently have access to very few studies of how firms act in practice to enforce their trade marks, apart from the records provided by the courts of the limited share of such enforcement actions that reach a court proceeding. One of the main gaps is knowledge about actions taken out of court by the issue of 'cease and desist' requests to other firms. What are the prospects of improving the number and scale of surveys devoted to generating data on enforcement activity?

The cheapest way to collect data is generally to add questions to an existing data collection process. Clearly in the field of registered trade marks, firms have to get in touch with a government agency or an intergovernmental registration authority when renewing their marks. It would be feasible to ask questions about what enforcement actions, in or out of court, they have taken over the duration of their mark and how successful these have been. Within Europe many countries engage in data collection for the Community Innovation Survey, which aims to monitor the innovative activities of firms. Here too the ownership and enforcement of IP assets could be the subject of ancillary enquiries attached to the main survey. Another route to improving data collection could be to invite firms to register their disputes on a website. This would provide firms with a mechanism by which to signal to other firms, not party to the current dispute, what their attitudes are to enforcement.

Key policy issue – identifying and addressing anti-competitive usage of brands

We have identified what we might call the 'deep pockets' (firm-size) issue, whereby larger firms with significant brands may act to threaten smaller firms that are disadvantaged by compliance with these orders, but do not have the resources to resist the bigger firm. Can the law courts, or other agencies such as competition authorities, distinguish between activities that constitute valid publicity and enforcement for a firm's brand and those that constitute threatening behaviour by firms with deep pockets?[50] Should other factors besides the narrow facts of the case be admissible evidence in the courts – for example should the prior record of behaviour by a particular firm in the field of enforcement of its IP rights be considered in a new conflict?[51] This might cause firms to consider more carefully whether a particular threat or sequence of threats would be worthwhile over the longer term.

Another way forward could be for the agencies of government themselves to issue 'cease and desist' letters to companies that are seen as being engaged in throwing their weight about within their markets. This could be done based on collaboration between the IP agencies and the competition authorities to monitor firms. A research unit on trade marks and brands would have as part of its remit the task of monitoring behaviour by owners of both longstanding, mature trade marks, and of marks that have experienced meteoric rises within particular product markets. This kind of activity would of course be more efficiently conducted if the data on enforcement had already been improved!

A further issue is of course the size of the remedies being imposed on firms that are found guilty of infringement. For example if newly trading firms attempt to free-ride on the existing reputation of a well-known trade mark, then there needs to be a disincentive to choosing such a closely related name or logo. One of the conclusions of the Bircham report of the recent UK government conference on brands was that:

[50] For example in Australia there is legal protection against unjustified threats, but this type of legislation is not universal. See, e.g., Trade Marks Act 1995 (Cth) s. 129.

[51] Of course this risks going against the principles generally in use to obtain a fair trial; for example the past criminal record of a defendant subject to a new trial is not admissible evidence within the trial, but is considered in both bail hearings and sentencing.

> Stronger punitive remedies need to be considered in respect of intellectual property infringement to discourage persistent infringement and ensure that infringement is not merely a commercial risk worth taking.[52]

However this has no impact for the majority of conflicts that do not get as far as the courts. Offering government advice and financial support to small and medium enterprises (SMEs) for enforcement has also been mooted as a remedy, with suggestions including public subsidy to litigation insurance schemes. However in the Greenhalgh *et al.* survey of smaller firms, few firms already had such insurance and other respondents were generally sceptical about the costs of such insurance ever being within their reach.[53]

Self help – actions by firms themselves

What can smaller firms do to help themselves in regard to preserving the competitive nature of their markets? Advertising by new entrants can be directly comparative, making named references to established brands within their own product launch. This type of behaviour is not welcomed by incumbents, who typically see this as an example of new entrants free-riding on their own reputation. Does a permissive attitude by the courts to comparative advertising help new entrants to gain a foothold in a market? In their discussion of this issue, Davis and Maniatis argue that comparative advertising is seen as helpful to overcoming barriers to entry into fields dominated by established brands. They point out that, both in the US Court of Appeal and the European Court of Justice, there have been a number of rulings that appear to favour comparative advertising.[54] There is also likely to be strength emanating from product comparisons performed by independent consumers' associations. The difficulty for public policy in this field is that neither firms nor government agencies can intervene without compromising the independence of such product evaluation agencies.

Can we rely on a sensible approach by firms to control the excessive use of litigation in the field of trade marks? There is perhaps a boundary that firms can recognise that they should not cross when engaging in attempts to suppress similar marks to their own. Thus according to Leong:

52 Intellectual Property Office (UK), *Branding in a Modern Economy: Conference Report*, Conference Report (2009) 14.
53 Greenhalgh *et al.*, 'Intellectual Property Enforcement', 1, 2.
54 Davis and Maniatis, 'Trademarks, Brands and Competition', in da Silva Lopes and Paul Duguid, *Trademarks*, 126–7.

> [For companies] it is equally important to guard against an indiscriminate policy to oppose all third parties' use of marks remotely similar, as this may generate substantial negative publicity and ultimately damage the equity in these brands, which businesses are trying so hard to protect.[55]

Certainly the publicity that the cases involving McDonald's in Singapore and Malaysia attracted may not have improved this firm's image in those countries.

[55] Susanna Leong, 'To brand or not to brand?', *Singapore Business Times* (Singapore) 29 August 2009, 43.

Part II

Personal reputation

3 Legal and cultural approaches to the protection of the contemporary celebrity brand in the Asia Pacific region

David Tan

I. Introduction

Celebrity sells. Madonna models for the Dolce & Gabbana global advertising campaign. Roger Federer fronts Rolex. David Beckham is synonymous with Adidas. Julianne Moore goes naked for Bulgari. Michael Phelps partners Subway. And the list goes on. Indeed consumer brands are willing to pay millions of dollars to be associated with prominent celebrities who are known to audiences around the world. As cultural studies scholar Graeme Turner observes:

> it is the pervasiveness of celebrity across the modern mass media that encourages us to think of it as a new development . . . The exorbitance of celebrity's contemporary cultural visibility is certainly unprecedented, and the role that the celebrity plays across many aspects of the cultural field has certainly expanded and multiplied in recent years.[1]

Bolstered by their ubiquitous presence in the mass media and the internet, the commercially valuable reputations of celebrities are often widely exploited. Celebrities have become brand names in their own right, with each well-known persona embodying a constellation of meanings specific to that persona.

This chapter examines how legal analysis and doctrinal development may benefit from observations and empirical research conducted in cultural studies on the celebrity personality and its relation to consumption behaviour. As cultural studies is a diverse discipline that incorporates perspectives from other areas such as anthropology, media studies, semiotics and sociology, this chapter will adopt a combination of resources based on revised, updated and reconstructed readings of the Frankfurt School, of British cultural studies and of some positions of postmodern theories. Instead of selecting a particular theory of cultural studies, this 'multiperspectival approach' is not only 'pragmatic contextualist' in its

[1] Graeme Turner, *Understanding Celebrity* (Sage, London, 2004), 4.

orientation, but can also yield 'more insightful and useful analyses than those produced by one perspective alone'.[2] Such an approach is evident in the celebrity studies of contemporary cultural scholars such as Richard Dyer, David Marshall and Graeme Turner,[3] and of Stuart Hall, whose writings constitute an invaluable resource for this research.[4] Over the last two decades, the research of Grant McCracken on the celebrity endorsement effect in economic consumption, drawing on semiotics and other cultural writings, has also influenced other scholars exploring the connection between the star aura and consumer behaviour.[5] These works will form the foundation of the cultural studies approach undertaken in this analysis.

Part II outlines the three key actions that celebrities have generally relied on to vindicate an unauthorised commercial use of their persona. In the US, a majority of state jurisdictions recognise various aspects of the human persona – like name, likeness and voice – as protectable indicia of identity, according to them the status of a proprietary right known as 'right of publicity'. Mere misappropriation is often sufficient to result in legal liability. Other common law jurisdictions such as the UK, Australia and Singapore do not recognise a right of publicity, but allow the protection of the celebrity persona through the passing off action, requiring the plaintiff to prove elements of goodwill, misrepresentation and damage. Moreover, the defamation tort, while rarely invoked in an advertising context, has been successfully employed on a number of occasions in Singapore against defendants for unauthorised commercial uses of identity.

[2] Douglas Kellner, *Media Culture: Cultural Studies, Identity and Politics between the Modern and the Postmodern* (Routledge, London, 1995), 26.

[3] For example Richard Dyer, *Stars* (British Film Institute, London, 1979); Richard Dyer, *Heavenly Bodies: Film Stars and Society* (2nd edn, Routledge, New York, 2004); P. David Marshall, *Celebrity and Power: Fame in Contemporary Culture* (University of Minnesota Press, Minneapolis, 1997); Turner, *Understanding Celebrity*.

[4] For example Stuart Hall, 'Encoding/Decoding', in Stuart Hall, Dorothy Hobson, Andrew Lowe and Paul Willis (eds.), *Culture, Media, Language: Working Papers in Cultural Studies, 1972–79* (Hutchinson, London, 1980), 128; Stuart Hall, 'The Rediscovery of "Ideology": Return of the Repressed in Media Studies', in Michael Gurevitch, Tony Bennett, James Curran and Janet Woollacott (eds.), *Culture, Society and the Media* (Routledge, London, 1982), 56.

[5] For example Grant McCracken, 'Who is the Celebrity Endorser? Cultural Foundations of the Endorsement Process' (1989) 16 *Journal of Consumer Research* 310. See also Sejung Marina Choi, Wei-Na Lee and Hee-Jung Kim, 'Lessons from the Rich and Famous: A Cross-Cultural Comparison of Celebrity Endorsement in Advertising' (2005) 34 *Journal of Advertising* 85; B. Zafer Erdogan, Michael J. Baker and Stephen Tagg, 'Selecting Celebrity Endorsers: The Practitioner's Perspective' (2001) 41 *Journal of Advertising Research* 39.

Part III highlights key aspects in cultural studies writings about the contemporary celebrity phenomenon to indicate how some of these may be relevant to the analysis of the elements of the passing off action. The usefulness of cultural studies to legal doctrine rests in its examination of the roles and meanings of celebrities in contemporary society, and how people consume them and incorporate them into their daily lives.[6]

Part IV demonstrates how these cultural insights may assist future development of the passing off action – the action most commonly relied on in the common law jurisdictions in the Asia Pacific region – in a more nuanced manner that takes into account the semiotic nature of the contemporary celebrity phenomenon. In particular, it argues that the concept of 'affective transfer' should form the basis of liability for unauthorised commercial uses.

Part V concludes that far from being just a theoretical discipline concerned with the politics of power and identity, cultural studies can provide a useful analytical framework for judges, scholars and lawyers to further their understanding of the extra-legal issues relating to the laws protecting the commercial value of the celebrity brand.

II. Right of publicity, passing off and defamation

(a) Right of publicity

The right of publicity, broadly defined as the 'inherent right of every human being to control the commercial use of his or her identity',[7] has been well established in the United States for over fifty years.[8] It protects the 'associative value' that celebrities bring to products and services.[9] Generally perceived to be a property right akin to an intellectual property

[6] I have previously made this argument in the context of the right of publicity. In essence the celebrity personality is constituted by the 'celebrity trinity' comprising the celebrity individual, the audience and the cultural producers. See David Tan, 'Beyond Trademark Law: What the Right of Publicity Can Learn from Cultural Studies' (2008) 25 *Cardozo Arts and Entertainment Law Journal* 913, 916.

[7] J. Thomas McCarthy, *The Rights of Publicity and Privacy* (2nd edn, West, Minnesota, 2000) § 3:1.

[8] It was first recognised by the Second Circuit in 1953 that baseball players had a 'right of publicity' in their images: *Haelan Laboratories Inc.* v. *Topps Chewing Gum Inc.*, 202 F 2d 866, 868 (2nd Cir, 1953). In the only right of publicity case ever to reach the US Supreme Court, the court affirmed the recognition of such an actionable right: *Zacchini* v. *Scripps-Howard Broadcasting Co.*, 433 US 562 (1976).

[9] Sheldon W. Halpern, 'The Right of Publicity: Maturation of an Independent Right Protecting the Associative Value of Personality' (1995) 46 *Hastings Law Journal* 853, 856, 859–60.

right,[10] the right of publicity has been invoked mainly by celebrities to prevent unauthorised commercial uses of their persona. The right of publicity is articulated in the Restatement (Third) of Unfair Competition as follows:

> [o]ne who appropriates the commercial value of a person's identity by using without consent the person's name, likeness, or other indicia of identity for purposes of trade is subject to liability.[11]

Injunctive and monetary relief may be granted for an appropriation of the 'commercial value' of a person's identity.[12]

What clearly sets the right of publicity apart from passing off and defamation is its treatment of indicia of identity as a limited-term proprietary right that is both assignable and descendible.[13] In practice, once identification of the plaintiff from the defendant's commercial use has been made out, liability is presumed, subject to statutory exclusions and the First Amendment defence; it is virtually a strict liability tort. Thus it is not surprising that other common law jurisdictions which do not share a robust First Amendment culture have rejected the right of publicity as it can overprotect the human persona.

(b) Passing off

Both right of publicity and passing off actions acknowledge that the law should protect the commercial interests of these individuals and prevent unlawful profiting. However, it is established law that a right of publicity claim does not require any evidence that a consumer is likely to be confused as to the plaintiff's association with or endorsement of the defendant's use.[14] Therefore it appears more expansive in its protection against an unauthorised use of identity compared to a common

[10] See for example *Comedy III Productions Inc.* v. *Gary Saderup Inc.*, 25 Cal 4th 387, 399 (2001).

[11] Restatement (Third) of Unfair Competition (1995) § 46.

[12] Restatement (Third) of Unfair Competition (1995) §§ 48–9.

[13] In 2009, twenty-eight states had provided their citizens with a remedy for infringement of the right of publicity. Eighteen states recognise publicity rights by way of common law, and of those, eight also have statutory provisions. Ten states provide only a statutory remedy: McCarthy, *Rights of Publicity*, § 6:3.

[14] Restatement (Third) of Unfair Competition (1995) § 46 cmt (c) § 47 cmt (a); McCarthy, *Rights of Publicity*, § 2:8; Melville B. Nimmer, 'The Right of Publicity' (1954) 19 *Law and Contemporary Problems* 203, 212; *Parks* v. *LaFace Records*, 329 F 3d 437, 460 (6th Cir, 2003) ('*Parks*'); *Abdul-Jabbar* v. *General Motors Corp*, 75 F 3d 1391, 1398 (9th Cir, 1996) ('*Abdul-Jabbar*'); *Rogers* v. *Grimaldi*, 875 F 2d 994, 1004 (2nd Cir, 1989) ('*Rogers*').

law passing off claim. Celebrities in common law jurisdictions such as Hong Kong,[15] as well as the UK and Australia, generally rely on the action of passing off and equivalent statutory claims if their identities have been used without their consent in advertising or trade as the right of publicity is not recognised in these jurisdictions.[16] In addition, s. 18 of the Australian Consumer Law, contained in sch. 2 of the Competition and Consumer Act 2010 (Cth), provides a statutory remedy for Australian plaintiffs.[17] Unlike in a right of publicity claim, it is necessary to show in passing off that consumers have been misled or deceived as to the celebrity's endorsement of, or association with, the defendant's products.

The classic common law tort of passing off was originally intended to protect against rival traders in the same field of business 'passing off' their products as the products of another competitor ('trading goodwill'), with its rationale being the prevention of commercial dishonesty.[18] Subsequently, passing off has broadened to protect goodwill 'not in its classic form of a trader representing his goods as the goods of somebody else, but in an extended form'.[19] In English law, it appears settled law that the extended action of passing off today does not require the plaintiff to

[15] See Chapter 4, in this volume.

[16] See for example *Irvine* v. *Talksport Ltd* [2002] 1 WLR 2355 ('*Irvine*'); *Pacific Dunlop Ltd* v. *Hogan* (1989) 25 FCR 553 ('*Crocodile Dundee*'); *Hogan* v. *Koala Dundee Pty Ltd* (1988) 20 FCR 314 ('*Koala Dundee*'); *Radio Corporation Pty Ltd* v. *Henderson* [1960] NSWR 279 ('*Henderson*'). It is important to note that the common law passing off action finds an equivalent in the US, where the broad language of the federal Lanham (Trademark) Act of 1946, 15 USC § 43(a) creates a civil cause of action against any person who identifies his or her product in such a way as to likely cause confusion among consumers as to the association of the producer of the product with another person or regarding the sponsorship or approval of the product by another person: 15 USC § 1125(a).

[17] This provision was previously set out in s. 52 of the Trade Practices Act 1974 (Cth) (TPA). In Australia, plaintiffs have often brought concurrent actions in passing off and for misleading or deceptive conduct under s. 52 of the TPA. The Australian High Court has addressed the issue of misrepresentation under both common law passing off and the TPA simultaneously: see for example *Parkdale Custom Built Furniture Pty Ltd* v. *Puxu Pty Ltd* (1982) 149 CLR 191, 219 ('*Puxu*'); *Hornsby Building Information Centre Pty Ltd* v. *Sydney Information Centre Pty Ltd* (1978) 140 CLR 216, 227.

[18] See for example *Reddaway (Frank) & Co. Ltd* v. *George Banham & Co. Ltd* [1896] AC 199, 204 ('*Reddaway*'); *Erven Warnink BV* v. *J Townend & Sons (Hull) Ltd* [1979] AC 731, 742 ('*Erven Warnink*'); *Irvine*, 2360. See also David Tan and J. Thomas McCarthy, 'Australia – Protecting Goodwill and Reputation', in J. Thomas McCarthy, *The Rights of Publicity and Privacy* (2010 edn, Thomson Reuters) § 6:158; Alison Laurie, 'The Big Sell: The Value and Effectiveness of Character Merchandising Protection in Australia' (2003) 54 *Intellectual Property Forum* 12, 14; Benjamin F. Katekar, 'Coping with Character Merchandising – Passing Off Unsurpassed' (1996) 7 *Australian Intellectual Property Journal* 178, 188.

[19] *Erven Warnink*, 739.

prove a common field of activity;[20] and the passing off action is capable of protecting the goodwill or valuable reputation of a person/business against any unauthorised claim of association or connection by another ('promotional goodwill').[21] This position resonates with the Australian cases.[22]

The passing off action does not recognise a proprietary interest per se in a name, likeness or other indicia of identity, but it protects goodwill as 'the attractive force which brings in custom'[23] by preventing a trader from gaining an unfair competitive advantage through associating itself or its products with a well-known personality. In order for a celebrity to obtain legal recourse for interference with his or her goodwill, the claimant must prove all the elements of the passing off tort. Despite there being no generally accepted definition of passing off, the element of misrepresentation or misleading/deceptive conduct is considered to be central to the tort.[24]

The elements of a common law passing off action in both the UK and Australia follow the position set out by the House of Lords in *Reckitt & Colman Products Ltd* v. *Borden Inc.*,[25] in that there are three key elements of goodwill or valuable reputation, deceptive conduct and damage.[26] Over the last two decades, the courts have increasingly recognised that it is a prevalent commercial practice 'whereby, to gain a competitive advantage, goods and services are marketed to the public by associating them with a well-known personality, real or fictitious . . . who has developed an identifiable reputation among potential purchasers . . . [thus appearing] more desirable to consumers'.[27] However, although it has been noted that 'passing off has been expanded further by Australian courts than most other countries . . . in keeping with the corresponding development in the practice of character merchandising',[28] the courts there, as well as

[20] See for example *Lego Systems A/S* v. *Lego M Lemelstrich* [1983] FSR 155, 183–7 ('*Lego*'); *Irvine*, 2368.

[21] See for example Samuel K. Murumba, *Commercial Exploitation of Personality* (Law Book Co., Sydney, 1986) 65. See also *Arsenal FC plc* v. *Reed* [2001] RPC 922, 930–1.

[22] For example *Campomar* (2000) 2002 CLR 45, 89 (Australian High Court unanimous decision). See also *Henderson*, 576; *Crocodile Dundee*; *Koala Dundee Pty Ltd.*

[23] *Inland Revenue Commissioners* v. *Muller & Co.'s Margarine Ltd* [1901] AC 217, 224 ('*Muller*'). See also *Federal Commissioner for Taxation* v. *Murry* (1998) 193 CLR 605, 615 ('*Murry*').

[24] See for example *ConAgra Inc.* v. *McCain Foods (Aust) Pty Ltd* (1992) 33 FCR 302, 356 ('*ConAgra*'); *Irvine*, 2360.

[25] [1990] 1 All ER 873 ('*Reckitt & Colman*').

[26] For example *Cadbury Schweppes Pty Ltd* v. *Pub Squash Co. Pty Ltd* [1981] 1 WLR 193 ('*Cadbury Schweppes*'); *Moorgate Tobacco Co. Ltd* v. Philip *Morris Ltd (No. 2)* (1984) 156 CLR 414 ('*Moorgate Tobacco (No. 2)*'); *Irvine*.

[27] Laurie, 'Big Sell', 12. [28] *Ibid.*

the English courts, have consistently rejected the recognition of a general tort of unfair competition.[29]

It is generally accepted that consumers are often influenced in their choice of products because of a perceived association between those products and a celebrity personality. As an Australian federal court judge remarked, the use of celebrities in advertising seeks to 'foster favourable inclination towards [the product], a good feeling about it, an emotional attachment to it' such that the product is 'better in [the] eyes' of consumers than a comparable product without such an association.[30]

However, over the last decade, there have been relatively few passing off claims by celebrities in the UK and Australia, just a handful in Hong Kong,[31] and virtually none in Singapore, compared to a flourish of right of publicity litigation in the US. The most high-profile case arguably is Formula 1 driver Eddie Irvine's claim against TalkSport Radio for using a digitally altered photograph of him holding a portable radio bearing the name of the radio station in a promotional brochure.[32] Irvine was awarded damages at first instance amounting to £2,000, but this was increased to £25,000 on appeal, being the 'reasonable endorsement fee' the defendant '*would have had to pay* in order to obtain lawfully that which it in fact obtained unlawfully'.[33] Laddie J.'s views at first instance appear to have been accepted by the English Court of Appeal.[34] His judgment indicates that the English courts may be prepared to go as far as the Australian courts in finding that impressionistic association may suffice as misrepresentation. In particular, Laddie J. observes:

> the court can take judicial notice that it is common for famous people to exploit their names and images by way of endorsement . . . those in business have reason to believe that the lustre of a famous personality, if attached to their goods or services, will enhance the attractiveness of those goods or services to their target market.[35]

The dicta suggest that courts may adopt, as evident in the *Crocodile Dundee* litigation in Australia,[36] a less stringent view of misrepresentation

29 For example *Campomar Sociedad Limitada* v. *Nike International Ltd* (2000) 202 CLR 45, 54–5; *Moorgate Tobacco (No. 2)*, 445; *Victoria Park Racing and Recreation Grounds Co. Ltd* v. *Taylor* (1937) 58 CLR 479, 509; *Erven Warnink*, 740; *L'Oréal SA* v. *Bellure NV* (2007) 73 IPR 629, 666–7.

30 *Crocodile Dundee*, 583–4 (Burchett J.).

31 Yu, Chapter 4, in this volume (discussing *Lau Tak Wah* v. *Hang Seng Bank Ltd* [2000] 1 HKC 280; *Tam Wing Lun Alan* v. *Hang Mei Record Co.* [1991] 2 HKC 384).

32 *Irvine*.

33 *Irvine* v. *Talksport Ltd (Damages)* [2003] 2 All ER 881, 903 ('*Irvine (Damages)*') (emphasis added).

34 *Ibid.* 887.

35 *Irvine*, 2368.

36 *Crocodile Dundee*, 553; *Koala Dundee*.

when the celebrity persona has been used by the defendant in advertising and merchandising.

(c) *Defamation*

The law of passing off in Singapore essentially follows the test established in *Reckitt & Colman*,[37] but in two cases decided in the 1990s, a well-known fashion model and a politician succeeded in bringing an action in defamation against unauthorised uses of their image in advertising.[38] Although they both appear to be a simple open-and-shut case of passing off – that the advertisement misrepresented their endorsement or association – the plaintiffs curiously relied on the tort of defamation to vindicate damage to their reputation. It is commonly accepted that the tort of defamation protects the dignitary, as opposed to the commercial, interests of the individual.[39] Damages are usually awarded as a solatium for the defamed plaintiff's lowered standing in the community and associated mental distress and suffering.[40]

In *Hanis Saini Hussey* v. *Integrated Information*, the image of the celebrity was used in an advertisement for an escort agency; this unauthorised use of persona undoubtedly would engender a likelihood of confusion as to the plaintiff's endorsement of, or association with, the defendant's escort services. While it is clear that the plaintiff would not encounter any problem proving goodwill, misrepresentation and damage, only an action in defamation was pleaded. In awarding her damages of S$30,000, the court remarked that there must have been members of the public who thought Hussey was either advertising for the defendant's escort agency or was in some way connected with it, using language evocative of passing off. Similarly, when Member of Parliament Chiam See Tong's image was used in an advertisement promoting a restaurant, he alleged that his reputation has been tarnished as a result of the association. Perhaps the broad interpretation of what constitutes defamatory meaning in Singapore jurisprudence and the balance struck in favour of

[37] For example *Tong Guan Food Products Pte Ltd* v. *Hoe Huat Hng Foodstuff Pte Ltd* [1991] 1 SLR 133; *Saga Foodstuffs Manufacturers (Pte) Ltd* v. *Best Food Pte Ltd* [1995] 1 SLR 739; *Pontiac Marina Pte Ltd* v. *CDL Hotels International Ltd* [1997] 3 SLR 726; *Nation Fittings (M) Sdn Bhd* v. *Oystertec Plc* [2006] 1 SLR 712.

[38] See *Chiam See Tong* v. *Xin Zhang Jiang Restaurant Pte Ltd* [1995] 3 SLR 196; *Hanis Saini Hussey* v. *Integrated Information Pte Ltd* [1998] SGHC 219.

[39] For example *Reynolds* v. *Times Newspapers Ltd* [2001] 2 AC 127, 201; *Review Publishing Co. Ltd* v. *Lee Hsien Loong* [2010] 1 SLR 52, 182 ('*Review Publishing*').

[40] See for example *Cassell & Co. Ltd* v. *Broome & Anor* [1972] AC 1027; *Uren* v. *John Fairfax and Sons Pty Ltd* (1966) 117 CLR 118; *Jeyaretnam Joshua Benjamin* v. *Lee Kuan Yew* [1992] 2 SLR 310 ('*JBJ*').

the protection of reputation,[41] and the ability of the court to award aggravated damages, has resulted in these well-known individuals choosing the tort of defamation over passing off to seek redress for the unauthorised commercial use of their persona. Generally, however, it would be more appropriate to have recourse to passing off if one is seeking damages for injury to goodwill or reputation in a commercial context, and leaving the defamation tort for situations where there is damage to the dignity of an individual through the 'lower[ing] of him [or her] as such in the estimation of right-thinking people in Singapore'.[42]

III. Cultural studies – deriving key insights

The focus here is on eliciting salient themes from the cultural writings on the contemporary celebrity and represents an effort to create a new interdisciplinary synthesis that investigates what cultural pragmatism can contribute to the law. Using key texts in cultural studies, this chapter adopts a pragmatic orientation towards inquiry that is both contextualist and instrumentalist.[43] Elsewhere I have explored these themes in greater detail.[44]

(a) The celebrity as defined by widespread public identification

Daniel Boorstin's influential reading of the superficiality of the celebrity in 1961[45] paved the way for future works on the nature of the contemporary celebrity personality. His elegant and oft-quoted phrase, '[a] celebrity is a person who is known for his well-knownness'[46] is an important starting point for a broad definition of a contemporary celebrity based on a ubiquitous media presence and public recognition. Cultural studies writings are notable in their overwhelming acceptance that the contemporary celebrity is 'characterized by an individual distinction, mass appeal, ubiquity and popular authorship'.[47]

[41] See for example *Jeyaretnam Joshua Benjamin* v. *Goh Chok Tong* [1983–1984] SLR(R) 745; *JBJ* [1992] 2 SLR 310. See also *Review Publishing*, 76–8, 178–9.

[42] *JBJ*, 323.

[43] For a more comprehensive analysis of the relevance of cultural studies on the celebrity phenomenon to laws protecting the commercial value of identity, see Tan, 'Beyond Trademark Law', 955–76.

[44] See for example Tan, 'Beyond Trademark Law'; David Tan, 'The Fame Monster Reloaded: The Contemporary Celebrity, Cultural Studies and Passing Off' (2010) 32 *Sydney Law Review* 291; David Tan, 'Political Recoding of the Contemporary Celebrity and the First Amendment' (2011) 2 *Harvard Journal of Sports and Entertainment Law* 1.

[45] Daniel J. Boorstin, *The Image: A Guide to Pseudo-Events in America* (Harper, New York, 1961).

[46] *Ibid.* 57.

[47] Tan, 'Beyond Trademark Law', 938.

Individuals from almost any field, be it film, sport, music, television, business or even cookery, can be elevated to the status of celebrity.[48] It is this widespread public identification – both of the visual image and the embodied values/ideals – that defines a celebrity, and consequently imparts to it a commercial value in the context of consumption.[49] In writing on why celebrities enhance brand familiarity and favourability, it was observed that celebrities 'have very high public awareness and people are able to visualize them very easily as they are so familiar with them'.[50] This evocative aspect of celebrity – through the 'marginal differentiation of their personalities'[51] that leads to easy audience recall – provides the impetus for the legal recognition and protection of the commercial value of the celebrity identity. The emotional affinity the audience may have with a particular celebrity often translates to some form of imitation,[52] where the consumer would purchase products associated with their favourite celebrities to become more like them.

(b) The celebrity as a cultural sign

According to Dyer, Marshall and many other cultural studies scholars, the celebrity is a sign that embodies particular meanings for the majoritarian public.[53] Celebrities can 'represent typical ways of behaving, feeling and thinking in contemporary society, ways that have been socially, culturally, historically constructed'.[54] Due to the meticulously constructed public personae of many celebrities – particularly the movie stars and sport icons – the semiotic sign of these well-known individuals is usually 'decoded' by the audience to represent a defined cluster of meanings.[55] A celebrity persona is like a well-known brand; each advertisement featuring a celebrity can be viewed as 'a contributory iteration of the brand' and its function is to attach the 'brand idea to advertised product or service in appropriate style'.[56] The concept of celebrity – with its attendant notions of well-knownness, adulation and popularity – is signified

[48] For example Irving Rein, Philip Kotler and Martin Stoller, *High Visibility: The Making and Marketing of Professionals into Celebrities* (NTC Publishing Group, Lincolnwood, IL, 1997).

[49] For example Rosemary J. Coombe, *The Cultural Life of Intellectual Properties: Authorship, Appropriation, and the Law* (Duke University Press, Durham, NC, 1998), 96.

[50] Hamish Pringle, *Celebrity Sells* (John Wiley & Sons, Chichester, West Sussex, 2004), 68–9.

[51] Boorstin, *The Image*, 65.

[52] For example Dyer, *Stars*, 17–18.

[53] For example *ibid.* 2–3, 53–61, 99–181, 183–4; Marshall, *Celebrity and Power*, 57.

[54] Richard Dyer, *Heavenly Bodies*, 15–16. See also Dyer, *Stars*, 3 (discussing how Hollywood, through its representation of movie stars, can reproduce the 'dominant ideology of Western society').

[55] For example Marshall, *Celebrity and Power*, 56–71, 185–99, 244–7; Turner, *Understanding Celebrity*, 14–15, 23–6, 89–108.

[56] Iain MacRury, *Advertising* (Routledge, Abingdon, Oxon., 2009), 50.

through, for example, an entertainer or athlete, and the resulting product is a semiotic sign replete with meaning in everyday culture. While movie stars are often represented as objects of aspiration, glamour and desire, the celebrity athlete signifies heroism, human transcendence and a love for the pure authentic game.

Thus the celebrity as a widely recognised cultural sign, can encourage the public who identify with such attributed ideological values to consume the celebrity itself as a commodity (for example by watching the movies of a particular actor) or products associated with the celebrity (for example by purchasing celebrity-endorsed products). On the other hand, the celebrity semiotic sign, as a result of its publicly identifiable encodings, also presents rich opportunities for alternative codings to challenge these 'typical ways of behaving, feeling and thinking in contemporary society'[57] representative of majoritarian ideals.

(c) Interim observations – the celebrity brand

Generally, cultural scholars have documented the ways in which notions of celebrity and fame are occupying increasingly prominent positions in contemporary society, with a recognition of the burgeoning commercial value that the celebrity persona brings to global advertising and merchandising. Despite the postmodern critique that there is 'no objective perception of a sign', the encoded meanings of the celebrity sign as widely recognised by audiences and consumers may nevertheless be determined by the average consumer test.[58] In essence, the celebrity personality is like a 'brand'. Although there is no agreed definition of a brand, as legal commentator Jennifer Davis observes, a brand is 'understood to have a value which transcends the product with which it is associated'.[59] Brands are often said to have a quality of transferability, in that they can transfer consumer loyalty between products because consumers invest affective meanings in brands.

The celebrity persona functions much like a well-known brand in contemporary consumption: it is often identified by distinctive visual elements, it embodies a bundle of affective values for the consumer, and its meaning is shaped by producers and consumers. In the context of

[57] Dyer, *Heavenly Bodies*, 15–16.

[58] Jennifer Davis, 'Between a Sign and a Brand: Mapping the Boundaries of a Registered Trade Mark in European Union Trade Mark Law', in Lionel Bently, Jennifer Davis and Jane C. Ginsburg (eds.), *Trade Marks and Brands: An Interdisciplinary Critique* (Cambridge University Press, Cambridge, 2008), 65, 71 fn. 24.

[59] *Ibid.* 80. See also Megan Richardson, 'Trade Marks and Language' (2004) 26 *Sydney Law Review* 193, 194–5; David Tan, 'Differentiating between Brand and Trade Mark: *City Chain* v. *Louis Vuitton Malletier*' [2010] *Singapore Journal of Legal Studies* 202, 202–3.

trade marks, Davis argues that in the case of the brand values which attach to certain marks, these 'have not been appropriated from the public domain'; rather they have been 'nurtured by the proprietor and, as such, the question is not whether they belong in the public domain, but to what extent they may be protected through trade mark registration'.[60] An analogy may be drawn with the right of publicity here. Although the audience-consumer has contributed to the production of a celebrity sign like David Beckham or Tiger Woods, it is arguable that the stable configuration of meanings embodied by these signs (brand values) as maintained by the celebrity individual (the proprietor) over time merits legal protection against unauthorised *commercial* uses that would take unfair advantage of their reputation or of the emotional attraction for the consumers.

IV. The celebrity brand and passing off: a cultural–legal approach

Using a celebrity in advertising, product merchandising and other commercial contexts is likely to have a positive effect on consumers' brand perceptions and purchasing decisions; this is commonly referred to as the 'positive halo effect' within branding and marketing research.[61] In buying a product associated with a celebrity, the consumer can buy into some of the glamour, self-indulgence and decadence of the charmed life of a movie star or into the athleticism and success of a sporting icon. Such symbolic celebrity images attempt to create an association between the products offered and the ideologically desirable traits in order to produce the impression that if one wants to be a certain type of person, then one should buy the particular product.[62] This is evident in the multimillion dollar endorsement contracts that globally recognised actors and athletes sign each year with brands as diverse as American Express, Louis Vuitton, Nike, Rolex and Gillette. While cultural scholars such as Dyer have acknowledged the commoditised status of the celebrity, it was Grant McCracken who in 1989 connected empirical socio-psychological and economic research with cultural studies writings on the semiotic significance of celebrities to consumption.[63] McCracken's conclusion that a celebrity sign is 'persuasive' to consumers because the sign is 'made up

[60] Davis, 'Between a Sign and a Brand', 81–2. *Contra* Rosemary Coombe, 'Objects of Property and Subjects of Politics: Intellectual Property Laws and Democratic Dialogue (1991) 69 *Texas Law Review* 1853, 1876 (arguing that trade mark owners have 'the ability to restrict and control meaning' because they 'own' the sign).

[61] For example Pringle, *Celebrity Sells*, 72.

[62] Kellner, *Media Culture*, 248.

[63] McCracken, 'Who is the Celebrity Endorser?'.

of certain meanings that the consumer finds compelling and useful' provided a good foundation for further investigative work on the impact of celebrities on contemporary consumption.[64]

The meaning–transfer model advanced by McCracken – that the symbolic affective values embodied by the celebrity sign is transferred to the product that the celebrity is associated with – supports the *raison d'être* of the right of publicity to prevent the commercial appropriation of the associative value of identity.[65] A similar cultural analysis has been made elsewhere in respect of the notion of associative value in a passing off claim.[66] In addition to perceiving the celebrity sign as embodying a bundle of meanings, it is argued that the cultural circuit of movement of meaning is complete when members of the public, in expressing their identification with a particular celebrity, consume the celebrity commodity by purchasing products associated with that celebrity. Generally, celebrity endorsements translate into better product sales only when consumers feel that whatever cultural meanings attached to the celebrity can shift along unimpeded paths from the celebrity to the product. In the words of Stuart Hall, this would be an idealised state where the advertiser assumes a 'dominant–hegemonic position' and the 'perfectly transparent communication' results in the audience's consumption of the product.[67]

(a) Goodwill and well-knownness of the contemporary celebrity

In a passing off claim, a celebrity has to show that he or she has a protectable commercial goodwill or reputation within a particular area or location in which the relevant misrepresentation is alleged to have taken place.[68] In other words, it is recognised that the reputation of a plaintiff

[64] Roobina Ohanian, 'The Impact of Celebrity Spokespersons' Perceived Image on Consumers' Intention to Purchase' (1991) 31 *Journal of Advertising Research* 46; B. Zafer *Erdogan*, '*Celebrity Endorsement*: A Literature Review' (1999) 15 *Journal of Marketing Management* 291.

[65] See David Tan, 'Affective Transfer and the Appropriation of Commercial Value: The Contribution of Cultural Pragmatism to the Right of Publicity' (2010) 9 *Virginia Sports and Entertainment Law Journal* 272.

[66] See David Tan, 'The Fame Monster Reloaded: The Contemporary Celebrity, Cultural Studies and Passing Off' (2010) 32 *Sydney Law Review* 291.

[67] Hall, 'Encoding/Decoding', 136. Hall has also defined the taking of an existing meaning and reappropriating it for new meanings as 'trans-coding'. Stuart Hall, 'The Spectacle of the "Other"', in Stuart Hall (ed.), *Representation: Cultural Representations and Signifying Practices* (Open University, London, 1997), 223, 270.

[68] In Australia, it is not necessary for the plaintiff to have a business presence in Australia; it is sufficient that he or she has a reputation among the persons there. For example *ConAgra*, 340–4. The specific thing in which goodwill is vested must also be identified. For example *Conan Doyle* v. *London Mystery Magazine Ltd* (1949) 66 RPC 312, 313–14 (goodwill only in existing stories and not generally in all aspects of Sherlock Holmes character).

in the forum is the source of his potential business there; and a 'sufficient reputation' to be actionable 'requires something more than a reputation among a small number of persons'.[69] For most individuals who have become well known to the public through their endeavours in the fields of sports, entertainment or popular culture, it appears that they will have no problem satisfying the first element of a common law passing off claim in Singapore, Hong Kong, the UK or Australia.[70] Expert evidence, survey evidence and results from focus groups are often admitted as evidence used to prove the subsistence of goodwill.[71] The ubiquitous circulation in contemporary society of an individual's name, image or other distinctive characteristics can result in that individual gaining an ever-increasing familiarity among members of the public, thus becoming 'well-known'.[72] The judicial evaluation of whether the plaintiff has established the requisite local goodwill or reputation takes into account precisely these channels of communication, considering a wide range of media exposure from print publicity to advertising circulation, as well as television audience figures indicated by ratings.[73]

By focusing on goodwill, the passing off action dispenses with the debate about the recognition of a *proprietary* right of publicity in evocative aspects of identity.[74] Nonetheless, courts still have to confront the question whether the plaintiff has been identified by the relevant group of consumers through the defendant's use. However, this inquiry may

69 *ConAgra*, 346.

70 See for example *Irvine* (F1 driver Eddie Irvine); *Crocodile Dundee* (actor Paul Hogan); *Hutchence* v. *South Sea Bubble Co. Pty Ltd* (1986) 6 IPR 473 ('*Hutchence*') (pop music group INXS); *Talmax Pty Ltd* v. *Telstra Corp. Ltd* [1997] 2 Qd R 444 ('*Talmax*') (swimmer Kieren Perkins); *Honey* v. *Australian Airlines* (1990) 18 IPR 185 (athlete Gary Honey); *Newton-John* v. *Scholl-Plough (Australia) Ltd* (1986) 11 FCR 233 (singer Olivia Newton-John). See also Huw Beverley-Smith, *The Commercial Appropriation of Personality* (Cambridge University Press, Cambridge, 2002) 61–70 (comparing the requirement of goodwill in UK and Australia).

71 However, courts are more reluctant to place great weight on expert testimony and survey evidence as proof of misrepresentation. See for example *Britt Allcroft (Thomas) LLC* v. *Miller* (2000) 49 IPR 7, 15–16.

72 A parallel argument has also been made in relation to satisfying the threshold requirement of identification in a right of publicity action. See David Tan, 'Much Ado about Evocation: A Cultural Analysis of Well-Knownness and the Right of Publicity' (2010) 28 *Cardozo Arts and Entertainment Law Journal* 317.

73 For example *Duff Beer case* (1996) 34 IPR 225, 230–2; *Irvine*, 2370–3.

74 For example *White* v. *Samsung Electronics America Inc.*, 971 F 2d 1395 (9th Cir, 1992); *Wendt* v. *Host International Inc.*, 125 F 3d 806, 814 (9th Cir, 1997). Arguably the controversy also surrounds the property right in a role or character. For example *McFarland* v. *Miller*, 14 F 3d 912 (3rd Cir, 1994); *Lugosi* v. *Universal Pictures*, 25 Cal 3d 813 (1979); *Nurmi* v. *Peterson* (CD Cal, WL 407484, 31 March 1989); Peter K. Yu, 'Fictional Persona Test: Copyright Preemption in Human Audiovisual Characters' (1998) 20 *Cardozo Law Review* 355.

sometimes be deferred to the misrepresentation stage, where the court would determine if, based on an overall impression, consumers were misled as to the celebrity plaintiff's approval of the product.

(b) Misrepresentation and affective transfer

Despite a general recognition that one may have a proprietary interest in goodwill that may be enforced through a passing off action – language that is evocative of the concept of misappropriation in a right of publicity claim – courts are nevertheless adamant that 'there is still a need to demonstrate a *misrepresentation* because it is that misrepresentation which enables the defendant to make use or take advantage of the claimant's reputation'.[75] Australian courts have also established that the finding of deceptive conduct must be assessed taking into consideration all the circumstances and the overall effect or impression on the consumers or potential consumers; the courts rely on 'a combination of visual impression and judicial estimation of the effect likely to be produced' by the defendant's conduct on consumers.[76]

However, the case law does not indicate clearly what type of misrepresentation must be alleged.[77] In Australia, Burchett J. of the Federal Court thought that the judicial focus should not be on determining the nature of 'precise representations', but rather on 'suggestions by [the trader] that may inveigle the emotions into false responses';[78] in particular, the 'subliminal effect of an advertisement . . . may be deceptive even without making any [explicit] untrue statement'.[79] This impressionistic approach, especially with the findings of misrepresentation in the parodic advertisement in the *Crocodile Dundee* case and in the get-up of the koala image in *Koala Dundee*, has led commentators to lament

75 *Irvine*, 2368 (emphasis added).
76 *Australian Woollen Mills Ltd* v. *FS Walton & Co. Ltd* (1937) 58 CLR 641, 659. Evidence of actual deception is not conclusive; ultimately it was 'a question of fact to be decided by considering what [was] said and done against the background of all surrounding circumstances'. *Taco Co. of Australia Inc.* v. *Taco Bell Pty Ltd* (1982) 42 ALR 177, 202 ('*Taco Bell*'); *10th Cantanae Pty Ltd* v. *Shoshana Pty Ltd* (1987) 79 ALR 299, 318. See also *Sydneywide Distributors Pty Ltd* v. *Red Bull Australia Pty Ltd* (2002) 55 IPR 354 ('*Red Bull*'); *Anheuser-Busch Inc.* v. *Budjovecky Budvar Narodni Podnik* (2002) 56 IPR 182; *Mark Foys Pty Ltd* v. *TVSN (Pacific) Ltd* (2000) 104 FCR 61. Although the English and Australian courts have not enumerated a list of factors to be examined, in practice, most of the *Downing* factors – in the context of a Lanham Act § 43(a) celebrity false endorsement claim – are considered: see *Downing* v. *Abercrombie & Fitch*, 265 F 3d 994, 1007–8 (9th Cir, 2001) ('*Downing*') (restating the *Sleekcraft* factors to be considered in the context of celebrity claims for an unauthorised use of identity).
77 See also Beverley-Smith, *Commercial Appropriation*, 72–97 (comparing different types of connection misrepresentation in the UK and Australia).
78 *Crocodile Dundee*, 584. 79 *Newton-John* (1986) 11 FCR 233, 235.

that 'mere *identification* was enough to suggest an association and therefore a misrepresentation'.[80] The unpredictability of this approach is also demonstrated in Olympic swimmer Kieren Perkins' claim against Telecom Australia for using a photograph of him wearing a swimming cap with the defendant's logo in an advertisement which allegedly highlighted Perkins' achievements to promote the sport of swimming. The Full Federal Court there reversed the trial judge's decision, finding that the advertisement misrepresented that Perkins 'was sponsored by it [and] had consented to its use of his name, image and reputation'.[81] More importantly, the court held that the relevant target audience in passing off included

> the astute and the gullible, the intelligent and the not so intelligent, the well educated as well as the poorly educated, men and women of various ages pursuing a variety of vocations, and [the plaintiff] could rely on any meaning which was reasonably open to a significant number of the newspaper readership.[82]

Thus, even in the absence of an explicit misrepresentation, it appears that courts are increasingly open to accepting that the overall or 'gestalt'[83] impression of the defendant's use can constitute misleading or deceptive conduct. As Burchett J. commented in the *Crocodile Dundee case*, '[i]t would be unfortunate if the law merely prevented a trader using the primitive club of direct misrepresentation, while leaving him free to employ the more sophisticated rapier of suggestion, which may deceive more completely'.[84] It is the transfer of affective meanings from the celebrity persona to the defendant's product as perceived by the audience that attracts liability.

As Marshall avers, '[t]he celebrity's power is derived from the collective configuration of its meaning . . . the audience is central in sustaining the power of any celebrity sign'.[85] One may therefore argue that

[80] Scott Ralston, 'Australian Celebrity Endorsements: The Need for an Australian Right of Publicity' (2001) 20(4) *Communications Law Bulletin* 9, 10 (emphasis in original). See also Mark Davison and Maree Kennedy, 'Proof of Deception and Character Merchandising Cases' (1990) 16 *Monash University Law Review* 111, 115 (this is a 'spectacular departure from the passing off requirement of factual misrepresentation'). It should also be noted that passing off is not made out 'merely because members of the public would be caused to wonder whether it might not be the case that two products come from the same source' (*Puxu* (1982) 149 CLR 191, 209).

[81] *Talmax*, 451. [82] *Ibid.* 446 (citing *Taco Bell*, 202).

[83] *Red Bull*, 366. [84] (1989) 23 FCR 553, 586.

[85] P. David Marshall, *Celebrity and Power: Fame in Contemporary Culture* (University of Minnesota Press, Minneapolis, 1997), 65. See also Francesco Alberoni, 'The Powerless Elite: Theory and Sociological Research on the Phenomenon of the Stars', in Denis McQuail (ed. and trans.), *Sociology of Mass Communications* (Penguin, Middlesex, 1972), 75, 93.

the touchstone for liability for the unauthorised commercial exploitation of a celebrity's identity, as pointed out by Laddie J. in *Irvine*, ought to take into account the *effect* of such a use on the audience-consumer. McCracken's observations, about how affective meaning that is conferred on the celebrity (Stage 1) may flow into the product that the celebrity is associated with (Stage 2),[86] are also relevant here. If one accepts that the celebrity identity has an associative value only because of the semiotic meanings conferred on it by the audience, then public perception becomes the natural reference point for the determination of liability.

Generally the advertisers can choose the particular configuration of culturally constituted meanings they wish to convey, and the relevance of which may be examined in passing off under the rubric of the intent of the trader.[87] But regardless of their intent:

> the final act of meaning transfer is performed by the consumer, who must glimpse in a moment of recognition . . . the cultural meanings contained in the people, objects, and contexts of the advertisement are also contained in the product.[88]

The more recent Australian cases have held that the plaintiff could 'rely on any meaning which was reasonably open to a significant number of the [target audience]'[89] thus directing the judicial focus in passing off to the impact of the unauthorised use on the audience-consumer.

If there is *no likelihood* that a typical consumer would be led to believe that a celebrity endorses or is connected to the defendant's product, then arguably *no* associative value has flowed to the product, and accordingly there should be no liability. In the co-present mode frequently employed in print advertisements where a celebrity is juxtaposed with a brand or product,[90] there may be no explicit indication of endorsement. Hence in this form of 'enhancement advertising', the endorsement can be 'by inference only, not in express words but by the association of a celebrity with a product, merely by them appearing together'.[91] It should therefore

[86] McCracken, 'Who is the Celebrity Endorser?'.

[87] For example *Irvine*, 2376–7; *Crocodile Dundee*, 575–6, 586. For Lanham Act § 43(a) cases, it is one of the factors to be considered in determining the likelihood of confusion. For example *Downing*, 1007–8.

[88] McCracken, 'Who is the Celebrity Endorser?', 314.

[89] For example *Talmax*, 446.

[90] McCracken, 'Who is the Celebrity Endorser?', 310. See also Tan, 'Beyond Trademark Law', 963.

[91] Hazel Carty, 'Advertising, Publicity Rights and English Law' (2004) 3 *Intellectual Property Quarterly* 209, 217. Carty, however, is reluctant to endorse a broad interpretation of misrepresentation, pointing out that '[m]erely taking something of value without paying is not a good reason to interfere with an unauthorised use of a celebrity persona' and the 'exposure of celebrities to such [enhancement advertising] use should be seen as the price of fame' (258).

be open to the court to determine whether, as a matter of impression, consumers are likely to be confused as to the celebrity's connection with the product when depicted in this manner. The fact is advertisers rely on the well-knownness of celebrities with global goodwill to lend their star aura to their brands and products by simply being present in the advertisement. No explicit endorsement message is required; the mere presence of the celebrity suggests an approval or association sufficient to persuade relevant segments of consumers to buy the product.[92]

V. Conclusions

Unlike in the right of publicity doctrine, which may generally impose liability for misappropriation – based on identification of a celebrity plaintiff from the defendant's unauthorised commercial use – the passing off action requires the plaintiff to prove misrepresentation of the celebrity's association with the defendant. Its focus on the impression that is created in the minds of consumers can overcome some of the doctrinal objections to characterising indicia of identity as personal property, and 'has the potential to acknowledge the existence of celebrity images in popular culture as a shared resource or heritage'.[93] Furthermore, as legal commentator Marshall Leaffer argues, there is potential to agree on 'an international norm for the protection of [a] personality right based on false endorsement'.[94]

The celebrity endorsement studies conducted by McCracken and other scholars have demonstrated that it is this impression of association that makes the defendant's products more attractive to a relevant group of consumers to whom a particular celebrity persona connotes positive affective meanings. If consumers perceive this association from the defendant's unauthorised use of the celebrity persona, then the impression engendered is a false one, and accordingly the defendant's conduct is misleading. The focus on *misrepresentation*, unlike *misappropriation* in right of publicity cases, directs courts to the moment at which harm or damage to the celebrity occurs. Hence the inquiry should be directed to the examination of whether there has been an unauthorised transfer of

92 In his analysis, Ellis Cashmore noted that advertising has 'moved away from the utilitarian approach in which product information was at the forefront. Many global brands avoid even mentioning products in an attempt to create synonymy between their brand and the celebrity' (*Celebrity/Culture* (Routledge, Abingdon, Oxon., 2006), 172).

93 Kirsten Anker, 'Possessing Star Qualities: Celebrity Identity as Property' (2002) 11 *Griffith Law Review* 147, 166.

94 Marshall Leaffer, 'The Right of Publicity: A Comparative Perspective' (2007) 70 *Albany Law Review* 1357, 1372. Leaffer also contends that the 'British court in the Irvine case got it right and its reasoning should be the current standard' (1372).

the semiotic meanings of the celebrity persona/brand to the defendant's product as a result of the product becoming more valuable in the eyes of the consumers. The perceived damage, in commercial terms, is the denial of a fee to the well-known individual for the use of his or her affective value in this manner.

Guided by the notion of affective transfer, the extended passing off claim as interpreted by the Australian courts not only appears to be adequate in protecting against unauthorised exploitation of the associative value of a celebrity's persona, but is also able to consider, in a more holistic manner than in a right of publicity claim, the interests of the audiences and cultural producers. In the absence of a statutory right of publicity, perhaps courts in Hong Kong and Singapore, and other common law jurisdictions in the Asia Pacific, can follow suit in expanding the passing off action to offer better protection to celebrity brands. However, one must also be cautious not to stifle creativity and entrepreneurship in the process. The celebrity individual should be accorded control over the associative value of his or her commercially valuable persona, but only in circumstances where his or her star aura is transferred to other commodities. The producers as commercial traders should be allowed to compete more freely, but not dishonestly. And the audiences who invest meanings in the celebrity personality should be examined not only as *consumers* but also as *participants* in the cultural process of coding, recoding and transcoding the celebrity brand.[95]

[95] See generally, David Tan, 'Political Recoding of the Contemporary Celebrity and the First Amendment' (2011) 2 *Harvard Journal of Sports and Entertainment Law* 1.

4 No personality rights for pop stars in Hong Kong?

Peter K. Yu

Referred to as 'the Pearl of the Orient' for generations, Hong Kong is a glamorous city known for its lavish lifestyle and the rich and famous. Its entertainment products – in particular movies, television programmes and Canto-pop music – are highly popular in not only Asia, but also different parts of the world. Notwithstanding this popularity, the region does not offer strong personality rights to celebrities. Such limited protection provides an interesting contrast to the United States, in which Hollywood actors and famous artists receive very strong protection of their name, likeness, image, voice or other personal attributes. The lack of protection in Hong Kong also contrasts strongly with the right of portrait protected under the Chinese civil code.

This chapter begins by tracing the origin of the right of publicity as an independent cause of action. It underscores the difference between this discreet American-born right and the type of protection available in Commonwealth jurisdictions. The chapter then discusses the leading case in Hong Kong, *Lau Tak Wah Andy* v. *Hang Seng Bank Ltd.*[1] It explores why Hong Kong has yet to offer strong personality rights despite having fertile conditions for such development. The chapter concludes by focusing on three areas of influence that may impact on the future development of personality rights in Hong Kong.

The right of publicity and its American origins

The right of publicity, which originated in the United States, protects individuals, mainly celebrities, against the unauthorised commercial use of their name, likeness, image, voice or other personal attributes.[2] As Melville Nimmer observed more than half a century ago:

[1] [2000] 1 HKC 280 ('*Lau Tak Wah*').

[2] Peter K. Yu, 'Fictional Persona Test: Copyright Preemption in Human Audiovisual Characters' (1998) 20 *Cardozo Law Review* 355.

> It is an unquestioned fact that the use of a prominent person's name, photograph or likeness (i.e., his publicity values) in advertising a product or in attracting an audience is of great pecuniary value. This is attested to by the now pervasive trade practice of paying well known personalities considerable sums for the right thus to use such publicity values. It is also unquestionably true that in most instances a person achieves publicity values of substantial pecuniary worth only after he has expended considerable time, effort, skill, and even money. It would seem to be a first principle of Anglo-American jurisprudence, an axiom of the most fundamental nature, that every person is entitled to the fruit of his labors unless there are important countervailing public policy considerations.[3]

By enabling celebrities to control the use of their identity through licenses or legal sanctions, the right of publicity protects the celebrities' personality interests from devaluation by virtue of overexploitation.[4]

Before the right of publicity was expressly recognised as an independent cause of action, an individual's identity was protected under the right to privacy. That right was proposed as a 'right to be let alone' by Samuel Warren and Louis Brandeis in a highly influential law review article entitled 'The Right to Privacy'.[5] The right was soon expanded to encompass a cause of action for the unauthorised commercial use of an individual's name and likeness. In *Pavesich* v. *New England Life Insurance Co.*,[6] the Georgia Supreme Court held that the right to privacy protected an individual against an insurance company's unauthorised use of his picture in an advertisement for its insurance policies. Stating that the use of the plaintiff's identity unreasonably infringed upon his personal privacy, the court afforded the plaintiff a remedy for his 'wounded feelings'.

Although arguments based on 'wounded feelings' worked well for people who were not well known, and therefore did not expect to be subject to public scrutiny, they failed to persuade courts in cases involving celebrities. For instance, in *O'Brien* v. *Pabst Sales Co.*,[7] the US Court of Appeals for the Fifth Circuit denied a well-known American football player relief from the unauthorised commercial use of his photograph on a football calendar featuring a beer advertisement. The court found that the plaintiff suffered no 'wounded feelings' or invasion of privacy, as he constantly sought publicity through the university's publicity department. As a result

[3] Melville Nimmer, 'The Right of Publicity' (1954) 19 *Law and Contemporary Problems* 203, 215–16.
[4] Mark F. Grady, 'A Positive Economic Theory of the Right of Publicity' (1994) 1 *UCLA Entertainment Law Review* 97, 98, 103.
[5] Samuel D. Warren and Louis D. Brandeis, 'The Right to Privacy' (1890) 4 *Harvard Law Review* 193.
[6] 50 SE 68 (Ga, 1905). [7] 124 F 2d 167 (5th Cir, 1941) ('*O'Brien*').

of *O'Brien*, celebrities became vulnerable to the unauthorised use of their identities in advertisements or in other commercial contexts.[8]

In the early 1950s, the momentum shifted when the US Court of Appeals for the Second Circuit recognised an independent cause of action at common law called 'the right of publicity'.[9] In *Haelan Laboratories Inc.* v. *Topps Chewing Gum Inc.*, the court held that, 'in addition to and independent of [the] right of privacy . . . a man has a right in the publicity value of his photograph, i.e., the right to grant the exclusive privilege of publishing his picture'.[10] As Judge Jerome Frank declared:

> it is common knowledge that many prominent persons (especially actors and ball-players), far from having their feelings bruised through public exposure of their likenesses, would feel sorely deprived if they no longer received money for authorizing advertisements, popularizing their countenances, displayed in newspapers, magazines, busses, trains and subways. This right of publicity would usually yield them no money unless it could be made the subject of an exclusive grant which barred any other advertiser from using their pictures.[11]

In the end, the court recognised a new right of publicity that provided individuals with incentives to enter the public scene and to undertake socially enriching activities.

Since *Haelan*, the right of publicity gradually gained acceptance in jurisdictions around the nation. In 1977, the US Supreme Court addressed the right of publicity for the first (and only) time in *Zacchini* v. *Scripps-Howard Broadcasting Co.*[12] In that case, the right of publicity of an entertainer was allegedly infringed when a television station showed the entire performance of his 'human cannonball act' on the evening news. Relying on the Lockean principle that an individual should enjoy 'the product of [his] own talents and energy, [and] the end result of much time, effort and expense', the Court held that the First and Fourteenth Amendments to the US Constitution did not immunise the news broadcaster when it showed a performer's entire 15-second act without his consent.[13]

The right of publicity was further expanded in *Carson* v. *Here's Johnny Portable Toilets Inc.*,[14] where Johnny Carson, the famous late-night talk-show host, sued the defendant for the unauthorised use of the phrase 'Here's Johnny' in marketing portable toilets. The US Court of Appeals for the Sixth Circuit rejected the defendant's contention that a common

[8] Arlen W. Langvardt, 'The Troubling Implications of a Right of Publicity "Wheel" Spun Out of Control' (1997) 45 *University of Kansas Law Review* 329, 333–4.

[9] *Haelan Laboratories Inc.* v. *Topps Chewing Gum Inc.* 202 F 2d 866 (2nd Cir, 1953) ('*Haelan*').

[10] *Ibid.* 868. [11] *Ibid.* [12] 433 US 562 (1977). [13] *Ibid.* 575.

[14] 698 F 2d 831 (6th Cir, 1983) ('*Carson*').

law right of publicity did not extend beyond an individual's actual name and likeness. Instead, the court found that Carson's right of publicity was infringed when the familiar introductory phrase merely conjured up his images.

The Ninth Circuit employed the same rationale in *White* v. *Samsung Electronics America Inc.*[15] In that case, Vanna White, the hostess of the 'Wheel of Fortune' game show, sued Samsung Electronics for infringing upon her right of publicity by appropriating her likeness in an advertisement. That advertisement depicted a robot standing in front of a set modelled after the game show. Although the court declined to find the robot constituting the hostess's likeness within the meaning of the California right of publicity statute,[16] it embraced the *Carson* rationale and held that the advertisement infringed upon the hostess's common law right of publicity by evoking her identity.

Today, the right of publicity has been expanded so greatly that, in some US jurisdictions (such as the celebrity-friendly State of California), virtually anything evoking an individual's personal identity can infringe upon the right of publicity. Nevertheless, many states offer much more modest protection. While some place severe limits on the right's applicability, transferability and descendability, others, such as the State of New York, do not even have a separate right of publicity statute. Instead, they rely on the right of privacy statute.[17]

As a result, the protection of the right of publicity in the United States continues to vary significantly from state to state. Notwithstanding these variations, US law provides the much-needed background to understand the need for protection of celebrities' identities. The US right of publicity also serves as an instructive reference point for evaluating the nature and extent of personality rights in Hong Kong.

Limited personality rights in Hong Kong

Having been a British colony from 1842 to 1997, Hong Kong draws its influence in developing intellectual property law from the United Kingdom and other Commonwealth jurisdictions. Thus far, English law has yet to recognise a discrete right of publicity – or, for that matter, any proprietary rights in a celebrity's identity. Instead, it offers protection through a wide array of legal devices, including copyright and trade mark laws, the tort of passing off, defamation, violation of advertising codes

[15] 971 F 2d 1395 (9th Cir 1992). [16] Cal Civil Code § 3344 (West 1997).
[17] NY Civil Rights Law § 51 (McKinney 2009).

and breach of confidence under contract law.[18] In the area of character merchandising and celebrity endorsement, until recently English courts have also 'maintained a strict requirement of misrepresentation'.[19]

It is therefore no surprise that commentators have widely criticised England for its limited protection of celebrities' identities. As Thomas McCarthy, the author of a leading treatise on US rights of publicity, has noted: 'English law often seems tied to the legal categories of the past and, up to the present, unable to accommodate itself to the modern commercial realities of licensing and merchandising'.[20] Likewise, Michael Pendleton and Alice Lee lament:

> The tort of passing off although flexible in its ability to deal with new and interesting scenarios has its limits . . . It would appear that in trying to allow a remedy under passing off for character merchandising actions, the courts have stretched the limits of passing off.[21]

In Hong Kong, the leading case implicating personality rights is *Lau Tak Wah*.[22] In this case, Hang Seng Bank, a well-known bank in Hong Kong, introduced a promotional campaign to provide customised credit cards and phonecards featuring the photos of popular entertainers. This turn-of-the-millennium campaign allowed card applicants to obtain both the StarSelect Mastercard and MegaStar Collectible Phonecards. Under the StarSelect program, applicants could choose one of the thirty-two photos featuring a local entertainer. One of the ten available entertainers was the plaintiff, Andy Lau, a famous local actor and Canto-pop singer who was involved in negotiations with other banks over the sponsorship of his concerts.[23] In addition to the StarSelect programme, the bank also offered the SelectImage programme, under which applicants supplied a photo of their own in one of three categories: people, scenery or pets.

To promote the StarSelect programme, an advertisement appeared in *Oriental Daily News*, with the following caption: 'Hang Seng StarSelect Mastercard TVB MegaStars rejoice the year 2000 with you And earn

[18] Hayley Stallard, 'The Right of Publicity in the United Kingdom' (1998) 18 *Loyola of Los Angeles Entertainment Law Journal* 565, 567.

[19] Michael Spence, *Intellectual Property* (Oxford University Press, Oxford 2007), 236.

[20] J. Thomas McCarthy, *The Rights of Publicity and Privacy* (2nd edn, Thomson West, St Paul, MN, 2001) § 6:147.5.

[21] Michael D. Pendleton and Alice Lee, *Intellectual Property in Hong Kong* (Lexis Nexis, Hong Kong, 2008), 32–3.

[22] [2000] 1 HKC 280.

[23] 'Andy Lau and Aaron Kwok Intend to Sue Hang Seng Bank' *Guangzhou Daily* (online) 8 March 1999, http://news.sina.com.cn/richtalk/news/movie/9903/030824.html. The other entertainers were Ekin Cheng, Sammi Cheng, Nick Cheung, Andy Hui, Aaron Kwok, Leon Lai, Gigi Leung, Michele Reis and Miriam Yeung.

Monthly Awards'.[24] The bank's promotional leaflet also stated: 'Choose your favourite from these 10 MegaStar images and print it on your Star-Select MasterCard'. All of the photos used in the promotional campaign were taken directly from the entertainers' performances in programmes produced by Television Broadcasts Limited (TVB), a terrestrial television broadcaster in Hong Kong. The bank obtained licences from TVB to use the copyrighted photos, and a copyright notice, which read 'Photo © TVB 1999', was placed on each photo and the promotional materials.

TVB, which was later joined as a third party in the action, claimed that it owned the copyright in the photos and had the right to use them for promotional purposes pursuant to contracts signed by the performers, including the plaintiff. Meanwhile, the plaintiff claimed that his likeness had been used without authorisation and TVB's contractual rights to use its photos were limited in both duration and scope. Specifically, the actor claimed that the photos taken during his TVB performances 'could only be used in advertising and exploiting the products of the plaintiff's services'.[25]

In March 1999, Lau filed a lawsuit based on the common law tort of passing off, asking the court for an interlocutory injunction to prevent further usage of his image. In the Court of First Instance of the High Court, Deputy Judge (and now Justice) Andrew Chung found that there was a 'serious question to be tried as to whether or not the plaintiff enjoys a reputation who might endorse a financial services product, namely, credit cards'.[26] Nevertheless, he noted that the plaintiff had failed to present a triable question concerning misrepresentation. As the court declared:[27] 'the law of passing off in Hong Kong (in the context of personality or character merchandising) includes an ingredient of a misrepresentation that the plaintiff has endorsed or licensed the defendant's products, or somehow can exercise quality control over them'.

In addition, Deputy Judge Chung questioned whether the plaintiff had made his case of misrepresentation:

> In my view, what the defendant has done is no more than offering to affix the plaintiff's photographs onto its credit cards or phonecards when members of the public decide to use the defendant's credit cards (out of a choice of other photographs, including the photographs of nine other artistes and photographs of the applicants' own choice). I do not consider that the public would consider the plaintiff has 'endorsed' the defendant's products. Some members of the public may consider there may be some link between the plaintiff and the defendant regarding these photographs 'in a vague and unfocused way' (as the defendant put it). However, this falls short of enabling one to reasonably imply that any

[24] *Lau Tak Wah*, 283. [25] *Ibid.* 289. [26] *Ibid.* 291. [27] *Ibid.* 286–7.

endorsement arrangement had been reached between the plaintiff and the defendant. I agree with the defendant's submissions that any unreasonable belief is to be disregarded.[28]

The court also found that 'the damages likely to be suffered by the plaintiff on the one hand (if the injunction is not granted) is [sic] as difficult to quantify as those likely to be suffered by the defendant on the other hand (if the injunction is granted)'.[29] After considering the first two elements in the action – namely, goodwill and misrepresentation – the court 'consider[ed] the balance of convenience to lean against granting an interim injunction order'.[30] The court dismissed the case at the interlocutory injunction stage, leaving the case for a final adjudication before the High Court.

To some extent, this dispute is similar to the dispute between actors George Wendt and John Ratzenberger on the one hand and the producer of the television series *Cheers* on the other.[31] This US case concerned the use of the 'Norm' and 'Cliff' characters as models for developing animatronic robots that were displayed in a chain of *Cheers*-themed restaurants. In that case, both the actors and the TV producer insisted they had a valid legal claim. While the TV producer contended that the fictional characters were copyrighted and therefore belonged to them, the actors claimed that their likeness, rather than the copyrighted characters, was the subject of litigation.

Because the use of fictional audiovisual characters often includes both the fictional persona (protected by copyright) and the human persona (protected by publicity or personality rights), the case presented a very challenging issue.[32] At first blush, the use of well-drafted entertainment contracts may help to avoid this type of dispute. In reality, however, contracts are unlikely to be helpful, because they tend to grant TV or movie producer rights in fictional characters while retaining in actors the rights to exploit their human persona. As a result, the contracts do not address the grey area in which the subject matter implicates both copyright and personality rights.

In Commonwealth jurisdictions, disputes implicating personality rights are even more complicated. If a claim of the tort of passing off is to be successful, misrepresentation must be shown. Unfortunately, showing misrepresentation is not always easy. In *Lau Tak Wah*, for example, the photos included both a copyright notice by TVB and Chinese characters denoting the programmes in which the actor had appeared. Although

[28] *Ibid.* 292. [29] *Ibid.* [30] *Ibid.* 293.
[31] *Wendt* v. *Host International Inc.* 125 F 3d 806 (9th Cir, 1997).
[32] Yu, 'Fictional Persona Test', 378–82.

the plaintiff insisted that the copyright notice and the additional Chinese characters were 'obscure and not easily noticeable',[33] the court found a number of additional facts that could help negate the plaintiff's claim of deception:

(a) the plaintiff has not expressly been portrayed as promoting the defendant's products individually;
(b) none of the artistes has been expressly represented by the defendant as having endorsed the defendant's products;
(c) not only was the plaintiff included as among a group, the theme of the campaign is to give the applicant of the card a choice of the image to be put onto the card;
(d) further, the choice is not limited to the 10 artistes. It extends to choosing the applicant's own favourite photograph, which may be one of three categories: 'people', 'scenery' or 'pets';
(e) the plaintiff's name only appears among the other nine artistes and only for the purpose of confirming his photograph was included.[34]

Moreover, deception is hard to prove, and unconsented use is not per se misleading. As Diane Zimmerman explains:

> It is quite possible to make unconsented uses of the identifying characteristics of well-known people to promote products in ways that are entirely truthful. For instance, if Jack Nicholson actually drinks Minute Maid orange juice, it is hard to argue that the company would have falsified anything if it were to say so in its ads.[35]

To be certain, celebrities can always claim the existence of deception over the associative link between the celebrity and the defendant's product or service.[36] However, such a task is more difficult than anticipated. As Professor Pendleton points out in his comment on *Lau Tak Wah*:

> What is problematic, as is well documented with character merchandising and sponsorship, is that, in order for the public to be deceived, the public needs to believe that a licence is required for character merchandising and sponsorship, which necessarily requires them to take view that the law requires a licence. Otherwise the public would have to assume that royalties and licences change hands for no reason. The public are not so naïve. Yet this public belief that the law requires a licence, and that no such licence in fact exists, becomes in all character merchandising and sponsorship cases the basis for the court's finding

33 *Lau Tak Wah*, 284. 34 *Ibid.* 291.

35 Diane Leenheer Zimmerman, 'Who Put the Right in the Right of Publicity?' (1998) 9 *DePaul–LCA Journal of Art and Entertainment Law* 35.

36 On the associative value of personality, see Sheldon W. Halpern, 'The Right of Publicity: Maturation of an Independent Right Protecting the Associative Value of Personality' (1995) 46 *Hastings Law Journal* 853.

of a legal right to character merchandise and sponsor. Necessarily this is logically circular . . . [37]

In sum, because the tort of passing off requires a showing of misrepresentation (in addition to goodwill and reputational damage), it is more difficult to protect a celebrity's personality right in Hong Kong than in, say, the United States, where misrepresentation need not be shown. While decisions on personality rights are rare in Hong Kong, with *Lau Tak Wah* remaining its leading case, there were a few other published cases involving the use of name, image or likeness of celebrity entertainers. Many of these cases involved the use of the celebrity's identity in marketing cassette tapes, CDs, laserdiscs, karaoke albums, VCDs or DVDs.

Among these published cases, one of the most widely discussed is *Tam Wing Lun Alan* v. *Hang Mei Record Co.*[38] In this High Court case, another highly popular Canto-pop singer (and sometimes actor) in Hong Kong claimed that the defendant had engaged in passing off in its sale of cassette tapes that included a collection of Tam's songs covered by unknown substitute singers. Those infringing tapes were sold for only a third of the original price – usually in hawker stalls in such places as Temple and Tung Choi Streets.[39]

Although this case, like *Lau Tak Wah*, did not involve claims based on personality rights, one can easily see how the defendant record company had exploited the singer's name and image in its effort to market the infringing tapes. As Master Patrick Chan declared:

> The basis of a passing-off claim is that the defendant has sold or put on the market, goods which are calculated to deceive or mislead the public. The wrong lies in the defendant's get-up and description of his goods which constitutes a false representation to the public and this is sufficient to find a claim in passing-off. It is not necessary for the plaintiff to show that the public had actually been deceived or misled.[40]

While the use of the singer's name might be needed to correctly identify the repertoire of the covered songs, such use could mislead consumers into purchasing products that they thought were sung, endorsed or licensed by the singer or his record company. Even more problematic, if consumers who purchased the covered version could not distinguish between that version and its original counterpart, the lower quality of the covered version might hurt the singer's reputation.

[37] Michael D. Pendleton, 'Character Merchandising, Personality and Sponsorship Rights Strike a Snag in Hong Kong: The *Andy Lau* Case' (1999) 21 *European Intellectual Property Review* 521, 522.

[38] [1991] 2 HKC 384. [39] *Ibid.* 392. [40] *Ibid.* 388.

In the end, the court found for the singer and provided a considerable damage award.[41] Although the defendant questioned whether the plaintiff had suffered actual damage to his goodwill due to his well-known status, the court rejected such an argument. Citing with approval the English case of *Draper* v. *Trist*, the court explained:

> In passing-off cases . . . the true basis of the action is that the passing-off by the defendant of his goods as the goods of the plaintiff injures the right of property in the plaintiff, that right of property being his right to the goodwill of his business. The law assumes or presumes that, if the goodwill of a man's business has been interfered with by the passing-off of goods, damage results therefrom. He need not wait to show that damage has resulted. He can bring his action as soon as he can prove the passing-off because it is one of the class of cases 'in which the law presumes that the plaintiff has suffered damage'.[42]

In sum, although Hong Kong offers protection to celebrities, such protection has been rather meagre. Except in cases of misrepresentation, celebrities rarely obtain protection for their name, likeness, image, voice or other personal attributes.

Fertile conditions for developing strong personality rights

The lack of protection of celebrities' identities in Hong Kong is rather intriguing. After all, Hong Kong provides four different sets of fertile conditions for the development of strong personality rights. This section discusses each of these conditions in turn.

To begin with, Hong Kong has been known as a place for the rich and famous. People within the region are highly conscious of image, brands and status symbols. From place to place, one can find local people using or wearing goods with luxury brands – Calvin Klein, Christian Dior, Dolce & Gabbana, Ermenegildo Zegna, Gianni Versace, Giorgio Armani, Gucci, Hugo Boss, Polo Ralph Lauren, Prada, you name it. This fascination with brands, indeed, has led to the development of an unhealthy culture in which local people are constantly tempted to consume fake-branded products, in part to conform to local brand-worshipping norms. High brand awareness also has made Hong Kong an attractive place for developing greater protection for celebrities' identities.

Second, while Western commentators tend to use Confucianism or other cultural reasons to account for the lack of protection of intellectual property rights among the Chinese,[43] culture does not prevent Hong

[41] *Ibid.* 392. [42] *Ibid.* 388 (citing *Draper* v. *Trist* [1939] 3 All ER 513, 526).
[43] On how Confucianism and other aspects of the Chinese political culture have prevented intellectual property rights from taking root in China, see William P. Alford, *To Steal*

Kong from developing stronger personality rights. In fact, when the lack of protection of celebrities' identities is compared against developments in other areas of intellectual property law, it becomes clear that such a lack is more the exception than the norm. For example, Hong Kong offers strong protection to both well-known trade marks and moral rights. The Trade Marks Ordinance allows the owner of a well-known mark 'to restrain by injunction the use in Hong Kong of a trade mark which, or the essential part of which, is identical or [confusingly] similar to his [or her] trade mark, in relation to identical or similar goods or services'.[44] The Copyright Ordinance further provides for the rights to be identified as the work's author or director, to object to its derogatory treatment, and to prohibit false attribution of the work.[45]

The weak personality rights in Hong Kong also contrasts interestingly with the strong right of portrait (*xiàoxiàng quán*) in China, thereby challenging the assumption that culture may have stifled the development of personality rights in Hong Kong. Drawing inspiration from German law, which 'recognized a "portrait right" as early as 1907',[46] art. 100 of the General Principles of Civil Code of the People's Republic of China provides: 'Citizens shall enjoy the right of portrait. The use of a citizen's portrait for profit without his consent shall be prohibited.' Article 120 stipulates further:

> If a citizen's right of personal name, portrait, reputation or honour is infringed upon, he shall have the right to demand that the infringement be stopped, his reputation be rehabilitated, the ill effects be eliminated and an apology be made; he may also demand compensation for losses.

With the growing popularity of commercial entertainment and professional sports in China, the right of portrait can only become more important in the near future.[47]

In fact, personality rights evolve naturally within the Chinese culture. As Harold Chee reminds us:

a Book Is an Elegant Offense: Intellectual Property Law in Chinese Civilization (Stanford University Press, Stanford, 1995); Peter K. Yu, 'Piracy, Prejudice, and Perspectives: Using Shakespeare to Reconfigure the US–China Intellectual Property Debate' (2001) 19 *Boston University International Law Journal* 1, 16–21.

[44] Trade Marks Ordinance (Hong Kong) Cap 559, s. 63(1).

[45] Copyright Ordinance (Hong Kong) Cap 528, ss. 89, 92, 96.

[46] F. Jay Dougherty, 'Foreword: The Right of Publicity – Towards a Comparative and International Perspective' (1998) 18 *Loyola of Los Angeles Entertainment Law Journal* 421, 425.

[47] Jeffrey F. Levine, 'Meeting the Challenges of International Brand Expansion in Professional Sports: Intellectual Property Right Enforcement in China through Treaties, Chinese Law and Cultural Mechanisms' (2007) 9 *Texas Review of Entertainment and Sports Law* 203, 223.

> Face is about one's self-respect and prestige and, crucially, about one's standing in the group. It is an essentially public phenomenon, though it has powerful (albeit secondary) emotional consequences. The emotions are about dignity and dignity's enemy, shame. This polarity runs deep in the lives of Chinese people.[48]

Because of the importance of face (*miànzi*) in the Chinese culture, public shaming provides an effective strategy for protecting intellectual property rights in China.[49] Public apology has also been considered one of the more important remedies for infringement of intellectual property rights.[50]

Third, Hong Kong has a very successful entertainment industry. Hong Kong movies and TV programmes, for example, have received wide acclaim in Southeast Asia and other parts of the world. In 2009 alone, 'Hong Kong films (including Hong Kong–Mainland co-productions) and artists won a total of 52 awards at 12 film festivals and competitions, held in the Mainland and overseas'.[51] Hollywood also actively recruits actors or directors from Hong Kong. Bruce Lee, Jackie Chan, Chow Yun Fat, Tony Leung, Michelle Yeoh, John Woo and Wong Kar Wai are all Hong Kong-based actors and directors that have achieved phenomenal success outside the region.

Taking account of such tremendous talent in the local entertainment industry, one therefore can safely assume the existence of a critical mass of stakeholders that will benefit from stronger personality rights. As I noted in the past, the existence of local stakeholders is the key to successful intellectual property law reforms.[52] By locating support from the inside, these reforms often result in more sustainable protection that is also well tailored to local needs, interests and conditions.

Finally, Hong Kong was an important jurisdiction that helped to establish protection of fictional characters within the Commonwealth. As Professor Pendleton points out, Hong Kong was a pioneer in granting protection in the area of character merchandising.[53] In the early 1970s, the Shaw Brothers, a major local film producer, successfully obtained protection for one of its characters, the One-armed Swordsman (*dúbì dāo*), in the movie of the same name.

48 Harold Chee with Chris West, *Myths about Doing Business in China* (Palgrave Macmillan, New York, 2004), 481.

49 James McGregor, *One Billion Customers: Lessons from the Front Lines of Doing Business in China* (Free Press, New York, 2005), 10.

50 Peter K. Yu, 'From Pirates to Partners (Episode II): Protecting Intellectual Property in Post-WTO China' (2006) 55 *American University Law Review* 901, 952–3.

51 *Hong Kong Yearbook 2009* (HKSAR Government, Hong Kong, 2010), 362.

52 Yu, 'Fictional Persona Test', 958–9; Peter K. Yu, 'The Copyright Divide' (2003) 25 *Cardozo Law Review* 331, 431–3.

53 Pendleton, 'Character Merchandising', 521.

In *Shaw Brothers (Hong Kong) Ltd* v. *Golden Harvest (H.K.) Ltd*,[54] a well-known action star, Wang Yu, played the single-armed protagonist in two trend-setting martial arts movies produced by the Shaw Brothers in the mid- to late 1960s.[55] Directed by famous Chinese film director Chang Cheh, these movies were followed a couple of years later by a reboot, 'The New One-armed Swordsman', with new stars and a different storyline.[56] Before the film was released, Wang reprised the role of the One-armed Swordsman in a Japanese movie 'Zatoichi Meets the One-armed Swordsman' – this time, fighting the famous blind masseur-swordsman in the wildly popular Zatoichi series, due largely to communication problems and a fatal misunderstanding.[57]

Shaw Brothers sued Golden Harvest, the Hong Kong co-producer, for infringement of the rights in both the name and the fictional character of 'the One-armed Swordsman', utilising the common tort of passing off and an alleged independent and new tort of unfair competition. Appearing for the plaintiff was E. P. Skone James, the noted co-author of *Copinger and Skone James on Copyright*. Patrick Yu, a highly respected local attorney, served as counsel for the defendant.[58]

This case is particularly interesting because the Commonwealth had yet to recognise the protection of fictional characters at the time of litigation. Although the defendant insisted that no property right in fictional characters existed in English law, the High Court found it

> hard to accept the absence of authority in this field of law as a factor of great weight, even if there were ground for believing that conduct such as that alleged against the defendants here had occurred before – and writers are more likely to find their works being pirated than their characters being adopted.[59]

As Judge Huggins noted in the form of a rhetorical question: '[W]hy should an author, playwright or film script writer not acquire a right of property in a fictional character which is his brain-child?'[60]

[54] [1972] RPC 559 ('*Shaw Brothers*').

[55] *Dubi Dao* ['The One-Armed Swordsman'] (directed by Chang Cheh, Shaw Brothers, 1967); *Dubi Daowang* ['Return of the One-Armed Swordsman'] (directed by Chang Cheh, Shaw Brothers, 1969).

[56] *Xin dubi dao* ['The New One-Armed Swordsman'] (directed by Chang Cheh, Shaw Brothers, 1971).

[57] *Shin Zatô Ichi: Yabure! Tôjin-ken* ['Zatoichi Meets the One-Armed Swordsman'] (directed by Yasuda Kimiyoshi, Daiei Motion Picture Co, 1971).

[58] On the life of Patrick Yu, see his autobiography, Patrick Yu, *Seventh Child and the Law* (Hong Kong University Press, Hong Kong, 1998).

[59] *Shaw Brothers*, 563–4.

[60] *Ibid*. 563.

To fill the void in English law, and to provide the basis for the decision, the court turned to the US *Lone Ranger* cases.[61] While the defendant correctly pointed to the difference between the American tort of unfair competition and the English tort of passing off, the court noted a 'close relationship' between American and English cases.[62] As Judge Higgins reasoned, 'the decisions in these American cases are good sense and that I find nothing in the English cases which is at all inconsistent with the reasoning of the American courts'.[63]

In the end, the court found for the plaintiff. In a broad statement towards the end of his decision, Judge Huggins declared: 'I think Equity will give them a remedy if a competitor unfairly appropriates what is indeed the spirit though not the actual substance of their work, namely a character they have succeeded in building up'.[64] *Shaw Brothers* therefore established 'one of the first instances of judicial recognition of rights in fictional character in Commonwealth jurisprudence'.[65]

Failure to provide strong personality rights

Given these fertile conditions for the development of stronger personality rights, one cannot help but wonder why celebrities do not obtain greater protection for their identities. There are at least four reasons.

First, being a former British colony, Hong Kong remains heavily influenced by not only English law, but also those of other Commonwealth jurisdictions. Such heavy influence is particularly obvious in the area of intellectual property law – a highly technical area with few reported local cases. This influence is important because the protection of personality interests remains weak in Commonwealth jurisdictions even today. As noted earlier, one of the distinguishing features between US and UK laws in the area of personality rights is the latter's reluctance to grant proprietary rights to a celebrity's identity. In *Lau Tak Wah*, for example, the court insisted on a showing of misrepresentation – a requirement that is absent from US law.

Second, the historical lack of privacy protection in Hong Kong has greatly limited the development of personality rights in the region.[66]

[61] *Lone Ranger* v. *Cox* 124 F 2d 650 (4th Cir, 1942); *Lone Ranger* v. *Currey* 79 F Supp 190 (MD Pa, 1948). On the *Lone Ranger* cases, see Pendleton, 'Character Merchandising', 523.

[62] *Shaw Brothers*, 564. [63] *Ibid.* [64] *Ibid.* 567.

[65] Pendleton and Lee, *Intellectual Property*, 32.

[66] On the protection of privacy in Hong Kong before 1997, see Raymond Wacks, 'Privacy', in Raymond Wacks (ed.), *Human Rights in Hong Kong* (Oxford University Press, Oxford, 1992), 319–49.

Although greater privacy protection is not always needed to strengthen personality rights – China being a very good example[67] – the right to privacy serves as a key substitute in countries that do not offer discrete publicity or personality rights. In addition, the more individuals are conscious of privacy intrusions, the more likely they are to demand stronger privacy or personality rights. To some extent, there is a 'unique historic relationship' between the protections of privacy and personality rights:[68] the two interrelated rights are mutually reinforcing.

Like the limited protection of personality interests, the lack of privacy protection in Hong Kong has a strong parallel in the United Kingdom, which offered rather limited protection before the enactment of the UK Human Rights Act 1998.[69] To be certain, privacy protection in Britain has been strengthened somewhat shortly after the untimely death of Princess Diana in a car accident following a paparazzi chase. However, such strengthening was done only indirectly through an amendment of the code of conduct of the Press Complaints Commission.[70] While the British newspaper and periodical industry, including journalists, may have taken the code seriously,[71] this code is soft law at best and does not have any direct legal effect.

In Hong Kong, the Personal Data (Privacy) Ordinance was not enacted until August 1995, shortly before China resumed sovereignty over the region in 1997. The Office of the Privacy Commissioner for Personal Data was only established in August 1996. Undoubtedly, the introduction of the Ordinance and the establishment of this new office have resulted in greater protection of individual privacy interests. In a report released shortly after the establishment of the office, for example, the Privacy Commissioner

> ruled that surreptitious videos taken of [a university student in her dormitory] were a contravention of data protection principle 1(2)(b) [in sch. 1 of the Ordinance] which requires that personal data be collected 'by means which are lawful and fair in the circumstances' and data protection principle 3 which provides that

[67] On the growing protection of privacy in China, see Cao Jingchun, 'Protecting the Right to Privacy in China' (2005) 36 *Victoria University of Wellington Law Review* 645. On the protection of reputation and privacy in the digital and virtual environments in China, see Anne S. Y. Cheung, 'A Study of Cyber-Violence and Internet Service Providers' Liability: Lessons from China' (2009) 18 *Pacific Rim Law and Policy* 323, 325–40.

[68] Rosina Zapparoni, 'Propertising Identity: Understanding the United States Right of Publicity and Its Implications – Some Lessons for Australia' (2004) 28 *Melbourne University Law Review* 690, 706.

[69] Carrie Rainen, 'The Right of Publicity in the United States and the United Kingdom' (2005) 12 *New England Journal of International and Comparative Law* 197, 226–7.

[70] Stallard, 'Right of Publicity', 586–7. [71] *Ibid.* 587.

personal data shall not, without the prescribed consent of the data subject, be used for any purpose other than that for which it was collected.[72]

Considering the videographer's conduct 'a serious intrusion on an individual's privacy', the Commissioner declared:

The act of observing the private actions of someone in a private place does not come within the coverage of the Ordinance. This is because observation alone does not result in the collection of personal data, which by definition must involve recorded information. However, a recorded image of a living individual from which it is practicable to identify that person and in a form to which access to or processing of the data is practicable is personal data of that individual. Hence, a recorded image of an individual held in any format, whether it is captured on a roll film, printed on a photographic paper, or embodied on a video tape, so as to be capable of being reproduced may fall within the definition of personal data.[73]

Although there has been growing awareness of privacy protection in Hong Kong since the introduction of the Ordinance in the mid-1990s, such greater awareness has yet to result in stronger personality rights. Moreover, a subsequent court decision has greatly undercut the Commissioner's ability to broaden the definition of 'data' to include photos, videos or other audiovisual content. As the Hong Kong Court of Appeals noted in *Eastweek Publisher Ltd* v. *Privacy Commissioner of Personal Data*, although the complainant 'would be entirely justified in regarding the article and the photograph as an unfair and impertinent intrusion into her sphere of personal privacy . . . the Ordinance does not purport to protect "personal privacy" as opposed to "information privacy"'.[74]

Third, the local media have a tight and highly concentrated structure. Until recently, there have been very limited advertising channels outside the print media. Fewer opportunities for the misuse of celebrities' identities exist as a result. Consider the television industry, for example. Until the early 1990s, there were only two television broadcasters in Hong Kong – TVB and Asia Television Limited (known as Rediffusion Television Limited before September 1982). Even today, these two broadcasters, which have both Chinese and English stations, are the only two terrestrial broadcasters in the region. Because many local entertainers have contracts with these broadcasters (in addition to their managers and producers), the industry structure provides additional safeguards

72 Raymond Wacks, 'Pursuing Paparazzi: Privacy and Intrusive Photography' (1998) 28 *Hong Kong Law Journal* 1, 4 n. 19.

73 Office of the Privacy Commissioner for Personal Data, *Report Published under Section 48(2) of the Personal Data (Privacy) Ordinance (Cap.486)*, Report No. R97–1948 (13 October 1997) available at www.pcpd.org.hk/english/publications/files/R97–1948.pdf.

74 *Eastweek Publisher Ltd* v. *Privacy Commissioner of Personal Data* [2000] 1 HKC 692, 705.

against the misuse of the entertainers' identities. After all, broadcasters are likely to be vigilant against the misuse of the identity of contracted artists in commercials broadcasted on their stations.

Moreover, the industry may fear that stronger personality rights would eventually make it more difficult – or, at least, more costly – for the broadcasters to promote their products or develop new revenue streams. Notably, *Lau Tak Wah* was not a case between the actor-singer and an unlicensed advertiser, who took a free ride on the entertainer's popularity. Instead, Hang Seng Bank purchased a licence from TVB. Thus, the case is better viewed as one between the actor and the TV producer over who should receive licence fees from a willing advertiser. Given these conflicting interests, it is understandable why TV producers may be reluctant to support the development of stronger personality rights.

Finally, although the protection and enforcement of intellectual property rights in Hong Kong has greatly improved in the past decade, the discourse of intellectual property protection remains rather limited. Except for copyrights, patents and trade marks, the three main branches of intellectual property rights, the region has yet to focus on developments in other less well-known branches, such as personality rights. As a result, there has yet to be a greater push for developments in the area, even though such developments could benefit local celebrities.

To complicate matters further, personality rights face the same challenge as the protection of luxury goods. It is, indeed, hard for celebrities – especially those wealthy ones – to earn public sympathy when they complain about the harm they suffer when their identities have been misused. Moreover, as shown in *Lau Tak Wah* and *Tam Wing Lun*, as well as in earlier US cases that seek to protect celebrities through the right to privacy, it is rather difficult to show *actual* damage to the celebrities' reputation, as opposed to *presumed* injury through the loss of goodwill. While lesser-known celebrities may benefit from additional exposure brought about by the unauthorised use of their identities, there may be limited harm to high-profile celebrities when their identities are appropriated in the marketing of products they are unlikely to sponsor.

The future of personality rights in Hong Kong

Given the limited development of personality rights in Hong Kong, one may wonder whether those rights will be strengthened in the near future. After all, Hong Kong artists and products already have an important presence in the global entertainment scene. With a booming Chinese economy and now even closer connections to its motherland, Hong Kong may greatly benefit from the development of stronger personality rights.

Looking forward, there are three possible influences that may affect future development in the area.

First, as Hong Kong artists take greater advantage of the Chinese market, they are likely to demand protection that is at least as strong as the right of portrait found on the mainland. Although China has been widely criticised by the United States and the European Union for its lack of enforcement of intellectual property rights, it does offer stronger protection of personality interests than Hong Kong. If such protection eventually diffused southwards to Hong Kong, such diffusion would provide a very interesting phenomenon in which Hong Kong strengthens its laws by transplanting models from the mainland.

Given the wide criticism of intellectual property protection in China, such transplantation would come in an opposite direction than what many commentators expect. To date, much of the transplantation in Hong Kong has come from the United Kingdom or other Commonwealth jurisdictions. In the recent proposals for digital copyright reform, the Hong Kong administration did not even consult Chinese law. Instead, it surveyed the laws of the United Kingdom, the United States, Singapore, Australia and New Zealand.[75]

The fact that stronger personality rights can be found in China is, indeed, not surprising. In the past two decades, attention to celebrities has grown considerably in China. While hero-worship and emphasis on symbols were common in China in the 1960s and 1970s,[76] economic reforms and media liberalisation in China have led to an ideal environment for nurturing and promoting celebrities both inside and outside the country.[77] Notable examples include NBA basketball player Yao Ming, kung-fu movie star Jet Li, film directors Feng Xiaogang and Zhang Yimou, actresses Gong Li and Zhang Ziyi, Olympic athletes Li Ning and Liu Xiang and pianists Lang Lang and Li Yundi.

Greater awareness of celebrities also makes sense in an environment where the government actively pushes for the development of national champions through its economic policies.[78] Such awareness also resonates well with the emerging brand consciousness and the rapidly

[75] Commerce and Economic Development Bureau, HKSAR Government, *Proposals for Strengthening Copyright Protection in the Digital Environment* (2009) available at www.cedb.gov.hk/citb/ehtml/pdf/consultation/Panel_Paper_Digital_Eng_Full.pdf.

[76] On China's celebrity culture, see Elaine Jeffreys and Louise Edwards, 'Celebrity/China', in Louise Edwards and Elaine Jeffreys (eds.), *Celebrity in China* (Hong Kong University Press, Hong Kong, 2010), 9–14.

[77] *Ibid.*

[78] Oded Shenkar, *The Chinese Century: The Rising Chinese Economy and Its Impact on the Global Economy, the Balance of Power, and Your Job* (Wharton School Publishing, Upper Saddle River, NJ, 2005), 158; Yu, 'Pirates to Partners', 998.

growing luxury market in China. As Ernst & Young stated in a study released in the mid-2000s:

> The Chinese luxury market . . . is expected to grow 20%, annually until 2008 and then 10% annually until 2015, when sales are expected to exceed US$ 11.5 billion. By 2010, China is expected to have a quarter-billion consumers who can afford luxury products, nearly 17 times the present number. By 2015, Chinese consumers could be as influential as the Japanese and account for 29% of all global luxury goods purchases.[79]

In fact, as Oded Shenkar points out, the growing brand consciousness among the Chinese can be seen as 'a legacy of Confucian hierarchy and of their imperial past where rank was prominently displayed on bureaucrats' clothing'.[80] Such consciousness also fits well with the Chinese language, which consists of pictorial characters and 'is strongly visual and semiotically promiscuous'.[81]

The second influence concerns the dramatic change of the media structure in Hong Kong. Such changes can be attributed to the arrival of new players such as i-Cable (formerly Wharf Cable) and Now TV (operated by PCCW Limited) as well as the advent of the World Wide Web, mobile telephony and other digital communications technologies. While the traditional media structure has provided an independent safeguard to protect against the misuse of celebrities' identities, the greater number of opportunities for advertising and other forms of commercial exposure both on- and off-line has made it difficult for celebrities to monitor the use of their identities.

Even more problematic, internet users have actively used celebrities' images in so-called user-generated content, such as blogs, mash-ups, fanvids, spoofs and parodies. Such use has raised new questions about the appropriate protection of a celebrity's identity. Commentators, for example, have identified the new phenomenon of 'virtual kidnapping', in which celebrities are forced to engage in 'lewd or violent acts' on the internet or in the virtual world.[82] The use of a celebrity's identity in internet domain names or Twitter's user names – either for the purposes

79 Ernst & Young, 'China: The New Lap of Luxury' (Report, EYG No. CP0006, September 2005), 1, available at www.ln.edu.hk/mkt/staff/gcui/EY-Luxurygoods.pdf.

80 Shenkar, *Chinese Century*, 157.

81 Bob Hodge and Kam Louie, *The Politics of Chinese Language and Culture: The Art of Reading Dragons* (Routledge, London, 1998), 8.

82 Alice Haemmerli, 'Whose Who? The Case for a Kantian Right of Publicity' (1999) 49 *Duke Law Journal* 383, 389 n. 21; Susan Kuchinskas, 'Image is everything', 18 June 1998, *Wired News*, available at www.wired.com/culture/lifestyle/news/1998/06/13075.

of deception, fan worship or criticism – has also become increasingly common.[83]

These new issues are particularly challenging, because it remains unclear whether online uses by individuals should be considered commercial or not. In fact, if infringement on personality rights is defined as the unauthorised *commercial* exploitation of an individual's identity, the use of such an identity in a *non-commercial* context could raise challenging legal questions by negating the commercial element. To some extent, these questions resemble those difficult ones in the internet file-sharing context, in which non-commercial activities have resulted in commercial impacts. While some courts, such as the one in *A&M Records Inc.* v. *Napster Inc.*,[84] have defined file-sharing activities as commercial in light of the fact that users reaped economic benefits by 'getting for free something they would ordinarily have to buy', commentators have widely criticised such grotesque distortion of the meaning of the term 'commercial'.

Indeed, the term's definition has become so controversial in recent years that it has been the root of a World Trade Organization dispute between China and the United States over the protection and enforcement of intellectual property rights.[85] Countries such as the United States and members of the European Union have also pushed for a redefinition of the term through bilateral, plurilateral and regional trade agreements.[86] Article 23.1 of the highly controversial Anti-Counterfeiting Trade Agreement, for example, states that 'acts carried out on a commercial scale include at least those carried out as commercial activities for direct or indirect economic or commercial advantage'.[87]

Third, and somewhat related to the second, the entertainment scene will be highly globalised in light of the many different advertising channels that have emerged as a result of the information revolution and changing business structures. Because of varying nation-based standards, the

[83] Jacqueline D. Lipton, 'Celebrity in Cyberspace: A Personality Rights Paradigm for Personal Domain Name Disputes' (2008) 65 *Washington and Lee Law Review* 1445; Jacqueline D. Lipton, 'Commerce versus Commentary: Gripe Sites, Parody, and the First Amendment in Cyberspace' (2006) 84 *Washington University Law Review* 1327; Jacqueline D. Lipton, 'Who Owns "Hillary.Com"? Political Speech and the First Amendment in Cyberspace' (2008) 49 *Boston College Law Review* 55.

[84] 114 F Supp 2d 896 (ND Cal, 2000).

[85] *China – Measures Affecting the Protection and Enforcement of Intellectual Property Rights – Report of the Panel*, WTO/DS362/R (26 January 2009) paras. 7.532–79; Peter K. Yu, 'The TRIPS Enforcement Dispute' (2011) 89 *Nebraska Law Review* 1046 (2011).

[86] For example, United States–Australia Free Trade Agreement art. 17.1.26(a), 18 May 2004.

[87] Anti-Counterfeiting Trade Agreement, opened for signature 1 May 2011 (not yet in force), art. 23.1. For a critical analysis of the agreement, see Peter K. Yu, 'Six Secret (and Now Open) Fears of ACTA' (2011) 64 *SMU Law Review* 975.

misuse of likeness in one region can also result in misuse in another.[88] This issue is particularly important in light of the wide geographical scope of diasporic communities that originated in Hong Kong (such as London, Los Angeles, Melbourne, New York, San Francisco, Sydney, Toronto and Vancouver). It is, therefore, no surprise that Professors Pendleton and Lee contended in their treatise on Hong Kong intellectual property law that 'it is a sensible progression to develop a new tort such as that of misappropriation of personality as in the USA or one of unfair competition as in Europe'.[89]

Although there has been a growing trend to harmonise intellectual property standards throughout the world, personality rights are unlikely to be the subject of such harmonisation. The reasons are twofold. First, countries remain deeply divided over how a celebrity's identity is to be protected. In light of these deep divisions, it is unlikely that an international consensus would emerge in the near future. Indeed, international harmonisation has been slow even in areas where there is greater consensus, such as the promotion of access to essential medicines in developing countries[90] and the protection of traditional knowledge and cultural expressions.[91] In the area of personality rights, one can only imagine how limited harmonisation will be in the near future.

Moreover, one of the major champions of international harmonisation – the United States – has yet to attain nationwide consensus on the protection of personality interests. As mentioned earlier, the scope and extent of protection under state rights of publicity vary from state to state. Although there have been proposals calling for the establishment of a federal right of publicity statute,[92] those proposals have yet to be adopted. With continuous disagreement among its states, the United States is unlikely to seek greater international harmonisation in the area in the near future.

[88] On conflict-of-law and jurisdictional issues concerning personality rights, see Dougherty, 'Foreword', 426–40.

[89] Pendleton and Lee, *Intellectual Property*, 33.

[90] Peter K. Yu, 'The International Enclosure Movement' (2007) 82 *Indiana Law Journal* 827.

[91] Peter K. Yu 'Cultural Relics, Intellectual Property, and Intangible Heritage' (2008) 81 *Temple Law Review* 433.

[92] Richard S. Robinson, 'Preemption, the Right of Publicity, and a New Federal Statute' (1998) 16 *Cardozo Arts and Entertainment Law Journal* 183 (1998); J. Eugene Salomon, Jr, 'The Right of Publicity Run Riot: The Case for a Federal Statute' (1987) 60 *Southern California Law Review* 1179; Steven C. Beer and Holly Pekowsky, 'Rights of Publicity after *Forest Gump*' *New York Law Journal*, 31 May 1995, 1.

Conclusion

Although Hong Kong has many successful entertainers and entertainment products, it has yet to offer strong personality rights. The lack of protection of celebrities' identities in Hong Kong provides a useful case study to understand the development of intellectual property protection in the Asia Pacific region. Through the historical British roots of Hong Kong intellectual property law, the study highlights the path-dependent nature of intellectual property development as well as the challenges confronting the establishment of new intellectual property rights. The limited protection of personality interests in Hong Kong also foreshadows the larger debate about the future of protection for brands and reputation in the Asia Pacific region.

While it remains unclear whether Hong Kong will eventually offer stronger personality rights, there is no doubt that the issue will deserve our close attention in the near future. There are, indeed, good reasons both for and against greater protection of personality interests in Hong Kong. Hopefully, this chapter will provide the much-needed groundwork to help us understand better the need for and challenge in strengthening protection in the region.

5 Fashioning personality rights in Australia

Megan Richardson and Andrew T. Kenyon

Introduction

Just over a century ago the celebrity writer H. G. Wells gave a public lecture entitled 'The discovery of the future' to the Royal Institution in London.[1] Curiously, since Wells was predominantly a science-fiction writer with no legal training or previously displayed interest in the law, the lecture had more to do with law than with science (or fiction). The futurist Wells was scathing about the lawyer's reliance on history, speaking of 'the legal or submissive type of mind' and saying 'let the dead past bury its dead' and contrasting the historicism of judges involved in developing common law with the futurism of legislators.[2] Despite Wells' questionable authority on matters of the law, it does seem that lawyers and judges in Britain and most of its former colonies have historically treated the past as a more reliable standard for regulating the present and future than any other standard, even while legislators in these same jurisdictions may have sought to break with former approaches and fashion rights directly for current social circumstances. These observations are particularly pertinent in the Australian treatment of personality rights. Here we find a clear disjuncture between statutory reformism and traditionalism of judges when it comes to development of the common law (including equity) to deal with new demands for personality rights in the face of new technologies and practices of media. Nevertheless, we conclude that for all these peculiarities Australian law has developed in a rather personality-rights sensitive way although current indications are still tentative, halting and inconclusive.

Thanks to Jason Bosland and Shaun McVeigh for helpful comments, and to Oscar O'Bryan for excellent research support.

[1] H. G. Wells, 'The discovery of the future', lecture given to the Royal Institution, London, 1902 and published in *Nature* (1902) 65; reprinted by BE Huebsch, New York, 1913.

[2] *Ibid.* 5–15ff.

Reformist legislation

A review of the various Australian statutes that regulate the individual's versus the group's control over professional and personal identity shows several instances of legislative efforts to frame a modern approach suitable for current social conditions. An example is the provisions regarding misleading or deceptive conduct in the consumer protection part of the Australian Trade Practices Act 1974 (Cth).[3] The principal provision, s. 52 of the Act, was framed in sufficiently broad terms to allow the 'local hero' Paul Hogan, creator and alter ago of the famous *Crocodile Dundee* character which he represented in Australian television and film productions, to object to a television advertisement that relied on a subtly confusing homage to the first and most famous *Crocodile Dundee* film in the case of *Hogan* v. *Pacific Dunlop Ltd*[4] – setting the scene for the provision's broad reading in later cases, supplementing and extending the common law. As observed by one commentator:

> Resorting to florid metaphor, the dedicated legal modernist may depict the common law and its causes of action as primeval broadacres grazed by slow-growing sauropods. Upon this landscape the action for misleading or deceptive conduct falls as a kind of statutory comet threatening significant reductions in the species number of fraud, negligent misstatement, passing off, defamation, collateral warranty and contractual representation.[5]

A further possible example is the provision made for protection of 'well-known' registered trade marks in s. 120(3) of the Trade Marks Act 1995 (Cth). The Australian High Court in *Campomar Sociedad Ltd* v. *Nike International Ltd*[6] said this provision gives more than extended statutory protection against deceptive uses of a registered trade mark that is well known in Australia, offering protection against 'dilution' by blurring or

[3] Section 52(1) of the Trade Practices Act 1974 (Cth), the Act's general provision on deceptive trading, stated that 'a corporation shall not, in trade or commerce, engage in conduct that is misleading or deceptive or is likely to mislead or deceive'. For the current provision (not limited to corporations) in the Australian Consumer Law, see sch. 2 of the Competition and Consumer Act 2010 s. 18.

[4] *Hogan* v. *Pacific Dunlop Ltd* (1988) 12 IPR 225 (Gummow J.); confirmed by a majority on appeal in *Pacific Dunlop* v. *Hogan* (1989) 23 FCR 553 (the decisions are collectively referred to as '*Hogan*'). And, for a discussion of the case in the context of the Australian film industry, see Megan Richardson, 'Larger than Life in the Australian Cinema: *Pacific Dunlop* v. *Hogan*', in Andrew Kenyon, Megan Richardson and Sam Ricketson, *Landmarks in Australian Intellectual Property* (Cambridge University Press, Melbourne and New York, 2009), 160.

[5] Robert French, 'A Lawyer's Guide to Misleading or Deceptive Conduct' (1989) 63 *Australian Law Journal* 250, 250.

[6] (2000) 202 CLR 45 ('*Campomar*').

tarnishment of the trade mark irrespective of confusion.[7] Some (although not all) Australian commentators have argued that it is not clear this was the legislator's intention or effect.[8] And it is unclear whether the High Court will continue to read the provision in such an apparently broad way.[9] But, if the original reading prevails in a relevant case, the provision may be taken as a legislative response to modern advertising practices of referencing to the recognisable imagery of popular culture in ways that are more subtle than traditional legal confusion standards may necessarily recognise. It is noteworthy that one of the few actual cases in which the provision has been utilised was one of referencing of this kind and also involved a (fictional) celebrity:[10] the defendant argued that his dressing up in the character of Nintendo's 'Super Mario' to play out his role as professional wrestler was not confusing but rather in the way of homage. Nevertheless the injunction sought to prohibit the conduct was awarded.

The above provisions do not distinguish between individual and other claimants. One aspect of this broader operation as far as personality rights are concerned has been to bring fictional persons under the scope of protection available to human personalities, treating them in an analogous way to human personalities. The *Hogan* and *Nintendo* cases are both examples of this, although in *Hogan* at least it was pointed out that a human creator and alter ego lay behind the fictional *Crocodile Dundee* character. On the other hand, the fact that the uniform Defamation Acts 2005–6 in general deny corporations the right to sue for defamation may suggest a narrower perception, namely that defamation law in Australia is viewed as a vehicle for individual human persons to claim protection from being subjected to unwarranted imputations that may harm their reputation (although corporations retain other avenues of recourse against imputations that may harm their reputation, including misleading or deceptive conduct and the common law actions for passing off and injurious falsehood).[11] Nevertheless it is not precluded that individuals involved in corporations may claim they are defamed by statements about

[7] See *ibid.* 65 [42] especially.

[8] See, for a survey, Jason Bosland and Megan Richardson, 'Competing Discourses of "Rights" and "Harms" in Trade Mark Law', in Kathy Bowrey, Michael Handler and Dianne Nicol (eds.), *Emerging Challenges in Intellectual Property* (Oxford University Press, Melbourne, 2011), 103.

[9] Although for an interesting reference to the 'monopoly' given by trade mark registration, see *E & J Gallo Winery* v. *Lion Nathan Australia Pty Ltd* (2010) 241 CLR 144 at [69], noted in Bosland and Richardson, 'Competing Discourses', in Bowrey *et al.*, *Emerging Challenges*, 103, fn. 79 .

[10] *Nintendo Co. Ltd* v. *Care* (2000) 52 IPR 34 ('*Nintendo*').

[11] See, e.g., Matt Collins, 'Protecting Corporate Reputations in the Era of Uniform National Defamation Laws' (2008) 13 *Media and Arts Law Review* 447.

and concerning the corporation that reflect on them, or that individuals claiming, for instance, that their created fictional character or fictional alter ego has been used in a manner that brings them personally into disrepute. More significant perhaps are reforms made to available defences to defamation under the uniform Acts. Now truth is a defence without the need also to show public interest, as previously required under the law of New South Wales (Australia's main centre for defamation claims).[12] The result is that the defamation law is now tailored to imputations that cannot be proven true. As a result, those who may previously have relied on defamation law as a vehicle to limit disclosure of embarrassing private facts and so control their public image[13] have lost that particular avenue of recourse.

The statutory incursions in the field of personality rights in Australia that we have discussed so far, although important and to an extent transformative are also patchy and confined to certain aspects of personality rights. In particular, there is no general statutory cause of action for invasion of privacy in Australia[14] and nor is there any general statutory right or rights of publicity, in the sense accepted in some US jurisdictions.[15] Moreover, the fact that successive Australian governments have resisted following the British, Canadian and New Zealand (and earlier United States) path of enacting a bill of rights means that nationally no signals are given by the legislature as to the preferred common law development around rights of privacy and reputation. The non-action of the Australian legislature has been heralded from time to time as a marker of Australian

[12] See Andrew T. Kenyon, *Defamation: Comparative Law and Practice* (UCL Press, Oxford, 2006), 6 and ch. 5.

[13] As, for instance, in *Ettinghausen* v. *Australian Consolidated Press Ltd* (1991) 23 NSWLR 443 and *Chappell* v. *TCN Channel Nine Pty Ltd* (1988) 14 NSWLR 153.

[14] Although Australia has a Privacy Act 1988 (Cth), which imposes certain privacy obligations with respect to collection and handling of information on government agencies and businesses; but this specifically exempts journalism and individuals acting in an individual capacity, as well as small businesses, although reform of the latter exemption has been proposed: see Australian Law Reform Commission, *For Your Information: Australian Privacy Law and Practice*, Report No. 108 (2008). In addition, legislation to provide a statutory cause (or causes) of action for address mediated invasions of privacy has been proposed: Australian Law Reform Commission, *ibid.*; New South Wales Law Reform Commission, *Invasion of Privacy*, Report No. 120 (2009), Victorian Law Reform Commission, *Surveillance in Public Places*, Final Report No. 18 (2010). This remains a live issue: see the Australian Government Issues Paper, *A Commonwealth Statutory Cause of Action for Serious Invasion of Privacy*, Commonwealth of Australia, Department of the Prime Minister and Cabinet, September 2011 (available online at www.dpmc.gov.au/privacy/causeofaction/docs/issues%20paper_cth_stat_cause_action_serious_invasion_privacy.pdf).

[15] See Chapters 3 and 4, in this volume. See also, for example, David S. Caudill, 'Once More into the Breach: Contrasting US and Australian "Rights of Publicity"' (2004) 9 *Media and Arts Law Review* 263.

independence, reflecting a society which is determinedly not about individual rights but rather the broader community. Ironically, however, we have acquired more the air of a former British colony which still takes an older legislative model while the United Kingdom moves on to embrace a more modern European discourse of rights of privacy, reputation and free speech.[16] Thus, while not going as far as to maintain that the law recognises a full image right,[17] United Kingdom courts acknowledge that individuals have rights of privacy and reputation as stated or implied in the Human Rights Act 1998 (UK), implementing the United Kingdom's obligations under the European Convention on Human Rights.[18] In the United Kingdom, these rights are reflected in the (largely) common law of breach of confidence and defamation, and so on; and may according to some recent cases have a more distinctly statutory and conventional character as well.[19] One consequence of these external influences, within and outside Australia, is that Australian courts are under pressure to determine the extent to which their common law (including equity) can and should be drawn on to accommodate new social demands for legal protection of personality.

Common law 'incrementalism'

Here it seems clear that Australian judges have not shown the same boldness as the legislature when it comes to reforming their law. The High Court in recent cases has articulated a 'historical' approach. As said in *Farah Constructions Pty Ltd* v. *Say-Dee Pty Ltd*, quoting Gummow J. in *Roxborough* v. *Rothmans of Pall Mall (Australia) Ltd*:

[16] Although the Australian Capital Territory has enacted a Human Rights Act 2004 and Victoria has its Charter of Human Rights and Responsibilities Act 2006, neither on their face changes the common law of Australia.

[17] In fact some English judges have disclaimed this (so far): see for instance *OBG Ltd and another* v. *Allan and others; Douglas and others* v. *Hello! Ltd and others (No. 3)*; *Mainstream Properties Ltd* v. *Young* [2008] 1 AC 1, 49 [124] (Lord Hoffmann).

[18] Human Rights Act 1998 (UK), implementing the European Convention on Human Rights, opened for signature 4 November 1950, ETS 5 (entered into force 3 September 1953).

[19] See, for instance, *McKennitt* v. *Ash* [2008] QB 73, 80–2 [8]–[11] (Buxton J.); *Mosely* v. *News Group Newspapers Ltd* [2008] EWHC 2341, Eady J. at [7] (breach of confidence extended and superseded by 'breach of privacy' under the terms of the ECHR) – but it may be wondered whether a majority of the House of Lords would accept this reasoning: see for instance *Campbell* v. *Mirror Group Newspapers Ltd* [2004] 2 AC 457 (breach of confidence flexibly construed to reflect ECHR's right of privacy) and Megan Richardson, 'Towards Legal Pragmatism: Breach of Confidence and the Right to Privacy', in Elise Bant and Matthew Harding (eds.), *Exploring Private Law* (Cambridge University Press, Cambridge, 2010), 109.

To the lawyer whose mind has been moulded by civilian influences, the theory may come first, and the source of the theory may be the writings of jurists not the decisions of judges. However, that is not the way in which a system based on case law develops; over time, general principle is derived from judicial decisions upon particular instances, not the other way around.[20]

Further, in *Campomar* the High Court made clear that that it would not accept any general action for 'unfair competition' that might give general protection against misappropriation on the basis that such an action ran counter to its historical approach of framing protection around traditional statutory and common law causes of action.[21] Similarly, in *Australian Broadcasting Corporation* v. *Lenah Game Meats Pty Ltd*,[22] Gummow and Hayne JJ doubted whether the Court's 'preferable legal method' allowed for the wholesale introduction 'of any general wrong of unjustified invasion of privacy' (although the option of a privacy cause or causes of action being declared further down the line was not precluded), especially given the protection already available to privacy under traditional doctrines.[23] Rather, these judges said, the preferable legal method permitted 'the development and adaptation of recognised forms of action to meet new situations and circumstances'.[24] This leads us to the question of where precisely this historical preference developed and also what it signifies for the developing protection of personality rights.

When the High Court in *Farah* characterises the approach of a 'system based on case law' as one in which 'general principle is derived from judicial decisions upon particular instances, not the other way around', distinguishing this from a European approach (and by implication perhaps the Europeanising British one), it ignores or overlooks the rather different approach of another 'system based on case law'. That is the American system. From around the beginning of the twentieth century and in a more formalised way after the First World War, this system came under the modernising impulse of the American legal realist movement. Although mostly associated with and attributed to a few key names,

[20] *Farah Constructions Pty Ltd* v. *Say-Dee Pty Ltd* (2007) 230 CLR 89, 158 [154] ('*Farah*'), citing *Roxborough* v. *Rothmans of Pall Mall (Australia) Ltd* (2001) 208 CLR 516, 544 [72] (Gummow J.). In the latter case Gummow J. also refers at [73] to (the American judge and lawyer economist) Richard Posner's classic article 'Legal Reasoning from the Top Down and from the Bottom Up: The Question of Unenumerated Constitutional Rights' (1992) 59 *University of Chicago Law Review* 433 – but in the quoted passage Gummow J. characterises the theorised approach as a 'civilian one'. (Posner may agree: he does not contend that US legal reasoning is completely 'top-down' but rather suggests that it represents a more nuanced version.)

[21] *Campomar*, 54 [3].

[22] (2001) 208 CLR 199, 250 [110] ('*Lenah*').

[23] *Ibid.* 255 [123], and further Gleeson CJ at 224–5 [34]–[39], arguing that 'if the activities filmed [in the case] were private then breach of confidence is adequate to cover the case'.

[24] *Ibid.* 250 [110].

including legal scholars Karl Llewellyn and Jerome Frank (later Justice Frank), there are many others before and after those influential scholars, including Justices Oliver Wendell Holmes, Louis Brandeis and Learned Hand, who have been associated with legal realism. Legal realism may be characterised as 'an effort to define and discredit classical legal theory and practice and to offer in their place a more philosophically and politically enlightened jurisprudence',[25] while not necessarily conceding the importance of the rule of law.[26] Personality rights offer a case in point. As discussed in the chapters in this book by Peter Yu and David Tan,[27] in many jurisdictions of the United States of America courts from the beginning of the twentieth century onwards moved to adopt common law rights of privacy and later rights of publicity (supplementing the statutory rights in some US states). These were framed directly in terms of the individual's right of control over privacy and publicity, although also qualified or made subject to the countervailing right of free speech provided for in the US Constitution. Importantly, rather than simply observing this position as organically developed through a line of judicial decisions, judges made law openly and reformist legal scholars provided impetus for the personality rights to emerge.

In some cases the process of reform began with legal scholars. Samuel Warren and Louis Brandeis' article entitled 'The Right to Privacy' published in the 1890 *Harvard Law Review*,[28] pointed to the impact of the then relatively new medium of photography for journalistic practices and individual, if bourgeois, expectations of privacy and argued that courts should now openly acknowledge the 'right to privacy' as a right of 'inviolate personality' and fashion law around that expressly. Following this, courts in several US jurisdictions inspired by Warren and Brandeis and observing the influences of radio and television on media and advertising practices, began to articulate new common law rights of privacy.[29] In the post-war years, American scholars working in the now pervasive tradition of realism offered an elaborated rubric of reasoning to account for and support and help shape the new rights as well as (in some states)

25 See William Fisher, Morton Horwitz and Thomas Reed, introduction to Fisher, Horwitz and Reed (eds.), *American Legal Realism* (Oxford University Press, New York, 1993) xi, xiii–xiv.

26 See generally *ibid.*, and further Brian Tamanaha, 'Understanding Legal Realism' (2008) 87 *Texas Law Review* 731, as well as Posner's interesting discussion of Holmes, 'Legal Reasoning', 450.

27 See Chapters 3 (Tan) and 4 (Yu).

28 Samuel Warren and Louis Brandeis, 'The Right to Privacy' (1980) 4 *Harvard Law Review* 193.

29 See, e.g., *Pavesich* v. *New England Life Ins. Co.* 120 Ga 190 (Ga Sup Ct, 1905); *Melvin* v. *Reid* 112 Cal App 285 (Cal Ct App, 1931).

a related right of publicity, defined as the right to the 'publicity value' to be obtained from the public exposure of their likenesses in advertising by Justice Frank in the 1953 case of *Haelan Laboratories* v. *Topps Chewing Gum*.[30] William Prosser in his 1960 article on privacy explained how the protection of Warren and Brandeis' right of privacy had been expanded in judicial decisions to embrace distinct rights of intrusion, disclosure, false light publicity and appropriation of name or likeness, and at the same time gave these labels to the torts and emphasised certain lines of reasoning.[31] Further, Randolph Nimmer and Thomas McCarthy, helped to identify and foster the right of publicity.[32] Their efforts were supplemented by the influential US Restatement (Second) of Torts[33] and Restatement (Third) of Unfair Competition,[34] enterprises in which Prosser and McCarthy participated. And judges deciding cases cited Prosser, Nimmer and McCarthy as well as the Restatements in fashioning law.

Was Australia not influenced by American legal realism? We suggest that in a similar way as Australia took more of its political and social culture from America after the Second World War, Australian judges had some consciousness of the evolving American legal culture as well and responded to it with their own theories of preferable legal development – although much more slowly, and with the future direction still not clear. One sign of the High Court's still developing approach can be found in *Lenah* itself. There Gummow and Hayne JJ not only articulated the High Court's preferred legal method as one that explicitly fashions law in reference to new situations and circumstances. They were at pains to observe that, notwithstanding that Australian courts do not fashion their doctrines directly as rights of privacy, rather preferring to develop their traditional doctrines in privacy-sensitive ways, there are similarities in the substantive protection offered to privacy. In particular:

> [I]n Australia, one or more of the four invasions of privacy [as identified in the American discourse and jurisprudence], to which reference has been made, in many instances would be actionable at general law under recognised causes of action. Injurious falsehood, defamation (particularly in those states where,

30 *Haelan Laboratories, Inc.* v. *Topps Chewing Gum, Inc.* 202 F 2nd 866 (2nd Cir, 1953).

31 William Prosser, 'Privacy' (1960) 48 *California Law Review* 383. Although Prosser did not highlight the effects of film, radio and television in the way that Warren and Brandeis did for photography, the article is littered with references to these media: see, for instance, 393, 393, 405.

32 Melville Nimmer, 'The Right of Publicity' (1954) 19 *Law and Contemporary Problems* 203; and J. Thomas McCarthy, 'Melville B Nimmer and the Right of Publicity: A Tribute' (1987) 34 *UCLA Law Review* 1703.

33 American Law Institute, Restatement (Second) of Torts (1979).

34 American Law Institute, Restatement (Third) of Unfair Competition (1995).

> by statute, truth of itself is not a complete defence), confidential information and trade secrets (in particular as extended to information respecting the personal and private life of the plaintiff, and the activities of eavesdroppers and the like), passing off (as extended to include false representations of sponsorship or endorsement), the tort of conspiracy, the intentional infliction of harm to the individual based on *Wilkinson* v. *Downton* and what may be termed a developing tort of harassment, and the action on the case for nuisance constituted by watching or besetting the plaintiff's premises, come to mind. Putting aside the special position regarding defamation to one side, these wrongs may attract interlocutory and final injunctive relief.[35]

Such benchmarking statements – also found in the other judgments in *Lenah* (with respect to privacy)[36] as well as in *Campomar* (with respect to dilution)[37] – suggest a rather more interesting picture of the preferred approach of Australian courts than the simple statement about bottom-up reasoning in *Farah*. And their reasoning also differs from older High Court decisions. Although Gummow and Hayne JJ in *Lenah* reference the High Court's 'preferable approach' to the judgment of Dixon J. in the 1937 case of *Victoria Park Racing and Recreation Grounds Co. Ltd* v. *Taylor*,[38] little support for incrementalism is to be found there, although there are a number of cases from the 1960s that support the current High Court's newly evolving 'traditional' approach.

No doubt one reason for citing Dixon J. in *Victoria Park Racing* is the tremendous authority conceded by Australian legal scholars and judges to this influential judge who served on the High Court for thirty-five years, including twelve as chief justice, and was actively engaged in fashioning his own version of a judge's role both in judgments and extra-judicial lectures and essays. Sir Owen Dixon's mythology as Australia's 'greatest jurist' seems unassailable.[39] Yet the preferable legal method that Dixon articulated in his lectures and essays was not one of deliberate development of the law to deal with new situations and circumstances but rather

35 *Lenah*, 255 [123]. As noted above, the defamation law of all Australian jurisdictions now provides that truth is a complete defence, which appears to reduce the degree to which the action might incidentally protect privacy.

36 See especially Gleeson CJ at 225–6 [40]–[42], citing Prosser and the US Restatement (Second) of Torts in comparing the Australian breach of confidence doctrine with a US-style tort of public disclosure of private facts.

37 *Campomar*, 65–6 [42]–[43].

38 (1937) 58 CLR 479 ('*Victoria Park Racing*'). See *Lenah* (2001) 208 CLR 199, 250 [110] (referring to 'the view taken by Dixon J. . . as to preferable legal method'). And see also *Campomar*, 54 [4] (Dixon J. provides 'an authoritative statement of contemporary Australian law').

39 David Ritter, 'The Myth of Sir Owen Dixon' (2004) 9 *Australian Journal of Legal History* 249.

one of 'an external standard . . . [to be] found in a body of positive knowledge which [the judge] regards himself as having acquired', which may permit 'legal development' concerning social ends but not 'deliberate innovat[ion] bent on express change of acknowledged doctrine'.[40] That was the legal positivist method, discussed by Sir Owen Dixon in a lecture delivered at Yale University in 1955 and containing many veiled criticisms of legal realism. And it was already evident in Dixon J.'s judgment in *Victoria Park Racing*. The case concerned a claim by a race ground to a legal entitlement to control practices of radio stations in the 1930s of broadcasting details of races taking place on private race grounds with the assistance of neighbours who permitted their use of viewing platforms built on their properties overlooking the grounds. The plaintiff's argument was framed first in terms of a broad reading of the common law of nuisance and/or statutory copyright (although less evidently relying on the equitable doctrine breach of confidence despite its longstanding authority and flexible character). Failing that, it was suggested, the High Court might develop a new misappropriation doctrine in the same way that the US Supreme Court in *International News Service* v. *Associated Press*[41] had developed a misappropriation doctrine to deal with cases of a news service's copying of news bulletins from a rival news service. The High Court's response to these arguments was that it had no authority to grant such control. As Dixon J. put it:

> [I]t is not because the individual has by his efforts put himself in a position to obtain value for what he can give that his right to give it becomes protected by law and so assumes the exclusiveness of property, but because the intangible or incorporeal right he claims falls within a recognized category to which legal or equitable protection attaches.[42]

Not all the High Court judges accepted the position, however.[43] For instance, Rich J. dissented on the basis that such a narrow reading of existing doctrine risked giving little protection against breaches of an individual's privacy occasioned by the surveillance of neighbours and pointed to television as exacerbating the problem – adding that this may

[40] Sir Owen Dixon, 'Concerning judicial method', lecture delivered at Yale on 19 September 1955, repr. in Judge Woinarski (ed.), *Jesting Pilate* (Law Book Co., Melbourne, 1965), 152, 157–8 especially.
[41] *International New Service* v. *Associated Press* 248 US 215 (1918) ('*International News Service*').
[42] *Victoria Park Racing*, 509.
[43] For a more extended discussion of the decision in *Victoria Park Racing* and its social context, see Jill McKeough, 'Horses and the Law: The Enduring Legacy of *Victoria Park Racing* v. *Taylor*', in Kenyon *et al.*, *Landmarks*, 53.

ultimately 'force the courts to recognise that protection against the complete exposure of the doings of the individual may be a right indispensable to the enjoyment of life'.[44] A second dissent came from Evatt J. who preferred the Supreme Court's approach in the *International News Service* case and made reference to Holmes J.'s concurring opinion in the case, where protection was premised not on a new misappropriation doctrine but rather a broad reading of the traditional common law doctrine of passing off construed to encompass cases where a news service implicitly represents news as its own when in reality it is gathered by a rival news service. Similarly, Evatt J. suggested, *Victoria Park Racing* could be characterised as a case where the radio station misrepresented its information about races gathered from a neighbour's property as coming from the race ground itself.[45]

Twenty years later Evatt J. contributed to another important decision of another court on the question of the preferred legal method of an Australian judge. After a period in office as a minister in the Australian Labor Government and leader of the Opposition in the 1950s (during which time he was instrumental in securing a provision for statutory protection against the unauthorised broadcasting on television of live games in the Broadcasting and Television Act 1942),[46] Evatt J. was handed the retirement position of Chief Justice of the New South Wales Supreme Court. In a case that came before the court in 1960, the same year as Prosser wrote his article entitled 'Privacy', this court was faced with a passing off case in the form of *Henderson* v. *Radio Corporation Pty Ltd.*[47] In that case, well-known professional ballroom dancers Mr and Mrs Henderson objected to the use of their image on ballroom dancing records manufactured and sold by the Melbourne-based Radio Corporation, providing evidence from a number of witnesses as to confusion. Although there was also evidence that Mr Henderson had engaged in some character merchandising in the past and had when he came to Australia from the United Kingdom sought a commercial arrangement with a phonograph company to sell his image for ballroom dancing records, he also indicated his disapproval of the particular use of his image in this case. More generally the Hendersons objected to the use of their personal image without their consent on the defendant's records. Having found there was sufficient evidence of public confusion to infer

44 *Victoria Park Racing*, 505. 45 *Ibid.* 518–19.

46 See the debate on the Broadcasting and Television Bill 1956, leading to the insertion of s. 115 into the Broadcasting and Television Act 1942–1956: Commonwealth of Australia, *Parliamentary Debates*, House of Representatives, 10 May 1956, 1981–7, and especially Dr Evatt.

47 [1960] SR (NSW) 576; 1A IPR 620 ('*Henderson*').

passing off (and rejecting the suggestion from English cases that a common field of activity was required between plaintiff and defendant before a successful action could be brought) Evatt CJ and Myers J. turned to the question of damage, holding that:

> The wrongful appropriation of another's professional or business reputation is an injury in itself, no less, in our opinion, than the appropriation of . . . goods or money.[48]

Although preferring to limit an assessment of damage to a more concrete assessment of the fee the plaintiffs might have charged, the third judge Manning J. similarly agreed with the majority that the law of passing off needed to accommodate 'new and altered methods of advertising and marketing' in the modern era of commercial radio and television – in particular in a case where 'the result of the defendant's action was to give the defendant the benefit of the plaintiff's recommendation and the value of such recommendation'.[49]

Framed in such terms, *Henderson* is one of Australia's leading decisions on personality rights. The doctrine relied on is still passing off, as pointed out in *Hogan* (which also entailed a claim for passing off alongside a more general statutory claim for misleading or deceptive conduct); thus the core of protection is still misrepresentation.[50] But there are parallels to be drawn with the US rights of publicity and privacy. The majority's highly flexible decision in *Henderson* straddles the borderline of the US privacy and publicity rights concerning the unauthorised use of name or image for advertising purposes. There is more emphasis than in the US publicity right and appropriation of name or image privacy right on the public's likely misconception, bringing the action closer doctrinally to Prosser's false light publicity privacy tort. On the other hand, there is no suggestion that passing off is to be viewed as simply about privacy, even in respect of claims involving the use of personal features in advertising (any more than a claim for misleading or deceptive conduct). Indeed, taking into account later cases such as *Hogan*, the question of when the public is likely to be confused can be given a very liberal construction. Thus the case stands alongside *Lenah* in not merely advocating but also adopting a flexible approach to traditional forms of action to deal with contemporary claims regarding rights of publicity and privacy.

Indeed, to revert to *Lenah*, this was a point implicitly recognised by Gummow and Hayne JJ in their discussion of the protection of personality

48 *Ibid.* 1A IPR, 638. 49 *Ibid.* 644–5.

50 See *Hogan* v. *Pacific Dunlop Ltd* (1988) 12 IPR 225; *Pacific Dunlop* v. *Hogan* (1989) 23 FCR 553; and generally Richardson, 'Larger than Life'.

rights in Australia. First, *Henderson* was cited for the proposition that passing off 'as extended to include false representations of sponsorship or endorsement' can serve a privacy-protection function equivalent to the American privacy torts (not merely the commercial function more commonly associated with the doctrine). Second, in talking about the preferred legal method Gummow and Hayne JJ cite not just Dixon J. in *Victoria Park Racing* but also Deane J. from the 1984 High Court case of *Moorgate Tobacco Co. Ltd* v. *Philip Morris Ltd (No. 2)*,[51] who articulated the method in terms of:

> the desirability of adopting a flexible approach to traditional forms of action when such an approach is necessary to adapt them to meet new situations and circumstances.[52]

But the one Australian authority cited in the latter case for this proposition is *Henderson* – not *Victoria Park Racing* (which is mentioned in relation to the 'rejection of a general action for "unfair competition" or "unfair trading"' by Australian courts).[53] So, if the statement of Deane J. in *Moorgate* approved by Gummow and Hayne JJ in *Lenah* is taken as a guide, it seems that *Henderson* as much as if not more than *Victoria Park Racing* has to do with the current legal method of the High Court – a method which although not as boldly reformist as American legal realism can be characterised as a form of legal realism, a form capable of fashioning law.

To conclude this brief discussion, then, we have argued that while statutes may be the obvious measure to reform the law when it comes to fashioning personality rights, the common law (including equity) can and has been developed by Australian courts to deal with new situations and circumstances, and the incremental method has been endorsed by several judgments in the Australian High Court. Although the legislature may have benefits when it comes to law reform, leaving matters there can also bring disadvantages.[54] That suggests the ability of Australian case law to fashion new approaches should not be forgotten.

[51] *Moorgate Tobacco Co. Ltd* v. *Philip Morris Ltd (No. 2)* (1984) 156 CLR 414.

[52] *Ibid.* 445. [53] *Ibid.*

[54] Including uncertainty and delay in the implementation of recommended legislative reforms: see, e.g., regarding recent calls to fashion statutory causes of action for privacy: above n. 14.

Part III

Brands and personality

6 Protection of reputation in the trade mark and copyright laws of Malaysia and Singapore

Divergence and a cultural exploration

Khaw Lake Tee, Tay Pek San and Ng-Loy Wee Loon

I. Introduction

Malaysia and Singapore are alike in many respects. Both are a melting pot of cultures from three main racial groups, namely, the Chinese, the Indians and the Malays. Both inherited the common law system, a legacy from the days when they were under British protection and rule.[1] Both were once within the same federation.[2] In the realm of intellectual property law, both countries have the same starting points for copyright (namely, the Imperial Copyright Act of 1911 (UK)),[3] for patents (in the form of a registration system of patents first registered in the UK),[4] and

[1] The following is a very brief account of British protection and rule in Singapore and Malaysia. Between 1826 and 1946 (except during the Japanese Occupation, 1941–5), the island of Singapore and two states in the Malay Peninsula (Malacca and Penang) were ruled by the East India Company, and later directly under British rule, as a Crown colony called the Straits Settlements. The other states in the Malay Peninsula – Negri Sembilan, Pahang, Perak, Selangor (forming the Federated Malay States) and Johor, Kedah, Kelantan, Perlis and Terengganu (forming the Unfederated Malay States) – were British protected states. After the Second World War in 1946, the British disbanded the Straits Settlements and set up Singapore as a separate Crown colony. Rule over Malacca and Penang was maintained by placing them, together with the other states within the Malay Peninsula, in a new entity called the Malayan Union. In 1948, the Malayan Union was reconstituted as the Federation of Malaya.

[2] This federation which was formed in 1963 comprised, apart from Singapore, the states of the Federation of Malaya, Sabah and Sarawak. Singapore left this federation to become a sovereign nation in 1965.

[3] The Imperial Copyright Act of 1911 (UK) continued to be the law in Malaysia and Singapore for many years after independence (1957 in the case of Malaysia and 1963 in the case of Singapore). This Act was repealed in Malaysia in 1969 and in Singapore in 1987 when the country enacted its own copyright legislation.

[4] No provision then existed for the local registration of patents which were not first registered in the UK. See the Registration of United Kingdom Patents Ordinance 1937 enacted by the Governor of the Straits Settlements. Similar provisions for the local registration of UK patents were provided in the Federated Malay States pursuant to the Inventions Enactment (FMS Cap 72) and in some states of the Unfederated Malay

for trade marks (via the common law action for passing off and a registration system modelled on the Trade Marks Act 1938 (UK)).[5] Both are also contracting parties to the Paris Convention for the Protection of Industrial Property[6] and the Berne Convention for the Protection of Literary and Artistic Works[7] and members of the World Trade Organization.

Yet in spite of these similarities, Malaysia and Singapore have different approaches when it comes to protecting reputation within their IP regimes. Under Malaysian trade mark law, following the decision in *McCurry Restaurant (KL) Sdn Bhd* v. *McDonald's Corp.*,[8] misrepresentation remains an essential requirement for a passing off action. Under the statutory regime of trade marks protection, Malaysia does not provide for dilution protection of the reputation of a trade mark. On the other hand, Singapore protects reputation in a trade mark against dilution regardless of the presence or absence of confusion. Under copyright law, Malaysia provides for moral rights which can protect the reputation of an author whereas Singapore has no equivalent system.

Dilution is often advanced as a 'modern trademark' theory.[9] Moral rights have been elevated to become fundamental human rights.[10] Looked at from these perspectives, one may characterise the Malaysian approach as being more traditional and moralistic. The Singaporean approach, on the other hand, is more utilitarian in a commercial sense. In particular, the absence of protection for moral rights *à la* art. 6*bis* of the Berne Convention is a result of the concern that the inalienable and

States. See the Registration of United Kingdom Patents Enactment 1937 (Johore En No. 7 of 1937), Enactment (No. 54) Inventions (Kedah En No. 54) and the Inventions Enactment 1928 (Kelantan En No. 11 of 1928).

5 See the Trade Marks Ordinance 1938 enacted by the Governor of the Straits Settlements. The Federated Malay States enacted the Federated Malay States Merchandise Marks Enactment 1917 which empowered the chief secretary to the government to make rules to provide for the establishment of a system of registration of trade marks. However, no rules were ever made for the registration of trade marks. The Unfederated Malay States did not have any legislation regulating trade marks prior to joining the Federation of Malaya in 1948, except for the state of Johor which modelled its Merchandise Marks Enactment 1918 on the Straits Settlements Merchandise Marks Ordinance 1917.

6 Malaysia acceded to the Paris Convention in 1989; Singapore acceded in 1995.

7 Malaysia acceded to the Berne Convention in 1990; Singapore acceded in 1998.

8 [2009] 3 MLJ 774 ('*McCurry*').

9 This 'modern' dilution theory is often credited to – or blamed upon, if you are a critic – Frank Schechter and his article published in the *Harvard Law Review*, in which he advocated that 'modern trademark protection' must take into account the value of 'modern trademark', namely, its 'selling power' that is acquired as a result of 'modern trade': see 'The Rational Basis of Trademark Protection' (1927) 40 *Harvard Law Review* 813.

10 See art. 27(2) of the UN Declaration of Human Rights: 'Everyone has the right to the protection of the *moral* and material interests resulting from any scientific, literary or artistic production of which he is the author' (emphasis added).

potentially perpetual nature of these rights will impede the commercial exploitation of the author's work. If these characterisations are accurate, it raises the question: does the moralistic Malaysian approach and the utilitarian Singaporean approach accord with the different religious and cultural underpinnings in the two countries? It has been mentioned that, culturally, Malaysia and Singapore are alike because of the presence of the same three ethnic groups in its population. At the same time, there is a material difference in that the dominant racial group in Malaysia is the Malays whereas the dominant racial group in Singapore is the Chinese.[11] As the Malays in Malaysia are Muslims,[12] it is not surprising that Islam is the official state religion of Malaysia.[13] Singapore, on the other hand, is a secular state whose leadership styles are steeped with paternalistic traditions often associated with Confucianism. This difference becomes important once we turn to academic research that suggests that Islam and Confucianism have teachings on the nature of IP protection: it has been said that teachings in Islam sanction the protection of moral rights but perhaps not the dilution theory, and that the very notion of authors having rights over their works is alien in Confucianism.

The structure of the rest of this chapter is as follows. Part II is on the protection of reputation under the trade mark law in Malaysia and Singapore. Part III is on the moral rights provisions in the Copyright Act 1987 (Malaysia) and the provisions in the Copyright Act 1987 (Singapore, Cap 63, 2006 Rev Ed) which provide some limited protection for moral rights. Part IV provides an overview of the academic writings on the influence of Islam and of Confucianism on copyright law and on trade mark law.

II. Protecting reputation in trade mark law: the dilution debate

(a) Malaysia

The primary means of protecting trade mark rights in Malaysia are the registered trade mark system and the common law of passing off

[11] The relative composition of these three racial groups in the two countries is as follows. In Malaysia, the population is made up of 65 per cent of Malays, 26 per cent of Chinese and 7 per cent of Indians. In Singapore, the population is made up of 75 per cent of Chinese, 14 per cent of Malays and 9 per cent of Indians.

[12] Islam is so integral to the Malay community that art. 160 of the Federal Constitution (Malaysia) deems Islam to be the faith of a person who is ethnically Malay.

[13] Article 3(1) of the Federal Constitution (Malaysia) provides that Islam is the religion of the Federation of Malaysia.

although, strictly speaking, passing off law protects the goodwill of the business that uses the trade mark rather than the trade mark itself.[14]

The foundation of Malaysian trade mark law, whether at common law or under the registration system, is the prevention of consumer confusion or misrepresentation in the marketplace. Thus, the only legally recognised function of a trade mark under Malaysian trade mark law is its indication of origin function.[15] The emphasis given to a trade mark's indication of origin function serves two purposes. First, only trade mark proprietors or persons authorised by them are allowed to create the link between the products which bear the marks and themselves. This protects the trade mark owner's goodwill. Second, through curbing the deceptive use of a trade mark, consumers are protected against misrepresentation created by third parties as to the origin of their goods.

In recent years, there have been cases where counsels have urged Malaysian judges to recognise that it is inadequate in today's market environment for the law to limit itself to a recognition of the indication of origin function only. The argument is that in the light of the needs of today's business community and international developments in trade mark protection, the boundaries of Malaysian trade mark law should be extended to encompass protection of the advertising function of trade marks, specifically the reputation of well-known trade marks. Proponents of this view assert that well-known trade marks possess an advertising function in addition to their indication of origin function. The advertising function recognises that well-known trade marks are commercial magnets which are able to draw customers to the marks themselves and, hence, to products bearing the marks. According to Frank Schechter, the father of American dilution law, the rational basis for trade mark protection is to prevent 'the gradual whittling away or dispersion of the identity and hold upon the public mind of the mark or name by its use upon non-competing goods'.[16] Radical though this may seem at that time, Schechter's dilution theory caught on, albeit slowly, and is now entrenched in the trade mark law of some major jurisdictions in the world.[17] The dilution theory, however, has not found its way into the

[14] *Star Industrial Co. Ltd* v. *Yap Kwee Kor* [1976] 1 MLJ 149, 150.

[15] See the definition of a 'trade mark' in s. 3(1) of the Trade Marks Act 1976 (Malaysia) which adopts the notion of a trade mark as an indicator of origin, even though the source may be anonymous. Other provisions of the Act, such as those dealing with applications for registration (s. 14(1)(a)), the protection of a trade mark owner's exclusive right (s(1)) and the maintenance of a trade mark on the Register of Trade Marks (s. 45(1)(a) read together with s. 37(b)) also place importance on the prevention of consumer confusion.

[16] Schechter 'Rational Basis', 825.

[17] For instance, the US Trademark Dilution Revision Act of 2006, Pub L No. 109–312, § 2, 120 Stat 1730, 1730–2 (2006), amending 15 USC § 1125(c) (1946); ss. 5(3) and

Malaysian trade mark regime. Sections (i) and (ii) below give a summary of the failed attempts to expand the trade mark law in Malaysia to include Schechter's dilution theory.

(i) At common law: passing off There are decisions dating back to the late 1990s in which Malaysian courts have recognised dilution of trade marks as a head of damage in passing off proceedings. In the first related case, *Service Master (M) Sdn Bhd* v. *MHL ServiceMaster Sdn Bhd* (‘*Service Master*’),[18] the High Court in dismissing the plaintiff's claim for passing off stated that ‘[t]he plaintiff has shown no inferior services or products by the defendants nor has it shown how there can be an erosion of its name’.[19] This statement suggests that trade marks may be protected against dilution if there is evidence of its erosion. Two years later, the High Court in *Scotch Whisky Association* v. *Ewein Winery (M) Sdn Bhd*[20] explicitly stated that the defendant's acts of passing off would dilute the meaning of ‘Scotch Whisky’. In that case, the defendants, who were a locally incorporated company carrying on the business of manufacturing liquor, had used the words ‘Scotch Whisky’ on the label of their product and had adopted features of get-up in visual representations which suggested Scottish origin. As is common knowledge, the term ‘Scotch Whisky’ denotes spirits distilled solely in Scotland in a regulated manner. In finding the defendants liable for passing off, the High Court stated that if locally produced whiskies were widely sold as ‘Scotch Whisky’, the meaning of ‘Scotch Whisky’ would be diluted and might eventually become generic to the detriment of real ‘Scotch Whisky’ producers.[21] Similarly, in *Petroliam Nasional Bhd (Petronas) & Ors* v. *Khoo Nee Kiong*,[22] it was held that the registration by the defendant of many domain names comprising the plaintiff's well-known trade mark ‘Petronas’ would result in an erosion of the exclusive goodwill in that trade mark and would, eventually, damage the reputation of the trade mark.

These cases became the backbone for the argument advanced in *McCurry*[23] to expand the scope of passing off. The plaintiff in this case was the well-known fast-food franchisor, McDonald's Corporation, which had outlets all around the world. The defendant conducted a restaurant which offered Indian and Malaysian cuisine under the trade name ‘McCurry Restaurant’. The defendant's signage had the words

10(3) of the Trade Marks Act 1994 (UK); and, arguably, s. 120(3) of the Australian Trade Marks Act 1995 (Cth).

[18] [1998] 5 MLJ 378. [19] *Ibid.* 392. [20] [1999] 6 MLJ 280.

[21] *Ibid.* 303. [22] [2003] 4 MLJ 216. [23] [2009] 3 MLJ 774.

'McCurry Restaurant' in white lettering and grey shading on a red background. Those colours were similar to the plaintiff's colour scheme. In its passing off action against the defendant, the plaintiff tendered evidence from consumer witnesses that they thought that the defendant was associated with the plaintiff. The trial judge took the view that a possibility of association, as opposed to actual confusion, was sufficient to satisfy the element of misrepresentation for a passing off action. Having found that the plaintiff's business goodwill had been generated by the prefix 'Mc' and that there was misrepresentation by the defendant's use of the same prefix, the trial judge held that the defendant was liable for passing off. She then proceeded to consider the issue of damage. Relying on the earlier case of *Service Master*, she held that the damage to the plaintiff included 'the loss of the exclusivity, distinctiveness and singularity attached to the prefix "Mc"'[24] and that 'the prefix "Mc" would cease to be a badge of recognition of the plaintiff's products'.[25] Clearly, the trial judge accepted that dilution protection of well-known trade marks was available under passing off law.

However, the trial judge's decision was reversed on appeal to the Court of Appeal. Essentially, the appeal proceeded on a determination of two points. First, whether Malaysian law recognises that passing off could be established without proof of a misrepresentation, *a fortiori*, whether dilution protection is available in Malaysia. Second, whether the defendant, in using the word 'McCurry', had passed off their goods as that of the plaintiff. In so far as the first point is concerned, counsel for the defendant submitted that Lord Fraser in *Erven Warnink* v. *Townend & Sons (Hull) Ltd*[26] had dispensed with the requirement of misrepresentation in a passing off action and urged the appellate court to rule that this did not represent Malaysian passing off law. Gopal Sri Ram JCA, who delivered the judgment of the court, disagreed with the counsel's interpretation of Lord Fraser's speech and stated that it was manifestly clear that the law lord in using the phrase 'falsely described' had imposed the requirement of misrepresentation as an essential element of the tort. In other words, the Court of Appeal refused to recognise any action for the misappropriation of a trade mark without proof of misrepresentation. In so doing, the Schechter's dilution theory was cast out from the law of passing off.

With regard to the second issue on whether the defendant's use of the word 'McCurry' was an act of passing off, the court held that there was no passing off for four reasons. First, the defendant's signage and presentation of business were distinctively different from that of the plaintiff. Second, all of the plaintiff's food items had the prefix 'Mc' but not the

[24] [2008] 9 CLJ 254, 272 [64]. [25] *Ibid.* 272 [65]. [26] [1979] AC 731.

defendant's items. Third, the type of food available at both parties' outlets was very different. Fourth, the category of customers who patronised the plaintiff's outlets was also different from those of the defendant. The plaintiff's further appeal to the Federal Court was dismissed.[27]

(ii) The registration regime: Trade Marks Act 1976 (Malaysia)
Apart from the outdated and limited manner of protecting well-known trade marks via the defensive registration provision of the Trade Marks Act 1976 (Malaysia) (TMA (Malaysia)),[28] the Act contains three specific provisions which deal with well-known trade mark protection. Sections 14(1)(d), 14(1)(e) and 70B(1) were incorporated into the Act in the year 2000 in response to Malaysia's international obligations under the Agreement on Trade-Related Aspects of Intellectual Property Rights (TRIPS).[29] In determining whether a trade mark is well known, s. 14(2) imports the guidelines provided in art. 16 of TRIPS. As a consequence, to qualify for well-known trade mark protection, it is not necessary that the mark must be well known to the general public. It is sufficient if the mark is well known to a relevant sector of the public.

The overall legal matrix of well-known trade mark protection in Malaysia is as follows. For applications to register a mark which is identical or similar to a well-known trade mark for the same goods or services of the well-known trade mark owner, the Registrar must refuse registration under s. 14(1)(d) of the TMA (Malaysia). This section applies to both registered and unregistered well-known trade marks. There is no requirement for the well-known trade mark owner to prove confusion because a likelihood of confusion is presumed to exist under such circumstances. In the case of the use in Malaysia of a mark which is identical or similar to a well-known trade mark in relation to the same goods or services, an injunction will be granted under s. 70B in favour of the well-known trade mark owner if they can show that the use was likely to deceive or cause confusion. Under both ss. 14(1)(d) and 70B, there is no requirement for the well-known trade mark owner to carry on business in Malaysia using that trade mark.

For applications to register a mark which is identical or similar to a well-known trade mark registered in Malaysia in relation to different goods or services, s. 14(1)(e) requires the Registrar to refuse registration

[27] An application for leave to appeal to the Federal Court was dismissed as the Court stated that the questions framed by the appellants did not arise from the judgment of the Court of Appeal.
[28] The defensive registration provision is laid down in s. 57 of the TMA (Malaysia).
[29] Agreement on Trade-Related Aspects of Intellectual Property Rights, opened for signature 15 April 1994, 1869 UNTS 299 (entered into force 1 January 1996).

if the applicant's use of the mark would indicate a connection with the well-known trade mark owner and his interests are likely to be damaged by such use. Thus, where the conflicting trade mark is in relation to different goods or services, the protection given to the well-known trade mark is narrower than that offered in s. 14(1)(a). This is understandable because, fundamentally, the exclusive right of a registered proprietor is the right to the use of the trade mark in relation to the goods or services in which he trades. There is a further requirement that the well-known trade mark must be registered before s. 14(1)(e) can apply, which means that the well-known trade mark must be used in Malaysia.

The TMA (Malaysia) does not contain any provision that prohibits a trader from unfairly using a trade mark which is identical or similar to a well-known trade mark in circumstances where the unfair use would cause dilution to the reputation of the well-known trade mark. In the recent case of *Aspect Synergy Sdn Bhd* v. *Banyan Tree Holdings Ltd*,[30] the High Court confirmed that protection against dilution is not embodied in the Act. That case concerned the use by a Malaysian housing developer (the applicant) of the name 'Taman Sri Banyan' for its high-end residential development project. The use of the word 'Banyan' was challenged by a Singapore company (the respondent) who was the registered proprietor in Malaysia of the 'Banyan Tree' trade mark and whose business concerned the management and development of resorts, hotels and spa. The applicant sought a declaration of non-infringement of trade mark while the respondent counterclaimed for passing off and trade mark infringement. The respondent claimed that its trade mark was well-known and that there was a likelihood of it being diluted. In support of this, the respondent relied on the Singapore High Court decision of *Amanresorts Limited & Anor* v. *Novelty Pte Ltd*[31] which was factually similar to the respondent's case, where the court recognised that dilution of the well-known 'Amanusa' name was likely to cause damage to the plaintiff. However, the Malaysian High Court rejected this submission on the ground that the Singapore Trade Marks Act 1998 (Singapore Cap 332, 2005 Rev Ed) (TMA (Singapore)) had a dilution provision but there was no corresponding dilution provision in the TMA (Malaysia).

[30] [2009] 8 CLJ 97.

[31] [2008] 2 SLR 32. Although the Singapore High Court decision of *Amanresorts* was subsequently appealed to the Court of Appeal, only the High Court decision was available at the time when *Aspect Synergy* was argued before the Malaysian High Court. The Singapore High Court decision was affirmed by the Court of Appeal in *Novelty Pte Ltd* v. *Amanresorts Ltd and Anor* [2009] 3 SLR(R) 216. See below n. 38 for a discussion of this case.

(b) Singapore

The dilution law was introduced into Singapore in 2004. In that year, the TMA (Singapore) was amended to include the following categories of prohibited acts:

	The nature of the prohibited act	Level of renown of the plaintiff's mark
Category A[32]	Defendant's use indicates a connection between the defendant's goods/services and the plaintiff, and causes damage to the plaintiff's interests	Well known in any relevant sector in Singapore
Category B[33]	Defendant's use causes dilution in an unfair manner of the distinctive character of the plaintiff's trade mark	Well known to the public at large in Singapore
Category C[34]	Defendant's use takes unfair advantage of the distinctive character of the plaintiff's trade mark	Well known to the public at large in Singapore

The rights in these three categories were available to trade marks, whether they are registered or not, provided that they satisfy the requisite level of renown stipulated for each category. In the case of the right in Category A, the level of renown need only be reputation within a relevant sector of the public in Singapore. In other words, proof of 'niche fame' is sufficient for the purposes of invoking the right in Category A. For Categories B and C, the level of renown is higher, namely, there must be reputation among the public at large in Singapore. This difference between the levels of renown required for Category A and Categories B/C is significant, and we shall return to this point in a little while.

From the start, it was clear as daylight that the dilution theory is found in the rights in Category B and Category C. In the case of 'dilution' used in Category B, this term is defined in the statute to mean the following:[35]

[T]he lessening of the capacity of the trade mark to identify and distinguish goods or services, regardless of whether there is –

(a) any competition between the proprietor of the trade mark and any other party; or
(b) any likelihood of confusion on the part of the public.

[32] TMA (Singapore) s. 8(4)(b)(i) and s. 55(3)(a).
[33] TMA (Singapore) s. 8(4)(b)(ii)(A) and s. 55(3)(b)(i).
[34] TMA (Singapore) s. 8(4)(b)(ii)(B) and s. 55(3)(b)(ii).
[35] TMA (Singapore) s. 2(1) (emphasis added).

What was not so clear was whether Category A was also part of the anti-dilution law – at least, it was not clear until the decision in *Novelty Pte Ltd* v. *Amanresorts Limited.*[36] In this case, the complainant was the operator of a chain of luxury resorts under the *Aman* name. Examples of these resorts are the *Amanpuri* resort in Phuket, Thailand and the *Amanusa* resort in Bali, Indonesia. So high end are these *Aman* resorts that they were described by the Court of Appeal as 'the playgrounds of the rich and famous – albeit with quiet understatement and elegant restraint'.[37] The complainant marketed the *Aman* resorts only among the elite in Singapore such as those who were holders of American Express's 'Platinum' card. As a result, the complainant enjoyed reputation and goodwill within the elite group in Singapore. The defendant was a property developer which started to market a not-so-luxurious condominium project located in a not-so-prestigious suburb in Singapore under the name *Amanusa*. The plaintiff sued, *inter alia*,[38] for infringement under the TMA (Singapore).

The complainant relied on its right in Category A. (Its case was not for infringement of its right in Category B or C because it was quite clear that the renown of its *Amanusa* name was limited to those within the elite group in Singapore. In other words, it only had 'niche fame' which was not sufficient for the purposes of Categories B and C.) The complainant argued that there was no need to prove likelihood of confusion for there to be infringement of its right in Category A, and that the defendant had tarnished the renown of the *Amanusa* mark by using it on a not-so-prestigious condominium and this tarnishment was a type of dilution that was caught by Category A. In essence, the complainant's case was that the dilution theory was found in Category A. This argument was rejected by the Court of Appeal. In coming to this conclusion, the appellate court noted the differing levels of renown required for Category A and for Categories B/C. There must be a reason for this differentiation. In

[36] [2009] 3 SLR(R) 216 ('*Novelty*'). [37] *Ibid.* 224 [6].

[38] The other cause of action was for passing off. This claim succeeded. On the first element of goodwill, the court was satisfied that, as a result of the plaintiff's selective marketing campaign aimed at the wealthy and the well-heeled in Singapore, there was sufficient exposure of the *Aman* name within this target group. On the second element of misrepresentation, the court found that it was likely that the well-heeled in Singapore would think that complainant was associated with the defendant's not-so-luxurious condominium. This 'initial confusion', the court explained, would not be dispelled because this elite group, who were not likely to be purchasers of units in this condominium, would not conduct any further investigations. On the third element of damage, the court found that the complainant's goodwill was likely to suffer damage as a result of, *inter alia*, the perception that it was the source of a residential project that was not quite of the same quality or class of its *Aman* resorts.

looking for this reason, the appellate court was conscious of the risk that the very strong trade mark protection created by the dilution theory could be 'disincentives to competition and distort the proper functioning of the free market economy'.[39] It was because of this risk, the appellate court decided, that the draftsman when introducing the three categories of rights in 2004 chose to limit the dilution protection to a special class of trade marks whose renown is very widespread, that is, those which are 'well known to the public at large in Singapore'. In short, the Court of Appeal held that the dilution theory in Singapore is limited to the rights in Categories B and C.

The Court of Appeal in *Novelty* also provided some guidelines about the scope of the dilution theory in Categories B and C. The first guideline relates to the class of trade marks entitled to dilution protection. This class was described by the appellate court as 'a rare and privileged few'.[40] The second guideline relates to the scope of the term 'dilute' in Category B. This term refers to a situation where the unauthorised use of the trade mark results in a harm to the reputation of the trade mark, and this harm may occur by 'blurring' or by 'tarnishing'.[41] The third guideline relates to the scope of the phrase 'takes unfair advantage' in Category C. This phrase refers to a situation where the unauthorised use of the trade mark results in a benefit to the defendant by 'free riding on the coat-tails' of the reputation of the trade mark.[42]

At the date of writing, there is no judicial decision in which the plaintiff successfully has established a case in Category B or in Category C in the absence of a likelihood of confusion.[43]

39 *Novelty*, 271 [144].

40 *Ibid.* 302–3 [229]. At 305 [233], these trade marks were also described as 'a rare and exclusive class'.

41 *Ibid.* 301 [225]. In coming to this conclusion, the Court of Appeal made reference to the WIPO Joint Recommendations for the Protection of Well Known Marks (1999) and the US law including the Supreme Court's decision in *Mosley* v. *V Secret Catalogue, Inc.* 537 US 418 (2003).

42 *Novelty*, 289 [193]. In coming to this conclusion, the Court of Appeal made reference to the WIPO Joint Recommendations for the Protection of Well Known Marks (1999) and the EU law including the Opinion of Advocate General in *Adidas-Salomon* v. *Fitnessworld Trading Ltd* (C-408/01) [2003] ECR I-12537. Since the Court of Appeal's decision, the ECJ in *L'Oréal SA* v. *Bellure NV* [2010] RPC 1 has endorsed the 'riding on the coat-tails' principle.

43 There is one case where the court found for the plaintiff in Category C, that is, the defendant had taken unfair advantage of the distinctive character of the plaintiff's trade mark. But this was a case where the court found that there was a likelihood of confusion arising from the defendant's unauthorised use of a mark that was similar to the plaintiff's trade mark. See *Clinique Laboratories LLC* v. *Clinique Suisse Pte Ltd* [2010] SGHC 189 (2 July 2010).

III. Protecting reputation in copyright law: the moral rights debate

(a) Singapore

Although Singapore is a member of the Berne Union, there is no provision in its current copyright law, namely the Copyright Act 1987 (Singapore, Cap 63, 2006 Rev Ed) (Copyright Act (Singapore)), which is the equivalent of art. 6*bis* of the Berne Convention. There are merely four provisions which have some implications on the protection of moral rights.

The first provision deals specifically with the statutory licensing scheme for making records of a musical work and making records of an adaptation of a musical work.[44] It is made clear that this statutory licensing scheme is not applicable in relation to a record of an adaptation of a musical work when the adaptation 'debases' the work.[45] The concept of 'debasement' allows the author of the musical work some protection that is akin to an infringement of his moral right of integrity. The limits of this protection are obvious. In particular, it cannot be invoked outside of the special statutory licensing scheme.

The other three provisions relate to a duty not to falsely attribute the authorship of a work.[46] These provisions protect the author's moral right of attribution – but to a very limited extent. They do not give the author a positive right to claim authorship.

(b) Malaysia

The main focus of copyright law in most common law jurisdictions is on economic rights which are exercisable at the option of the copyright owner. There is lesser emphasis on moral rights which are granted to recognize and respect the work and the author's relationship to the work on the basis that the created work is seen as an extension of the author's personhood. Malaysia, however, has accorded statutory recognition of moral rights, or more specifically, the rights of attribution and integrity, since the enactment of its first unified national copyright system under

[44] This statutory licensing scheme is permitted by art. 13 of the Berne Convention.
[45] Copyright Act (Singapore) s. 56(2).
[46] Copyright Act (Singapore) s. 188 (duty not to attribute falsely authorship of a work or identity of performer of a performance); s. 189 (duty not to represent altered work or recording of performance as unaltered); s. 190 (duty not to falsely attribute authorship of reproduction of an artistic work).

the former Copyright Act 1969 (Malaysia) and now under its Copyright Act 1987 (Malaysia) (Copyright Act (Malaysia)). In other words, Malaysia's protection for moral rights was not a matter of complying with international obligations. This part examines the scope of these moral rights provisions, and also the extent to which these provisions could be deployed to afford protection for the reputation of a mark against dilution.

The former Copyright Act 1969 (Malaysia) granted the author of a literary, musical or artistic work, or a cinematograph film, the right, during his lifetime, to claim authorship as well as to object to any distortion, mutilation or other alterations which would be prejudicial to his honour or reputation. These rights were similar to those found under art. 6*bis* of the Berne Convention.

Under the current Copyright Act (Malaysia), the rights of attribution and integrity under s. 25 of the Act are couched in a negative manner prohibiting any person from doing or authorising the doing of any of the following acts:

(i) The presentation of a work, by any means whatsoever, without identifying the author or under a name other than that of the author;[47] and
(ii) The distortion, mutilation or other modification of the work[48] if the distortion, mutilation or modification significantly alters the work and is such that it might reasonably be regarded as adversely affecting the author's honour or reputation.[49]

The above statutory rights, as is normally the case, are exercisable at the option of the author of the work,[50] for so long as copyright in the work subsists, and are applicable to copyright works as defined under the Act,[51] that is, literary, musical and artistic works, films, sound recordings and broadcasts. Accordingly, the author falling within the ambit of s. 25 may not necessarily be a natural person; it could be a corporate author[52] as in

47 Originally, there was no provision for the identification of the author, only the right to prohibit the attribution of authorship to a third party. The former was inserted by the Copyright (Amendment) Act 1997 (Malaysia).
48 Prior to the Copyright (Amendment) Act 1997 (Malaysia), the prohibition was against the presentation of a work in a 'modified form' with no clarification as to its meaning or scope.
49 Copyright Act (Malaysia) s. 25(2)(a) and (b).
50 Copyright Act (Malaysia) s. 25(4).
51 Copyright Act (Malaysia) s. 7(1). The former provisions under the former Copyright Act 1969 (Malaysia) applied only to literary, musical and artistic works and cinematograph films.
52 Section 3 of the Copyright Act (Malaysia) defines 'author' in relation to each category of protected works, including films, sound recordings and broadcasts. While the author of a literary, artistic or musical work, by reason of the provisions of the Act, would seem to refer to a natural person, that of a film, a sound recording or a broadcast may refer

the case of sound recordings and broadcasts, although conceptually, the inclusion of corporate authorship may not be in alignment with the basis for which moral rights are granted, that is, to protect the personhood of the author.

There are no exceptions with regard to commissioned works or works created in the course of employment.[53] In such cases, s. 26(2) expressly provides that copyright is transferred or vested in the commissioner or employer, as the case may be. Notwithstanding such transfer or vesting, and in the absence of express provisions to the contrary, the commissioned or employee author retains the right to exercise his moral rights under s. 25.[54] As there are no provisions which allow for a waiver[55] or assignment of moral rights, the position of a commissioned or employee author would appear to be quite strong, although, from a practical standpoint, it may be unlikely for such author to assert his statutory rights.

To the extent that some marks, such as pictorial marks, three-dimensional shapes, slogans and melodies, may also qualify as artistic, literary or musical works under copyright, several observations can be made with regard to the above statutory rights and their possible application or otherwise to such trade marks.

First, the author has the right to be named or identified when a work is presented by any means whatsoever. 'Presentation by any means whatsoever' is not defined but it is sufficiently broad to encompass activities such as publication, performance, exhibition, broadcasting and transmission of the work. In addition to the right of attribution, there is also the right to prevent the work from being attributed to someone else. However,

to either a natural or a corporate person. In *Rock Records (M) Sdn Bhd* v. *Audio One Entertainment Sdn Bhd* [2005] 3 MLJ 552, the court held that the author of a sound recording was the recording company which made the arrangements for the recording (see 561, 569).

53 No exception is also made with respect to works created under the direction or control of the government, which are vested initially in the government and not the author: s. 26(3) of the Copyright Act (Malaysia).

54 As was evident in the first case brought under s. 25 by the Malaysian artist Syed Ahmad Jamal against the Mayor of the Kuala Lumpur City Council for alterations done to a public sculpture which he had been commissioned to create by a bank in 1985 and which was subsequently bequeathed to the city of Kuala Lumpur. For the infringement of his moral rights, the artist was awarded a sum of RM750,000: see *Syed Ahmad bin Jamal* v. *Dato Bandar Kuala Lumpur* [2011] 2 CLJ 569 ('*Syed Ahmad Jamal*'); also Yuen Meikeng, 'KL mayor to pay RM750,000 for "vandalism"', *The Star* (online), 22 May 2010 http://thestar.com.my/news/story.asp?file=/2010/5/22/nation/6319984&sec=nation.

55 While s. 25(3) of the Copyright Act (Malaysia) recognises that there may be circumstances where in order to publish, reproduce, perform in public or communicate to the public a work, an assignee or licensee may have to modify the work, and is permitted to do so, yet it is expressly stated that nothing in the subsection shall be taken to authorise a modification that contravenes any of the moral rights granted.

there is no right to prevent a work from being falsely attributed to the author, which may have, in some circumstances, an impact on his honour or reputation. In such cases, the author's recourse may be in defamation or passing off.[56]

Second, and of more relevance to the issue of reputation is the right of integrity, which can be invoked but only upon the fulfilment of the following three requirements, that is, there must be a distortion, mutilation or other modification of the work, which must have altered the work significantly, resulting in an adverse effect on the author's honour and reputation.

The words 'distortion, mutilation or other modifications' are not defined although when coupled with the requirement that such acts must significantly alter the work, they would seem to suggest that there must be physical changes, alterations or other modifications to the work,[57] such as where a similar, instead of an identical, trade mark is used. However, if interpreted more liberally, the subsection may not be restricted to acts resulting in physical changes or alterations. A distortion may occur without there being any physical changes made to the work. Yet, at the same time, it may result in a significant alteration to the meaning or essence of the work. For instance, an artistic work may be placed or used in an inappropriate manner; a literary or musical work may be misrepresented or presented or interpreted in a manner contrary to the original intentions of the author or which does not accord with the beliefs of the author or in a manner not intended by the author.[58] In such instances, the work may be significantly altered so as to adversely affect the reputation of the author even in the absence of any alterations or changes to the work. In the context of this chapter with its focus on reputation and dilution of this reputation, such a situation may also occur where a trade mark is altered, parodied or cast in an unflattering light or associated with an inferior or unseemly product.[59]

[56] The Copyright Act (Malaysia) recognises that there may be some other right of action or remedy available to the author in cases where his honour or reputation may have been violated, and provides in clear terms that nothing in the subsection shall be construed as requiring any damages recovered for breach of statutory moral rights to be disregarded in assessing damages in any proceedings other than by virtue of this section.

[57] In *Syed Ahmad Jamal* [2011] 2 CLJ 569, the Kuala Lumpur City Council replaced the sculpture's ceramic glass slabs with stainless steel plates, fixed steel tubing along the perimeters of the sculpture and substituted the blue tiles with black ones, committing what one of the plaintiff's witnesses termed as 'institutional vandalism' (see 577 B).

[58] On the interpretation of the UK position in this regard, see Hugh Laddie, Peter Prescott and Mary Vitoria, *The Modern Law of Copyright and Designs* (2nd edn, Butterworths, London, 1995), vol. 1, 1015 [27.17].

[59] In particular, see the concept of dilution by tarnishment which occurs when prospective consumers conjure up negative or unsavoury associations with regard to the goods or

The final requirement is that regardless of its extent or significant impact, a distortion, mutilation or other modification will not be caught by s. 25 if it may not be reasonably regarded as adversely affecting the honour or reputation of the author.[60] In assessing whether injury has been done to the honour or reputation of the author, the test is not necessarily an objective one as was evident in the case of *Syed Ahmad Jamal*.[61] The artist had claimed, *inter alia*, that the changes to his sculpture had altered 'the character and spirit' of his work, elements which the court appeared to have taken into account in deciding in favour of the artist.

Applying the moral rights provision to a dilution situation may not necessarily have the desired effect. What is sought to be protected in a dilution situation is the reputation of the trade mark itself and not the reputation or honour of the author or the creator of the trade mark, which may also be a copyright work. Resorting to moral rights in this situation requires a conflation of the reputation and honour of the creator of the mark and that of the mark itself, not to mention the interests sought to be protected, which may not necessarily coincide. While there may be cases where the reputation or honour of the creator of a trade mark may be adversely affected by the changes to the trade mark, this may not necessarily tarnish or dilute the trade mark, and vice versa. Even assuming there are convergent interests, the author may not necessarily be the trade mark or copyright owner, and as moral rights are not assignable, the trade mark owner's recourse to these statutory rights to protect the dilution of his mark may be limited.

Outside the moral rights provisions, a trade mark owner may be able to sue for copyright infringement as when the mark is copied whether in its original or derivative form. However, where the copying involves a parody of the mark so as to affect the reputation of the mark, the remedy offered by copyright is limited as, under s. 13(2)(b), parody is a defence to copyright infringement.

IV. The perspectives of Islam and Confucianism on dilution and moral rights

This part explores the impact of teachings in Islam and of Confucianism on the dilution and moral rights debates.

services of the well-known trade mark owner as a result of another person's use of that trade mark.

[60] Changes that enhance the reputation or honour of the author would appear to be outside the scope of s. 25 of the Copyright Act (Malaysia).

[61] [2011] 2 CLJ 569.

One Islamic law scholar has noted that, while confusion-based trade mark law is consistent with Islamic law (Shari'a),[62] the dilution theory may face certain hurdles.[63] There are two doctrines which arguably conflict with the dilution theory. First, there is the doctrine of *Mysar* which prohibits gaining profit without labour. When this is applied to the special protection that the dilution theory advocates for famous marks, the argument is that this special protection results in the famous marks continuing to enjoy fruits that exceed the actual time, effort and expense invested in promoting the trade mark proprietors' goods or services.[64] Second, there is the doctrine of *Maslaha* which calls for distributive justice 'for the good of all'. The argument is that the special protection for famous marks concentrates large profits earned from the goodwill associated with famous trade marks in the hands of a few.[65] Protection of moral rights, on the other hand, is seen to be consistent with the principles of Shari'a.[66] In fact, one scholar has submitted that the moral rights of attribution and of integrity are key to ensuring the purity of the protected knowledge of Islam.[67] Thus, this scholar argues:

> the Islamic right of attribution demands that no man-made verse be attributed to God, nor any verse of the *Qu'ran* be attributed to man [and in] the case of the *Sunna*, the right of attribution preserves the authenticity of the Prophet [Muhammad]'s decisions, statement, and comments.[68]

Further, the Islamic right of integrity

> safeguards the protected knowledge from innovations, repudiation, internal disrespect, and external assaults [and it] also protects the honor of the Prophet who served as the sole medium to transmit the protected knowledge to the world.[69]

In light of these scholarly views of Islamic law, it may be surmised that the presence of moral rights protection and the absence of dilution protection in Malaysia is in harmony with Islamic teachings. While it is clear from the

[62] There are two primary sources of Shari'a, namely, the Qu'ran the Holy Scripture, and the Sunna the record of the sayings and deeds of the Prophet Muhummad.

[63] Amir H. Khoury, 'Ancient and Islamic Sources of Intellectual Property Protection in the Middle East: A Focus on Trademarks' (2003) 43 *IDEA* 151. For another scholar who shares the view that confusion-based trade mark law is consistent with the Shari'a: Heba A Raslan, '*Shari'a* and the Protection of Intellectual Property – The Example of Egypt' (2007) 47 IDEA 497.

[64] Khoury, 'Ancient and Islamic Sources', 184–8. [65] *Ibid.* 188–9.

[66] Raslan, '*Shari'a*', 544; Steven D. Jamar, 'The Protection of Intellectual Property under Islamic Law' (1992) 21 *Capital University Law Review* 1079, 1097; Ida Madieha Azmi, 'Authorship and Islam in Malaysia: Issues in Perspective' (1997) 28(5) *International Review of Intellectual Property* 671, 677.

[67] Ali Khan, 'Islam as Intellectual Property: "My Lord! Increase Me in Knowledge"' (2000–1) 31 *Cumberland Law Review* 631.

[68] *Ibid.* 655. [69] *Ibid.* 657–8.

Parliamentary debates during the passing of the TMA (Malaysia) and the Copyright Act (Malaysia) as well as their subsequent amendments that Islamic teachings and philosophy do not provide any underlying impetus or inspiration for the enactment of any provisions of these statutes, the situation which currently prevails in Malaysia appears to sit happily with the country's stature as an Islamic state.

In the case of Singapore, we turn to Confucius. Among his teachings, there is one proclamation which has implications in the area of IP. The philosopher is known to have proclaimed that 'I transmit rather than create'.[70] One way in which this philosophy manifested itself (and continues to do so) in Chinese culture was the desire of artists and calligraphers for faithful replication or imitation of the master's works. Outside of Chinese painting and calligraphy, Confucius' proclamation was intended to convey his thought that his writings were not to be original to him; they were merely a transmission of the teachings in the ancients.[71] To put it in another way, Confucius rejected the concepts of originality and authorship. And if I am not the creator of the work, I alone cannot be attributed as its author or be the sole guardian of its integrity and honour. From this perspective, the lack of protection for moral rights in Singapore accords with this teaching of Confucius.

[70] Daniel Burkitt, 'Copyrighting Culture – The History and Cultural Specificity of the Western Model of Copyright' (2001) 5(2) *Intellectual Property Quarterly* 146, 177.

[71] Peter Feng, *Intellectual Property in China* (2nd edn, Sweet & Maxwell, Hong Kong, 2003), 62.

7 Reproduction rights in US trade mark law

Graeme W. Austin

I. Introduction

Among the many benefits of the study of the humanities described by *New York Times* columnist David Brooks in a 2010 editorial is an ability to understand 'the language of emotion'.[1] That understanding, Brooks explained, will equip humanities graduates to do many useful things, one of which is to create attractive brands:

> In an information economy, many people have the ability to produce a technical innovation . . . Very few people have the ability to create a great brand . . . Branding involves the location and arousal of affection, and you can't do it unless you are conversant in the language of romance.[2]

To protect a great brand doubtless still requires some understanding of trade mark law, but, at least according to David Brooks, romance is key to creating it in the first place. Presumably, it does not take a humanities degree to locate and arouse affection, but Brooks' point seems to be that study of the body of creative work associated with the humanities – philosophy, art, poetry, novels, music – will help at least some of us learn to translate native romantic instincts into something of commercial value: the great brand to which all marketers aspire.

Brands are aggregations of many types of creative expression. To be sure, underlying all branding strategies is a trade mark, to which trade mark law necessarily applies, but the other ingredients of a great brand might include arresting designs, fictional characters, narratives, images, songs, dramas, and the like. To choose among them in order to build a brand, and, most importantly, to choose *well*, requires the kind of knowledge and creativity that study of the humanities can engender.

Hopefully no intellectual property rights are *necessary* to encourage romance; doubtless many other drivers exist. But there is nevertheless

[1] David Brooks, 'History for dollars', *New York Times* (New York), 8 June 2010, A27.
[2] *Ibid.*

much common ground between the kinds of things that copyright typically protects and the phenomena that brands have become. Indeed, if we were going to choose one type of intellectual property that is most clearly associated with this kind of creativity, copyright would probably be it. Like many copyright-protected works, brands tell stories; they tell us that we're worth it; they tell us that we're cool; they amuse us; they arouse our jealousies; assuage our anxieties. This is what it takes, marketers think, to *move* us – hopefully, to buy, to be loyal, perhaps even to fall in love.

Focusing on US trade mark law,[3] this chapter argues that in many contexts the right to reproduce, the core prerogative of copyright owners, is as important as trade marks' conventional role of 'marking' a 'trade' with an exclusive sign, and, by so doing, signalling a specific source of goods or services. Aiming only to describe the *extent* to which the right to reproduce a mark has become relevant to the bundle of rights comprising a trade mark, this chapter sidesteps the difficult normative issues that have been distilled by concerns about trade mark law's expansion. Even so, analysis of the extent to which a trade mark right protects against unlicensed reproduction of trade marks is relevant to these debates, which typically concern the extent to which trade marks are becoming valuable, and enforced, as things in their own right – in addition to the conventional rationale of protecting trade marks as (mere) designators of source. The exclusive right to copy is the core right attaching to a copyright for the very reason that the 'value' copyright protects is the value of the work *as embodied in a copy*. By prohibiting copying, copyright vindicates the economic value of the copy itself. The legal rights protecting against copying do not require the copy to signal anything else; in copyright, the reproduction is protected for its own sake. Whether a trade mark should be protected on the basis that it is an economic and cultural artefact that has value apart from, or in addition to, its conventional role of signalling the source of goods or services distils the central normative controversy in modern trade mark commentary: whether, through the vehicle of *trade mark* rights, that kind of value ought to be protected.

Much contemporary legal scholarship laments the expansion of trade mark rights beyond their role of designating the source of goods and

3 This development is not unique to the United States. See for example Annette Kur, 'Fundamental Concerns in the Harmonization of (European) Trademark Law', in Graeme Dinwoodie and Mark Janis (eds.), *Trademark Law and Theory: A Handbook of Contemporary Research* (Edward Elgar, Cheltenham; Northampton, MA; 2008), 151 (noting that French trade mark law traditionally took for granted that rights vested in a trade mark were essentially no different from other intellectual property rights, such as copyrights and patents).

services into areas traditionally understood as governed by copyright.[4] Some commentators argue that intellectual property law need not offer firms any enhanced protections to encourage them to build and develop brands in this way – to use them as vehicles for telling compelling stories or creating arresting and attractive images. Professor Rochelle Dreyfuss has urged, for instance, that firms already have a forceful incentive to do so: selling stuff.[5] Trade mark law need offer no further encouragements. The commentary is not, however, all one way. In an important article, one of the editors of this volume, Professor Megan Richardson has argued that the 'utilitarian justification for copyright protection, lying in providing incentives for artistic and cultural development for the broader social benefit, can be extended to th[e] new cultural items' that trade marks have become.[6] While these debates are enlightening, it may also be a useful endeavour to attempt to tease out the doctrinal developments that are relevant to the changes with which the more normatively focused commentary is concerned. An appreciation of modern trade mark law's concern with protecting trade mark owners against reproduction of trade marks might provide a modest contribution to this broader set of concerns.

II. Trade marks and copyrights

To many, the suggestion that trade mark rights protect a right of reproduction will seem heterodox, to say the least. After all, trade mark law is not meant to be concerned just with copying. Trade mark infringement

[4] Graeme B. Dinwoodie, 'The Rational Limits of Trademark Law', in Hugh Hansen (ed.), *US Intellectual Property Law and Policy* (Edward Elgar Cheltenham, 2002); Jessica Litman, 'Breakfast with Batman: The Public Interest in the Advertising Age' (1998–9) 108(7) *Yale Law Journal* 1717; Mark A. Lemley, 'The Modern Lanham Act and the Death of Common Sense' (1998–9) 108(7) *Yale Law Journal* 1687; Rudolf Rayle, 'The Trend Toward Enhancing Trademark Owners' Rights: A Comparative Study of US and German Trademark Law' (2000) 7 *Journal of Intellectual Property Law* 227.

The classic statement – more descriptive and analytical than lamenting – on the expansion of trade marks beyond the traditional function of avoiding consumer confusion is by Frank Schechter: 'Any theory of trade-mark protection which . . . does not focus the protective function of the court upon the good-will of the owner of the trade-mark, inevitably renders such owner dependent for protection, not so much upon the normal agencies for the creation of goodwill, such as the excellence of his product and the appeal of his advertising, as upon the judicial estimate of the state of the public mind. This psychological element is in any event at best an uncertain factor' (*The Historical Foundations of the Law Relating to Trade-Marks* (Columbia University Press, New York, 1925), 166 (citations omitted)).

[5] Rochelle Cooper Dreyfuss, 'Expressive Genericity: Trademarks as Language in the Pepsi Generation' (1990) 65 *Notre Dame Law Review* 397.

[6] Megan Richardson, 'Trade Marks and Language' (2004) 26 *Sydney Law Review* 193, 211–13.

typically involves reproduction or colourable imitation of a mark,[7] but, according to traditional conceptions of trade mark rights, reproduction is not generally sufficient to establish liability. Rather, trade mark liability requires that the defendant's use of a mark cause, or be likely to cause, legally relevant consumer confusion. Copying, or making colourable imitations of the trade mark owner's mark, may be a means to that end – but, conventionally, trade marks are not protected for their own sake. They are protected only to maintain the accuracy of information that circulates in consumer markets about the sources of goods and services. Trade marks 'mark' a 'trade' in this sense, because they signal the trade source from which goods and services derive. That is a trade mark's job. Trade marks are protected because they do this job, and, ideally, only to the extent that they do.[8]

But how firm is the distinction between trade marks and copyrights? The Supreme Court seemed quite emphatic about it in the famous 1879 *Trade-Mark Cases*, reasoning that a federal trade mark statute was not empowered by the Intellectual Property Clause in the United States Constitution[9] on the ground that trade marks exhibited none of the creativity required by copyright law[10] – nor, the Court also observed, did they share anything in common with the kind of inventive work required by patent law. It should not be too quickly assumed, however, that *The Trade-Mark Cases* provides a firm grounding for the separation of trade marks and copyrights. The Court's analysis concerned the problem of identifying the appropriate constitutional power on which the statute could be based. The statute flunked under the Intellectual Property Clause because no creativity of any kind was required by the challenged statute, not because trade marks categorically are bereft of *any* creativity. After observing that trade marks are 'simply founded on priority of appropriation', the Court identified the fatal flaw: 'We look in vain in the statute for any other qualification or condition'.[11] To the extent that Justice Miller's reasoning provided a more general exegesis

[7] In rare instances, conceptual, rather than physical similarity between the salient parts of the marks might be sufficient. See for example *American Home Products Corp* v. *Johnson Chemical Co.*, 589 F 2d 103, 107 (2nd Cir, 1978) ('Roach Motel' conceptually similar to 'Roach Inn' for insect traps).

[8] See for example *Peaceable Planet Inc.* v. *Ty Inc.* 362 F 3d 986 (7th Cir, 2004) (reasoning that trade mark rights should be tethered to the reasons for protecting trade marks).

[9] Article 1 § 8 cl. 8: Congress shall have power 'to promote the progress of science and useful arts by securing for limited times to authors and inventors the exclusive right to their respective writings and discoveries'. In *The Trade-Mark Cases* 100 US 82 (1879), the Court held that the statute could not be empowered by the Commerce Clause (art. 1 § 8 cl. 3), on the ground that the statute did not distinguish between intra- and inter-State uses of trade marks (92–3).

[10] *The Trade-Mark Cases*, 100 US 82, 94 (1879).

[11] *Ibid.*

on the creativity involved in developing a trade mark or on distinctions between this kind of creativity and that involved in other forms of intellectual property, it was dictum. The Court had nothing dispositive to say about marks that *do* manifest (sufficient) creativity.

Moreover, 'copyright' was not itself then a stable legal entity or construct against which the characteristics of trade marks could be set off. Copyright has itself undergone a slow evolution from protecting a narrow set of tangible products – 'maps', 'charts' and 'books', according to the first US federal copyright statute;[12] it now protects a very large, and largely amorphous, body of original creative expression. For modern marketers, the idea that creating a brand does *not* involve 'novelty, invention, discovery, or any work of the brain', to quote Justice Millar again,[13] would seem laughable, if not insulting. But copyright law has only gradually evolved in a manner that has equipped it to respond to and protect creativity in this more general sense – apart from the tangible things (books, etc.) with which it was originally concerned.[14] Accordingly, we should not derive too much enduring significance from various dicta that appear to assume that the two bodies of law are distinct. More generally, courts' ruminations on the distinctions and similarities between trade marks and other forms of intellectual property at this time mostly centred on technical questions about the characteristics of the cause of action for trade mark infringement – initially to establish that trade marks could be infringed without an intention to deceive, and then to resist liability theories that were tantamount to treating trade marks as rights in gross.[15] Concerns focused on characteristics of different forms of intellectual property were not ventilated in order to provide a thoroughgoing exposition of the characteristics of each species of legal rights. As César Remirez-Montes has compellingly argued,[16] nineteenth-century trade mark law did not pursue deeper theoretical commitments. The judiciary's principal impulse was to negotiate a balance between consumer and trader interests, rather than to distil any all-encompassing theory on the characteristics of the relevant rights. If courts served no ideological master, it is also highly unlikely the jurisprudence was informed

[12] Copyright Act of 1790, 1 Stat 124. [13] 100 US 82, 94 (1879).

[14] See generally Lionel Bentley and Brad Sherman, *The Making of Modern Intellectual Property* (Cambridge University Press, Cambridge, 1999).

[15] See generally Lionel Bentley, 'From Communication to Thing: Historical Aspects of the Conceptualization of Trade Marks as Property', in Dinwoodie and Janis, *Trademark Law and Theory*, 3.

[16] Cesar Ramirez-Montes, 'A Re-Examination of the Original Foundations of Anglo-American Trademark Law' (2010) 14 *Marquette Intellectual Property Law Review* 91, 116–17.

by any thoroughgoing understanding of the proper boundaries between different types of intellectual property.

Over the decades since the *Trade-Mark Cases*, courts have sometimes invoked copyright as a limit to curb the expansion of trade mark rights. Such curbs may be needed because concepts such as 'likelihood of confusion' do not provide sufficient internal controls on the scope of these rights, an issue that has been exacerbated by the increasing range of things about which the law assumes that consumers can be confused.[17] According to the US federal trade mark statute, the Lanham (Trademark) Act of 1946 (Lanham Act),[18] consumers are not only susceptible to confusion as to the origin of goods and services, but also as to affiliation, connection, association, sponsorship and approval.[19] Added to these grounds are judge-made rules imposing liability for creating a likelihood of post-sale[20] and initial interest confusion.[21] The impulse to impose limits on trade mark rights might also be a response to the Supreme Court's rejection of ontological limits on trade mark subject matter. The Court declared in 1995 that 'almost anything at all that is capable of carrying meaning'[22] can qualify as a trade mark. The Court itself later tempered this broad statement, reasoning (without any supporting empirical analysis) that consumers typically do not respond to product designs as designators of source, and that these designs therefore require secondary meaning to function as trade marks.[23] But these expansions of trade mark subject matter have left lower courts with few categorical limits on the kinds of things that can qualify as a trade mark. Inhibiting trade mark rights from trespassing into areas governed by copyright may be one way of keeping at least some types of intellectual property within manageable limits.

Even so, legal taxonomies are seldom ends in themselves. Even Justice Holmes' famous and emphatic statement in *Prestonettes Inc.* v. *Coty*, that a trade mark 'is not a copyright',[24] was made in the context of a more urgent concern to preserve the accuracy of information in consumer markets, and ensure that exorbitant assertion of trade mark rights did not inhibit traders from accurately describing the components of their products. The case concerned the defendant's accurate description of

[17] See generally, Graeme W. Austin, 'Tolerating Confusion about Confusion: Trademark Policies and Fair Use' (2008) 50 *Arizona Law Review* 157.

[18] 15 USC §§ 1051–1072, 1091–1096, 1111–1129, 1141 (2002).

[19] Lanham Act § 43(a) (references hereinafter are to the Lanham Act, not the US Code).

[20] *Adidas-Salomon AG* v. *Target Corp.*, 228 F Supp 2d 1192, 1211–12 [16] (D. Ore, 2002).

[21] *Academy of Motion Picture Arts & Sciences* v. *Creative House Promotions Inc.*, 944 F 2d 1446, 1455 (9th Cir, 1991).

[22] *Qualitex Co* v. *Jacobsen Products Co. Inc.*, 514 US 159, 162 (1995).

[23] See *Wal-Mart Stores Inc.* v. *Samara Brothers Inc.*, 529 US 205 (1999).

[24] *Prestonettes Inc.* v. *Coty*, 264 US 359, 368 (1923) ('*Prestonettes*').

its product as an admixture of different substances, including the plaintiff's trade marked cosmetics. Holding that the defendant was entitled to refer to the plaintiff's trade mark in describing the former's product, the Court's reasoning foreshadowed later cases in which courts have affirmed traders' rights to use others' trade marks in after markets, such as second-hand products[25] and repair services.[26] In more recent cases, many of these concerns have crystallised under the (judge-made) defence of 'nominative fair use'.[27]

Another example of a court invoking the distinction between copyrights and trade marks for broader policy reasons is offered by a 2001 decision in *Oliveira* v. *Frito-Lay Inc.*[28] where the Court of Appeals for the Second Circuit rejected the argument by Brazilian singer Astrid Gilberto that her trade mark rights were infringed by the use of a recording of her 1964 hit song, the 'The Girl from Ipanema', during a television advertisement. Gilberto contended that the public recognises the recording as a mark that designated her as a singer; according to Gilberto, this meant that her song could not lawfully be used in an advertisement without her permission. Much of the Court of Appeals' analysis focused on maintaining a distinction between the copyright in the underlying recording and any trade mark rights Ms Gilberto might claim in her 'signature' song. The court seemed especially concerned that assertions of trade mark rights should not unravel the *lex mercatoria* that had emerged in the context of the licensing of musical compositions. In so far as copyright is concerned, performing artists typically work under a work-for-hire platform; as a result, copyright in the sound recording vests in the record label. The Court of Appeals recognised that were it to rule otherwise, '[i]mmense unforeseen liabilities might accrue, upsetting reasonable commercial expectations',[29] no doubt diminishing the value of the underlying copyrights if their title could later be burdened by the assertion of trade mark rights. Again, this was not a case about categorical distinctions between copyright and trade mark. Instead, the court was principally concerned to avoid 'altering the commercial world's understanding of the scope of trade mark rights in this fashion'.[30]

Policy concerns, as much as intellectual property heuristics, also informed the Ninth Circuit's engagement with the respective domains of copyright and trade marks in its 2000 decision, *Comedy III Productions*

[25] *Champion Spark Plug Co.* v. *Sanders*, 331 US 125 (1946).
[26] *Volkswagenwerk Aktiengesellschaft* v. *Church*, 411 F 2d 350, 352 (9th Cir, 1969).
[27] *New Kids on the Block* v. *News America Publishing Inc.*, 971 F 2d 302, 308 (9th Cir, 1992).
[28] 251 F 3d 56 (2nd Cir, 2001) ('*Oliveira*'). [29] *Ibid.* 61. [30] *Ibid.* 63.

Inc. v. *New Line Cinema.*[31] At issue was the use of a few seconds from a classic Three Stooges film, *Disorder in the Court* by New Line Cinema in its 1996 film, *The Long Kiss Goodnight.* Because the copyright in the former film had expired, the owner of the intellectual property rights in The Three Stooges could not claim that the unlicensed use of the film clip constituted copyright infringement. Instead, it argued that the clip operated as a trade mark, grounding its claims on trade mark dilution and on the theory that the use of the film clip

> constitute[d] a false designation of origin of Defendant's goods and services or a false description or representation of Defendant's goods and services, and . . . creates a likelihood of confusion among prospective purchasers and because it induces purchasers and others to believe, contrary to fact, that Defendant's services and products are performed, manufactured, approved by or otherwise connected in some way to [The Three Stooges].[32]

Had the case been permitted to go to trial, it could have been decided on the basis that no secondary meaning was established in any of the characteristics of the Three Stooges which were manifest in the film clip – or that consumers simply didn't see the connections that the plaintiff alleged. Instead the court reasoned, as a matter of legal *principle*, that '[i]f material covered by copyright law has passed into the public domain, it cannot then be protected by the *Lanham Act* without rendering the *Copyright Act* a nullity'.[33]

That proposition led the Court of Appeals to draw a number of quite arbitrary distinctions. For example, the court acknowledged that '[h]ad [the defendants] used the likeness of The Three Stooges on t[ee]-shirts which it was selling, [the plaintiff] might have an arguable claim for trademark violation'.[34] As a factual matter, it might be true that consumers more readily assume that the use of images on T-shirts needs to be licensed, and that legally cognisable confusion will arise if they are not. But the court offered no factual basis for the distinction. Due to the procedural posture of the case, the plaintiffs were never able to establish likelihood of confusion on the facts: it might well be, for instance, that consumers' expectations as to film clip use are similar to those that exist in respect of T-shirts. According to the Ninth Circuit, use of a film clip in a movie is properly – and exclusively – the domain of copyright law. Use of a celebrity's image on a T-shirt could, however, plausibly be the concern of trade mark law. But the logic breaks down if the T-shirt

[31] 200 F 3d 593 (9th Cir, 2000).
[32] *Comedy III Productions Inc.* v. *New Line Cinema* 46 USPQ 2d 1930 (CD Cal, WL 334866, 6 January 1998) slip op 3.
[33] 200 F3d 593, 595. [34] *Ibid.*

hypothetical involved a reproduction of a pen-and-ink portrait that had also fallen into the public domain qua copyright. Its protection under trade mark law would appear to fall squarely within the court's prohibition against using the Lanham Act in a manner that would render the Copyright Act a 'nullity'. It seems more likely that the Ninth Circuit's purpose was to shut down the derivation of licensing income from films that had fallen into the public domain. The policy problem to which the court's analysis appears to be directed was the risk of extending the life of expired copyrights through the vehicle of trade mark law.[35]

Notwithstanding the *Prestonettes* Court's admonition that a trade mark is 'not a copyright', it seems that the determination of courts to keep copyrights and trade marks separate has seldom been motivated by a firm commitment to the heuristic boundaries between different kinds of intellectual property. Instead, as this brief survey suggests, distinctions between copyrights and trade marks are more often invoked in order to further some collateral policy, other than avoiding consumer confusion, such as facilitating established copyright licensing practices. Indeed, as the following section suggests, in many doctrinal contexts, there is already much in common between copyrights and trade marks.

III. The significance of reproduction in trade mark jurisprudence

In modern trade mark law, there are a number of contexts in which reproduction is a significant element in establishing liability. Even in the 'core' area of trade mark infringement – use of the mark so as to create a likelihood of consumer confusion – the defendant's deliberate copying of the mark is often the most significant factor in establishing liability. Similarly, in the trade mark dilution context, the defendant's use of an identical mark provides key circumstantial evidence that dilution is likely to occur. A defendant's deliberate copying of the mark can also help establish secondary meaning, which is often critical to the enforcement of trade mark rights that allegedly subsist in descriptive matter. In the merchandising context, the enforcement of trade mark rights sometimes comes very close to protecting rights in gross. Merchandising rights have been bolstered by recent developments in the aesthetic functionality doctrine. Finally, the relaxation of the rules on trade mark licensing and

[35] Similar concerns arguably underlie the Court's more recent decision in *Dastar Corp* v. *Twentieth Century Fox Film Corp.*, 539 US 23 (2003), which held that the Lanham Act could not be used to provide a right of authorial attribution for works that had fallen into the public domain. The Court's apparent fear was that the assertion of attribution rights might inhibit the free marketing of works that were otherwise in the public domain.

assignments suggest that in commercial transactions, the rights being bought and sold are not so much directed to marking the underlying goodwill or 'trade', but are treated like commercial entities in their own right.

(a) Likelihood of confusion

The core right attaching to a trade mark is the right to seek legal relief against uses of their marks that are likely to cause consumers to be confused as to (among other things) the source of goods and services. In US federal law, to test whether consumer confusion is likely, courts apply a number of factors. Application of these factors is a substitute for a more complex psychological inquiry – 'are consumers likely to be confused in some legally cognisable way?'. The Third Circuit's list is typical:

(1) the degree of similarity between the owner's mark and the alleged infringing mark;
(2) the strength of the owner's mark;
(3) the price of the goods and other factors indicative of the care and attention expected of consumers when making a purchase;
(4) the length of time the defendant has used the mark without evidence of actual confusion;
(5) intent of the defendant in adopting the mark;
(6) evidence of actual confusion;
(7) whether the goods, though not competing, are marketed through the same channels of trade and advertised through the same media;
(8) the extent to which the targets of the parties' sales efforts are the same;
(9) the relationship of the goods in the minds of consumers because of the similarity of function; and
(10) other facts suggesting that the consuming public might expect the prior owner to manufacture a product in the defendant's market or that he is likely to expand into that market.[36]

These factors help establish, by circumstantial evidence, whether legally cognisable confusion is likely to occur as a result of the defendant's conduct.

Professor Barton Beebe has established that federal courts' application of these factors have not typically resulted in a nuanced factual inquiry

[36] In the Third Circuit, these are known as the 'Lapp' factors, after *Interpace Corp* v. *Lapp Inc.*, 721 F 2d 460, 463 (3rd Cir, 1983). For other Circuits' lists, see for example *Polaroid Corp.* v. *Polarad Elecs Corp.*, 287 F 2d 492, 495 (2nd Cir, 1961) (the 'Polaroid factors'); *AMF Inc.* v. *Sleekcraft Boats*, 599 F 2d 341, 348–9 (9th Cir, 1979) (the 'Sleekcraft factors').

that balances all the factors.[37] Instead, courts take short cuts, weighing some factors much more heavily than others. Invoking decisional heuristics theory, Beebe argues that this narrowing of the factors is a predictable human response to complex phenomena.[38] As Beebe suggests, the application of the factors is itself simplified. Facially, at least, copying by the defendant is only one factor among many, but, as Beebe's analysis attests, the factors are not all equally weighed: the extent of similarities between the mark used by the defendant and the plaintiff's trade mark is by far the most important factor. It would be going too far, of course, to draw from Beebe's path-breaking work the conclusion that the basic cause of action for trade mark infringement is now entirely grounded in reproduction. But the research nevertheless underscores the significance of copying to the liability analysis in this core liability theory.

The significance of reproduction in the application of the factors is consistent with older US theories of trade mark infringement. The drafting of the current governing statutory provision setting forth the requirements for trade mark infringement, s. 32 of the Lanham Act, facially requires that the infringing use be both a 'reproduction, counterfeit, copy, or colourable imitation' *and* be likely to cause confusion or mistake, or deceive. In contrast, the 1906 statute contained a provision rendering the defendant liable simply for using a 'reproduction, counterfeit, copy, or colourable imitation of the registered mark on goods of the same descriptive properties'.[39] At that time, the liability theory in trade mark cases did not reach uses in the context of similar goods.[40] Over time, courts came to construe the statute so as to incorporate a broader concept of consumer confusion, particularly in cases involving related but non-competing goods.[41] That change is now reflected in s. 32.

One question distilled by Barton Beebe's research is whether this has made much of a difference, given the importance that is now accorded to the reproduction of the trade mark owner's mark. Of course, some of the likelihood of confusion factors have nothing to do with reproduction,

[37] Barton Beebe, 'An Empirical Study of the Multifactor Tests for Trademark Infringement' (2006) 94(6) *California Law Review* 1581.

[38] See generally Gerd Gigerenzer and Reinhard Selten (eds.), *Bounded Rationality: The Adaptive Toolbox* (MIT Press, Cambridge, MA, 2002).

[39] The relevant standard set forth in TRIPS is similar, but a little more exacting: 'In case of the use of an identical sign for identical goods or services, a likelihood of confusion shall be presumed' (Agreement on Trade-Related Aspects of Intellectual Property Rights (TRIPS), opened for signature 15 April 1994, 1869 UNTS 299 (entered into force 1 January 1996), art. 16(1)).

[40] *Aunt Jemima Mills Co.* v. *Rigney & Co.*, 247 F 407, 408 (2nd Cir, 1917), *certiorari denied, Rigney & Co* v. *Aunt Jemima Mills Co.*, 245 US 672 (1918).

[41] Graeme Dinwoodie and Mark Janis, *Trademarks and Unfair Competition: Law and Policy* (2nd edn, Aspen Publishers, New York, 2007), 450.

and instead focus on the wider marketing context. But Beebe's analysis does draw attention to the extent to which the defendant's reproduction of the mark sometimes *dominates* in the likelihood of confusion analysis. To that extent, the scope of rights attaching to a trade mark can, in some contexts at least, be determined by whether or not the defendant reproduced the mark. In such cases, therefore, rights of a trade mark owner can be vindicated in much the same way as rights in a copyright can be enforced.

(b) Dilution

The right to be protected against dilution of a famous mark is not equivalent to a reproduction right; even so, in the application of dilution doctrine, the reproduction of the plaintiff's trade mark can be particularly relevant to establishing liability. Trade mark dilution is most typically relevant when the defendant uses a famous mark in a commercial context that is sufficiently remote from the context in which the trade mark rights were established that it cannot necessarily be established that consumers would likely be confused. For example, a defendant's use of Rolls-Royce for marshmallows is almost certainly not actionable under likelihood of confusion theory; but the trade mark owner might still secure relief under trade mark dilution.

Dilution is of course not truly a right to prevent reproduction of a famous mark in conjunction with the marketing of goods and services: the plaintiff must, at least formalistically, also establish that the use would likely be dilutive. That said, *how* courts go about establishing a likelihood of dilution on the facts of a case does underscore the importance of reproduction in this liability context. Prior to the Trademark Dilution Revision Act of 2006,[42] the Supreme Court had held in *Moseley* v. *V Secret Catalogue Inc.*[43] that liability under federal dilution law required a showing of *actual* dilution, rather than a likelihood of dilution.[44] The 2006 Act reinstated 'likelihood of dilution' as the basis for granting legal relief. The

[42] 15 USC § 1125(c)(2)(C)(2006) ('2006 Act').

[43] 537 US 418 (2003) ('*Moseley*').

[44] *Ibid.* As I have suggested elsewhere, facially at least, the impact of the *Moseley* holding was itself diluted by Justice Kennedy's concurrence, in which it was pointed out that even if actual dilution is required, a trade mark owner would be entitled to an injunction based on the fear that the defendant's conduct would result in the harm of actual dilution, based on the familiar principle that plaintiffs in torts cases do not need to wait until the harm is consummated before seeking legal relief. In this respect, '*Moseley* might only have served to replace "fear of likelihood of the lessening of the capacity to distinguish" with "fear of actual lessening of the capacity to distinguish" as the test for dilution – hardly a momentous contribution to doctrinal clarification' (Austin, 'Tolerating Confusion', 172).

new statute describes dilution by blurring as 'association arising from the similarity between a mark or trade name and a famous mark that impairs the distinctiveness of the famous mark'.[45] The underlying factual inquiry appears to concern whether, as a result of the defendant's conduct, the mark is likely to be less distinctive for consumers who perceive it. As in other parts of trade mark law, however, courts do not ascertain the likely occurrence of this psychological state occurring (or, indeed, how widespread it might be) by somehow peering into the minds of a sufficient number of ordinarily prudent consumers to see how their attitudes might have changed as a result of the defendant's actions. Instead, to determine whether dilution is likely, a court may consider 'all relevant factors', including six statutory factors that are set forth in the 2006 Act.[46] Given the difficulties associated with ascertaining whether the requisite state of mind is likely to result from the defendant's activities, it was predictable that courts should turn to proxies to assist in their analysis. Indeed, they were encouraged to do so by the *Moseley* Court. In *Moseley*, the Court confirmed that empirical evidence would not always be needed to establish dilution, and admitted that circumstantial evidence may reliably prove dilution in some instances. According to the Court, 'the obvious case' where circumstantial evidence could be relied upon to establish dilution would be one 'where the junior and senior marks are identical'.[47] Referring to the leading judicial exegesis on the mental state required to establish dilution – in a Fourth Circuit case involving the use of 'The Greatest Snow on Earth' in conjunction with the 2002 Winter Olympics hosted by the State of Utah – the Court observed:

> We do agree . . . with that court's conclusion that, at least where the marks at issue are not identical, the mere fact that consumers mentally associate the junior user's mark with a famous mark is not sufficient to establish actionable dilution. As the facts of that case demonstrate, such mental association will not necessarily

[45] 15 USC § 1125(c)(2)(B) (2006).

[46] In determining whether a mark or trade name is likely to cause dilution by blurring, 15 USC § 1125(c)(2)(B) provides that the court may consider all relevant factors, including the following:

(i) The degree of similarity between the mark or trade name and the famous mark;
(ii) The degree of inherent or acquired distinctiveness of the famous mark;
(iii) The extent to which the owner of the famous mark is engaging in substantially exclusive use of the mark;
(iv) The degree of recognition of the famous mark;
(v) Whether the user of the mark or trade name intended to create an association with the famous mark;
(vi) Any actual association between the mark or trade name and the famous mark.

[47] *Moseley*, 434.

reduce the capacity of the famous mark to identify the goods of its owner, the statutory requirement for dilution under the [Federal Trademark Dilution Act]. For even though Utah drivers may be reminded of the circus when they see a license plate referring to the 'greatest snow on earth', it by no means follows that they will associate 'the greatest show on earth' with skiing or snow sports, or associate it less strongly or exclusively with the circus.[48]

Dilution is thus not mere 'mental association', but rather a mental state in which the capacity of the mark to distinguish has been diminished. This is a very fine distinction, underscoring, perhaps, just how stylised trade mark law can sometimes seem. Indeed, fine distinctions such as these arguably reflect a more basic definitional problem: considerable controversy remains as to what 'dilution' actually means. But the Court emphasised that drawing such distinctions need be done only 'where the marks are not identical'. It is not surprising therefore that some lower courts welcomed the suggestion that use of a trade mark that is identical to the plaintiff's mark may provide a critical piece of circumstantial evidence relevant to determining if dilution has actually occurred.[49] Some have even held that deliberate copying of the plaintiff's mark gives rise to a prima facie case of dilution.[50] Some judges apparently prefer the task of distinguishing between different marks to that of distinguishing between different mental states that consumers might experience.

To be sure, some courts have emphasised that 'mere similarity' between the marks would not necessarily suffice to establish circumstantial evidence of dilution. Moreover, 'the issue of whether the marks are identical will be context-and/or media-specific and factually intensive in nature'.[51] Even so, the emphasis on reproduction in the dilution context suggests that, for some courts at least, whether the defendant reproduced the plaintiff's mark can go a long way towards addressing the definitional problem of establishing what dilution *is* and, then, whether, on the facts of the case, it is likely to occur. The defendant's copying can thus serve as a proxy for the psychological inquiry that is otherwise required by the dilution cause of action. It is doubtless easier to determine if the defendant has copied the mark than to ascertain whether the defendant's action

48 *Ibid.* 433–4, discussing *Ringling Brothers Barnum & Bailey Combined Shows Inc.* v. *Utah Division of Travel Development*, 170 F 3d 449 (4th Cir, 1999).

49 *GMC* v. *Autovation Techs Inc.*, 317 F Supp 2d 756, 764 (ED Mich, 2004) ('GM's evidence establishes actual dilution in that Defendant has used marks that are identical to the world-famous GM Trademarks').

50 See for example *Savin Corp* v. *Savin Group*, 391 F 3d 439,452 (2nd Cir, 2004) (surveying case law on this point, and concluding that defendant's use of an identical trade mark provides per se evidence of actual dilution). The fact that defendant's use of plaintiff's mark was 'in commerce' and that the use followed plaintiff's were not at issue.

51 *Ibid.* 453.

is likely to cause consumers to have a diminished capacity to apprehend the distinctive qualities of the plaintiff's trade mark.

(c) Establishing secondary meaning

Disputes concerning the subsistence of secondary meaning in otherwise descriptive terms offer another illustration of the relevance of reproduction to establishing and enforcing trade marks. Under US law, descriptive terms cannot be enforced as trade marks until secondary meaning has been established.[52] To do so, a trade mark owner must show that consumers understand the mark not only as a term that describes goods or services or their characteristics but *also* as a designator of a particular source of goods or services. As with likelihood of confusion and dilution, the secondary meaning inquiry is an inquiry into consumers' mental state, this time in order to establish that the trade mark actually functions as a mark. The inquiry might be critical to establishing the grounds for legal relief: a defendant can avoid liability if it is established that the mark alleged to have been infringed is merely descriptive. Without secondary meaning, a descriptive term simply does not operate as a trade mark, and the plaintiff has no legal basis for its infringement claims.

The 'major inquiry' in this context is thus 'the consumer's attitude toward the mark'.[53] Once again courts typically ascertain that attitude by looking to a variety of factors to determine whether the mark has achieved secondary meaning. Relevant circumstantial evidence includes: the amount and manner of advertising, volume of sales, length and manner of any use[54] and concurrent use by other traders. All of these factors might be relevant to ascertaining the plaintiff's effectiveness in 'altering the meaning of [the term] to the consuming public'.[55] Also relevant, however, is '[p]roof that a competing seller has intentionally copied a designation previously used by another'.[56]

The importance of the latter factor – the defendant's copying of the mark – was recently underscored by a complex decision by the Fourth Circuit that involved allegations of trade mark infringement under US law in respect of a mark that had been used principally in foreign commerce.[57]

52 The Lanham Act makes provision for marks to become incontestable after five years, precluding challenge on the basis that a mark is merely descriptive and has not achieved secondary meaning: *Park 'N Fly Inc.* v. *Dollar Park and Fly Inc.* 469 US 189 (1985).

53 *Zatarain's Inc.* v. *Oak Grove Smokehouse Inc.*, 698 F 2d 786, 795 (5th Cir, 1983).

54 *Ibid.* See also Restatement (Third) of Unfair Competition (1995) § 18 cmt (e).

55 698 F 2d 786, 795.

56 Restatement (Third) of Unfair Competition (1995) § 18 cmt (e).

57 *International Bancorp* v. *Societe Des Bains De Mer Et Du Cercle Des Etrangers A Monaco*, 329 F 3d 359 (4th Cir, 2003), *certiorari denied*, 540 US 1106 (2004).

The defendant had used the mark Casino de Monte Carlo in internet commerce, offering various kinds of web-based gambling services in a manner that gave the impression that there was a connection between its services and those offered by the famous casino. The difficulty for the foreign trade mark owner was that no relevant trade had been undertaken using the mark in United States commerce. The Fourth Circuit noted that a mark must be considered distinctive by US consumers before Lanham Act protection can be available. Examining the factors that are relevant to establishing secondary meaning, the Court of Appeals, like the district court,[58] accorded particular weight to the defendant's deliberate copying of the plaintiff's trade mark. Given the absence of US-based trade using the plaintiff's trade mark, this case comes close to suggesting that the defendant's copying of the mark *creates* legally enforceable rights in the plaintiff's mark.

(d) Merchandising rights and aesthetic functionality

In the merchandising goods context, once again we see some courts' conceptualising trade mark rights as including a right to reproduce the mark. *Boston Professional Hockey Association Inc.* v. *Dallas Cap & Emblem Manufacturing*[59] is perhaps the most notorious case of this kind. The Fifth Circuit found the plaintiff's trade marks in its professional hockey team emblems to be infringed by the defendant's manufacture and sale of embroidered cloth patches that depicted the trade marks. The embroidered emblems were not applied to any goods sold by the defendant; instead, purchasers of the patches were meant to apply them to their own clothing or other items. The district court had recognised the problem that protecting the embroidered emblems would be tantamount to creating a copyright monopoly for designs that were not copyrighted.[60] This did not deter the Court of Appeals, however, which granted relief under the Lanham Act on the basis that 'the defendant duplicated the protected trade marks and sold them to the public knowing that the public would identify them as being the teams' trademarks'.[61] According to the Court of Appeals' analysis, the 'certain knowledge of the buyer that the source and origin of the trade mark symbols were the plaintiff['s] satisfies the requirements of the [A]ct'.[62] Two key factors established liability under

[58] *International Bancorp* v. *Societe Des Bains De Mer Et Du Cercle Des Etrangers A Monaco*, 192 F Supp 2d 467 (ED Va, 2002) (deliberate copying of the mark establishes secondary meaning).

[59] 510 F 2d 1004 (5th Cir, 1975) ('*Dallas Cap*'), *certiorari denied*, 423 US 868 (1975).

[60] *Boston Professional Hockey Association Inc.* v. *Dallas Cap & Emblem Manufacturing Inc.*, 360 F Supp 459 (ND Tex, 1973).

[61] 510 F 2d 1004, 1012. [62] *Ibid.*

the Lanham Act: (1) the defendant's reproduction of the mark; and (2) consumers' understanding that the defendant's goods reproduced the original emblems. Of course, the same theory might also apply to a considerable amount of copyright piracy. Sale of a pirated version of the latest DVD also reproduces the original, and the unlicensed reproduction is attractive to consumers precisely because they recognise the DVD as a copy of the original.

The liability theory announced in *Dallas Cap* is not uncontroversial. One court has characterised the case as setting forth an 'extreme' liability standard, according to which 'use of a mark with the knowledge that the public will be aware of the mark's origin' will be sufficient basis for establishing liability.[63] Another has observed that *Dallas Cap* transforms trade mark rights into rights in gross; it was unable to endorse this 'extraordinary extension of the protection heretofore afforded trademark owners'.[64] The case does, however, indicate how far into the area of copyright some courts are prepared to take trade mark liability in the merchandising context – a context in which consumers often respond to trade marks as artefacts in and of themselves, as much as designators of any particular source of products or services.[65]

Broadly similar issues have arisen in the aesthetic functionality context. It is axiomatic to US trade mark law that trade mark protection is withheld from functional aspects of products.[66] The doctrine has been extended to cases of aesthetic functionality,[67] and, broadly, precludes enforcement of trade mark rights if the prohibition on use of an aesthetic aspect of a product would place other firms at a 'significant non-reputation-related disadvantage'.[68] In *Au-Tomotive Gold Inc.* v. *Volkswagen of America Inc.*[69]

63 *Board of Governors of the University of North Carolina* v. *Helpingstine*, 714 F Supp 167, 172 (MD NC, 1989).

64 *International Order of Job's Daughters* v. *Lindeburg & Co.*, 633 F 2d 912, 919 (9th Cir, 1980).

65 See also *University of Georgia Athletic Association* v. *Laite*, 756 F 2d 1535, 1546 (11th Cir, 1985) (accepting that trade mark liability need not be based on confusion as to source, and, adopting the analysis in *Dallas Cap* for the proposition that trade mark infringement can occur when the connection with the trade mark proprietor is the 'triggering mechanism' for the sale).

66 See *In Re Morton-Norwich Products Inc.*, 671 F 2d 1332 (CC PA, 1982).

67 See *Wallace International Silversmiths Inc.* v. *Godinger Silver Art Co. Inc.*, 916 F 2d 76 (2nd Cir, 1990), *certiorari denied*, 499 US 976 (1991).

68 *See TrafFix Devices Inc.* v. *Marketing Displays Inc.*, 532 US 23, 27 (2000). In contrast, application of the 'functionality' doctrine outside of the aesthetic context (i.e. assertions of trade mark rights to protect functional aspects of products) precludes the extension of trade mark rights to aspects of products which are essential to their use or purpose or where they affect their cost or quality. Outside of the aesthetic functionality context, there is no need to consider the non-reputational–disadvantage issue, but this may be relevant to determining whether the product component at issue is indeed functional.

69 457 F 3d 1062 (9th Cir, 2006) ('*Au-Tomotive Gold*').

the Ninth Circuit declined to extend the 'aesthetic functionality' doctrine so as to deny trade mark protection to the owner of famous marks used in the automotive industry where the defendant had manufactured automobile accessories, such as licence plates and key chains, to complement specific makes of cars, including Cadillac, Ford, Honda, Lexus, Jeep and Toyota.

The defendant, whose accessories all bore the car firms' trade marks, argued that the trade marks that it used on its accessories served only a decorative function, and that consumers might want a Volkswagen licence plate or an Audi key chain simply because they own Volkswagens or Audis. The defendant urged, therefore, that the aesthetic functionality doctrine precluded the enforcement of the trade marks in these kinds of contexts. Writing for the court, Judge McKeown acknowledged that the plaintiffs' claims reflected the extension of trade marks beyond their traditional functions:

> Famous trademarks have assumed an exalted status of their own in today's consumer culture that cannot neatly be reduced to the historic function of trademark to designate source. Consumers sometimes buy products bearing marks such as the Nike Swoosh, the Playboy bunny ears, the Mercedes tri-point star, the Ferrari stallion, and countless sports franchise logos, for the appeal of the mark itself, without regard to whether it signifies the origin or sponsorship of the product.[70]

Despite her recognition of the extension of trade mark rights into this aesthetic domain, Judge McKeown was not prepared to adapt the aesthetic functionality doctrine to limit the scope of the plaintiffs' rights in the marks. Reasoning that the aesthetic functionality doctrine applied only where the aesthetic purpose of the item was 'wholly independent of any source-identifying function',[71] the court ruled in favour of the plaintiff car firms. In the court's view, the function of car logos was to designate the source of the firms' products. The defendant's liability for affixing these marks to accessories was grounded on the reality that customers purchased the accessories because of their association with the trade-marked cars. In the court's analysis, the 'entire significance' of the contested product features resided in their connection with the original trade marks.[72] This was a sufficient basis for establishing liability.

Au-Tomotive Gold appears to accept that the merchandising role of trade marks comes within the trade mark owner's prerogatives. A number of scholars have debated whether the court's application of the aesthetic

[70] *Ibid.* 1067. [71] *Ibid.* 1073.
[72] *Ibid.* 1074, quoting Restatement of Torts (1938) § 742 cmt (a).

functionality doctrine is analytically sound.[73] For present purposes, the holding offers another example of trade mark law's concern with reproduction. The court is protecting the seemingly endless reproduceability of brands, the right to reproduce the mark in different marketing contexts, so long as consumers' purchasing motivations derive from their attraction to the brand itself. While the holding in *Au-Tomotive Gold* was arguably limited to products closely associated with vehicles, the underlying *theory* of the case – that trade mark proprietors are entitled to the value attaching to consumers' desire to own something depicting the famous brand – has no such limitations. It might reach, for example, the use of Volkswagen trade marks sculptured into the shape of earbobs. Once again, invoking consumers' recognition of the connection between the item depicting the mark and the original trade marks imposes only a flimsy bulwark preventing the trade mark from operating like a reproduction right. This is not meant as a criticism of the Ninth Circuit's analysis: its holding may simply be a tacit recognition of the importance of reproduction to vindication of the value that firms and perhaps consumers see in cultural artefacts that are essentially reproductions of trade marks. The DVD example is apposite once again: most consumers purchase copies of copyright-protected works precisely because they derive, and consumers know that they derive, from the original source: the underlying copyright-protected work.

(e) Limitations on assignments and licensing

The evolution of doctrine surrounding the assignment and licensing of trade mark rights provides a final example. In US trade mark law, because trade marks do not exist apart from the goodwill they symbolise, marks cannot be assigned unless accompanied by that goodwill. Attempts to assign marks without the goodwill the marks represent risk characterisation as 'assignments in gross', and they have sometimes been held to be ineffective in transferring the mark. In turn, if the assignor ceased to use the mark and has no intention to resume use, the assignor could be considered to have abandoned the trade mark.[74] Similar restrictions accompanied the licensing of trade marks. It was originally thought that the licensing of trade marks destroyed their significance as designators of the source of the products or services. Licences were declared invalid as

[73] See for example Michael Grynberg, 'Things are Worse Than We Think: Trademark Defenses in a "Formalist" Age' (2009) 24 *Berkeley Technology Law Journal* 897, 921ff.

[74] J. Thomas McCarthy, Thomson Reuters, *McCarthy on Trademarks and Unfair Competition* (4th edn, 2010) ('*McCarthy on Trademarks*') § 18:17.

a fraud on the public. They were sometimes held to abandon the mark.[75] The traditional rules helped to ensure that trade marks were protected only to the extent that they operated as designators of source.

Consistent with developments in other jurisdictions, the US rules on assignments and licensing have relaxed considerably. Thus assignment of the goodwill of the relevant part of the business may be achieved in the traditional manner, by, for example, accompanying the assignment of the trade mark with the transfer of the relevant part of the business to the assignee. But some courts have held that an assignment is valid if the assignor ceases to manufacture goods under the mark.[76] Moreover, the assignment of trade marks does not necessarily require that the assignee's goods be identical to those of the assignor. The Second Circuit held in *Topps Co. Inc.* v. *Cadbury Stani SAIC* that consumers' expectations will be met even if the goods are 'substantially similar'.[77] The Court in this case acknowledged the development in the law of a 'more flexible definition of the goodwill necessary to avoid the prohibition against assignments in gross'.[78] In the service mark context, courts have adopted an even more flexible attitude, focusing on the continuity of consumers' experiences rather more than technical requirements as to the accompanying assignment of underlying business assets.[79] Since at least 1948,[80] US courts have recognised that licensing is valid, and does not effect an abandonment of the mark, so long as the licensor exercises quality control over the goods or services to which the mark is applied. This standard has been further relaxed by case law that holds a licence to be valid if the licensor had the right to control, even if the right is not in fact exercised.[81]

In general, the direction of the law has been towards loosening requirements grounded in a trade mark's traditional function of designating the source of goods and services.[82] In that sense, in transactions involving trade marks, trade marks are treated less and less as ciphers that 'mark'

[75] See generally Restatement (Third) of Unfair Competition (1995) § 33 cmt (a).

[76] *McCarthy on Trademarks*, § 18:24. [77] 526 F 3d 63 (2nd Cir, 2008). [78] *Ibid*. 71.

[79] See for example *Iskenderian* v. *Iskenderian*, 144 Cal App 4th 1162, 1173, 51 Cal Rptr 3d 163 (2nd Dist, 2006).

[80] *E I Du Pont de Nemours & Co* v. *Celanese Corp. of America*, 167 F 2d 484 (CC PA, 1948).

[81] See for example *Stanfield* v. *Osborne Industries Inc.*, 52 F 3d 867 (10th Cir, 1995), *certiorari denied*, 516 US 920 (1995). See also *McCarthy on Trademarks*, § 18:28. As a recent decision of the Seventh Circuit confirms, however, licensing without any quality control may be characterised as 'naked licensing' (*Eva's Bridal Ltd* v. *Halanick Enterprises Inc.* (CA 7th Cir (Ill), WL 1756163, 10 May 2011), slip op 1).

[82] Some limitations remain, however, such as the prohibition against sublicensing of trade mark licences. Trade mark licences are treated as personal, due to the power to control the quality of goods and services which remain vested in the licensor (*Tap Publications Inc.* v. *Chinese Yellow Pages (New York) Inc.*, 925 F Supp 212, 218 (SD NY, 1996)).

the 'trade'. Fewer restrictions now require that the trade mark symbolise the trade in respect of which the rights in the mark were originally established. As a matter of commercial reality, the goodwill may expand as a result of licensing and franchising, but the connections with the firm whose 'trade' was originally 'marked' by the trade mark may be quite tenuous. The increasing flexibility seen in the assignment case law allows the trade mark to migrate to new commercial contexts, again with increasingly flimsy connections to the original goodwill that underlies the mark. Licensees and assignees seem to be buying not so much the right to share in the goodwill symbolised by the mark, but rather the ability to *depict* the trade mark in some new business context.

IV. Conclusion

This brief survey of key doctrines in US trade mark law indicates that an emphasis on reproduction has crept into US trade mark jurisprudence in a number of contexts. The growing emphasis on the right to reproduce a mark probably enhances the strength of the rights attaching to a trade mark. A trade mark is 'psychological property'; in theory, its scope and strength depend on what consumers think. Ascertaining what consumers actually think about trade marks is a notoriously difficult task. Elsewhere, I have described trade mark liability as based on a kind of 'inchoate empiricism'.[83] For a variety of reasons, courts cannot peer into consumers' minds. The strength of trade mark rights is therefore partly a product of the readiness with which courts will accept other evidence of changes that are likely to occur in consumer perceptions as result of the defendant's actions. In contrast, determining whether the defendant has copied the trade mark is a relatively easy thing to do, and this may in turn make trade mark rights easier to sustain and enforce.

Whether the bundle of rights attaching to a trade mark includes a reproduction right is relevant to many of the broader themes that are explored elsewhere in this book. Marketers' key aspiration for their trade marks is to transform them into 'brands' – symbols to which consumers have strong emotional connections, and that ideally are valued in their own right, not merely as designators of source.[84] Trade mark law's orthodox role of protecting the veracity of information that circulates in the consumer marketplace cannot hope to address a firm's concern to

[83] Graeme W. Austin, 'Trademarks and the Burdened Imagination' (2003–4) 69 *Brooklyn Law Review* 827, 866.

[84] See for example Mark A. Lemley, 'Modern Lanham Act', 1688 (observing that trade marks are protected 'as things valuable in and of themselves, rather than for the product goodwill they embody').

protect the brand value that has been established through advertising and marketing. Rightly or wrongly, the emerging emphasis on reproduction suggests that trade mark rights are evolving in ways that match trade mark owners' aspirations for their brands. Firms want brands to be destinations; traditionally, trade marks have been understood only as road signs.

The task of resolving the various normative issues distilled by various kinds of expansion in the scope and strength of trade mark rights can be left to others. The descriptive approach adopted in this chapter betrays some scepticism as to the extent to which legal actors are likely to be influenced by engagement with grand theoretical controversies. Of course, it is possible that some relevant judicial disquiet might be provoked by (yet) more invective on trade mark law's departure from its conventional rationales – but that possibility seems decidedly remote, given the many normative and structural critiques of trade mark law's expansion by many distinguished commentators that have already been advanced in the scholarly literature. Attempts to confine trade mark rights, based on one or other theoretical commitment as to the 'core' purpose underlying purposes of this body of law, also seem to belie the messiness of grappling with individual facts which comprises the workaday world of the courts. That said, the descriptive approach adopted here might nevertheless illuminate some of the underlying normative issues that animate much of the recent scholarship that argues for constraining trade mark rights. Knowing how far the horse has bolted is surely relevant to the chances of ever again tethering it.

To the extent that this chapter has any prescriptive purposes at all, they are more modest. It might, for example, be useful to ask whether, if trade marks are coming closer to copyrights, other *copyright* doctrines – particularly limiting doctrines such as fair use – could be relevant to the shape and the scope of trade mark rights. Put another way, if – rightly or wrongly – trade marks have already evolved to encompass rights against reproduction, the orderly development of trade mark doctrine may be as well served by acknowledging that reality as by attempts to constrain the expansion of trade marks in the light of categorical or normative distinctions. To some extent, that work has already begun: Professor Jane Ginsburg notes, for example, that the influence of copyright on trade mark can partly be found in copyright law's limiting doctrines, most particularly fair use.[85] It should be no surprise that many of the trade mark

[85] Jane C. Ginsburg, 'Of Mutant Copyrights, Mangled Trademarks and Barbie's Beneficence: The Influence of Copyright on Trademark Law', in Dinwoodie and Janis, *Trademark Law*, 481.

defences that have a decidedly 'copyright' flavour to them – different forms of fair use, and, in the dilution context, defences for news reporting, parody, and other forms of purely informational or descriptive uses – have grown up broadly contemporaneously with trade mark doctrine's willingness to protect against 'copying' in a variety of contexts.

On the assumption that constraining trade mark rights is, at least in some contexts, a worthwhile endeavour, more might be achieved by taking a harder look at what trade mark doctrine protects, how it is protected, and then tailoring limitations to that reality. Doing so might also bring its own normative payoff. Significantly, many of the constraining doctrines offered by copyright law require that defendants have themselves engaged in creative communicative activity.[86] The leeway offered by copyright law to purely consumptive uses, for example, is quite small.[87] Creative activity is the kind of thing copyright generally encourages: if a defendant in a trade mark case has engaged in creative activity, this should also balance the equities in a defendant's favour. Focusing on the extent of the *defendant's* creative work might also help distinguish cases such as *Au-Tomotive Gold* (where the defendant's creative input was arguably quite minimal) from cases involving uses of trade marks in the context of parodies and satire.[88] For many legal actors, focusing on the degree and quality of the creative work performed by defendants might prove a more attractive prospect than unravelling a significant body of doctrine that has, in a number of contexts, already moved trade marks closer to copyright. To return to David Brooks' branding-informed paean to the humanities: if an understanding of the humanities can help to create a brand, then the kind of creative work associated with the humanities – and the appreciation for that creativity that is already embedded in copyright law – might better serve to limit the legal rights that protect it.

86 This theme is developed by the Supreme Court in *Campbell* v. *Acuff-Rose Music Inc.* ('*Campbell*'), 510 US 569 (1993). The defendants' taking of a considerable amount of the plaintiff's copyright-protected work might be excused because of the non-consumptive, creative endeavour involved in the defendants' creation of its own parody.

87 See *Campbell*.

88 The Dilutiuon Act of 2006 enacted a specific defence for uses of trade mark 'identifying and parodying, criticizing, or commenting upon the famous mark owner or the goods or services of the famous mark owner' (§ 43(c)(3)(A)(ii). There are no equivalent statutory defences for confusion-based liability theories.).

8 From magic charms to symbols of wealth

Well-known trade marks in Indonesia

Christoph Antons

I. Introduction: trade mark laws in the post-colonial context of developing countries

Different from articles that focus in particular on the protection of foreign well-known trade marks in Indonesia,[1] this chapter will also examine famous local brands in their socio-economic context. The role of trade marks according to intellectual property textbooks is to signify the origin of goods or services, the quality of the product, to advertise it and to provide consumers with information about the product.[2] We can detect some significant differences in these roles, however, if we examine trade marks in the context of young post-colonial nation states. Such differences have much to do with the nature of the local economy, with the role of foreign corporations and with attempts to strengthen and build up domestic enterprises.[3] In the immediate post-colonial period, this leads to a tension between the continuing trading interests of the departing colonial power and new nationalist governments.[4] In countries with peaceful decolonisation processes, these tensions are to some extent dissolved via foreign investment laws into arrangements where local companies are allowed to share in the continuing domestic operation of a

[1] Christoph Antons, 'The Recognition and Protection of Well-known Trade Marks in Indonesia', 3 *Journal of Intellectual Property Law and Practice* 185.

[2] Jill McKeough, Andrew Stewart and Philip Griffith, *Intellectual Property in Australia* (3rd edn, Lexis Nexis Butterworths, Chatswood, 2004) 498.

[3] Christoph Antons, 'Japan as a Model? Comparing Law and Development in Japan, Singapore and Indonesia', in Christoph Antons (ed.), *Law and Development in East and Southeast Asia* (RoutledgeCurzon, London and New York, 2003), 216; Onofre D. Corpuz, *An Economic History of the Philippines* (University of the Philippines Press, Quezon City, 1997) 257–61.

[4] See for example Richard Robison, *Indonesia: The Rise of Capital* (Allen & Unwin, Sydney, 1986), ch. 2; Amando Doronila, *The State, Economic Transformation and Political Change in the Philippines, 1946–1972* (Oxford University Press, Singapore and New York, 1992), ch. 3; Anne Booth, *The Indonesian Economy in the Nineteenth and Twentieth Centuries: A History of Missed Opportunities* (Macmillan, Basingstoke; St Martin's Press, New York, 1998), 313–14.

former colonial trading company.[5] However, in those countries where decolonisation occurred after an armed struggle, foreign trading interests and intellectual property often were simply nationalised and taken over by local companies, operated privately or by branches of the national government.[6] The latter scenario applies to Indonesia, where the Dutch colonial power granted independence only after an armed struggle lasting from Indonesia's declaration of independence in 1945 to 1949. Although Dutch enterprises were initially allowed to continue their operations in Indonesia, tensions between Indonesia and the Netherlands grew again at the end of the 1950s over the remaining Dutch territory in West New Guinea.[7] As a result, there were spontaneous takeovers of Dutch companies by workers and unions at the end of 1957, which subsequently came under the supervision of the Indonesian military and were endorsed by Parliament a year later.[8] The Ministry of Justice ordered the expulsion of 46,000 Dutch citizens and a large number of Dutch enterprises were expropriated and transformed into state corporations. The Indonesian government then simply nationalised the remaining Dutch trading interests in the country.[9] Foreign trade marks associated with Dutch colonial companies were discontinued and replaced with new national names or symbols. One of the Dutch trade marks affected by this development was the beer brand Heineken. In 1936, Heineken had become a majority shareholder in Indonesia's first brewery established in 1929, after which the company changed its name into Heineken Nederlands Indische Bierbrouwerijen Maatschapij.[10] As with other Dutch companies, the brewery was nationalised in 1957 and the name changed into Perusahaan Bir Bintang. After the change of government in Indonesia and the introduction

[5] On Malaysia's policies on gaining independence, see Constance Mary Turnbull, *A Short History of Malaysia, Singapore and Brunei* (Cassell Australia, Stanmore, 1980), 246–7; Jomo K. S. and Chang Yii Tan, 'The Political Economy of Post-colonial Transformation', in Jomo K. S. with Wong Sau Ngan (eds.), *Law, Institutions and Malaysian Economic Development* (NUS Press, Singapore, 2008) 22, 23–7; Jomo K. S., 'Investment and Technology Policy: Government Intervention, Regulation and Incentives', in Jomo with Wong, *Law, Institutions*, 177, 178–9.

[6] As to the different post-colonial policy approaches in various parts of South-East Asia, see Norman G. Owen, 'Economic and Social Change', in Nicholas Tarling (ed.), *The Cambridge History of Southeast Asia, Volume Two: The Nineteenth and Twentieth Centuries* (Cambridge University Press, Cambridge and Melbourne, 1992 edn) 467, 497–9.

[7] Merle Calvin Ricklefs, *A History of Modern Indonesia Since c.1200* (3rd edn, Stanford University Press, Stanford, 2001), 291, 305.

[8] *Ibid.* 316–17.

[9] Robison, *Indonesia*, 62–3, 71–8; Ricklefs, *History of Modern Indonesia*, 316–17; Booth, *Indonesian Economy*, 64–5.

[10] Multi Bintang Indonesia, *Bintang Story*, Bir Bintang www.birbintang.co.id/en/inside_beer_history.htm.

of the Foreign Capital Investment Law of 1967,[11] Heineken returned to Indonesia to become a joint venture partner in Multi Bintang Indonesia, after which the beer was named 'Bir Bintang Baru' ('the new Bintang beer'),[12] today one of Indonesia's most popular beers.

II. The emergence of local well-known brands in Indonesia

Governments of newly independent countries with a history like that of Indonesia probably prefer a completely new beginning for domestic commerce and related laws like intellectual property law rather than to continue the colonial administration of the system.[13] But such a completely new beginning is usually not possible, because trade has to continue and it takes time to draft new laws.[14] Therefore, a residue of the colonial period also continues in particular within those local businesses that were able to achieve a relatively prominent role during colonial times. Here, it is important to understand the social and economic stratification of Indonesian society during colonial rule. The Dutch had administered so-called interpersonal or intergroup laws that kept the various population groups in the colony apart from each other and that gave them varying degrees of access to trade and to commercial law.[15] Only the Europeans and people legally 'equalised' with Europeans were fully subjected to Dutch laws. Indonesians on average were subjected to their own various customary laws and to Islamic law, if they were Muslims.

[11] Christoph Antons, 'Japan as a Model? – Law and Development in Japan, Singapore and Indonesia', in Antons, *Law and Development*, 234.

[12] Multi Bintang Indonesia, *Bir Bintang Website* www.birbintang.co.id; Multi Bintang Indonesia, *About Us* www.multibintang.co.id/about_us_cp.htm; see also at *The History of Heineken*, Heineken International, www.heinekeninternational.com/content/live/files/downloads/History%20of%20Heineken.pdf.

[13] On attempts to rid the Indonesian legal system of Dutch influence during the years of the Sukarno presidency, see Sudargo Gautama, 'Legal Developments in Independent Indonesia (1945–1970)' (1970) 2 *LAWASIA* 157; Daniel Lev, 'The Lady and the Banyan Tree: Civil-Law Change in Indonesia' (1965) 14 *American Journal of Comparative Law* 282; Sudargo Gautama and Robert N. Hornick, *An Introduction to Indonesian Law: Unity in Diversity* (Penerbit Alumni, Bandung, rev. edn, 1983), 181–7; Soetandyo Wignjosoebroto, *Dari Hukum Kolonial ke Hukum Nasional: Dinamika Sosial-Politik dalam Perkembangan Hukum di Indonesia* (RajaGrafindo Persada, Jakarta, 1994), ch. 10.

[14] Gautama and Hornick, *Introduction to Indonesian Law*, 181–2; Christoph Antons, 'Legal Culture and History of Law in Asia', in Christopher Heath (ed.), *Intellectual Property Law in Asia* (Kluwer Law International, London, 2003) 13, 20–1.

[15] The classical and most detailed source on this subject matter is Sudargo Gautama, *Hukum Antargolongan: Suatu Pengantar* (11th edn, PT Ichtiar Baru Van Hoeve, Jakarta, 1993). See also Gautama and Hornick, *Introduction to Indonesian Law*, ch.1; Christoph Antons, 'Ethnicity, Law and Development in Southeast Asia', in Frans Hüsken and Dick van der Meij (eds.), *Reading Asia: New Research in Asian Studies* (Curzon, Richmond, Surrey, 2001), 3.

This, the lack of access to capital and foreign trading networks, largely confined them to a role in farming and small-scale artisan production of batik and other crafts.[16]

In between the European trading houses, on the one hand, and a predominantly farming-oriented local population on the other hand, were the trading interests of people that the Dutch called the 'foreign orientals', a group that included Chinese, Arab and Indian traders and traders from elsewhere in Asia.[17] These traders played a role in particular in the intermediate trade between Dutch companies and the population in the interior and rural parts of the colony.[18] After the departure of the colonial power, such Chinese- and Arab-owned companies stayed. They became an important part of the Indonesian economy and remain nowadays the main remaining link to colonial era trade. Since the days of the colony, they manufacture and trade in local products such as traditional medicine, crafts, tobacco, food and beverages.

Some of the most famous companies and oldest trade marks in Indonesia today are to be found in the industrial production of jamu, traditional Indonesian medicine used as household remedies for common ailments such as influenza, as beauty products and for energy drinks. Among the oldest trade mark in this field is 'Nyonya Meneer', a company set up by women of mixed Chinese and Indonesian descent, called Peranakan in the Malay-speaking countries, in 1918.[19] Not only did these Peranakan Chinese have easier access to Western commerce and to capital because of their legal status as 'foreign orientals', but they also had access to traditional remedies and recipes from their Indonesian mothers.[20] These different influences are visible from the Nyonya Meneer trade mark, which reveals the identity of the owner: 'Nyonya' is a term for a Peranakan woman. 'Meneer' is often misunderstood as referring to the Dutch word for 'Mister', but the website of the company explains that it in fact refers to her first name derived from the Javanese word for 'crushed rice'. Successful jamu companies owned by

16 Robison, *Indonesia*, 23–7.

17 Charles A. Coppel, 'The Indonesian Chinese as "Foreign Orientals" in the Netherlands Indies', in Timothy Lindsey (ed.), *Indonesia: Law and Society* (Federation Press, Sydney, 1999), 33, 33–41; Christoph Antons, 'The History of Intellectual Property Law in Indonesia: From Colonial to National Law' (1991), 22 *International Review of Industrial Property and Copyright Law* 359.

18 Robison, *Indonesia*, 19–21.

19 For a detailed history of this company, see Asih Sumardono, Tities Ahayuningtyas, Nunung Husnul Chatimah and Indriaty, *Perjalanan Panjang Usaha Nyonya Meneer* (PT Grasindo, Jakarta, 2002).

20 Onghokham, 'Beberapa Aspek Agama Cina', in Th. Sumaratana, E. Darmaputera, D. Effendi, D. Dhakidae and Z. Lubis (eds.), *Pergulatan Mencari Jati Diri* (Penerbit Interfidei, Jakarta, 1995), 141, 144.

ethnic Indonesians emerged after independence. They took a different approach from peranakan companies by focusing in particular on cosmetics and by stressing their descent from royal Javanese households, who in Java are the guardians and owners of the most highly regarded jamu recipes. The most famous company and trade mark in this field is 'Mustika Ratu', a company founded by a granddaughter of the Sultan of Surakarta in Central Java. Again, the trade mark reveals the identity of the owner, as 'Ratu' is the Indonesian word for 'Queen'.[21]

A further aspect that is important in understanding well-known trade marks and trade marks more generally in Indonesia, is the relative simplicity of local marks, the initial absence of sophisticated marketing techniques and the restrictions in the use of symbols in a society that wants to break away from a colonial past and that wants to return to some form of pre-colonial identity. The lack of access Indonesians had to modern forms of commerce and law during colonial times was mentioned earlier. Those Indonesian companies that started afresh after independence, therefore, had to establish their businesses in an environment in which modern marketing companies did not yet exist, prospective consumers were neither rich nor particularly demanding with regard to the sophistication of the products, and in which the use of many foreign symbols and words was politically inappropriate, because they were tainted by their association with the colonial period. Not surprisingly, Indonesians turned in their trade mark symbolism to mysticism or to the pre-colonial past. The first group of such locally established marks may be regarded as good luck charms for their owners. They use, for example, symbols that a spiritual adviser or practitioner of Javanese mysticism recommends as most likely bringing luck to the business. Indonesian trade marks that appear odd or little related to the product they are advertising sometimes have such origins. Examples are the most well-known cigarette brands with strange names and symbols such as 'salt storehouse' ('Gudang Garam'), 'root' ('Bentoel') or 'needle' ('Djarum'). In a case in the early 1980s, the Indonesian Supreme Court had to decide on the likelihood of deception between the 'Golden Rabbit-Goat Trade Mark', the 'Golden Rabbit-Deer Trade Mark' and the 'Goat-Ant Trade Mark'.[22]

[21] For more details on these and other jamu companies, see Christoph Antons and Rosy Antons-Sutanto, 'Traditional Medicine and Intellectual Property Rights: A Case Study of the Indonesian *jamu* industry', in Christoph Antons (ed.), *Traditional Knowledge, Traditional Cultural Expressions and Intellectual Property Law in the Asia-Pacific Region* (Kluwer Law International, Alphen aan den Rijn, 2009), 363.

[22] Supreme Court, 2391K/Sip/79 of 31 August 1983, as reported in Christoph Antons, *Intellectual Property Law in Indonesia* (Kluwer Law International, London, 2000), 230–1.

Such trade marks are frequently owned by Indonesians of Chinese descent, who also use lucky numbers, sometimes in a Chinese dialect, for their trade marks. Indonesia's oldest cigarette brand 'Djie Sam Soe' (the '2–3–4' brand) is an example. This trade mark is famous for *kretek* cigarettes, the popular and traditional Indonesian cigarettes that mix tobacco with cloves. The first 'Djie Sam Soe' was created in Surabaya in 1913 by Liem Seeng Tee, a Chinese migrant from Fujian province, who was also the founder of PT HM Sampoerna Tbk, now one of the major cigarette manufacturers in Indonesia. The brand '2–3–4' adds up to his lucky number 9 and it uses 9 stars on its logo. In fact, so strong is the belief in the magic of number 9 that in its production in Sampoerna House Surabaya, PT Sampoerna employs exactly 234 workers.[23]

Many other companies use names and characters from ancient Javanese mythology and from *wayang*, the Javanese shadow play based on epic stories, such as the *Mahabharata* or *Ramayana*. Frequently used for trade marks are, for example, the names of Arjuna and Bima, two heroes of the *Mahabharata*. Another very popular choice is the more local shadow play character of Semar. Typical Indonesian symbols such as the Javanese dagger, the keris, are also common. Two of the most famous batik brands in Indonesia today are 'Batik Keris' and 'Batik Semar'.[24] However, because such names and symbols are so widely used, they often have little distinctive quality as trade marks.

The story is not much different with other well-known Indonesian trade marks that do not refer to symbolism based on tradition or mythology. They were also often established at a time when sophisticated marketing concepts were not yet available on the Indonesian market and part of their success is their simplicity. There are many examples for very simple trade marks that have become very successful. One of the biggest success stories in the food industry is a brand of instant noodles, simply called 'Supermi'. 'Mi' refers to 'bakmi', the word for noodle and 'super' is an indicator of the quality promised to a consumer. The most successful local Indonesian beverage is bottled Javanese tea. The company that developed this concept markets the drink under the trade mark 'teh botol', which means 'tea bottle' in Indonesian. Finally, the first successful brand of bottled water was put onto the market under the trade mark 'Aqua'. In view of the simplicity of these marks, it is not surprising, that many of their owners initially had to wage court battles against

23 On the history of this trade mark, see *Djie Sam Soe* (24 March 2011) Wikipedia http://id.wikipedia.org/w/index.php?title=Dji_Sam_Soe.

24 Batik Semar has been produced since 1947: see *Batik Semar History* (2009) Batik Semar www.batik-semar.com/profile/PROFILE-INGG.php.

competitors that were seeking cancellation of their marks because of lack of distinctiveness. They succeeded, however, in establishing their brands, often relying on an old principle from Dutch trade mark law ('het woord is merk geworden')[25] and arguing acquired distinctiveness because of continuous and widespread use in trade.[26] Once the trade mark was established on this basis, many of these companies took successful legal action to have their marks recognised as well known and thereby acquire enhanced protection against local competitors.[27]

III. The arrival of foreign well-known marks during the period of the 'New Order' government

The immediate post-colonial period with its anti-colonialism and heightened nationalism came to an end in the mid-1960s, when Indonesia's first President Sukarno was replaced by former General Suharto's military backed government, which is widely known in Indonesia as the 'New Order' government. The new government initiated a radical break with Sukarno's anti-Western policies and opened the country to foreign investment. With the Western businesses that were attracted to the populous Indonesian market came their brands and marketing strategies. They encountered, however, a rather basic trade mark law from

25 '[T]he word has become a trade mark'.

26 The principle 'het woord is merk gewoorden' was applied in several cases as early as 1938 by the *Raad van Justitie Batavia* (see Sudargo Gautama, *Hukum Merek Indonesia* (2nd edn, Penerbit Alumni, Bandung, 1986), 31–2). Acquired distinctiveness was successfully argued in the *Supermi* case, District Court of Central Jakarta, No. 904/1970 of 30 January 1971, in Sudargo Gautama and Rizawanto Winata, *Himpunan Keputusan Merek Dagang* (Penerbit Alumni, Bandung, 1987), 57–62; in the case of the cigarette brand '555', District Court of Central Jakarta, No. 323/1968 G. of 22 July 1969, in Direktorat Jenderal Hukum dan Perundang-undangan Departemen Kehakiman, *Keputusan-keputusan Pengadilan tentang Sengketa Merek 1964–1970* (Direktorat Jenderal Hukum dan Perundang-undangan, Departemen Kehakiman, Jakarta, 1980) 51–5; for the zip-fastener brand 'YKK', Supreme Court No. 217K/Sip/1972 of 30 October 1972, in Gautama and Winata, *Himpunan Keputusan Merek Dagang*, 41–8; by a trade mark named 'jempol' (thumb), Supreme Court No. 178K/Sip/1973 of 9 April 1973, in Sudargo Gautama and Rizawanto Winata, 63–75; by 'Kraft', District Court of Central Jakarta, No. 281/1956 G. of 9 January 1957, *Hukum* No. 5–6, 1957, 106; and by the bottled-water brand 'Aqua', Supreme Court No. 757K/Pdt/1989 of 30 March 1992, in Sudargo Gautama, *Himpunan Jurisprudensi Indonesia yang penting untuk praktek sehari-hari (Landmark Decisions) berikut komentar*, vol. 5 (Penerbit PT Citra Aditya Bakti, Bandung, 1993), 1–19. See also Antons, *Intellectual Property Law*, 224–8.

27 See, e.g., Supreme Court No. 217K/Sip/1972 of 30 October 1972, '*YKK*', in Gautama and Winata, *Himpunan Keputusan Merek Dagang*, 41–8; Commercial Court Central Jakarta No. 56/Merek/2002/PN.Niaga.Jkt.Pst of 4 March 2003, '*Aqua*', in Tim Redaksi Tatanusa (eds.), *Himpunan Putusan-putusan Pengadilan Niaga dalam Perkara Merek*, vol. 3 (PT Tatanusa, Jakarta, 2004), 403–30.

1961 that was largely a translation of the former Dutch colonial law of 1912 and in which the right to a mark was based on first use, whereas registration provided only rebuttable evidence of first use and the right to a mark. Abuse of the system via token sales was common. Foreign companies also became the victims of a parasitic 'trade in marks' by so-called 'trade mark entrepreneurs', who registered whole portfolios of foreign trade marks that were not yet represented on the Indonesian market in their own names. In the booming economic climate of the 1970s and 1980s, it was only a question of time until at least some of these foreign trade mark owners would decide to extend their operations to Indonesia. Once they were setting up their offices in Jakarta, they were soon to discover that their trade marks were already registered in the name of an Indonesian owner. With no real intention to use the mark, however, the Indonesian owner usually could be easily persuaded against payment of a fee to abandon the mark. In the early 1990s, the prices for such buy-back arrangements reportedly ranged from US$10,000 to US$100,000 depending on the fame of the mark.[28]

Many foreign well-known trade marks thus entered the Indonesian market in the late 1960s and early 1970s. At the same time and in a rather disturbing development for local Chinese businesses, the new government initially took a hostile attitude to expressions of Chinese identity and the use of the Chinese language. After a coup attempt in 1965, the Indonesian Communist Party, allegedly with backing from mainland China, was held responsible. However, Indonesians of Chinese descent were targeted, too. Chinese language schools were closed down and citizens of Chinese descent were asked to assimilate and to change their names to Indonesian names.[29] As a result of this development, trade marks that used Chinese language, names or symbols or originated in China could be prohibited from registration as marks that were contravening the public order. This happened, for example, in the

[28] Aries Margono, G. Sugrahetty, Siti Nurbaiti and Indrawan, 'Menyapu Mafia Pedagang Merek', *Tempo* 1 August 1992, 38–9; Peter Rouse and Didi Dermawan, 'Indonesia: A Fresh Look at the Protection and Enforcement of Trademarks, Part 2: Enforcement' (1991) 38 *Trademark World* 25. See also Christoph Antons, 'The Protection of Well-known Marks in Indonesia', in Heath and Kung-Chung (eds.), *The Protection of Well-known Marks in Asia* (Kluwer Law International, 2000), 199, 199–201; Antons, 'Recognition', 185–6; Antons, *Intellectual Property Law*, 269.

[29] James Austin Copland Mackie, 'Anti-Chinese Outbreaks in Indonesia, 1959–1968', in James Austin Copland Mackie (ed.), *The Chinese in Indonesia: Five Essays* (Thomas Nelson, 1976), 77, 111–28.

'Flying Wheel' case with regards to a trade mark that was initially registered by a company from Shanghai.[30] After Indonesia and the People's Republic of China resumed their diplomatic relationship in 1990, trade marks using Chinese characters could again be registered like any other foreign trade mark in Indonesia.[31] Nevertheless, it is probably safe to assume that many trade marks using Chinese language or symbols would have been affected during the earlier period.

IV. Recognition of well-known trade marks in Indonesian courts and in legislative reforms

A breakthrough, especially for foreign owners of well-known trade marks, came with the '*Tancho*' decision of the Supreme Court in 1972, which cancelled the local registration of a Japanese trade mark in Indonesia.[32] The Supreme Court declared that first use in Indonesia, which under the first-to-use system at the time was decisive for the trade mark right, had to be 'first use in good faith'. As a consequence, the registration of the mark by an Indonesian joint venture partner that suspiciously used the trade name Tokyo Osaka Co and had tried to pass off locally made products as foreign had to be cancelled for lack of good faith. During the 1980s, use and registration in bad faith became one of the best arguments for owners of well-known marks to achieve the cancellation of competing registrations.[33]

Indonesian trade mark law changed from the first user system to a 'first-to-file' system with the Trade Marks Act 1992 (Indonesia) (Trade Marks Act), which came into force in 1993 and was revised in 1997. The new laws and several accompanying government decrees with specific relevance for well-known trade marks brought an increasingly clear protection for well-known marks, as long as they were used for identical or similar goods or services.[34] The situation has remained ambiguous,

[30] District Court of Central Jakarta, No. 33/1972 G. of 3 October 1973, in Direktorat Jenderal Hukum dan Perundang-undangan Departemen Kehakiman, *Keputusan-keputusan Pengadilan tentang Sengketa Merek 1971–1977* (Direktorat Jenderal Hukum dan Perundang-undangan, Departemen Kehakiman, Jakarta, 1981), 117–29.

[31] Christoph Antons, *Intellectual Property Law*, 220–1.

[32] Supreme Court No. 677K/Sip/1972 of 13 December 1972, in Gautama and Winata, *Himpunan Keputusan Merek* Dagang, 1–23.

[33] See for example District Court of Central Jakarta No. 205/1980 G. of 18 November 1980, '*Bata*', in Gautama and Winata, *Himpunan Keputusan Merek Dagang*, 109–15; No. 353/1980 G. of 3 February 1981, '*Seven Up*', in *ibid.* 243–51; No. 542/1980 G. of 21 August 1981, '*Dunhill*', in *ibid.* 97–108; Supreme Court No. 1269K/Pdt/1984 of 15 January 1986, '*Hitachi*', in *Yurisprudensi Indonesia*, vol. 1 (PT Ichtiar Baru Van Hoeve, Jakarta, 1989), 16–23.

[34] Antons, *Intellectual Property Law*, 244–6.

however, for dissimilar goods or services. Article 6(1)(b) of the current law of 2001 clearly protects well-known trade marks for goods and/or services of the same kind and art. 6(2) offers the same protection for dissimilar goods in accordance with a government regulation. This government regulation, however, has never been issued, so that in relation to dissimilar goods, well-known trade marks remain unprotected. So far, the government has left it to the courts to decide about the issue.

The most straightforward cancellation cases for the courts related to well-known marks are of course those where the competing mark is used for goods or services of the same kind. However, it can be observed that in cases where bad faith of the competitor in registering the mark is argued in addition to the well-known character of the mark, many courts avoid the decision about the well-known mark and cancel the competing registration on the basis of the bad faith argument.[35] A further reason why bad faith is so commonly argued is that it allows the courts to ignore time bars for cancellation claims that would otherwise apply. Cancellation claims actually have to be made within five years after the registration of a mark.[36] The time bar does not apply, however, for claims to cancel registrations in conflict with religious morality, decency and public security.[37] An explanatory memorandum of the Indonesian government accompanying the provision points out that an incidence of bad faith is included in the understanding of that which conflicts with public security. This has become a convenient argument in many Commercial Court cases to ignore the time bar,[38] especially after the Supreme Court has accepted this approach.[39]

The courts have much greater difficulties with cases involving use of the well-known trade mark for dissimilar goods or services. Such use is very common in a society, in which foreign products are regarded as

[35] Commercial Court Central Jakarta No. 11/Merek/2001/PN.Niaga.Jkt.Pst of 26 March 2002, '*Santa Barbara Polo & Racquet Club*', in Tim Redaksi Tatanusa, *Himpunan Putusan-putusan Pengadilan Niaga dalam Perkara Merek*, vol. 2 (PT Tatanusa, Jakarta, 2002), 1–19. For further examples, see Antons, 'Recognition', 189. The requirement that an applicant for registration must not be acting in bad faith is now to be found in art. 4 of the current Indonesian Trade Marks Act, see *ibid.* 188–9.

[36] Trade Marks Act 2001 (Indonesia) art. 69(1).

[37] Trade Marks Act 2001 (Indonesia) art. 69(2).

[38] See, e.g., Commercial Court of Central Jakarta, No. 35/Merek/2002/PN.Niaga.Jkt. Pst of 17 September 2002, '*Cesare Pacioti*', in Tatanusa, *Himpunan Putusan-putusan Pengadilan Niaga dalam Perkara Merek*, vol. 3, 283–318. For further examples, see Antons, 'Recognition', 190, fn. 29.

[39] See, e.g., Supreme Court No. 09K/N/HaKI/2002 of 7 August 2002, '*Polo*', in Tim Redaksi Tatanusa (eds.), *Himpunan Putusan-putusan Mahkamah Agung dalam Perkara HaKI*, vol. 1 (PT Tatanusa, Jakarta, 2003), 85–94. For further examples, see Antons, 'Recognition', 190, fn. 30.

exotic and famous foreign brands become symbols and synonyms for luxury and quality as well as for the wealth and success of the individual consumer using the brand. The passing off of local products as foreign occurs at the high end of the market, but also at the lower end on village markets and in rural settings. Here, the foreign flavour is often more important than an accurate depiction of the 'real thing' and imitators create this flavour in particular by copying the get-up and packaging of the famous brand. Depending on whether the get-up is part of the trade mark or not, it can be used in assessing deceptive similarity.[40] In case of slavish copying of get-up and packaging that is not part of the trade mark, Dutch colonial courts applied the tort of wrongful harm (*onrechtmaatige daad*) and this approach has occasionally been adopted in Indonesian courts.[41]

Legal action based on the Trade Marks Act is largely confined to claims for the cancellation of infringing registrations, because the courts have shown a great reluctance to grant injunctions or to award damages.[42] In cases concerning claims for cancellation of infringing registrations of well-known trade marks for dissimilar goods, the courts can no longer avoid the decision about the well-known character of the mark. In the case of Swiss watch manufacturer *Audemars Piguet*,[43] the court decided on the well-known character of the mark by using criteria listed in an explanatory memorandum of the Indonesian government accompanying the provision on well-known marks.[44] The criteria are knowledge of the public about the mark in the relevant branch of enterprise, reputation because of unceasing promotion, investment in several countries and proof of registration in several countries. The court then overcame the hurdle that the mark was used for dissimilar goods by pointing to art. 16(3) of the WTO–TRIPS Agreement with its provision that

40 See, e.g., Supreme Court No. 1596K/Pdt/1983 of 19 January 1985, '*Crocodile*', in *Yurisprudensi Indonesia*, vol. 1 (PT Ichtiar Baru-Van Hoeve, Jakarta, 1989), 1–15. For further examples, see Antons, *Intellectual Property Law*, 236, fn. 125–7.

41 District Court of Central Jakarta, 333/1972 G. of 13 March 1973, '*Fortuna*', in Direktorat Jenderal Hukum, *Keputusan-keputusan* 1971–7, 92–100.

42 Antons, 'Recognition', 193; Christoph Antons, 'Specialised Intellectual Property Courts in Southeast Asia', in Annette Kur, Stefan Luginbühl and Eskil Waage (eds.), '*. . . und sie bewegt sich doch!' – Patent Law on the Move* (Carl Heymanns Verlag, Cologne-Berlin-Munich, 2005), 287. For the historical reasons for this reluctance, see Christoph Antons, 'Patent Enforcement in Indonesia', in Reto Hilty and Kung-Chung Liu (eds.), *The Enforcement of Patents: Comparing the Asian, European and American Experiences* (Kluwer Law International, Alphen aan den Rijn, 2011, in print).

43 Commercial Court Central Jakarta No. 06/Merek/2001/PN.NIAGA.JKT.PST of 27 February 2002, in Tim Redaksi Tatanusa (eds.), *Himpunan Putusan-putusan Pengadilan Niaga dalam Perkara Merek*, vol. 1 (PT Tatanusa, Jakarta, 2002), 131–54.

44 Trade Marks Act 2001 (Indonesia), art. 6(1)(b).

art. 5bis of the Paris Convention was to be applied, *mutatis mutandis*, to dissimilar goods or services

> provided that use of that trademark in relation to those goods or services would indicate a connection between those goods or services and the owner of the registered trademark and provided that the interests of the owner of the registered trademark are likely to be damaged by such use.[45]

Finally, the court reconnected the argument derived from TRIPS again with the established jurisprudence that registrations applied for in bad faith had to be cancelled and decided that this was the case here, where the registration aimed at making a connection with a foreign well-known trade mark. This approach has since been used in a majority of cases.[46] A variation of this line of argument was developed in the case of *Morgan*, in which the Commercial Court decided that the lack of government regulation to provide the details for well-known trade marks and dissimilar goods meant that there was a legal void (*kekosongan hukum*) which had to be filled by turning to art. 16(3) TRIPS directly. It was then no longer necessary to discuss the bad faith of the owner of the competing registration.[47] In the case of 'Aqua', which in Indonesia is often used as a generic word for bottled water, the Commercial Court decided about the well-known character of the mark based on its widespread notoriety at the national level.[48] A rather straightforward case in the eyes of the courts is further where the well-known trade mark is also the trade name of the claimant, as this further enhances the argument that the competing registration was obtained in bad faith.[49]

[45] Agreement on Trade-Related Aspects of Intellectual Property Rights (TRIPS), opened for signature 15 April 1994, 1869 UNTS 299 (entered into force 1 January 1996), art. 16(3).

[46] For more recent decisions, see Commercial Court Central Jakarta, No. 20/Merek/2005/PN.Niaga.Jkt.Pst of 28 July 2005, '*Superboy*' and Commercial Court Central Jakarta No. 21/Merek/2005/PN.Niaga.Jkt.Pst of 28 July 2005, '*Superman*', in Tim Redaksi Tatanusa (eds.), *Himpunan Putusan-putusan Pengadilan Niaga dalam Perkara Merek*, vol. 11 (PT Tatanusa, Jakarta, 2008), 287–306 and 307–25; Commercial Court Central Jakarta No. 53/Merek/2005/PN.Niaga.Jkt.Pst of 12 December 2005, '*Breadstory*' and Commercial Court No. 59/Merek/2005/PN.Niaga.Jkt.Pst of 30 January 2006, '*Longchamp*', both in Tim Redaksi Tatanusa (eds.), *Himpunan Putusan-putusan dalam Perkara Merek*, vol. 13 (PT Tatanusa, Jakarta 2008) 87–113 and 163–94. For further examples of similar decisions, see Antons, 'Recognition', 189, fn. 26.

[47] Commercial Court Central Jakarta No. 09/Merek/2001/PN.Niaga.Jkt.Pst of 12 March 2002, '*Morgan*', in Tim Redaksi Tatanusa, *Himpunan Putusan-putusan*, vol. 1, 237–56. For further examples of this line of argument, see Antons, 'Recognition', 190, fn. 37.

[48] Commercial Court Central Jakarta No. 56/Merek/2002/PN.Niaga.Jkt.Pst of 4 March 2003, '*Aqua*', in Tim Redaksi Tatanusa, *Himpunan Putusan-putusan*, vol. 3, 403–30.

[49] Commercial Court Central Jakarta No. 033/Merek/2003/PN.Niaga.Jkt.Pst of 22 July 2003, '*Ferragamo*', in: Tim Redaksi Tatanusa (eds.), *Himpunan Putusan-putusan Pengadilan Niaga dalam Perkara Merek*, vol. 5 (PT Tatanusa, Jakarta, 2005), 307–24;

V. Conclusion

Owners of well-known trade marks, therefore, can finally be relatively sure that the Indonesian courts will protect their trade marks.[50] However, in spite of the existence of domestic well-known marks, cases that come before the courts concern mainly foreign companies operating in Indonesia.[51] One reason for this could be that many Indonesian trade marks are relatively strong marks with a well-established reputation, because they are for products that are rather unique to a regional market, such as *kretek* cigarettes or *jamu*. Strong marks for such products may have few competitors in the minds of Indonesian consumers, who will prefer the quality that the brand seeks to guarantee. Seen from this angle, defending well-known marks may be a problem encountered predominantly by foreigners.

However, the criteria of international fame that the courts now routinely apply in assessing the character of a mark as well known also seem to apply in a more straightforward manner to foreign brands. Typical Indonesian products such as *jamu* or *kretek* may be consumed by millions of people, but, depending on the size of the company, the owners of relevant brands may not always be able to show investment and registration in many different countries.[52] The courts have used other criteria in such cases to protect the locally well-known mark. The regulation of well-known marks is a good example of a famous feature of the Indonesian legal system that more controversial details of the law are often left open in the actual legislation to be filled in at a later stage via governmental regulations and other subsidiary type of regulation.[53] In the past, this

Commercial Court Central Jakarta No. 43/Merek/2005/PN.Niaga.Jkt.Pst and No. 44/Merek/2005/PN.Niaga.Jkt.Pst of 28 November 2005, '*Cesare Paciotti*', in Tim Redaksi Tatanusa (eds.), *Himpunan Putusan-putusan Pengadilan Niaga dalam Perkara Merek*, vol. 12 (PT Tatanusa, Jakarta, 2008), 249–72 and 273–91.

50 For a controversial decision see Christoph Antons, 'Indonesia', in Paul Goldstein and Joseph Straus (eds.), *Intellectual Property in Asia: Law, Economics, History and Politics* (Springer, Verlag, Berlin and Heidelberg, 2009), 87, 106–7.

51 Two cases on well-known trade marks involving local companies concerned trade marks discussed in the first part of this chapter, such as '*Aqua*' (above n. 27) and '*Mustika Ratu*', Commercial Court Central Jakarta No. 57/Merek/2003/PN.Niaga.Jkt.Pst of 23 October 2003, in Tim Redaksi Tatanusa (eds.), *Himpunan Putusan-putusan Pengadilan Niaga dalam Perkara Merek*, vol. 6. (PT Tatanusa, Jakarta, 2005), 293–334.

52 'PP Merek Terkenal Harus Perhatikan Pemegang Merek Lokal', *Hukumonline*, 25 September 2006, http://hukumonline.com/detail.asp?id=11897&cl=Berita.

53 Christoph Antons, 'Law Reform in the "Developmental States" of East and Southeast Asia: From the Asian Crisis to September 11, 2001 and Beyond', in Christoph Antons and Volkmar Gessner (eds.), *Globalisation and Resistance: Law Reform in Asia since the Crisis* (Hart, Portland, OR, 2007), 81, 90–2. For the difficulties of judicial review of such regulations, see Simon Butt and Tim Lindsey, 'The People's Prosperity?

approach to law-making has often allowed the Indonesian government to meet international demands for new legislation, while retaining time and flexibility to work on the fine-tuning. However, if there is no follow-up within a reasonable period of time, then cases related to the gaps in the legislation inevitably end up in the courts or in administrative agencies. Indonesia is a civil law country and its judges and administrators tend to stay close to the letter of the law and related government guidelines. For new procedural features of the current IP laws such as injunctions, a lack of guidelines for judges has meant that they are not applied.[54] For the problem area of well-known trade marks used for dissimilar goods, the courts are now routinely applying government guidelines that make it relatively easy for brands registered and promoted in many countries to pass the test. This could become problematic, if too many brands are granted this rather exceptional status, which under the 'bad faith' test almost certainly leads to the further conclusion that a competing registration is infringing. In view of this very strong position for well-known brands, a mechanical application of the criteria must be avoided and the long-promised government regulation of the matter would be helpful.

Indonesian Constitutional Interpretation, Economic Reform and Globalization', in John Gillespie and Randall Peerenboom (eds.), *Regulation in Asia: Pushing Back on Globalization* (Routledge, Abingdon, Oxon. and New York, 2009), 270, 274–5.

54 Djamal, *Hukum Acara Hak Kekayaan Intelektual (HKI) di Indonesia* (Pustaka Reka Cipta 2009), 121; A. Suryadhi, 'MA Terbitkan Peraturan Penyitaan Sepihak untuk Kasus HKI', *Arsip Berita* (online), 16 December 2009, www.dgip.go.id.

9 Names as brands

Moral rights and the 'unreasonable' pseudonym in Australia

Elizabeth Adeney

I. Introduction

In his play *Romeo and Juliet* Shakespeare has his heroine, Juliet, lament the inconvenient surname that her lover, Romeo, bears:

> 'Tis but thy name that is my enemy; . . .
> What's Montague? It is nor hand nor foot,
> Nor arm nor face, nor any other part
> Belonging to a man. O be some other name!
> What's in a name? That which we call a rose,
> By any other word would smell as sweet . . . [1]

In doing so Shakespeare emphasises the disjunction between name and substance, a person's essence or individuality transcending the mere label that the person bears. In delinking the name from the person, Shakespeare was playing on a theme that has been returned to constantly in the ensuing centuries. Not only does a name in its classificatory function[2] poorly represent individuality, but the name under which a work is published may also be a poor indicator of the work's origins. Periodically the point is made – whether tacitly or expressly – that the name of the so-called 'author' is a mere arbitrary label whose attachment to the work is neither necessary nor particularly informative.[3] What is important

All translations are by the author, unless where otherwise indicated.

1 William Shakespeare, *Romeo and Juliet in The Oxford Shakespeare: Romeo and Juliet* (Oxford University Press, Oxford and New York, 2000) act 2 scene 2, 201.

2 In this case classifying the person according to family background.

3 See, for example, comments by Jacob Grimm in 1811:

> the poetry of the people emerges from the spirit of the Whole whereas what I call art poetry emerges from the individual. For this reason the new poetry names its poets, the old poetry knows no poets to name. It is not made by one or two or three people but is a sum of the whole . . . It is unthinkable to me that there was ever such a person as Homer or a writer of the Nibelungenlied. (Excerpt from a letter to Achim von Arnim, 20 May 1811, in Reinhold Steig and Hermann Grimm (eds.), *Achim von Arnim und die ihm nahe standen* (J. G. Cotta'schen Buchhandlung, first published 1904, republished by Herbert Lang, Bern, 1970), vol. 3, 116.)

is the expression contained in the work itself and perhaps also its representation of cultural thought. At other times and in other contexts, however, the attachment of a name to a work seems essential in the interests of maintaining human rights and ensuring the authenticity of the material.[4] The two conflicting impulses seen here – to discard or devalue the name or to require and value its presence – seem to meet and be partially reconciled in the allowance that is made for authors to publish their work either anonymously or under a pseudonym. These days the protection of pseudonymity is typically, though not exclusively, contained in the moral rights provisions of our legislation. The protection of anonymity may or may not be a part of moral rights.

This chapter examines how the moral rights system in Australia protects but also limits the use of assumed names or pseudonyms by authors and performers. Such limitation on the freedom to choose a designation is imposed through the requirement that the assumed name be 'reasonable',[5] yet no guidance is given by the legislature on what 'reasonable' is intended to mean. The chapter considers what might be a reasonable choice of name by an author or performer, a name to which the reputation of the person concerned can legitimately attach. It further suggests what types of name should never be classified as reasonable.

II. The moral rights system in Australia

Moral rights are the product of an individualist and human-rights-based movement in artistic thought. They are, in a nutshell, the non-property-based, non-economic rights of the author or performer. They are enjoyed in relation to the works (namely literary, dramatic, musical, and artistic works and films) or to the performance of the rights-holder. They are distinct from copyright, which is a statutorily created form of property and economic in nature, despite its capacity on occasion to protect the author and the author–work relationship in less commercial ways. They are also distinct from the statutory, economic rights of the performer.

During the Middle Ages the great Passion Plays and Corpus Christi cycles were practically never associated with particular named authors. More recently, Michel Foucault has written of the essential irrelevance of authorial naming: 'What is an Author?' (Josué V. Harari trans.) in Paul Rabinow (ed.), *The Foucault Reader: An Introduction to Foucault's Thought* (Parthenon Books, New York, 1984), 101.

[4] This has been particularly the case since the early nineteenth century and the rise of the notion of authors' natural rights over their work. For the history of moral rights, see generally, Elizabeth Adeney, *The Moral Rights of Authors and Performers* (Oxford University Press, Oxford and New York, 2006), chs. 1 and 2; and, for more recent thinking, Sam Ricketson, 'The Case for Moral Rights' (1995) 25 *Intellectual Property Forum* 37, 40–1.

[5] Copyright Act 1968 (Cth) ss. 195(2)(b), 195ABC(2)(b) ('Copyright Act').

The moral rights system in Australia was introduced in its current form in 2000 for the benefit of authors of literary, dramatic, musical or artistic works and films.[6] In 2007 it was extended to protect the interests of performers in live or recorded performances.[7] It is designed with the personal interests of the author and performer at heart. It is also designed to bring Australia into compliance with the country's obligations under the Berne Convention and the WIPO Performances and Phonograms Treaty (WPPT).[8]

Moral rights and reputation – the legislative scheme

In Australia the author and the performer are protected through three kinds of provision, one of whose practical effects is the maintenance and enhancement of reputation. Indeed this is probably the most significant of their functions, though certainly not the only one.

One set of provisions – embodying the right of attribution of authorship or performership – ensures that the author's or performer's name will always be mentioned when the work or performance is used in a way that would make it available to the public.[9] In other words, the so-called 'paternity' of the work is recognised; the recipient or audience should never be unaware of who has created the work or acted in the performance. This in turn means that, if the material is considered to be good, the author or performer will either have her existing reputation enhanced or she will start to accrue a desirable reputation. She will be judged by others through the material she has produced. Once the reputation is gained, that reputation will then flow through to and influence the public reception of later material that she produces. The work's value as perceived by the public is transferred to the author, and the author's perceived qualities are then anticipated in future works.

It is within this right of attribution of authorship or performership that the protection of the pseudonym is situated. The author or performer is free, quite simply, to assume a name and therefore to attach the reputational advantage accruing from the work to that name. The second set of

[6] Copyright Amendment (Moral Rights) Act 2000 (Cth), amending Copyright Act 1968 (Cth).

[7] Copyright Legislation Amendment Act 2004 (Cth), amending Copyright Act 1968 (Cth) Part IX.

[8] Revised Explanatory Memorandum, Copyright Amendment (Moral Rights) Bill 1999 (Cth) Outline (taking account of amendments made by the House of Representatives to the Bill as introduced); Explanatory Memorandum, US Free Trade Agreement Implementation Bill 2004 (Cth), 73 [306].

[9] Copyright Act ss. 193 and 194; ss. 195ABA and 195ABB.

provisions – containing the right against false attribution of authorship or performership – is complementary to the first and extends the 'paternity' idea.[10] The provisions are drafted to produce two effects. First, they help to ensure that the author's or performer's work will not be presented to the public as the work of another person.[11] So they guard against another person wrongfully appropriating the advantage of the creator's reputation through plagiarism. Second, they ensure that the author's or performer's work, if altered by a third party without the creator's authorisation, will not be presented to the public as the unaltered work of the author or performer.[12] In other words the author or performer will not have to take public responsibility for amendments to the work/performance that she did not make, and that may have been badly made. The author's or performer's reputation will not be 'diluted' by association with substandard alterations.

The third set of provisions, containing the right of integrity of authorship or performership, focuses on: (1) certain types of treatment of the work or performance; and (2) the negative effect on the author or performer resulting from that treatment. The author or performer may take legal action if the work or performance is 'derogatorily treated'.[13] Derogatory treatment occurs if the work or performance is 'materially distorted, mutilated or materially altered' (and, in the case of an artistic work, if it is destroyed) in a way that is prejudicial to the reputation of the performer or the 'honour or reputation' of the author.[14] The right is further infringed if the work or performance is reproduced or disseminated in forms that show the derogatory treatment.[15] Again the maintenance of authorial or performer reputation is safeguarded. The value of this reputation then flows through to and maintains the value of the person's future products.

The trade mark function of a name

Within this moral rights scheme, the name and the work of the author or performer are protected because they embody the personality and spirit of the individual creator. This protection, however, has the inevitable

[10] Copyright Act ss. 195AC, 195AD, 195AE, 195AF, 195AG and 195AH; ss. 195AHA, 195AHB and 195AHC.
[11] Copyright Act ss. 195AD–195AF and 195AHB.
[12] Copyright Act ss. 195AG–195AH and 195AHC.
[13] Copyright Act ss. 195AI and 195ALA.
[14] Copyright Act ss. 195AJ–195AL and 195ALB.
[15] Copyright Act ss. 195AQ and 195AXC.

effect of maintaining both commercial reputation (through safeguarding the integrity of the work) and the authorial or performer name (through safeguarding the badge of origin). The latter function can be, and frequently is, described as a trade mark function.[16] Because the author or performer is free to appear to the public in the form of a verbal avatar or alter ego (the assumed identity), this alter ego inevitably represents the reputation and goodwill that accrue from the public exposure and that are protected by the integrity right and the right against false attribution. The author who chooses a name thus engages, for whatever purpose, in a form of self-branding.

The existence of this trade mark function of an authorial or performer name can, in turn, suggest to us ways in which some of the provisions governing the rights of attribution can or should be interpreted.

III. Names, pseudo-names and other identifiers – a historical perspective

While most authors will choose to publish under their inherited or given name, Western culture has long recognised the entitlement of the author (or indeed any other person) to either choose a form of designation or to forgo any particular form of designation for certain purposes. In other words, it has recognised the entitlement to use a designation both positively as an indication of origin and negatively as a mask behind which identity can be concealed.

Some accepted uses of pseudonymity and anonymity

When anonymity and pseudonymity were judicially discussed in the United States in a 1995 case the following general statements were made. They looked back in time and identified the use by authors of a masking device as an aspect of the freedom of speech which had long been protected by the Constitution:

> Great works of literature have frequently been produced by authors writing under assumed names. Despite readers' curiosity and the public's interest in identifying the creator of a work of art, an author generally is free to decide whether or not to disclose his or her true identity. The decision in favor of anonymity may

[16] See Laura Heymann, 'Authorship and Trademark Law' in Peter K. Yu, *Intellectual Property and Information Wealth* (Praeger, Westport, CT, 2007), vol. 3, 191, and her distinction between the author's name and the 'authornym'. Also Jane C. Ginsburg, 'The Author's Name as a Trademark: A Perverse Perspective on the Moral Right of "Paternity"?' (2005–6), 23 *Cardozo Arts and Entertainment Law Journal* 379.

be motivated by fear of economic or official retaliation, by concern about social ostracism, or merely by a desire to preserve as much of one's privacy as possible. Whatever the motivation may be, at least in the field of literary endeavor, the interest in having anonymous works enter the marketplace of ideas unquestionably outweighs any public interest in requiring disclosure as a condition of entry. Accordingly, an author's decision to remain anonymous, like other decisions concerning omissions or additions to the content of a publication, is an aspect of the freedom of speech protected by the First Amendment.[17]

The assumed or masked identity allows an author to challenge religious or political norms at less risk to personal safety than might otherwise be the case. The masking function of the designation also allows experimentation and risk taking, permitting authors to take a step beyond what they can be sure is currently acceptable to their public. Without risking their current reputation, they can build the foundations of a new one.

It was on the apparently unquestioned entitlement to manipulate his public identity that Sir Walter Scott relied in the nineteenth century when, for many years, he declined to publish his novels under his given and inherited names, preferring instead to identify himself by reference to his previous publications, for example as the 'Author of Waverley'. His purposes were not merely self-protective.

In his preface to a late edition of the Waverley Novels Scott gave a number of reasons for his decision. Initially he had feared embarrassment should the novels fail. Later, his place in society assured, he had no particular need of fame, or so he said. The use of another identity ensured that he did not seem to monopolise the public attention. Scott's anonymity (or perhaps rather pseudonymity) further created for him a wraith-like freedom of movement, with the effect that

I could appear, or retreat from the stage at pleasure, without attracting any personal notice or attention, other than what might be founded on suspicion only. In my own person also, as a successful author in another department of literature, I might have been charged with too frequent intrusions on the public patience; but the Author of Waverley was in this respect as impassable to the critic as the Ghost of Hamlet to the partisan of Marcellus.[18]

Moreover the mystery surrounding his identity exercised a useful influence on the buying public:

[17] Opinion of the majority in *McIntyre, Executor of Estate of McIntyre, Deceased* v. *Ohio Elections Commission* 514 US 334, 336 (1995).

[18] Walter Scott, *Waverley Novels* (Adam and Charles Black, Edinburgh, 1862), vol. 1, General Preface, xi.

Perhaps the curiosity of the public, irritated by the existence of a secret, and kept afloat by the discussions which took place on the subject from time to time, went a good way to maintain an unabated interest in these frequent publications. There was a mystery concerning the author, which each new novel was expected to assist in unravelling, although it might in other respects rank lower than its predecessors.[19]

Scott's analysis of the public reaction indicates that he had discovered, even in quasi-anonymity, a relatively sophisticated marketing function. Association of the unnamed person with the previous works acted as a fully adequate identifier, tapping in admirably to the reputation built up through publication of the previous novels. Even without naming himself in any way, Scott was, in trade marks terms, using the reference to *Waverley* to denote a certain quality of writing, to symbolise goodwill, to motivate consumers to buy and to differentiate his products from those of other authors. He was also teasing and tantalising the public. The public desire to identify the works' provenance being what it was, the incompletely attributed works remained before the public eye and accretions to the œuvre functioned as clues in a literary paper chase. They were entertainments even before the first page had been turned.

The treatment of the pseudonym in copyright law

The US court in *McIntyre* was not wrong in pointing to the longstanding tolerance in legal circles of anonymity and pseudonymity. Copyright jurists have repeatedly stated that a fictionalised or incompletely revelatory authorial designation has equal status and value with the 'true' given or inherited or legally acquired names of the author. Not only is the assumed identifier seen in some contexts as protecting freedom of speech, but it has long been recognised as performing the same function in the marketplace as the 'real' name does. (Indeed, judging by Scott's experience, it may have a considerably enhanced function.) Certainly there is no basis for according it an inferior claim to protection. The point appears to have been particularly thoroughly canvassed in Italy and was well made in the 1923 case of *Mariani* v. *Bletti Publishing House*, decided in the Court of Milan. There it was stated that:

The pseudonym and the inherited name both serve to identify the intellectual activity of individuals; they therefore have the same function and consequently the same juridical value . . . [I]n this domain protection is not accorded to the inherited name as such, but only by reference to the fact that the person who

[19] *Ibid.*

bears it uses it to identify his intellectual activity... [T]he name is intended to characterise by an external sign the intellectual activity of the individual.[20]

The designation is an external identifier of the source of intellectual activity and to be respected as such.

This perception of equality was already well established in 1923. Rosmini noted in 1888 that the commentator, Amar, had maintained that 'principles of justice and equity compel equal protection for known and unknown authors'.[21] Also in 1888, the conference of the Association littéraire et artistique internationale (ALAI) at Venice proposed that works signed with a pseudonym should be protected in the same manner as if they had been signed with the real name of the author.[22] This proposal was then put into effect in the Berne Convention for the Protection of Literary and Artistic Works. The provision makes arrangements for the legal protection of anonymous or pseudonymous works whose author is known, works which are published but whose author is unknown and works which are unpublished and whose author is unknown.[23]

Pseudonymity and moral rights

The principles in favour of allowing authorial choice of a designation existed and had made themselves felt independently of and even in the absence of moral rights protection. Witness the acceptance of this choice in the US, which has never had fully-fledged moral rights provisions.[24] Nevertheless, the introduction of moral rights to the majority of countries around the world has provided a convenient vehicle for the perpetuation, codification and extension of these principles. Thus, it is not unusual in moral rights legislation, including the legislation of the Asia Pacific region, to find a clause that allows the author a freedom to choose the form of designation required and hence to determine the tag to which the reputation derived from the work will attach.

In Japan, for example, Article 19(1) of the Copyright Law states:

[20] See Note, 'Italie' [Italy] (1926) *Le Droit d'Auteur* 83, 83.

[21] Henri Rosmini, 'Droits des auteurs sur leur pseudonyme' (1888) *Le Droit d'Auteur* 16, 17.

[22] Actes de la Conférence réunie à Paris du 15 avril au 4 mai 1896 (Bureau International de l'Union, Berne, 1897) 78.

[23] *Berne Convention for the Protection of Literary and Artistic Works*, opened for signature 9 September 1886, as last revised at Paris on 24 July 1971, 1161 UNTS 3 (entered into force 10 October 1974), art. 15 (previously art. 11).

[24] Copyright Act of 1976, 17 USC § 302. Currently in the US the only statutory rights that could be described as 'moral rights' relate to narrowly defined 'works of visual art'.

The author shall have the right to determine whether his true name or pseudonym should be indicated or not, as the name of the author, on the original of his work or when his work is offered to or made available to the public.[25]

The copyright Acts of Korea, New Zealand and Canada also provide expressly for the use of pseudonyms.[26]

In Australia the author's right to choose the desired designation is given in s. 195 of the Copyright Act 1968 (Cth); the performer's right is given in s. 195ABC(2)(b).

Negative aspects of the right to a pseudonym, and a legislative solution

The use of a pseudonym or other chosen designation has, however, its negative aspects. For one thing, the pseudonym chosen may be intrinsically objectionable in its social context – for its obscenity, for example, or its tendency to incite hatred. Furthermore, although the majority of pseudonyms are necessarily and intentionally deceptive, there may be deceptions that are unacceptable in the circumstances of the case. It is clear, moreover, that the half-imagined,[27] half-real safety of the mask tempts some authors to push at the boundaries of legality, defaming those who are normally protected by defamation law, publishing material which is injurious to persons, to social groups, to corporations or states.[28]

No doubt in order to guard against problems of these kinds, and perhaps also in a recognition that, if the name is to operate as a trade mark, then it should be subject to limitations, just as trade marks are, the

[25] Copyright Law of Japan (Japan) Act No. 48 of 1970 [Yukifusa Oyama *et al.*, trans., *English Translation of Copyright Law of Japan* (2010) www.cric.or.jp/cric_e/clj/clj.html].

[26] Copyright Act (Korea), Act No. 3916 of 1989, art. 12(1) [UNESCO Collection of National Copyright Laws translation, *English Translation of Copyright Act of Korea* (2003) http://portal.unesco.org/culture/en/files/37872/12221640381KOREAN_COPYRIGHT_ACT.pdf/KOREAN_COPYRIGHT_ACT.pdf]; Copyright Act 1994 (NZ) s. 95(2); Copyright Act, RSC 1985, c C-42, s. 14.1(1).

[27] Even to the extent that they are 'reasonable' and protected, anonymity and pseudonymity are always fragile protections – only as good as the secrecy of those who are in the author's confidence. Like the common or natural law principles which allowed authors to rename themselves in the past, this is not a regime which guarantees the maintenance or effectiveness of the mask.

[28] See for example the case of an Australian defamer who posted online under the name 'Witch'. He was sued after a court ordered disclosure of his identity: Tony Wright, 'Libel "witch" hunt: Cyber detective nabs south-west man for defamation', *The Standard* (online), 25 February 2010, www.standard.net.au/news/local/news/general/libel-witch-hunt-cyber-detective-nabs-southwest-man-for-defamation/1760543.aspx.

Australian legislators have given the author the right to determine the designation only to the extent that it is 'reasonable in the circumstances':

Copyright Act 1968 (Cth), s. 195:
(1) Subject to subsection (2), the author of a work may be identified by any reasonable form of identification.
(2) If:
(a) the author of a work has made known, either generally or to a person who is required under this Part to identify the author, that the author wishes to be identified in a particular way; and
(b) the identification of the author in that way is reasonable in the circumstances;
the identification is to be made in that way.

A counterpart provision establishes the same principles for performers.[29]

The reasonableness concept that is of interest to us here is contained in sub-section (2)(b) above. Unlike the reference in sub-section (1)[30] this requirement of reasonableness, which appears to be unique to Australia, indicates that authorial desires should be acceded to only if they are of a certain acceptable standard.

The existence of the reasonableness criterion has the potential to impose a significant limit on the range of designations supported by the Act. The unreasonableness of a pseudonym would give the publisher or gallery or production company, for example, a reason to refuse to use the name on the work or performance. It would further block an authorial or performer action against those who wished to use the author's or performer's real name in relation to the work or performance.

But the question remains what 'reasonable' means when applied to a person's choice of a pseudonym.

Reasonable in the circumstances?

The term 'reasonable' must be interpreted in its context in the Copyright Act and taking into account the purposes of the Act.[31] The immediate context of the term is the protection of moral rights, and, through moral rights, of authorial or performer reputation, among other things. More broadly it is a context in which the interests of: (1) authors/performers; (2) copyright owners or other commercial interests; and (3) consumers of

29 Copyright Act s. 195ABC(2).
30 Which appears to impose an obligation of the person using the work to ensure that the designation is reasonable – presumably reasonable for effective attribution purposes. The focus is not here on the reasonableness of the form of attribution chosen by the author.
31 Acts Interpretation Act 1901 (Cth) 15AA and 15AB(1)(b)(ii).

the creative or created material are balanced for the purpose of ensuring that none of the trio of interests unacceptably dominates the others.

The question of 'reasonableness in the circumstances' has not been judicially discussed in relation to authorial designations in Australia and it is not yet clear what range of considerations it would embrace. In this sense 'reasonableness' in the choice of a designation is treated very differently from the defence of 'reasonableness' in the context of moral rights infringement actions, where extensive lists of factors to be considered are offered to the decision maker.[32] Nevertheless, in both cases the reasonableness of a given act is for the tribunal to decide in an exercise of its discretion.

Touchstone values In determining what a reasonable pseudonym might be it is necessary to consider again the accepted purposes for which pseudonyms may be used. It would seem relatively uncontentious to say that we as a society want the pseudonym to protect the vulnerable author against persecution. The pseudonym ought to be able to protect the author against oppression from government, religious bodies, or from other groups or individuals. Such protection is in turn likely to encourage the production of works and performances, and to enable a certain amount of literary, artistic or even musical risk taking. On the other hand the pseudonym should not itself come to serve the forces of oppression or to facilitate seriously antisocial behaviour.

We accept that, if a pseudonym is to be protective, it must also, of necessity, be either positively deceptive or at least no more than semi-informative. On the other hand we presumably do not want the pseudonym to be part of the mechanism by which forgeries, misrepresentations and calumnies are passed off on the public.

Apart from its protective effect, we are quite happy to accept the pseudonym as a marketing tool and as a means by which a playful author may tease and tantalise the public. We are always willing to be entertained by a minor mystery. We are not even necessarily averse to the odd literary or artistic hoax as long as it results in no more harm than a pricking of certain bubbles of pretension.[33]

These values need, however, to be translated into some legal form.

[32] For example, Copyright Act s. 195AR.

[33] Few Australians would seriously wish that 'Ern Malley' had never existed to bamboozle a gullible public. For a short account of the Ern Malley hoax, see Samela Harris and Sheryl-Lee Kerr, *Angry Penguins* (2003) Ern Malley: Official Website www.ernmalley.com/angry_penguins.html.

The legal tools at hand If called on to do so, it is probable that a tribunal would look to trade marks law for initial guidance on how to deal with problematic authorial or performer designations. The overlap between the functions of a pseudonym and a trade mark would suggest as much. As a first step, the tribunal might well filter out those designations which could be described as 'scandalous', just as the Australian Trade Marks Act expressly filters out such marks.[34] Those signs which are, for example, offensive to ordinary persons, and even a particular class of person, may be denied protection under the Act,[35] though the playfully risqué trade mark is accepted readily enough by the trade mark Examiners.[36] The *Trade Marks Office Manual* indicates that 'Trade marks incorporating words and images which appear to condone and/or promote violence, racism or sociopathic behaviours fall within the ambit of "scandalous" marks.'[37] One might expect a similar logic to apply under the Copyright Act.

In addition to considering the position under Australian law, a tribunal might further look to United States law and its mode of distinguishing between acceptable and unacceptable trade marks. It might take note of s. 2(a) of the Lanham Act:

> No trademark . . . shall be refused registration on the principal register on account of its nature unless it – (a) Consists of or comprises immoral, deceptive, or scandalous matter which may disparage or falsely suggest a connection with persons, living or dead, institutions, beliefs, or national symbols, or bring them into contempt or disrepute.[38]

This formulation is significantly broader than the bare word 'scandalous' used in the Australian Act.

Second, those names whose use would be 'contrary to law' by breaching Australian legislation (or common law) – for example through being overtly misleading and deceptive in falsely indicating an attachment of the work or performance to another author or performer – would, almost of necessity, be as unreasonable under the Copyright Act as they are unregistrable under the Trade Marks Act.[39] What is unreasonable might therefore be interpreted as that which allows a competing authorial or performer reputation to be unnecessarily damaged and that which allows

[34] Trade Marks Act 1995 (Cth) s. 42(a) (Trade Marks Act).

[35] IP Australia, *Trade Marks Office Manual of Practice and Procedure*, Pt 30, para. 2.3 (10 March 2011) IP Australia, www.ipaustralia.gov.au/pdfs/trademarkmanual/trade_marks_examiners_manual.htm.

[36] This can be ascertained by a simple search for the 'f' word on the Australian (or US) online register.

[37] IP Australia, *Trade Mark Office Manual*, para. 2.9.

[38] Lanham (Trademark) Act of 1946, 15 USC.

[39] Trade Marks Act s. 42(b).

another person's legitimate commercial interests in the exploitation of their creation to be impinged upon. The rights of a given author or performer are naturally limited by the rights of other authors and performers. Where the motive for choosing a particular name appears to be a desire to appropriate another person's reputation, and particularly where this is done for commercial motives, it is hard to see how the use of the pseudonym could be justified.

Third, given the broader context of the provision – namely its position in a Copyright Act – it might also be thought that any pseudonym which had a negative impact on the saleability of a work or performance so as to prejudice the interests of a producer or copyright owner might also be considered unreasonable. The selection of a name capable of sabotaging the commercial operation would tend to upset the equilibrium which exists between the interests of the creator and those of the the exploiter of the material. And, after all, it is in no sense *necessary* that a particular pseudonym be chosen out of the infinite number available, so no injustice is done in the denial of the name. While moral rights are of their nature opposable against the copyright owner, the extent to which they may be used in this way is clearly intended by the legislators to be subject to limits. This is why defences to moral rights infringement are elsewhere built into the system.[40]

Fourth, certain words that have a special and reserved significance in government, religious, political or economic circles would hardly be reasonable pseudonyms, just as some of them are expressly listed as unregistrable trade marks.[41]

The deception dilemma The most difficult question is whether the principle enshrined in s. 43 of the Australian Trade Marks Act might be equally applicable in the establishment of reasonable and unreasonable author/performer designations:

> An application for the registration of a trade mark in respect of particular goods or services must be rejected if, because of some connotation that the trade mark or a sign contained in the trade mark has, the use of the trade mark in relation to those goods or services would be likely to deceive or cause confusion.

As noted above, pseudonyms are of necessity deceptive and confusing in some way. Yet intellectual property systems generally show a deep aversion to names or marks which deceive or cause confusion. Not only is this evidenced in s. 43 of the Trade Marks Act, but it is also indicated,

[40] Copyright Act ss. 195AR, 195AS, 195AT, and ss. 195AXD and 195AXE.
[41] Trade Marks Act s. 39.

in the moral rights context, by the fact that no reasonableness defence is allowed to a person who misattributes the author's work to a person who did not author it or who misattributes a performer's performance to another person.

We therefore need to examine further what deceptions might be regarded as acceptable and what might be regarded as unacceptable. This is an area in which the tribunals will have little material to assist them.

Truths and untruths in naming

Where something purporting to be the name of a human being identifies a product's origin a conflict develops between the truth-telling and the marketing functions of the name.

Inherited surnames and also patronymics, by their nature, are instruments of familial and cultural coalescence. In their primary function, they identify the individual with a parent, a family, an occupation or a cultural group as the case may be. Given or first names, on the other hand, are a much more malleable quantity than inherited names or patronymics. Their choice is often dictated by no more than parental taste, though often within cultural confines. Even at their most arbitrary, however, they too carry more or less subtle indications about society and background.

No legal rules require that any of these personal names be retained throughout life, and some societal rules allow or require them to be changed or exchanged.[42] But, by and large, names borne by persons are expected by the public at large to indicate some truth about cultural or civic identity. Truth telling, it might be thought, is a more fundamental function of language than artifice. This expectation that truth will be told is paired with a persistent desire to *know* the truth, illusory as the 'truth' may be in the artistic field. This was what Walter Scott had observed among his readership – the assumption that, once the name of the author is known, some vital truth about the work has been revealed. The tendency has also been commented upon by Foucault in his 'What Is an Author?'[43]

The expectation that a name will deliver a truth about provenance sits uncomfortably with the expectation predominant in commercial practice

[42] A woman's maiden name is commonly exchanged for the husband's surname in Western cultures. Names can also be formally altered by deed poll.

[43] Foucault, *Foucault Reader*, 101–20. As a construct, according to Foucault, a name must necessarily be to some degree misleading and false. Any naming of the author is also a type of masking of the true and diffuse nature of the authorship. The name is in a sense always a pseudonym.

that the name to be associated with a product (as an emblem of both origin and reputation) will be chosen primarily to enhance the marketability of the product. It should speak persuasively about the product's desirability, and attract consumer attention. The expectation also sits uncomfortably with the fact that, for centuries, pseudonyms have been chosen with the aim of addressing consumer expectations, prejudices and desires in order to achieve the optimal distribution of the product and to protect the author. This was particularly evident in nineteenth-century England when a number of leading female novelists, fearing that they would not achieve success as women, chose to publish under male pseudonyms.[44] It was also evident in the twentieth century with the choosing of more alluring screen names for the actors of Hollywood.[45] Even today the desirability of the product in a particular segment of the market may be most easily established through its association with a particular gender or age of person, or with an interesting or topical social or ethnic group.

The question of the acceptability and hence reasonableness of a given pseudonym becomes most vexed when the assumed identity is that of an embattled or insufficiently understood minority. (Little question is raised, apparently, when a member of the minority wishes to assume the identity of the majority; the aspiration to coalesce with the dominant group seems to be taken for granted and generally approved.)[46] In most if not all populations the potential exists for the exchange of inherited identity with chosen identity to cause offence, and this appears to be recognised in s. 2(a) of the US Lanham Act when it refers to marks 'which may . . . falsely suggest a connection with persons, living or dead' or 'beliefs'. It is argued here that these factors may have an impact on the reasonableness of the name.

The problematic pseudonym – Australian cases in point In Australia one of the most notable recent cases of the problematic pseudonym was that of Helen Darville, the daughter of English immigrants to Australia. In 1994 she achieved first fame and then notoriety when she published a novel, *The Hand that Signed the Paper*,[47] telling a story of Ukrainian experiences during the Second World War. The pseudonym under which

[44] For example the Brontë sisters published under the gender-free names Currer, Ellis and Acton Bell; Mary Ann Evans later published under the name George Eliot.

[45] For example, Michael Caine for Maurice Joseph Micklewhite; Diana Dors for Mavis Fluck; James Garner for James Scott Bumgarner; and Judy Garland for Frances Ethel Gumm.

[46] Witness the names typically assumed in the past by aspiring filmstars: Kirk Douglas for Issur Danielovitch Demsky; Doris Day for Doris Mary Ann von Kappelhoff, Charles Bronson for Charles Buchinsky.

[47] Allen & Unwin, St Leonards, NSW, 1994.

she chose to publish the book (and which the publishers apparently took to be her 'real' name) was 'Helen Demidenko', this alter ego being the supposed child of an illiterate Ukrainian immigrant. Darville went further, and appeared and was interviewed in public wearing Ukrainian national costume – dressing her avatar, as it were – and embracing the identity which accompanied the pseudonym. With the book she won the Australian/Vogel prize for young authors, the Miles Franklin Award and the Gold Medal of the Australian Literary Society. This critical success appears to have been partly due to the perceived 'authenticity' of the story which Darville related. The subsequent notoriety of the work was generated partly by the discovery of its author's invented identity and partly by allegations of historical inaccuracy with an anti-Semitic slant.

When the veil was lifted the work was branded as a hoax, a label typically applied to works which cause acute embarrassment in literary or artistic circles due to their having initially been taken at face value and rated highly. In Australia commentators made comparisons with the earlier 'Ern Malley' hoax, where a fictional author was attached to poems apparently written with the intention of misleading, mocking and embarrassing a gullible literary establishment.[48] It was not suggested, however, that mockery was the primary purpose of 'Demidenko'.

The assumption of Ukrainian identity was something of a curiosity in Australia. More frequent are the cases of white Australians taking on the personae of indigenous Australians. Between 1994 and her death in 2000, Elizabeth Durack, a well-known artist of European descent and member of a prominent pioneering family, painted and exhibited under the name of 'Eddie Burrup', a fictitious Aboriginal painter.[49] When the true origin of the 'Burrup' paintings was revealed the substitution caused anger in the indigenous community and was decried by the art galleries which had shown the work as Aboriginal art.[50]

The following, by way of explanation, is to be found today at the Elizabeth Durack website:

> Eddie Burrup is a *maban*, a Man of High Degree, a stockman, a painter, a story teller and performer. He is the brush and pen name of the artist Elizabeth Durack

[48] See above, n. 33.

[49] Interestingly, Durack did not retreat so far into the character of Eddie Burrup that she abjured all attribution of the works to herself. According to an entry in Wikipedia 'Elizabeth Durack [asserted] the moral right to be identified as the substituent of Eddie Burrup' (*Eddie Burrup* (accessed 26 December 2010) Wikipedia http://en.wikipedia.org/wiki/Eddie_Burrup).

[50] Susan McCulloch, 'Blacks blast Durack for her art of illusion', *Weekend Australian* (Sydney), 8 March 1997, 1.

and an integral part of the prodigious body of work she produced over a period of some 70 years.

First and foremost an ingenious work of art, the invention of Eddie Burrup initially was a device for Elizabeth Durack to obtain independent assessment of a breakthrough in work and ideas that had been gestating for years.

The persona himself appeared quite unexpectedly . . . Soon after that Eddie Burrup asserted his individuality and before long had taken possession of his creator . . .

Detractors and gatekeepers have disparaged the Eddie Burrup phenomenon. They describe it variously as a fiction, a hoax, a fraud, even a crime. They denounce Elizabeth Durack and contend she has appropriated Aboriginal culture . . .

From an historical viewpoint, the phenomenon of Eddie Burrup belongs to several well-documented traditions – to that of:

1. creative females resorting to the use of a male pseudonym in order to communicate original work and ideas
2. a writer or actor creating, or recreating, a character and in the process becoming that character
3. artists employing allegory or satire in order to comment on the follies and mistakes of those with power and influence.[51]

The traditions mentioned here are real enough, though these days the assumption of a female rather than male identity is sometimes thought to be the more productive move. For example, in a partial reversal of the Durack situation, it was revealed in 1997 that the prize-winning 'aboriginal' writer 'Wanda Koolmatrie' was in fact a non-Aboriginal man, Leon Carmen,[52] who claimed to have taken the name and identity of an Aboriginal woman in order to have his work published,[53] women and Aborigines being impliedly favoured in this regard.

The question, however, is whether our legislators have intended these various uses of a name, including that embraced by Durack, to be 'reasonable in the circumstances', so that the name can be assumed by the author as of right and will achieve the protection of moral rights. Also, regardless of what the legislators intended, is it desirable from a policy

[51] *Eddie Burrup* (2011) Elizabeth Durack (1915–2000), Australian Artist, An Archival Website www.elizabethdurack.com/burrup_1_intro.php.

[52] In 1996 the author won the Nita May Dobbie Award, intended for a first published work by a female writer.

[53] These cases were discussed widely in the media in early 1997. See, for example, Fiona Harari, 'The word's out: it's an epidemic', *The Australian* (Sydney), 14 March 1997, 1–2 and Adrian Bradley, 'Duped Publisher Calls in Lawyers', *Weekend Australian* (Sydney), 15–16 March 1997, 3.

point of view for such names to receive legal protection under our moral rights provisions?

The unimportance and importance of authenticity Cases of the type described here are generally deplored, either by a public that feels fooled by the deception (especially if it has extended some sort of special interest or sympathy to the author on account of the assumed identity) or by the cultural group whose name has been taken by a non-member of it. The cultural group may feel that the reputation of its genuine products has been diluted or contaminated by association with the pseudonymous works. But should all such designations be categorised as unreasonable due to the consumer or the group concern?

One way of thinking about the issue is to ask what the 'product' is, the reputation of which the name will embody. Does it in any way include the authorial identity and, if it does, for what period of time does it do so?

Is the product the novel, for example, or is it a novel by a certain person from a certain background – a second-generation Japanese or Ukrainian or Indian immigrant? Is it a novel by a man as opposed to a woman, or by a 20-year-old rather than an octogenarian? The answer of the arts world should surely be that the product – and the centre of interest – is the work itself, regardless of who wrote it. It would surely make no difference, artistically speaking, if *War and Peace* had been written by a Russian woman, if the *Mona Lisa* had been painted by an Albanian or if Beethoven had turned out to be Chinese.[54]

Yet perhaps such a response is simplistic in cases where the work is to be seen as embodying a historical or social or cultural truth – where the pre-eminent or even merely incidental purpose of the work is the communication of truths by its author. This is less likely to be the case, generally speaking, with musical works and even visually artistic works, where the dominant impact of the work is of human feeling translated into perceptible form. It will, however, be true when part of the importance of the art or the music lies in its being representative of a particular tradition. It is even more likely to be the case, at least for a time, with literary works.

In our societies the preponderant use of words is to relate facts. Most novels alternate fiction and fact, with the element of fact more important in some than in others. Many are designed to relate experiences which the

[54] In relation to the Burrup incident, one NSW gallery director stated, 'We're not judging the artist, we're judging the work of art. So really what name is appended to it I don't think matters a great deal' (McCulloch, 'Blacks blast Durack', 1).

authors have had or of which they are intimately aware. For a time, the interest and social value of the work depends to a substantial degree on its authenticity. This will be so until the events related become so historically remote to their readership that it is of little significance whether they are true or not. At this point, stripped of several layers of meaning, the story is reduced to a pure expression of human thought or emotion. Nobody is particularly concerned these days whether Shakespeare has given us an authentic account of the life of Macbeth or of the character of Richard III. On the other hand, if an Anglo-Saxon Australian were to write a purportedly first-hand account of the life of an Afghan refugee, most of the interest which the work might have to its readership would evaporate as soon as the identity of the author was known.

To be sure, the reading public is tolerant. Ostensibly truthful autobiographies, for example, are notorious for sliding into fiction without creating very much of a stir. But in areas where a real value is placed on authenticity, where the public expects more of a story than an exercise in storytelling, and where the promise of a particular insight is made but the insight then turns out to be illusory, it might be thought that there is a sufficient element of deception conveyed by the assumed name for it to be called 'unreasonable'.[55]

The trade mark function as a formal solution to the deception dilemma?

Perhaps one way of resolving the issue in a principled way is to return to the function that the name on the work performs and, in doing so, to borrow from trade marks law. The function of a trade mark is to distinguish the goods or services of one person from those of another. To use a name on goods or services as a trade mark is to use that name in order to connect the goods or services with the source.[56]

In the context of moral rights it might be said that any name which was being used genuinely to connect the work with the author is reasonable (as long as the name is not scandalous, contrary to law or reserved for other purposes). The deception necessarily involved in the masking function of the name is within acceptable bounds. The name John Le Carré (for John Cornwell) is a case in point. Even if the true name of the author were not known, the name would be unproblematic. The same could be said of the name 'Ern Malley'.[57] While it was used to perpetrate a literary hoax it is not in itself unreasonable.

[55] This has been recognised elsewhere. See Heymann, 'Authorship', 202.

[56] Trade Marks Act s. 17.

[57] See Harris and Kerr, *Angry Penguins*.

The problematic names, on the other hand, are those that purport to connect the work with persons other than the author. At the less problematic end of the spectrum (in today's world) the name might connect the work with a person of a different gender, class or age. At the extremely problematic end of the spectrum are names which connect the work to a different race, nationality, culture or religion. The more embattled that race, nationality, culture or religion, the more questionable the association of a work with it. The work is a cuckoo in the cultural nest.

How the spectrum is imagined will, of course, be culturally determined and will vary according to time and place. What is acceptable in one age may not be acceptable in another. Acceptability may also depend on the circumstances in which the inquiry takes place. Accurate information about age and gender are, for example, a great deal more significant in the context of personal online communications than they are in the context of artistic publishing. This needs to be taken into account in judging reasonableness.

Connection to a particular family (a connection implied by most pseudonyms) may or may not be problematic. In the trade marks world a mark has enhanced capacity (greater inherent adaptability)[58] to distinguish the rarer it is. Therefore those who wish to register a name will do a search of Australian surnames to try to gauge the distinctiveness of the name. On the other hand, the rarer the family name is, the greater the likelihood of deception or confusion. In other words, if the pseudonym suggests an association with a particular family, and especially a family that is well known for certain attributes, the name may seem unacceptably deceptive. On the other hand, if the name is so common that the bearer of the pseudonym need not necessarily be related to any other person bearing the name, the pseudonym would be unproblematic.

The name chosen will be most unacceptable and 'unreasonable' if its deception is apt to cast a particular light on other legitimate bearers of the name. If the name is clearly identifiable with a culture, the light may be cast onto the culture or race as a whole. Most harm will accrue to the group if the application of the name reflects negatively upon it, but I would suggest that the pseudonym will be unreasonable even if the group is cast in a positive light. Cases in point are the 'Demidenko', 'Burrup' and 'Koolmatrie' cases in Australia – all instances of an individual purporting to reveal insights which were associated, through the

[58] Trade Marks Act s. 41.

name, with the cultural group.[59] Moral rights around the world protect the individual against false attribution of authorship, ie the attribution of the author's work to another person. In the UK and New Zealand moral rights even protect non-authors from having the authorship of a work attributed to them.[60] While only an individual can enjoy moral rights, it would nevertheless be a strange thing if moral rights law (with its human rights connotations) were actively to sanction the attribution of a work to a social group which had not authored it, particularly if this were detrimental to the interests of individuals within the group.

One of the most chilling cases in point is that of *The Protocols of the Elders of Zion*, a forged/plagiarised document attributed by its possibly Russian 'authors' to the 'Elders of Zion' and instrumental in promoting the anti-Semitism that led to the Holocaust and beyond.[61] If one were inclined to see the use of assumed names as merely harmless and amusing, this instance of misattribution should give pause for thought. In cases of plagiarism and forgery, as in other cases, the name that is used to indicate the source of the work will be critical to its reputation, its reception and ultimately its social influence. The crime lies not solely in the plagiarism but in the attribution.

Thus it is suggested that a pseudonym will be most unreasonable when it strays from the simple trade mark function of attaching an author to a work or body of works. The same may be said of a performer's stage name. While a degree of deception is essential, that deception should not extend to attaching the work to a person, entity or social group that can be seriously misrepresented by their association with it. If this happens, the attributional or trade mark function of the name has been exceeded and the liberty to use the name abused.

IV. Conclusion

The express protection of pseudonymity under the current Australian Copyright Act challenges our concept of a name's purpose – what a name really is, what the moral rights system really protects and what it should

[59] While it was the Jewish rather than the Ukrainian community that saw most to object to in the Demidenko book, the propensity to misrepresent the community whose voice was assumed should not be underplayed.

[60] Copyright, Designs and Patents Act 1988 (UK) s. 84; Copyright Act 1994 (NZ) s. 102.

[61] See Maurice Joly, *The Dialogue in Hell between Machiavelli and Montesquieu: Humanitarian Despotism and the Conditions of Modern Tyranny* (John S. Waggoner ed. and trans., Lexington Books, Lanham, MD, 2003), ch. 11. [trans of: *Dialogue aux enfers entre Machiavel et Montesquieu* (first published 1864)].

protect. All the moral rights are intended to protect the authorial or performer reputation in different ways. However, the common assumption that the attribution right and the right against false attribution ensure that the public will know about the true origin of the work gives way to a more nuanced truth. In some cases deception is promoted for the greater good of society and its individual members. Yet what bounds are to be put on this state-sanctioned deception remains unclear. This chapter has been an attempt to tease out the implications of the protection of reputation through pseudonymity and to establish principles on which the reasonable use of a pseudonym might be distinguished from uses that are unreasonable to the point of harm.

Part IV

Measures

10 The use of survey evidence in Australian trade mark and passing off cases

Vicki Huang, Kimberlee Weatherall and Elizabeth Webster

I. Introduction

Consumer confusion lies at the heart of many actions for trade mark infringement, and under the common law tort of passing off and its statutory equivalents. The question on which liability often turns in both kinds of case is whether consumers would be confused as a result of the conduct of the respondent or alleged infringer, although the type of confusion varies with the cause of action brought. To establish liability in passing off, the applicant must first show that they have a 'reputation', or goodwill,[1] that attaches to the applicant's get-up (for example insignia, brand name, or packaging) such that the get-up is recognised by the public as distinctive of their goods and services.[2] The applicant must also prove that consumers are being misled into thinking there was some connection between applicant and respondent due to the respondent's misuse of the applicant's get-up.[3] Registered trade mark owners, however, do not have to establish reputation, as the registration is prima face evidence of distinctiveness. They only have to establish that the respondent's mark is 'deceptively similar' to theirs, this being measured by looking at whether consumers would have been confused as a result of its use.[4] Despite differences of language and legal tests, at their core,

[1] Lord MacNaghten in *Inland Revenue Commissioners* v. *Muller & Co.'s Margarine Ltd* [1990] AC 217, 223–4 describing goodwill as 'the attractive force which brings in custom'.

[2] *Reckitt & Colman Products Ltd* v. *Borden Inc.* (1990) 17 IPR 1, 7 ('*Jif Lemon Case*').

[3] *ConAgra Inc.* v. *McCain Foods (Aust) Pty Ltd* (1992) 33 FCR 302 ('*ConAgra*').

[4] This is determined by asking whether a consumer would be 'caused to wonder' whether goods sold under the infringing mark might come from the same source as those under the registered mark: *Southern Cross Refrigerating Co* v. *Toowoomba Foundry Pty Ltd* (1954) 91 CLR 592, 595. Thus reputation plays a lesser – and more complicated – role in registered trade mark cases, in part because the benefit of registering a trade mark is meant to be that a party does not, if they hold a registered mark, have to establish that consumers associate that mark with them. In a limited number of cases – where marks are identical or substantially identical and the defendant is operating in the market in which the trade mark is registered – the question of confusion will not arise.

both actions, statutory and common law, depend vitally on the mental associations consumers will make on seeing some brand, mark or insignia.

It might be expected that consumers would be the best source of evidence about how consumers perceive, process and are confused by trade marks.[5] But obtaining that evidence is not straightforward. Applicants could (and often do) seek evidence of instances of actual confusion, such as cases where consumers have asked for, or purchased, goods under a mistaken impression as to their origin. They may call witnesses from the relevant trade or profession, or consumers or members of the public, to give direct evidence of their confusion, or put into evidence documents (such as letters or order forms) indicative of such confusion. Such evidence is said to have 'great weight',[6] although it is not clear that it should. Too often such evidence amounts to anecdotal evidence from a few people,[7] who do not, in basic statistical terms, constitute a representative sample.[8]

We ought to be using more rigorous methods to test consumer responses to marks. Surveys[9] can potentially be used to establish a range of facts relevant to the overriding legal question whether consumers are likely to be confused. Depending on how they are worded, surveys can establish the degree of recognition of a complainant's mark,[10] how

[5] The alternative is a 'judicial estimation of the effect likely to be produced in the course of the ordinary conduct of affairs' by factors such as the similarity of the goods, of the marks, the sophistication of the audience at which those goods and marks are targeted, etc. (*Australian Woollen Mills Ltd* v. *FS Walton & Co. Ltd* (1937) 58 CLR 641, 659 ('*Australian Woollen Mills*')). Or, more pejoratively, 'judicial speculations and assumptions about what consumers believe' (Graeme W. Austin, 'Trademarks and the Burdened Imagination' (2004) 69 *Brooklyn Law Review* 827, 834).

[6] *Australian Woollen Mills*, 658.

[7] See, e.g., *ibid.*, where Justices Dixon and McTiernan state that '[e]vidence of actual cases of deception, if forthcoming, is of great weight', but in the very next sentence state that '[i]n the present case a few people said that they mistook a newspaper advertisement of the respondent for an advertisement of the appellant. But their evidence amounted, we think, to very little . . . [the learned primary judge] was right in refusing to act on an account of the mental processes set up by perusing a newspaper advertisement, an account given by witnesses long after the occurrence of what must have been a casual and unimportant mental experience' (*ibid.* 658).

[8] *State Government Insurance Corporation* v. *Government Insurance Office of NSW* (1991) 28 FCR 511, 528–9 ('*State Government Insurance Corporation*'). For a nice summary of the issues with such evidence, see James Lahore, James Dwyer and Ann Dufty, *Patents, Trade Marks & Related Rights* (Butterworths: Sydney, 1996), vol. 1 A (at Service 72) [85,020].

[9] We understand surveys to range from basic attitudinal questionnaires to more complex, controlled, consumer perception studies.

[10] See, e.g., *Sterling Pharmaceuticals Pty Ltd* v. *Johnson & Johnson Australia Pty Ltd* (1990) 18 IPR 309 ('*Sterling Pharmaceuticals*'); *Kellogg Co.* v. *PB Foods* [1999] FCA 1610 ('*Kellogg*').

consumers encounter marks or make their purchase decisions,[11] and, by testing individuals' responses to an alleged infringer's mark, whether consumers are likely to be confused.[12] Participants in a properly conducted survey should constitute a representative sample, and statistical techniques can be used to correct for sampling biases. This allows us to draw inferences from the sample about the whole population. Thus the use of the survey technique can allow a range of views to be accounted for without the expense of calling multiple witnesses, and without taking up court time. In the US, Beebe notes that it is 'generally thought that survey evidence is the best evidence of actual confusion, and indeed, that a good survey has the potential to supersede' other forms of evidence; quoting an American Bar Association statement that surveys are 'traditionally one of the most classic and most persuasive and most informative forms of trial evidence that trade mark lawyers utilize'.[13]

There has been some research into the effectiveness of surveys in trade mark cases in the US. In 2004, Graeme Austin published an 'impressionistic' review of ten years of decisions, finding that survey evidence 'carries weight in trade mark infringement cases relatively infrequently'.[14] Surveys were proffered around 57.4 per cent of the time. In 2006, Barton Beebe published a more detailed empirical study of the range of factors that influence a finding of confusion in the US,[15] which sought to ascertain which factors were most important in supporting a finding of likely consumer confusion. Beebe found that survey evidence was addressed in only 20 per cent of the court decisions in his sample.[16] More recently, Sarel and Marmorstein conducted a study of trade mark infringement cases decided between 2001 and 2006 in US district courts,[17] looking particularly at whether surveys made a difference depending on the similarity of the applicant's and respondent's trade marks. They concluded, perhaps unsurprisingly, that surveys were more valuable where marks were less similar.

In Australia, surveys have, however, been the subject of various concerns. Historically surveys were viewed as mere hearsay: this view was

[11] See, e.g., *Playcorp Group of Companies Pty Ltd* v. *Peter Bodum A/S* (2010) 84 IPR 542.
[12] *State Government Insurance Corporation.*
[13] Barton Beebe, 'An Empirical Study of the Multifactor Tests for Trademark Infringement' (2006) 94 *California Law Review* 1581, 1641.
[14] Austin, 'Trademarks', 834. The study examined cases decided between May 1993 and May 2003.
[15] Beebe, 'Empirical Study'. [16] *Ibid.* 1641.
[17] Dan Sarel and Howard Marmorstein, 'The Effect of Consumer Surveys and Actual Confusion Evidence in Trademark Litigation: An Empirical Assessment' (2009) 99 *Trademark Reporter* 1416.

only rejected in 1990.[18] The practitioner-oriented literature is replete with horror stories about the expense of obtaining such evidence, and about trials made lengthy by disputes over survey evidence.[19] Before embarking on a survey, a party cannot guarantee favourable results, but under Federal Court practice, the court expects that notice should be given, in writing, by the party proposing the survey to other parties in the proceeding.[20] The practitioner literature also asserts that courts will not view survey evidence favourably:[21] whether owing to criticisms of the methodology; because it is 'overly elaborate' and hence a waste of resources,[22] or, more fundamentally, because the question of consumer confusion is for the judge to determine,[23] unless the consumers in the 'target market' are some kind of 'special group' into whose minds a judge may not have insight (for example, pre-teenage girls).[24] In short, the belief has been expressed that 'in many cases [survey] evidence can create more problems than it solves'.[25]

Given these beliefs, and the risks and costs of conducting a survey, it is natural for parties to be interested in how courts use and rely (or do not rely) on surveys. There has been no study of which we are aware of these questions in Australia in recent times. This chapter plugs this gap in our knowledge, by examining the population of trade mark and passing off cases decided in Australia in the period 1 January 1990 to 1 April 2010. We have sought to assess the influence of survey evidence on the probability of winning a trade mark or a passing off dispute in court. The remainder of this chapter proceeds as follows: Part II outlines the methodology of the study; Part III provides a descriptive analysis of

18 *Arnotts Ltd* v. *Trade Practices Commission* (1990) 24 FCR 313, 360–1 ('*Arnotts*').

19 Lahore, *Patents, Trade Marks* [85,030]; *State Government Insurance Corporation.*

20 Federal Court of Australia, *Practice Note CM 13 – Survey Evidence*, 25 September 2009. Even this process does not guarantee the court will accept the resulting evidence. In *Optical 88 Ltd* v. *Optical 88 Pty Ltd (No. 2)* [2010] FCA 1380, the applicant's survey was given to the respondent's solicitors for criticism and comment. Some minor changes were made but a number of issues remained between the parties. After 9,164 consumers were approached (460 giving a complete interview), the court found the survey failed to 'measure whether and, if so, to what extent, members of the chosen population of interest were misled' ([406]).

21 See, e.g., Mark Davison, Tracey Berger and Annette Freeman, *Shanahan's Australian Law of Trade Marks and Passing Off* (4th edn, Lawbook, Pyrmont, 2008), 284–5.

22 *Neutrogena Corp.* v. *Golden Ltd* [1996] RPC 473, 485–6 (Jacob J.); *Sterling Pharmaceuticals Pty* (1990) 18 IPR 309, 328; *Cadbury Schweppes Pty Ltd* v. *Darrell Lea Chocolate Shops Pty Ltd* (2006) 228 ALR 719, 726 [30]–[31] (Heerey J.).

23 *Arnotts*, 362; *Interlego AG* v. *Croner Trading Pty Ltd* (1992) 39 FCR 348 at 387 ('*Interlego*'); *Cadbury Schweppes Pty Ltd* v. *Darrell Lea Chocolate Shops Pty Ltd (No. 8)* (2008) 75 IPR 557 at 573–74 ('*Cadbury (No. 8)*').

24 *Pacific Publications Pty Ltd* v. *Next Publishing Pty Ltd* (2005) 222 ALR 127; *Gas Corporation* v. *Phasetwo Nominees Pty Ltd* [1998] FCA 773.

25 Lahore, *Patents, Trade Marks* [85,035].

the data; and Part IV presents the results from the empirical model. Part V offers thoughts on why surveys are rarely relied on. Part VI concludes with some policy suggestions.

II. Methodology

The data for this study is the population of 353 trade mark infringement and passing off cases decided by both state and federal Australian courts[26] over the period 1 January 1990–1 April 2010. Relevant trade mark infringement and passing off cases were located by undertaking broad keyword searches in the LexisNexis legal database[27] and then read and coded by a legally trained researcher. Results were checked and confirmed by a second legally trained researcher. The population comprised, broadly speaking, all cases in the tort of passing off and/or trade mark infringement. Coded variables comprised:

- **Bibliographic data**. The date and citation of the judgment; the court; judge; the nature of the case (trade mark infringement and/or passing off), whether the case was a trial, appeal or an appeal from the Australian Trade Marks Office.
- **Outcome** (win, partial win, or loss). A complete win for the applicant was defined as when they were successful on all issues pleaded; a complete loss was a loss on those issues; and a 'partial' win was defined as when the applicant won on only a subset of the issues. If a win/loss was unclear (for example if the case was sent back to a lower court on remitter) then the cases was also recorded as 'partial'.

26 A case was 'decided' if there was resolution of the case, whether interlocutory, summary or final following a trial.

27 The searches undertaken were full text searches, looking for the terms 'trade marks act' and 'infringement' or 'passing off' using 'All Subscribed Australian Case Sources' in the relevant period. This search identified 2,180 cases. Duplicates were removed. We also removed cases that focused on procedural issues, ownership disputes, discovery, costs, damages, or on copyright, patents, designs law or contract interpretation. Some appeals from trade mark oppositions were also excluded, where based on issues other than confusion, for example, rejection under s. 41 (distinctiveness) or s. 27 (ownership). We included appeals from opposition decisions based on s. 44 and s. 60, treating these as, in effect, disputes over conflicting marks. Cases that turned on whether the respondent 'used' the applicant's mark as a trade mark were also discarded as not being concerned with confusion. We have also not included cases of misleading or deceptive conduct under s. 52 of the Trade Practices Act. While some s. 52 cases are akin to the trade mark infringement cases being considered here, many are not, and it was too difficult to separate them out. Our belief is that *most* cases which are of the kind considered in trade mark infringement and passing off – where the concern is that consumers are likely to be misled as to the origin of the goods – passing off will be pleaded and hence the case will be caught in our keyword search.

- **Trade mark similarity** (more similar or less similar). The degree of similarity between the trade marks or between the get-ups.[28]
- **Market information**. Whether the case involves counterfeit goods or is an 'ordinary' trade mark infringement case,[29] whether the respondent was involved in the same market as the applicant (or something 'related' but not directly competing), and the company status of the applicant and respondent.
- **Evidence**. Whether evidence was tendered to establish confusion and/or reputation; whether survey evidence[30] or expert evidence[31] was tendered; whether evidence in the form of surveys and experts was relied on, partially relied on or not relied on by the court. It is important not to put too much weight on this variable, as it was extremely difficult to code consistently. In assessing reliance, we looked at whether the judge relied on the evidence (such as the survey or expert) in proving an issue; that is, to prove consumer confusion or to prove the existence of reputation. If it wasn't clear whether the judge did or did not rely on the evidence, it was coded as 'partially relied on'. If the judge admitted the evidence but did not rely on it, then it was coded as 'no reliance'. If the evidence was described as persuasive then it was coded as 'relied on'.[32]

Over the 1990–2010 period, only 33 (or 10.4 per cent of the non-counterfeiting) cases discussed survey evidence.[33] This small absolute

[28] Similarity of marks is a necessary but not sufficient condition for the establishment of liability. This variable recognises that similarity is a matter of degree. Similarity was coded based on the judgment of the reader, based on the approach of Sarel and Marmorstein, 'Effect of Consumer Surveys', 1435. Trade marks or get-ups were coded as either 'More Similar' or 'Less Similar' where 'More Similar' marks are 'identical or very close in aural and visual similarity' for example MAGNILITE and MAGNI-LIGHTS. Cases that were not classed as 'More Similar' were coded as 'Less Similar'. For example, 'BIG APPLE DELI' and 'BIG BAGELS DELI' are 'Less Similar'.

[29] For a description of this distinction and its significance in trade mark litigation in Australia, see Jason Bosland, Kimberlee Weatherall and Paul Jensen, 'Trade Mark and Counterfeit Litigation in Australia' (2006) 4 *Intellectual Property Quarterly* 347.

[30] See above n. 9.

[31] An 'expert' was a witness that was referred to in the judgment as an 'expert'. An expert witness is impartial and has an overriding duty to the court. See, e.g., Federal Court of Australia, *Practice Note CM 7 – Expert Witnesses in Proceedings in the Federal Court of Australia*, 29 September 2009.

[32] Determining whether the court relied on particular evidence to prove a particular issue was often difficult. This was especially so in appellate cases where evidence is not reviewed *de novo*. We had to make inferences as to whether the appellate court followed the trial judge's treatment of the original evidence. Another problem was that many of the cases were interlocutory decisions, not involving a final determination of the merits of the case.

[33] 38 surveys were discussed in 33 cases.

Table 10.1 *Case Type, Australian trade mark and passing off cases, 1990–2010*

	Case Type			
Counterfeit?	Trade mark infringement & passing off	Passing off only	Trade mark infringement only	Total
No	85	168	64	317
Yes	14	0	22	36
Total	99	168	86	353

Source: Australian Trade Mark Case Database, 1990–2010. Includes counterfeiting cases.

number both limits the conclusions which can be drawn from a straightforward statistical analysis, and itself warrants explanation: if survey evidence has the potential to be the best source of information about likely consumer reactions to marks, why is it not used more often? In order to answer this question, we have analysed the courts' comments on evidence in trade mark cases.

III. Descriptive analysis

In Table 10.1 we show that of the 353 cases, 36 were counterfeiting. Of the non-counterfeiting cases, 168 were passing off only, 64 were trade mark infringement only and 85 were both. Since almost all of the counterfeiting cases were straightforward cases of infringement (in 34 of the 36 cases the applicant achieved either a partial or complete win), we exclude these cases from further analysis.[34] This leaves 317 cases of which 260 were first instance decisions.

Figure 10.1 presents the number of cases involving survey evidence each year and compares this with the total number and the number involving expert witness evidence. It reveals a clear downward trend in the use of survey evidence with a slight rising preference for expert witnesses.

In Table 10.2 we indicate the percentage of cases in which either survey or expert evidence was tendered (bearing in mind there are

[34] On average counterfeiting cases took 1.1 hearing days, compared with 2.4 days for passing off and trade mark infringement, which illustrates the less complicated nature of the former. To similar effect, see Bosland *et al.*, 'Trade Mark and Counterfeit Litigation'.

Table 10.2 *Percentage of trade mark and passing off cases tendering survey or expert evidence by win status, Australia, 1990–2010*

Type of evidence tendered	Loss[a] for applicant (% of all loss cases)	Win or partial win[b] for applicant (% of all win cases)	Both outcomes (% of all cases)
Type of evidence tendered by *applicant*			
Survey	8.6	6.7	7.6
Expert	21.6	12.9	16.7
Type of evidence tendered by *respondent*			
Survey	2.9	3.4	3.2
Expert	12.9	10.1	11.4

Notes: [a] Applicant lost on all issues. [b] Applicant was successful on at least some issues pleaded or if the outcome was unclear (for example if the case was sent back to a lower court on remitter).
Source: Australian Trade Mark Case Database, 1990–2010. Excludes counterfeiting cases.

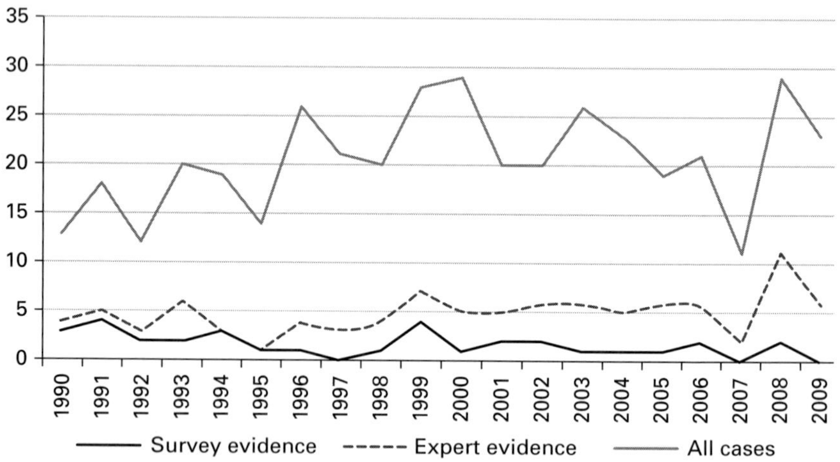

Figure 10.1 Number of trade mark cases using survey or expert witness evidence; all Australian courts, 1990–2009
Note: The chart excludes 2010 as the data for 2010 are incomplete.
Source: Australian Trade Mark Case Database, 1990–2010. Excludes counterfeiting cases.

317 cases in total). This data is further disaggregated according to whether the final decision involved a win or partial win for the applicant or a loss. According to this data, only 7.6 per cent of applicants and 3.2 per cent of respondents tendered survey evidence.[35] Expert evidence, which is apt to be cheaper, was more frequent at 16.7 and 11.4 per cent respectively. We note that these tables do not say that the remaining majority of cases involved no evidence at all. The remaining cases could have involved evidence of the less-than-rigorous kinds criticised earlier in this chapter – such as single instances of consumer confusion or, perhaps, marketing figures to establish the distinctiveness of indicia to the applicant. The point, rather, is that such a low proportion of cases are going beyond these 'evidential bits and pieces'. Note too that according to law and economics theory, the cases that we are looking at – those that make it all the way to court – ought to be the 'borderline' cases which could go either way: the very cases in which one would expect evidence would be necessary.[36]

Table 10.3 shows that about one-third of applicants led evidence, of any type, to prove confusion and slightly more led evidence on reputation.[37] There was little variation in this 'led evidence' rate by win status. However, applicants were twice as likely to lead evidence on either confusion or reputation as respondents. Again there was no difference (statistically speaking) in the percentages across both parties according to whether they won or lost the case. Given the importance of establishing distinctiveness in passing off only cases, we also examined this data for this group (results not presented). While we expected that reputation would be almost axiomatic for this group, we found that the percentage leading survey or expert evidence to establish reputation was still under 50 per cent.[38]

Table 10.4 shows the percentage of cases where the court relied on a piece of evidence in their decision. Although the reliance data was problematic, two points can be inferred: the first is the very low rate of reliance on either survey or expert evidence. Part of this low rate stems from the low rate at which the evidence is tendered (see Table 10.2). The

35 Even taking the lower US estimates concerning the use of survey evidence, the utilisation rate in Australia is less than half the rate of use of such instruments in the US: 3 or 7 per cent depending on the party, as compared to closer to 20 per cent of cases according to Beebe's US study ('Empirical Study').

36 See generally George Priest and Benjamin Klein, 'The Selection of Disputes for Litigation' (1984) 13 *Journal of Legal Studies* 1.

37 Four additional cases were 'led on confusion' but were not classified by whether this was led by the counsel for the applicant or respondent. Two additional cases were 'led on reputation' but were not classified by whether this was led by the counsel for the applicant or respondent.

38 Similarly for first instance passing off cases.

Table 10.3 *Percentage of trade mark and passing off cases according to issue to prove by win status, Australia, 1990–2010*

Issue to prove	Loss[a] for applicant (% of all loss cases)	Win or partial win[b] for applicant (% of all win cases)	Both outcomes (% of all cases)
Evidence led by *applicant* to prove			
Confusion	33.1	34.8	34.1
Reputation	36.0	40.0	38.2
Evidence led by respondent to counter			
Confusion	14.4	15.2	14.8
Reputation	15.8	12.4	13.9

Notes: [a] Applicant lost on all issues. [b] Applicant was successful on at least some issues pleaded or if the outcome was unclear (for example if the case was sent back to a lower court on remitter).
Source: Australian Trade Mark Case Database, 1990–2010. Excludes counterfeiting cases.

Table 10.4 *Percentage of trade mark and passing off cases according to evidence court relied on by win status, Australia, 1990–2010*

Type of evidence relied upon	Loss[a] for applicant (% of all loss cases)	Win or partial win[b] for applicant (% of all win cases)	Both outcomes (% of all cases)
Applicant's evidence relied upon by *court*			
Survey	2.2	1.1	1.6
Expert	8.6	5.6	6.9
Respondent's evidence relied upon by *court*			
Survey	0.0	0.6	0.3
Expert	7.9	3.9	5.7

Notes: [a] Applicant lost on all issues. [b] Applicant was successful on at least some issues pleaded or if the outcome was unclear (for example if the case was sent back to a lower court on remitter).
Source: Australian Trade Mark Case Database, 1990–2010. Excludes counterfeiting cases.

second point that can be inferred is that the parties' evidence does not appear to affect a party's chance of success. For example, the applicants' survey evidence was relied on in 2.2 per cent of the cases where the applicant lost but only 1.1 per cent of cases where the applicant won (or partially won). A similar pattern is apparent for respondents.

Table 10.5 *Percentage of trade mark and passing off cases tendering evidence by type and similarity of market, Australia, 1990–2010*

	Similarity of Market			
Type of evidence relied upon	Same[a] (% of same cases)	Similar[b] (% of similar cases)	Different[c] (% of different case)	All markets (% of all cases)
Type of evidence tendered by *applicant*				
Survey	9.3	1.6	7.9	7.6
Expert	15.8	17.2	21.1	16.7
Type of evidence tendered by *respondent*				
Survey	4.7	0.0	0.0	3.2
Expert	11.6	7.8	15.8	11.4

Notes: [a] 'Same' would be an applicant and respondent in the 'Restaurant' services business. [b] 'Similar' would be an applicant in the 'Game Manufacturing' business vs. a respondent in the 'Game Reconditioning' business. [c] 'Different' would be an applicant in 'Hotel services' vs. a respondent in 'Restaurant services'.
Source: Australian Trade Mark Case Database, 1990–2010. Excludes counterfeiting cases.

Table 10.5 shows that survey evidence is more likely to be tendered by the applicant when the market is different or the same but has been only tendered by the respondent when the market is the same. Although the use of surveys is limited, respondents are using them when their case is more tenuous. It suggests that they understand the role of objective evidence in bearing upon a case that is more difficult to prove.

Finally, Table 10.6 presents data on evidence led by the business status of both applicants and respondents. It reveals that surveys are most likely to be tendered by Australian public companies (that is, incorporated with ASIC). Overseas companies only tendered a survey when they are the applicants, and 'other' unincorporated business entities never tendered a survey.

IV. Empirical model

Use of survey evidence by either party should indicate that the applicant believes he or she has a strong case and, in addition, it should also add substance to the case such that he or she is more likely to prove their case.[39] In addition, given the *raison d'être* of the trade mark system is to

[39] We think this is true owing to a combination of three facts. First, theory predicts that an applicant who makes it all the way to court likely believes their case is strong: otherwise they would be more likely to settle earlier on: Priest and Klein, 'Selection of Disputes'. Second, to tender a survey the applicant must be confident about it strengthening the

Table 10.6 *Percentage of trade mark and passing off cases tendering evidence by type and business status, Australia, 1990–2010*

Applicant Status	Overseas Company (% OS company)	Private Company[a] (% private company)	Public Company[a] (% public company)	Other[b] (% other)	All businesses (% all cases)
Type of evidence tendered by *applicant*					
Survey	8.3	3.8	14.1	0.0	7.6
Expert	18.1	13.1	26.8	7.1	16.7
Type of evidence tendered by *respondent*					
Survey	0.0	1.8	9.3	0.0	3.2
Expert	25.0	9.0	16.0	4.2	11.4

Note: [a] Public company includes subsidiaries. [b] Comprises individuals and unincorporated organisations.
Source: Australian Trade Mark Case Database, 1990–2010. Excludes counterfeiting cases.

prevent consumer confusion, we also expect counsel that led evidence beyond the anecdotal on the issue of confusion or reputation and those that provide survey evidence of likely confusion should also be more likely to win.

However, we also expect the outcome to be affected by other factors – which we call control variables – such as other forms of evidence or the similarity of the industry or market. We do not believe that the financial resources of the two parties should affect the decision since the latter should be determined on a point of law. While the reality is that wealthier litigants are more able to sustain a dispute and therefore to end up in court, once there, wealth should not affect the outcome. However, to test our proposition that wealth and financial resources do not matter, we include the business status of each party in our control variables.

Before we launch into the estimations, we need to discuss what statisticians call 'selection issues'. Not all cases end up in court – the overwhelming majority are settled 'privately'.[40] In these settlements, survey

case: first, because conducting a survey according to Federal Court practice (that is, giving the other side prior notice) holds some risk unless a party is confident of the result, or, second, if Federal Court practice was not followed (note the majority of cases came from the Federal Court), and prior notice to the other side was not given, the survey would not have been tendered at all unless it was of assistance (a party will not tender evidence they consider unhelpful to their case).

40 For empirical confirmation in IP cases (in the US), see William Landes, 'An Empirical Analysis of Intellectual Property Litigation: Some Preliminary Results' (2004) 41 *Houston Law Review* 749. No similar research has been done in Australia in relation to trade mark, but for a similar result in patent litigation in Australia, see Fiona Rotstein and Kimberlee Weatherall, 'Filing and Settlement of Patent Disputes in the Federal Court: 1995–2005' (2007) 68 *Intellectual Property Forum* 65.

evidence may be produced and be used to settle the case. We do not have any data on how often this occurs or what role survey evidence has played in the final outcome. We can deduce however that the cases that end up before the courts are unlikely to be representative of the whole population of trade mark disputes.[41] This means that there may be biases in our estimations. Without data to be able to compare the whole population of disputes with our dataset, we are unable to give further guidance on whether this biases matters and in what direction.

We modelled the court's decision as a single equation with 'clustering' on the case identifier.[42] The unit of analysis is the characteristics of each party to each dispute. The dependent variable – the winability of the case, which we call *Win** – is modelled as a function of: whether counsel for each party tendered survey evidence (*Survey*); the quality of the survey evidence as indicated by whether the court relied on this survey evidence (*SurveyRely*) and whether counsel led evidence on confusion (*ConfusionLed*) or reputation (*ReputationLed*).

As mentioned, we also include a set of control factors (called *X*) – comprising other forms of evidence such as the use of expert evidence (*Expert*); the quality of this evidence as indicated by whether the court relied on this expert evidence (*ExpertRely*); the similarity of the industry or market (*SimilarMarket*); whether the trade mark is assessed by the authors as being more or less similar (*SimilarTM*); and the business status of the applicant and respondent (*Overseas company*, *Private company*, *Public company*, *Other*).

We model winability (*Win**) as:

$$Win_i^* = \beta_1 Survey_i + \beta_2 SurveyRely_i + \beta_3 ConfusionLed_i + \beta_4 ReputationLed_i + \boldsymbol{\beta} X + \varepsilon_i \quad (1)$$

$$Win_i = \begin{cases} 1 & \text{if } Win^* > 0 \\ 0 & \text{if } Win^* \leq 0 \end{cases} \quad (2)$$

41 While some cases may be driven by vexatious litigants – who have motives other than a 'win' on their mind – most cases will end up in court because *both* parties believe that their own probability of winning multiplied by the value of winning exceeds the value of the counterfactual (being the probability of losing multiplied by the costs of losing). Since the default position in the case of IP litigation usually involves continuation of the alleged infringing behaviour, considerable profits must be at stake for the applicant to pursue the case to court. In addition, both parties must have the means to sustain a court case. Essentially, therefore, the cases before us should represent more valuable trade marks, disputes close to the knife edge of a win or loss, and disputes between parties with assets. On the relevant theory, see Priest and Klein, 'Selection of Disputes'.

42 Clustering is a statistical process that accounts for the fact that our pair of observations for each case share common unobservable factors and therefore the error term in equation (1) will be correlated.

The dependent variable, *Win*, has been coded as binary so we estimate it as a discrete dependent variable model. Each case has two observations – one for each party. The dependent variable and the explanatory variables are constructed in the manner described below but for a complete description of the questions used in the construction of each variable, refer to Table A1 in Appendix A (at the end of this chapter).

Dependent variable. As mentioned, our dependent variable – *Win* – was coded =1 if the party was successful on at least some issues pleaded or if the outcome was unclear (for example if the case was sent back to a lower court on remitter). *Win* was coded =0 if the party lost on all issues.

Explanatory variables. *Survey* was coded =1 if counsel for that party tendered survey results as evidence, =0 otherwise. *SurveyRely* was coded as =1 if the courts indicated that they relied on the survey evidence, =0 otherwise; *ConfusionLed* was coded as =1 if counsel led evidence to prove confusion, or misrepresentation, =0 otherwise; *ReputationLed* was coded as =1 if counsel led evidence to prove reputation grounds and it was a passing off case only, =0 otherwise.

Control variables. *Expert* was coded =1 if counsel for that party tendered expert evidence, =0 otherwise. *ExpertRely* was coded as =1 if the courts indicated that they relied on the expert evidence, =0 otherwise; *SimilarMarket* was manually coded =3 if the party alleging infringement was considered to be in the same market as the alleged infringer; =2 if the suing party was in a similar market as the alleged infringer; =1 if in a different market. *SimilarTM* was based on the Sarel–Marmorstein test: =1 if, judged by this test, the party alleging infringement had a trade mark that was similar to the alleged infringer, =0 otherwise. The business status of the party (*OverseasCompany*, *PrivateCompany*, *PublicCompany*, '*Other*') was manually coded from the name given on the court records. All private companies which were subsidiaries of public companies were coded as *PublicCompany*. Company structure was identified from ASIC and IBISWorld databases and the internet.

Table 10.7 presents these results from the estimations using first all the cases (columns 1 and 2), second, first instance cases only (column 3) and third, cases that were exclusively passing off (column 4). The first column, which provides estimates for the coefficients on all variables, clearly shows that tendering survey evidence did not affect the probability of winning the case. This is quite a strong result and holds regardless of the number and type of other co-variates.

The easiest way to read the table is to look at the sign of the coefficients [the β_s from equation (1)] and their statistical significance (as indicated by whether there is an *, ** or *** beside it). If there are no asterisks, then one can assume that the variable had no influence over whether

Table 10.7 *Determinants of a win or partial win (to either party)*

Dependent variable: Win or partial win	(1) All cases	(2) All cases	(3) First instance cases	(4) Passing off cases exclusively
Explanatory variables				
Survey	–0.0731			
	(0.268)			
SurveyRely	–0.449			
	(0.614)			
ConfusionLed	0.0661			
	(0.129)			
ReputationLed	0.207*	0.205*		0.345**
	(0.124)	(0.120)		(0.165)
Control variables				
Expert	–0.372**	–0.291**	–0.383*	–0.307
	(0.183)	(0.142)	(0.196)	(0.189)
SurveyRely	0.172		0.332	
	(0.241)		(0.249)	
SimilarMarket	0.0270		0.136	
	(0.0786)		(0.0867)	
SimilarTM	0.546***	0.543***	0.568***	0.736***
	(0.139)	(0.139)	(0.155)	(0.198)
Overseas company	0.264	0.188	0.270*	
	(0.175)	(0.143)	(0.160)	
Private company	0.123			0.375***
	(0.133)			(0.133)
Other (inc individual)$_i$	–0.269*	–0.356***	–0.347**	
	(0.159)	(0.132)	(0.147)	
Constant	–0.299	–0.152*	–0.416**	–0.565***
	(0.201)	(0.0793)	(0.189)	(0.132)
Observations	622	622	508	326

Notes: Probit estimation. Standard errors in parentheses. *** $p<0.01$, ** $p<0.05$, * $p<0.1$. Base case = Public company.
Source: Australian Trade Mark Case Database, 1990–2010. Excludes counterfeiting cases.

or not the party won the case. Given this, we can see that neither the coefficient for *Survey* (–0.0731) or *SurveyRely* (–0.449) have asterisks and are therefore statistically insignificant. This means that *we cannot reject the hypothesis that tendering or relying on survey evidence had no effect on the judgement*.

The results also show that leading evidence on reputation, having a similar looking mark, being an overseas company (in first instance cases),

Table 10.8 *Marginal effects on the probability of a win or partial win (to either party) statistically significant variables only*

Dependent variable: Win	Percentage point change
Explanatory variables	
ReputationLed	8.0
Control variables	
Expert	−10.8
SimilarTM	21.6
Other (incl. individual)$_i$	−14.7

Notes: Derived from the estimate in Table 10.8, column (2)
Source: Australian Trade Mark Case Database, 1990–2010. Excludes counterfeiting cases.

and being a Australian private company (in exclusively passing off cases) had a positive effect on winning. The coefficients for these variables are positive and statistically significant. However, tendering expert evidence and being an 'other' business type (such as an individual or unincorporated entity) tended to have a negative effect on winning. The coefficients for these variables are negative and statistically significant. Table 10.8 converts these coefficients into changes to the probability of winning. It shows for example that leading evidence on reputation, versus not leading on reputation, raises the probability of winning by 8.0 percentage points. If the party alleging infringement had a similar looking trade mark to the other party, the probability of winning that was 21.6 percentage points higher. Tendering expert evidence, versus not tendering expert evidence, was associated with a probability of winning that was 10.8 percentage points lower. This may be due to expert evidence being tendered in only weak cases but may also be associated with the calibre of the evidence.

V. Commentary: why so little survey evidence, and so little reliance?

Our figures show that the initial enthusiasm for surveys after *Arnotts Ltd* v. *Trade Practices Commission*[43] in 1990 has rapidly declined; and that

[43] (1990) 24 FCR 313, 360–1 (Full Federal Court).

survey use is now infrequent. Our analysis also suggests that surveys have limited impact on the results in these cases. These facts are clearly related. We think that parties are rationally deciding not to bother with costly surveys that will not be used by the courts. This decision is made easier by the fact that the courts have not provided complainants with any real incentive to obtain survey evidence. Courts have made it clear that they are prepared to make decisions on the likelihood of consumer confusion, without any empirical evidence, on the basis of their own inferences and judicial 'common sense', from looking at the competing marks, marketing budgets and activities. Judges have insisted that it is their right and duty to make that determination.[44] In most cases where judges comment on the absence of survey evidence they express little concern.[45] Indeed, in some cases judges suggest that such evidence is inappropriate. In *Interlego*, for example, Justice Gummow notes that it is inappropriate to tender 'evidence of prospective purchasers that they would be deceived', because this contravenes the rule prohibiting opinion evidence on the very question the judge must decide.[46] Strictly, this rule of evidence is no longer the law,[47] but doubts about evidence of likely confusion persist.[48] Only very occasionally is that absence detrimental, and these cases tend to have particular characteristics, for example, the market is a special one where judicial 'common sense' is perhaps inapplicable.[49]

A review of the comments made by judges about survey evidence generally, or particular surveys, confirms the difficulties faced by a party seeking to tender such evidence. No doubt some occasions where courts reject survey evidence are justified. In some cases, there are good reasons

44 *Arnotts*, 362–3; *State Government Insurance Corporation*, 513; *Johnson & Johnson Australia Pty Ltd* v. *Sterling Pharmaceuticals Pty Ltd* (1991) 21 IPR 1, 15; *Cadbury (No. 8)*, 574.

45 See, e.g., *Pacific Publications Pty Ltd* v. *IPC Media Pty Ltd* (2003) 57 IPR 28; *Natural Waters of Viti Ltd* v. *Dayals (Fiji) Artesian Waters Ltd* (2007) 71 IPR 571, 579 ('*Natural Waters of Viti*'); *Twentieth Century Fox Film Corporation and Anor* v. *South Australian Brewing Co. Ltd* (1996) 66 FCR 451, 471–2; *TGI Friday's Inc.* v. *TGI Friday's Australia Pty Ltd* (1998) 42 IPR 444; *United Realty Co. Pty Ltd* v. *BSP & GS Property Group Pty Ltd* [2003] NSWSC 419.

46 (1991) 25 IPR 65, 107–8.

47 See Evidence Act 1995 (Cth) s. 80; discussed in *Cadbury Schweppes Pty Ltd* v. *Darrell Lea Chocolate Shops Pty Ltd* (2007) 72 IPR 261, 274–5.

48 *Natural Waters of Viti* (2007) 71 IPR 571, 579–80 (noting that evidence from consumers of reputation is unproblematic, but evidence of confusion is more problematic, and citing *Interlego* for that proposition).

49 For example *Pacific Publications Pty Ltd* v. *Next Publishing Pty Ltd* (2005) 222 ALR 127 (target consumers were 'tween' girls whose likely response to similarities between magazines was not something a judge could determine).

for a judge to refuse to rely on survey evidence tendered by a party: the sample may be too small or unbalanced;[50] the methodology may not be explained;[51] the survey may read more like a petition than evidence;[52] or the questions may be poorly worded.[53] In other cases, the problem is timing. In passing off litigation, the risk of confusion is considered as at the time the impugned conduct started. In one recent case, the impugned conduct commenced in 1993, but the legal proceedings did not commence until 2006 and the survey – on which the court did not rely – was not conducted until 2009.[54] Other occasions, however, are less obviously justifiable. For example, the courts have often critiqued surveys for placing consumers in artificial circumstances, removed from the context in which goods or services are actually purchased, such that no reliance can be placed on the results.[55] Such comments deserve to be questioned. Is evidence of a carefully conducted psychological experiment or survey, designed by an expert to test the impact of a mark, and conducted according to high standards[56] really so artificial as to reduce its reliability? More importantly, is it any more artificial than the mechanisms of which courts *do* more happily rely on, such as single instances of confused consumers, or judicial intuition?

Nor have the courts made available much guidance to practitioners on how best to provide survey evidence. For example, the Federal Court

[50] *CA Henschke & Co.* v. *Rosemount Estates Pty Ltd* (1999) 47 IPR 63; *Cadbury Schweppes Pty Ltd* v. *Darrell Lea Chocolate Shops Pty Ltd (No. 4)* (2006) 69 IPR 23 ('*Cadbury (No. 4)*'); *ConAgra*; *Armor All Products Corporation* v. *CRC Chemicals Australia Pty Ltd* (1993) 28 IPR 77 (247 people approached but only 15 gave statutory declarations).

[51] *Re Castlemaine Perkins Ltd* v. *Power Brewing Company Limited* [1992] FCA 638.

[52] *Osgaig Pty Ltd* v. *Ajisen (Melbourne) Pty Ltd* (2004) 63 IPR 156. The complainant restaurant tendered a list of people who claimed to have eaten at the applicant's restaurant, had noticed the respondent's sign, and immediately thought the new restaurant was connected to the applicant's restaurant.

[53] *South Australian Brewing Co. Pty Ltd* v. *Carlton & United Breweries Ltd* (2001) 185 ALR 719 (questions did not sufficiently distinguish between use of the word Showdown as a mark, and use of the word to refer to certain AFL games).

[54] *Optical 88* v. *Optical 88 (No. 2)* [2010] FCA 1380. For other cases where timing has been an issue, see *South Australian Brewing Co. Pty Ltd* v. *Carlton & United Breweries Ltd* (2001) 185 ALR 719 (survey conducted shortly after media publicity of an interlocutory injunction in the relevant proceedings); *Kellogg* [1999] FCA 1610 (survey conducted in 1998 but impugned conduct started in 1992); *Sydney Markets Ltd* v. *Sydney Flower Market Pty Ltd* [2002] FCA 124 (survey conducted in 2000, after applicant had commenced promotional activities).

[55] See, e.g., *Interlego* (1991) 21 IPR 373, 412; *Cadbury (No. 4)*, 37; *Kellogg* [112]; *The Ritz Hotel Ltd* v. *Charles of the Ritz Ltd* (1988) 12 IPR 417, 474; *State Government Insurance Corporation*, 528–9.

[56] Standards that likely exceed the standards applied to the many market surveys actually acted on by companies in designing marketing campaigns.

of Australia Practice Note on Survey Evidence[57] is concerned with procedure only. In essence, it states that parties intending to obtain survey evidence should give notice of that intention, and the details of the survey, to their opponents and attempt to reach agreement on how the survey is to be conducted. It is also frequently ignored,[58] and no wonder: based on the decision in *Eveready* v. *Gillette*, failure to comply with the Practice Note does not make survey evidence inadmissible.[59] In that case, in fact, the Federal Court allowed the opponent to tender expert evidence critiquing a survey – although the opponent made no such comments during the opportunity offered during the Practice Note process.[60] For as long as this judicial attitude prevails, there is little reason for an opponent to seek to improve the other party's evidence by offering critique prior to the survey being conducted.

Parties must feel as if they are damned if they test consumer confusion – and damned if they do not. However, given that courts do not treat survey or empirical evidence of confusion as necessary, parties are *less* likely to be damned, perhaps, if they do not. This present situation concerning the use of surveys of all kinds is unsatisfactory. Courts' equivocal attitudes increase the likelihood of wasted costs, both in obtaining evidence that will be largely ignored, and in court and expert time arguing over admissibility and weight. The very low usage of surveys over the last decade (10.4 percent) indicates that parties are responding rationally to this situation by simply avoiding such evidence altogether.

VI. Policy proposals

Richard Posner has suggested a rule that weak statistical evidence should be excluded from evidence to avoid confusing judges who have difficulty understanding statistics.[61] We do not think that limiting or ignoring survey evidence is a good solution. We understand the reluctance of the courts to turn questions of everyday consumer behaviour into battlegrounds for experts,[62] with the costs attendant on such a development. However, we do not believe that the best answer is to refuse

[57] Now Federal Court of Australia, *Practice Note CM 13 – Survey Evidence*, 25 September 2009.

[58] *Cadbury Schweppes Pty Ltd* v. *Darrell Lea Chocolate Shops Pty Ltd* [2006] FCA 364; *Re Castlemaine Perkins Ltd* v. *Power Brewing Company Limited* [1992] FCA 638.

[59] *Eveready Australia Pty Ltd* v. *Gillette Australia Pty Ltd* (1999) 47 IPR 327.

[60] *Ibid.*

[61] Richard Posner, 'The Law and Economics of the Economic Expert Witness' (1999) 13 *Journal of Economic Perspectives* 91.

[62] *Cadbury (No. 8)*, 578; *Cat Media Pty Ltd* v. *Opti-Healthcare Pty Ltd* [2003] FCA 133 [55].

such evidence. As aptly stated by Jacob Schmookler, 'we have a choice of using . . . statistics cautiously and learning what we can from them, or not using them and learning nothing about what they alone can teach us'.[63] The Full Federal Court stated in *Arnotts*, 'information is preferable to intuition'.[64] It cannot be the case that psychologists' and marketers' increasing insights into how consumers process and respond to different aspects of marketing are irrelevant to the application of laws which have as their key goal preventing the deception or confusion of consumers.

We suggest that a better approach would be for courts to state more clearly their requirements for acceptable market research evidence. The last judgment of the Full Federal Court giving serious guidance on the use of surveys in trade mark or passing off cases, *Interlego*, is now twenty years old, and precedes both important changes to the law of evidence,[65] and, no doubt, refinements in market research techniques and cognitive psychology. It might even be possible to develop model questions and sampling methods to help parties design their process for gathering evidence. For proposals such as model survey questions or guidelines for the preparation of survey evidence to work, it would likely be necessary to include them in the court's guidelines to practitioners. This could be done by development of the existing Federal Court of Australia Practice Note on Survey Evidence.[66]

This would require a dialogue between lawyers and experts in psychology. The learning would not, we expect, be all in one direction. Lawyers could afford to learn more about how consumers respond, both consciously and unconsciously, to various aspects of branding. They could also learn more about the methods which have been developed to ensure that, so far as possible, individual responses to surveys are an accurate reflection of the individual's untutored response to stimuli like brands or product packaging. In turn, cognitive psychologists and marketing experts could learn more about the limits to the law's concern about consumer confusion. Not every form of consumer confusion will justify the law's intervention. An open discussion between these differing areas of expertise could help in two ways. It could perhaps help the clearer, more coherent development of legal rules relating to trade mark infringement and passing off. Most importantly, it could help ensure decisions are made based on the best available evidence.

[63] Jacob Schmookler, *Invention and Economic Growth* (Harvard University Press, Cambridge, MA, 1966), 56.

[64] *Arnotts*, 362 (Lockhart, Wilcox and Gummow JJ).

[65] See above n. 47.

[66] Now Federal Court of Australia, *Practice Note CM 13 – Survey Evidence*, 25 September 2009.

Appendix A – Variable definitions

Table A1. *Variable definitions*

Variable	Value	Definition
Win	Yes=1 if a complete or partial win, No=0	If the party was successful on all issues pleaded (issues being either TM infringement or s. 52/passing off), then a win was recorded by a 'Yes'. Conversely a loss on those issues was recorded by a 'No'. If the party won on only a subset of the issues, then it was recorded as 'Partial'. If a win/loss was unclear (for example if the case was sent back to a lower court on remitter), then the cases was recorded as 'Partial'.
Similar market	Same=3 Similar=2 Different=1	Manually coded. An example of 'Same' would be an applicant and respondent in the 'Restaurant' services business. An example of 'Similar' would be an applicant in the 'Game Manufacturing' business vs. a respondent in the 'Game Reconditioning' business. An example of 'Different' would be an applicant in 'Hotel services' vs. a respondent in 'Restaurant services'.
SimilarTM	More similar=1 Less similar=0	Coding was based on the Sarel–Marmorstein test. Trade marks or get-ups were coded 'More' if marks are 'identical or very close in aural and visual similarity' for example MAGNILITE and MAGNI-LIGHTS. All other cases were coded as 'Less'; for example 'BIG APPLE DELI' and 'BIG BAGELS DELI' are 'Less'.
First instance or appeal	Forced choice: Trial/Appeal/ Remittance	Where the case was a first hearing (including an interlocutory hearing), then the case was coded as 'First Instance'. Where the case was an appeal from a lower court (but not an appeal from the ATMO), the case was coded as 'Appeal'. Where the case was a remittance from a higher court, the case was coded as 'Remittance'. Note that appeals from the ATMO were coded separately.
Case type	TM infringement, passing off, both	If the case had a TM infringement argument but not a passing off/s. 52 argument, then it was recorded as 'TM Infringement'. If the case had a s. 52 or passing off argument, then it was coded as 'Passing Off'. If the case had both a TM infringement and a s. 52/passing off argument then it was coded as 'Both'.

(*cont.*)

Table A1. (*cont.*)

Variable	Value	Definition
Counterfeit Y/N	Yes=1, No=0	Counterfeit cases were classified according to Note 14 of the TRIPS agreement which states that '(a) "counterfeit trademark goods" shall mean any goods, including packaging, bearing without authorization a trademark which is identical to the trademark validly registered in respect of such goods, or which cannot be distinguished in its essential aspects from such a trademark, and which thereby infringes the rights of the owner of the trademark in question under the law of the country of importation'.
Survey Expert	Yes=1, No=0	Each case was scanned to determine whether an expert or survey evidence was used. Multiple pieces of evidence could be recorded for each case. Each piece of evidence was defined according to whether it was tendered by the applicant or respondent.
SurveyRely *ExpertRely*	Yes=1, No=0	Each case was scanned to determine which evidence was relied in the court's decision.
ConfusionLed *ReputationLed*	Yes=1, No=0	Each case was scanned to determine whether evidence was led to prove confusion, or misrepresentation; or reputation.
Overseas Company, *PrivateCompany*, *PublicCompany*, *'Other'*		The business status of the party was manually coded from the name given on the court records. All private companies which were subsidiaries of public companies were coded as Public Company. Company structure was identified from ASIC and IBISWorld databases and the internet. 'Other' includes unincorporated entities such as individuals, statutory bodies, etc.

11 The place of expert evidence in unfair competition cases

The Australian experience

Sam Ricketson

I. Introduction

The use of expert evidence in Australian unfair competition cases is a matter of some controversy. Widely differing views have been expressed as to the utility of such evidence in assisting courts in their determinations. At one extreme, it is said that expert opinion on such matters as reputation, likely consumer reactions and questions of damage can rarely, if ever, be helpful to a court in determining what are ultimately matters of common-sense judgement. At the other end of the spectrum, however, there is the equally strongly expressed view that such determinations can only properly be made in the light of opinion evidence from such experts as marketers, advertisers and behavioural psychologists.

The purpose of this chapter therefore is to examine the present law and practice in Australia relating to the use of expert evidence in unfair competition cases, having regard to the provisions of the old common law and the newer provisions of the Evidence Act 1995 (Cth) ('Evidence Act'), as well as relevant rules of court and practice guidelines. Are such matters as reputation and likelihood of confusion really susceptible to expert evidence, and in what respects, if any, is such evidence likely to assist? In this regard, it may be helpful to refer to the use of expert evidence in other areas of more traditionally recognised expertise, such as patents, construction and medico-legal cases, as well comparing what is done in other areas where the relevant expertise is of a more qualitative and qualified kind, such as economic evidence in trade practices cases and accounting evidence in valuation cases. It will be seen that

At the outset, the author should indicate that he was involved as counsel in one of the cases discussed in this essay, namely *Cadbury Schweppes Pty Ltd* v. *Darrell Lea Chocolate Shops Pty Ltd* (2006) 228 ALR 719 and the following appeals and further hearings. He also takes this opportunity to acknowledge his thanks to Colin Golvan, SC and the Hon. Peter Heerey, QC for reading this chapter in draft form and for their useful comments and insights. However, the opinions expressed herein, and any errors, are the responsibility of the author alone.

there is no single approach that fits all cases, and it will be argued that expert evidence, however framed, can only have a limited role to play in cases involving brands and reputation. In such cases, the issues before courts turn ultimately on purely factual matters, such as the volume and extent of sales, the volume and scale of advertising and promotion, length of use, and so on. In the absence of actual evidence of confusion, the legal inferences that can reasonably be drawn from such evidence are quintessentially matters for judicial determination and the assistance to be gained from expert opinion evidence applies only within a narrow compass.

II. The role of expert evidence – facts and opinion

It is trite to say that typical court cases in an adversary system will involve the following steps:

1. The ascertainment of a set of facts.
2. The formulation of some claim arising from that set of facts, that is, a question that will require resolution in favour of one party or another.
3. The identification of relevant legal rules or principles that will be capable of resolving the question or questions raised under 2.
4. The application of those rules or principles to the particular set of facts identified under 1.

There may be a certain amount of overlap or interaction between these different steps, in particular 1 and 2, as the facts dictate the kind of claim that can be made, but the initial identification of those facts will be clearly influenced by the kind of question a plaintiff wants to ask, informed, no doubt, by an understanding of what are the relevant legal principles under step 3. Nonetheless, step 1 remains the most critical, and none of the others will be possible without a proper factual foundation.

If all this sounds too simplistic, consider its application in a typical unfair competition case involving protection of a 'brand' in a common law jurisdiction (and the same is probably true in civil law jurisdictions as well). To succeed, the plaintiff will usually have to point to:

1. the existence of a reputation or goodwill in the marketplace that attaches to a particular sign, mark or getup used by the plaintiff – in lay terms, that its 'brand' is well recognised and understood by consumers in the relevant market;
2. instances of consumer confusion arising in relation to use of some similar form of indicia by another party (possibly, but not necessarily, a competitor), or at least the likelihood that some confusion might

arise, in the sense that consumers will be led to believe that the goods or services so branded are those of, or are in some way associated with, the plaintiff; and

3. the 'damage', or likelihood of such damage, to the plaintiff as a consequence of the defendant's conduct.

There will be a series of further questions or refinements to each of these principal requirements that may differ from jurisdiction to jurisdiction. For example:

(a) How widely is the notion of insignia or brand to be drawn? Does it, for example, extend to shapes, colours, sounds, etc.?
(b) How is the notion of confusion is to be defined? For example, does this require a mistaken belief that D's goods are those of Y, or is a simple representation of affiliation or sponsorship enough? What is the position if consumers are simply uncertain whose goods or services are whose, and is it necessary that the parties be in direct competition?
(c) How is the question of damage to be quantified? For example, is it something as concrete as loss of sales, or as ephemeral as some kind of notional 'blurring' or tarnishing of the plaintiff's wider repute?

A further question is whether it is necessary to show that the defendant has acted with some kind of intention or even fraud, and the effect that such a finding may have.

Essentially, all these questions involve legal determinations of one kind or the other, influenced, no doubt, by policy considerations. Nonetheless, while the shape and precise contour of these rules may differ somewhat from jurisdiction to jurisdiction, they will all require a firm factual foundation before they can be brought into play in favour of a plaintiff, and this will involve the adducing of evidence going to each of the three main issues identified above: (a) reputation; (b) confusion; and (c) damage. In a typical case, how is this to be achieved?

Unlike many kinds of civil litigation, such as a vehicle collision case, the 'facts' in an unfair competition case have a nebulous character. For example, in a vehicle collision case, the primary fact observed by a witness or witnesses may be that the car driven by D collided with the car driven by P. Proof of these facts may be confirmed by admissions from P and D that they were driving their respective cars at the time of the collision. Damage to each of the cars and/or occupants may be equally capable of ascertainment by direct observation. The legal question so far as liability in such a case may be whether D was driving her car with due care, but again there may be directly observable primary facts that will assist here, for example: that she went through a red light, was driving on the wrong side of the road, had an excess blood alcohol reading, etc. These facts may then assist the court in drawing an inference of negligence, and hence liability, on the part of D.

By contrast, in a typical unfair competition case, the 'facts' are difficult to ascertain directly. What, for example, is 'reputation' or 'goodwill'? Legal definitions may suggest that this is the 'drawing power' of a brand or the 'attractive force which brings in custom'[1] – the elusive element in the brand that identifies the branded goods or services to consumers as being those of the particular trader or business. 'Market recognition' or 'market presence' may be other useful ways of describing what is meant here. But factual support for the existence of 'reputation' will largely be a matter of inference from other facts that can be more readily established, such as:

- the volume of sales or transactions in goods or services bearing the relevant brand;
- the period over which these transactions have taken place, as well as the territories where this has occurred (for example, in Australia historically some brands of beer widely sold in one state were unknown in other states);
- the price point at which the goods or services are supplied;
- the channels through which the parties' goods or services are distributed;
- the way in which such distribution occurs and consumers purchase those goods or services;
- the scale and geographical spread of advertising of the branded goods or services (brochures, mailbox drops, newspapers, radio and television, internet, etc.);
- 'peer recognition' of the brand, as revealed through trade and other publications, awards, etc.; and
- market surveys of consumers showing their awareness of the brand.

Likewise, in the case of 'confusion', there is a range of evidence that will assist in the drawing of inferences of confusion or likely confusion, ranging from instances of actual consumer confusion (the most obvious being purchases of D's goods or services in the belief that they are those of P or logs of mistaken telephone or email inquiries) to surveys of consumer reactions both in real life settings and in hypothetical scenarios. Finally, there is a range of other evidence that will assist in drawing the inference of damage to the plaintiff's reputation or goodwill, such as a specific drop in sales commensurate with the period of the defendant's entry into the relevant marketplace (or reduction in anticipated sales), evidence that

[1] As per Lord MacNaghten in *Commissioners of Inland Revenue* v. *Muller & Co.'s Margarine Limited* [1901] AC 217, 223.

the quality and price of the defendant's goods or services are inferior to those of the plaintiff, and the loss of commercial opportunities through distributors and consumers refusing to deal with the plaintiff.

All the above are factual matters from which inferences of reputation, confusion and damage may be drawn by a court, although contrary inferences may also be drawn from evidence produced by a defendant, for example:

- any disclaimers on their products or in their advertising;
- price differentials between the parties' products (suggesting that they are operating in different segments of the market);
- the presence of third parties in the marketplace that use similar branding; and
- other differences in the markets in which the parties respectively operate.

In general, courts have little difficulty in dealing with these kinds of evidence, and experienced practitioners are well versed in the preparation of such evidence (which may often be a time-consuming and costly exercise). What, then, is the role of expert evidence in all of this? As a starting point, such evidence breaks the general rule that excludes evidence of opinion – what someone thinks about something – rather than evidence of a fact directly observed. In Australia, this is now contained in s. 76(1) of the Evidence Act:

> Evidence of an opinion is not admissible to prove the existence of a fact about the existence of which the opinion was expressed.

In a crude sense, this means that the only person entitled to reach an opinion in a case is the court itself, in drawing whatever inference is reasonably open to it in light of the factual evidence adduced. In a medical negligence case involving a surgical operation, therefore, where P is suing the surgeon, it will not be open for P's neighbour, W, who had the same operation, to give evidence of his opinion that D had not performed the operation as well as his own.[2] Likewise, in an unfair competition case, a plaintiff's witness should not be able to say that, in light of the extent of sales made by the plaintiff's business and the close similarities in the plaintiff's and defendant's brands, it is likely that consumers will be likely to be confused – this would be an inadmissible opinion for the purposes of proving the ultimate issue of whether such a likelihood of confusion would arise (a matter for the court to decide and no one else). However, there are various exceptions to the opinion rule that may assist in these

[2] This example is given in the statutory note to Evidence Act s. 79.

kinds of cases. One of these is the 'lay opinion' rule in s. 78 which allows for the giving of evidence of an opinion by a person where:

(a) the opinion is based on what the person saw, heard or otherwise perceived about a matter or event; and
(b) evidence of the opinion is necessary to obtain an adequate account or understanding of the person's perception of the matter or event.

The other exception, more relevant for present purposes, is the expert opinion rule, which is contained in s. 79(1):

If a person has specialised knowledge based on the person's training, study or experience, the opinion rule does not apply to evidence of an opinion of that person that is wholly or substantially based on that knowledge.

This needs to be read in conjunction with s. 80 which abolishes the former common law rules precluding the giving of expert opinion on the 'ultimate issue' in a case or on matters of 'common knowledge':

Evidence of an opinion is not inadmissible only because it is about:
(a) a fact in issue or an ultimate issue; or
(b) a matter of common knowledge.

As will be seen, this provision expands the scope for the offering of expert opinion evidence. In particular, it cannot be said by a trial judge, 'Oh, this evidence is of no relevance or assistance to me because the matters before me that I have to determine are matters of everyday experience and there is no need for expert opinion on this.' Sensible as such a rule may be in cases involving ordinary consumer reactions in relation to the purchase of everyday goods and services, such as may arise in many unfair competition cases,[3] s. 80 now enjoins Australian courts to have regard to it, if offered (what they then do with it is quite another matter). It should be noted that this provision, enacted in 1995 as a Commonwealth statute and as a template for corresponding state legislation, was reviewed in

[3] See, for example, *Dalgety Spillers Food Ltd* v. *Food Brokers Ltd* [1994] FSR 504, 527–8, where Blackburne J. of the UK Chancery Division ruled such evidence to be inadmissible, stating that:

[b]roadly, the test in such cases must be whether the experience which a judge must be taken to possess as an ordinary shopper or consumer will enable him, just as well as any other, to assess the likelihood of confusion. If it will, then the evidence will not be admissible. If, for whatever reason it will not, then such evidence will be admissible.

To similar effect, see *Symonds Cider & English Wine Company Ltd* v. *Showerings (Ireland) Ltd* [1997] IEHC 1 at [20] (Laffoy J.). However, it should be noted that in both these cases, the judges acknowledged that particular markets involving special categories of consumers may require expert evidence to inform a trial judge as to how such consumers go about their purchasing decisions.

2005 in a joint report by the Australian Law Reform Commission and the New South Wales and Victorian Law Reform Commissions, and its retention was recommended.[4] In the Commissions' view, s. 80 removed doubts under the common law about the admissibility of expert evidence on such matters as expert evidence from psychiatrists or psychologists about human behaviour or on child development.[5] They also noted that it complemented s. 79, which requires that the expert opinion should be based 'wholly or substantially' on expert opinion, not on matters of common knowledge, and that the discretionary power conferred under s. 135 (see further below) provided a mechanism for excluding such evidence where appropriate.[6]

As for s. 79 itself, it will be seen that this embodies a number of requirements for its application. These were spelt out in their most stringent form by Heydon JA (as he then was) in the NSW Court of Appeal in *Makita (Australia) Pty Ltd* v. *Sprowles*,[7] a case involving expert engineering opinion in relation to an injury occurring on stairs that were allegedly faulty. His Honour said (in a passage much quoted by counsel in subsequent cases):

> In short, if evidence tendered as expert opinion evidence is to be admissible, it must be agreed or demonstrated that there is a field of 'specialised knowledge'; there must be an identified aspect of that field in which the witness demonstrates that by reason of specified training, study or experience, the witness has become an expert; the opinion proffered must be 'wholly or substantially based on the witness's expert knowledge'; so far as the opinion is based on facts 'observed' by the expert, they must be identified and admissibly proved by the expert, and so far as the opinion is based on 'assumed' or 'accepted' facts, they must be identified and proved in some other way; it must be established that the facts on which the opinion is based form a proper foundation for it; and the opinion of an expert requires demonstration or examination of the scientific or other intellectual basis of the conclusions reached: that is, the expert's evidence must explain how the field of 'specialised knowledge' in which the witness is expert by reason of 'training, study or experience', and on which the opinion is 'wholly or substantially based', applies to the facts assumed or observed so as to produce the opinion propounded. If all these matters are not made explicit, it is not possible to be sure whether the opinion is based wholly or substantially on the expert's specialised knowledge. If the court cannot be sure of that, the evidence is strictly speaking not admissible, and, so far as it is admissible, of diminished weight. And an attempt to make the basis of the opinion explicit may

[4] Australian Law Reform Commission and the New South Wales and Victorian Law Reform Commissions, Uniform Evidence Law, ALRC Report No. 102, NSWLR Report 112 and VLRC Final Report (2005) [9.137].

[5] *Ibid.* [9.134]. [6] *Ibid.* [9.136].

[7] (2001) 52 NSWLR 705 ('*Makita*'). This decision related to the corresponding provision in the Evidence Act 1995 (NSW).

reveal that it is not based on specialised expert knowledge, but, to use Gleeson CJ's characterisation of the evidence in *HG* v. *The Queen* (at 428 [41]), on 'a combination of speculation, inference, personal and second-hand views as to the credibility of the complainant, and a process of reasoning which went well beyond the field of expertise'.[8]

According to Heydon JA, there are six requirements that expert evidence should meet under s. 79 of the Evidence Act:

1. there must be a field of 'specialised knowledge';
2. there must be an identified aspect of that field in which the witness demonstrates that by reason of specified training, study or experience, the witness has become an expert;
3. the opinion proffered must be 'wholly or substantially based on the witness's expert knowledge';
4. so far as the opinion is based on facts 'observed' by the expert, they must be identified and admissibly proved by the expert, and so far as the opinion is based on 'assumed' or 'accepted' facts, they must be identified and proved in some other way;
5. it must be established that the facts on which the opinion is based form a proper foundation for it; and
6. the opinion must demonstrate the scientific or other intellectual basis of the conclusions reached: that is, the expert's evidence must explain how the field of 'specialised knowledge' in which the witness is expert by reason of 'training, study or experience', and on which the opinion is 'wholly or substantially based', applies to the facts assumed or observed so as to produce the opinion propounded.

Heydon JA went on to state[9] that his six propositions corresponded to the views of the Full Federal Court in *Ocean Marine Mutual Insurance Association (Europe) OV* v. *Jetopay Pty Ltd*.[10] However, it should be noted that in that case the Full Court had ruled the claimed expert evidence inadmissible because none of them was shown by the evidence to be experts in marine engineering (the relevant area in that case).[11] The Court also stated that:

> The further requirement that an opinion be based on specialised knowledge would normally be satisfied by the person who expresses the opinion demonstrating the reasoning process by which the opinion was reached. Thus, a report in which an opinion is recorded should expose the reasoning of its author in a way that it would demonstrate that the opinion is based on particular specialised

[8] *Ibid.* 733–4. [9] *Ibid.* 744–5 [86].
[10] (2000) 120 FCR 146, 151 [21]–[23] (Black CJ, Cooper and Emmett JJ).
[11] *Ibid.* 150 [19], 151 [25], 152 [27]–[28] and [32].

knowledge. Similarly, opinion evidence given orally should be shown, by exposure of the reasoning process, to be based on relevant specialised knowledge.[12]

Subsequent to these cases, a differently constituted Full Federal Court (Branson, Weinberg and Dowsett JJ) in *Sydneywide Distributors Pty Ltd* v. *Red Bull Australia Pty Ltd*[13] explained how Heydon JA's views should be applied in the context of a trial, noting that the matters referred to by his Honour would more usually go to weight rather than admissibility. Thus, Weinberg and Dowsett JJ stated:

> The use of the phrase 'strictly speaking' in the last sentence [of Heydon JA] should not be overlooked. It may well be correct to say that such evidence is not strictly admissible unless it is shown to have all of the qualities discussed by Heydon JA. However many of those qualities involve questions of degree, requiring the exercise of judgment. For this reason it would be very rare indeed for a court at first instance to reach a decision as to whether tendered expert evidence satisfied all of his Honour's requirements before receiving it as evidence in the proceedings. More commonly, once the witness's claim to expertise is made out and the relevance and admissibility of opinion evidence demonstrated, such evidence is received. The various qualities described by Heydon JA are then assessed in the course of determining the weight to be given to the evidence. There will be cases in which it would be technically correct to rule, at the end of the trial, that the evidence in question was not admissible because it lacked one or other of those qualities, but there would be little utility in so doing. It would probably lead to further difficulties in the appellate process.[14]

Branson J. noted[15] that Heydon JA's approach should be understood as 'a counsel of perfection', and adopted a similar approach to that of Weinberg and Dowsett JJ.[16] There is some practical appeal in this more flexible approach, and one that underlines the distinction between issues of admissibility and issues of weight. In civil proceedings, there may be no great harm in allowing in evidence which may not strictly satisfy all of the *Makita* criteria, with the court dealing with issues of weight down the track after it has heard all the evidence on the case and received submissions from counsel. It is therefore quite conceivable that an expert's opinion evidence could be admitted, but be subsequently found to be of little or no significance (or 'weight') because, for example, the expert's reasoning is shown to be faulty on cross-examination, the facts assumed to be the case for the purposes of the opinion are not ultimately established, and so on. An initial decision to exclude is therefore a more

[12] *Ibid.* 151 [23]. To similar effect, see the later Full Court decision in *Cadbury Schweppes Pty Ltd* v. *Darrell Lea Chocolate Shops Pty Ltd* (2007) 159 FCR 397 ('*Cadbury (Full Court)*'), 419–20 [101]–[110], in particular [106]–[108].

[13] (2002) 55 IPR 354 ('*Red Bull*'). [14] *Ibid.* 379 [87].

[15] *Ibid.* 356–7 [7]. [16] *Ibid.* 357 [10].

'final' matter in that it rules out that evidence from consideration altogether, although, for the sake of completeness, it should be noted that the Evidence Act provides for a general residual statutory discretion under s. 135 for a court to exclude evidence if its probative value is substantially outweighed by the danger that the evidence might:
(a) be unfairly prejudicial to a party; or
(b) be misleading or confusing; or
(c) cause or result in undue waste of time[17]
Accordingly, there will be, in theory at least, two stages at which the admissibility of expert evidence is open to attack: (a) initially, on the basis that the expert does not have the required expert knowledge, and (b) subsequently, on the basis that it falls within the court's general discretion to exclude under s. 135. A case arising under (b) would be where it is shown that the facts relied upon by the expert in formulating his or her opinion are irrelevant or cannot be proved or are unlikely to be proved. In such an instance, as the Full Federal Court has observed:

> It should not be for a cross-examiner to endeavour to elicit the facts or assumptions upon which an opinion is expressed, and it would be unfair to leave such matters to the cross-examiner. Except in a straightforward, uncomplicated case, where the facts are admitted or otherwise readily identified, opinion evidence would normally be rejected under s. 135 if the facts or assumptions upon which the opinion is based are not expressly stated.[18]

III. Applying the rules in a brand protection case

How do these rules play out in the context of brand protection? Identifying experts is not as obvious as, for instance, in a patent case involving biotechnology, or in a personal injury case where specialist medical knowledge will be critical in understanding the extent of the injury and degree of impairment. In such cases, the relevant expert disciplines are more sharply defined, as is the extent of assistance that the non-expert court may acquire from the expert opinion. In an unfair competition case involving brands, the relevant expert discipline or disciplines is or are less obvious, and, even when identified, they may appear 'softer' and more speculative than those possessed by an expert biochemist, surgeon

[17] Evidence Act s. 135.
[18] *Cadbury* (*Full Court*), 420 [108]. For a recent copyright infringement case involving architectural plans, see *Barrett Property Group Pty Ltd* v. *Dennis Family Homes Pty Ltd* [2011] FCA 246 (18 March 2011) [215]–[218] (Dodds-Streeton J.) (lack of proper factual foundation for expert witness's opinions on general architectural and design trends in the project home industry).

or marine surveyor ('real' experts). In a brands case, what are the matters on which the provision of an 'expert' opinion might be of material assistance to a court? As the analysis above suggests, there are three areas that the court will typically be required to investigate: reputation, confusion and damage. The practical limitations on factual evidence in each of these areas have been noted: to what extent, then, can expert opinion evidence assist the court in making these determinations?

The scope and extent of the plaintiff's reputation

As noted above, this is something that can only be 'proved' by inferences from other primary facts, such as volume of sales, transactions, advertising expenditure et cetera. But each case arises within a specific industry context, and it may well be that there is a place for evidence of industry practice that places the plaintiff's brand usage within that context. For instance, if the plaintiff is seeking protection for a particular colour or set of colours used on its goods, or a particular kind of shape or device, it would be helpful for a court to have evidence of whether such colours, shapes or devices are commonly used elsewhere in that particular market. The expert in question here may well be someone well versed in that industry, who can give such evidence on the basis of his or her experience and observations over a period of time. They will clearly be offering opinions on the basis of this acquired practical expertise,[19] but this may be of substantial assistance to a judge who has had no direct experience, for example, of marketing and distribution practices in, say, hardware retailing or supermarkets (apart from what he or she may have observed as an ordinary consumer, of which more below). Such 'practical' experts may also be able to offer meaningful opinions on such matters as the placement of brands on products, the way in which products are best promoted in particular settings, the efficacy of particular kinds of advertising campaigns, and so on. The utility of such experts in a courtroom setting might be tested by asking, how would such advice be treated by a company that was seeking to launch a brand for the first time? The extent to which such business decisions are guided by the opinions of those already well versed in the particular industry underlines the potential significance of the assistance that a court may

[19] There may well be an argument here that this is more correctly described as 'lay opinion' evidence within s. 78, rather than expert opinion evidence within s. 79, on the basis that the witness is providing opinion based on what he or she has observed. On the other hand, such a witness will still be bringing to bear a great deal of other practical experience and knowledge that will inform the expression of those opinions and the admissibility of such evidence is therefore more appropriately within the scope of s. 79.

likewise derive in determining the success of a plaintiff in building up the reputation of its brand.

The 'practical' expert, therefore, is one kind of potential expert in this area, but is there a broader range of expertise that may be brought to bear here as well? Many universities today have marketing departments, usually within their business and commerce schools or faculties, and there are certainly sufficient objective criteria to indicate that marketing is a well-established academic discipline, with specialist journals and conferences, structured undergraduate programmes and postgraduate qualifications, and associated professional organisations. In the particular context of brands, there is a significant body of academic literature that points to the existence of an organised set of principles and framework of knowledge that may be relevant to the issues of reputation and brand recognition. This undoubtedly amounts to a 'body of specialized knowledge' within s. 79 of the Evidence Act and the first of the *Makita* principles, and therefore indicates that there may well be scope for opinion evidence from a person possessed of that knowledge, being something perhaps of more general application than the kind of detailed industry-specific knowledge possessed by the 'practical expert' discussed above. Thus, a person acquainted more generally with the academic literature on marketing should potentially be able to offer opinions relevant to the development of brands, say, in the chocolate products market, even if he or she has no direct experience of that market. Such opinions will, of course, require to be based on the appropriate foundation of actual or assumed facts (of which more below), but their lack of 'hands-on' experience should be no barrier to their acceptance as experts. Thus, in the *Red Bull* case, the plaintiff's expert had no direct experience of the sports-drink market, but was accepted as being appropriately qualified in the discipline of marketing. Depending on the way in which such an expert is instructed, he or she may therefore be able to provide useful insights on the reputation of a particular brand.

Confusion

As noted above, in the absence of actual evidence of confusion, the likelihood of confusion will be a matter for inference from primary facts, particularly in relation to the way in which competing products are branded, marketed and otherwise dealt with. It is difficult to see how the discipline of marketing referred to in the preceding paragraphs will assist here, apart from the primary consideration that those who design brands and branding strategies will clearly be concerned to ensure their brands remain distinctive and become more so. However, here we are dealing with the conduct of competitors and the reactions of consumers, and the kind of expertise described above is not directed at addressing such issues, otherwise than, perhaps, providing evidence of what an experienced person, faced with the same evidence as the court, might think on these matters. In some instances, of course, such evidence might well be valuable, for example, where a market is a specialised one and/or the consumers are of a particular kind and where the judge him- or herself may have no experience as an ordinary consumer as to how consumers in that market might react.[20] On the other hand, in the more usual and everyday kind of cases, such an opinion is no different than that of the judge who, moreover, does have a particular expertise not possessed by the expert, namely that of evaluating evidence and drawing inferences from it. For the expert's opinion to offer something more in this context, therefore, it will need to draw upon further insights not otherwise at the court's disposal. And in this context there is a range of expertise that is possessed by some marketing academics that may well be of assistance to a court. On the one hand, at the purely empirical level, there are those who are experienced in designing, carrying out and evaluating consumer surveys and other inquiries into consumer reactions. While such evidence has its own difficulties, not relevant to the present discussion,[21] expert opinion evidence on how such investigations are to be interpreted is potentially very helpful on the issue of likely confusion. At the other end of the spectrum is more abstruse expertise in such areas as behavioural psychology and neuro-psychology which, again, may cast light on the way consumers view certain stimuli such as insignia, colours, and the like, and the way in which such mental processes operate. Such evidence may potentially be of assistance to a court, but it will clearly need to be based on a proper factual foundation before it can be anything other than speculation or mere hypothesis.

Damage

Once again, this remains a matter for inference from primary facts, such as loss of sales or other commercial opportunities, and so on. It is not

[20] As acknowledged by Blackburne J. in *Dalgety Spillers Foods Ltd* v. *Food Brokers Ltd* [1994] FSR 504, 527. To similar effect, see *Sodastream Limited* v. *Thorn Cascade Company limited* [1982] RPC 459 (Kerr OLJ) (evidence from persons in a specific market, that of refillable carbon dioxide cylinders, as to how persons in that market might react to the defendant's similarly coloured product) and *Guccio Gucci SpA* v. *Paolo Gucci* [1991] FSR 89, 90–1 (Browne-Wilkinson VC) (a case involving designer goods of a kind not normally purchased by the judge). See also *Taittinger SA* v. *Allbev Limited* [1993] FSR 641, 663 (Peter Gibson LJ).

[21] For example, issues of hearsay.

immediately obvious what expert evidence can add here to the court's armoury. Anecdotal evidence of what has happened in other similar cases (and might therefore occur in the case before the court) is one possible suggestion, but the factual foundation for such evidence may often be flimsy. Psychological evidence of what may happen when consumers mentally process misleading information is another suggestion, but is this sufficient? How can a court be satisfied that a hypothetical possibility, however attractively framed, will, or will be likely to occur, in the case before it? Can, or should, a judge in such circumstances allow an expert's opinion to displace his or her own role as the ultimate finder of fact?

IV. Some relevant Australian cases

Red Bull

These questions have only received piecemeal attention to date by Australian courts in the unfair competition context, but the cases amply illustrate the difficulties involved in receiving and applying such evidence.

The first appellate court decision in which the role of opinion evidence from marketing experts was considered at length is the *Red Bull* case, already referred to above.[22] This concerned the insignia and colouring used on competing cans of 'energy drinks'. While expert evidence from both sides was received without objection at trial, its admissibility was raised on appeal, particularly the evidence of the respondent (plaintiff) that had postulated the notion of a 'gestalt' or general image that had been copied in the appellant's product, albeit with various differences. There are several notable aspects of this case for present purposes:

1. It put paid to any intuitive or 'feel it in my waters' objection that marketing is not an area for expert evidence in the first place, and therefore fails to meet the requirements of s. 79 of the Evidence Act, as explained by Heydon JA in *Makita*. In the words of Weinberg and Dowsett JJ:

   It cannot be seriously suggested that marketing (including the mechanics and effects of advertising) is not an area of expert study. The very large amounts of

[22] It should not be assumed that this was the first unfair competition/brand protection case in Australia where such evidence had been presented and admitted: it is certainly clear that this had occurred in a number of previous first instance decisions in the Federal Court of Australia and one commentator, indeed, has referred to this as a 'long standing practice' of that court: see Caron Beaton-Wells, 'Do Judges Buy Chocolate and Does It Matter?' (2006) 14 *Trade Practices Law Journal* 228 (a comment on the decision of Heerey J. in *Cadbury Schweppes Pty Ltd* v. *Darrell Lea Chocolate Shops Pty Ltd (No. 4)* (2006) 228 ALR 719, which is discussed in the principal text below).

money notoriously spent on advertising make such a proposition unlikely. Dr Beaton's curriculum vitae demonstrates that marketing is an organized area of study. In par. 2 of his curriculum vitae (AB 576) he says:

> 'As part of my Masters of business administration at the University of Witwatersrand, I studied the subject organizational behaviour which subject is based on an understanding of how human beings behave in various settings. These settings include, for example, the underpinnings of marketing including an analysis of how consumers behave in response to the marketing stimuli of marketers and their competitors.'

He has had substantial experience in the commercial world with advertising, packaging and other marketing issues and has done research in the area. The evidence demonstrates an area of specialized knowledge and Dr Beaton's training and experience in that area. The close relationship between such expertise and the matters in issue in this case is obvious.[23]

2. Given that the expert evidence (from both sides) had been received at trial without objection, the Full Court now viewed any further arguments on appeal against its admissibility with some caution. However, this was not to say that proper objections could not have been made at trial, the problem now being that, on appeal, it was difficult to show that the trial judge had placed undue or incorrect weight on that evidence in making his findings. In other words, the opportunity for challenge had been present at trial, but had not been taken up then, either by way of submission or relevant cross-examination of the witness. These matters are important for two very practical reasons indicated in both s. 79 and *Makita*:
   (i) The expert's opinions must be based on a factual foundation. In particular, these will include the facts of the particular case, but may also extend to other 'facts' on which broader opinions are expressed, for example, the results of empirical research in the general area. It may well be the case that these facts will need to be 'assumed' to exist, at least in part, and will need to be established by the plaintiff through other evidence before the conclusion of the trial. However, unless the opinion relates squarely to these facts, it will be of no value to the court, and may well end up being excluded for lack of relevance or given little or no weight. Exclusion under the discretion contained in s. 135 may also be possible, if the criteria listed in that provision are satisfied.
   (ii) The expert's process of reasoning on these facts must be clearly articulated and explained. In simple terms, the expert must explain what he or she has done.

[23] *Red Bull*, 377–8 [82]–[83].

3. In *Red Bull*, it was difficult for the appellant to raise meaningful objections based on the matters listed in the preceding paragraph. There was nothing in the evidence of Beaton (the plaintiff's expert) that would have justified a finding by the Full Court that he had not based his opinion on an appropriate factual foundation or that his reasoning had not been properly exposed. Any doubts about these issues required exploration through cross-examination at trial, but this had not been done.
4. Beaton's expert evidence as to the notion of 'gestalt', a concept embracing more than just the particular insignia applied to its products by Red Bull but also matters of colouring, placement and shape, was therefore accepted by the Full Court. How significant this was is hard to say, but it did provide a marketing framework that was held to be consistent with traditional passing off principles in relation to get-up and presentation and to go no further than what the law allowed. Accordingly, it might be possible to argue that the evidence made no difference to the outcome of the case, in particular as there was clear evidence that the appellant had deliberately sought to imitate the Red Bull product. On the other hand, it can be said that the expert evidence, particularly as it was unchallenged, provided clear confirmation to the plaintiff's claim: it is always useful to be able to say that 'scientific' opinion underpins the legal conclusion. An important consequence, therefore, of the *Red Bull* case, was that expert evidence could now be seen as a useful part of an unfair competition case: could one indeed properly proceed without such evidence?

The Cadbury *litigation over the use of the colour purple*

This was clearly the view taken by the applicants in another important case involving a claim in passing off and contravention of the misleading and deceptive conduct provisions of the Trade Practices Act 1974 (TPA)[24] by the leading chocolate manufacturer, Cadbury-Schweppes Ltd ('Cadbury'), against another, smaller chocolate manufacturer, Darrell Lea Chocolate Shops Pty Ltd ('Darrell Lea'). The subject of this proceeding was the use by Darrell Lea (for a limited period of time) of the colour purple (referred to as 'Cadbury purple') on its products and on and within its retail premises.[25] Along with extensive evidence of its

[24] These provisions are now contained within the Australian Consumer Law, Competition and Consumer Act 2010 (Cth) sch. 2 s. 18.

[25] The author was involved in this litigation as junior counsel for the respondent, Darrell Lea Chocolate Shops Pty Ltd.

use of purple (but none of any actual consumer deception or confusion), Cadbury filed expert opinion evidence from a number of marketing academics. Several of these witnesses taught and researched in the area of marketing generally, with some knowledge of retail marketing though not specifically in relation to confectionary or chocolate products, but one of the witnesses had expertise in behavioural psychology and gave evidence as to the effect of colour on consumer decision-making processes. In general, the evidence was directed at providing the opinions of these experts on the issues of reputation and confusion arising out of the experts' review of much of the Cadbury factual evidence of its use of the colour purple on its products and in the light of their own experience and knowledge (most notably in the case of the witness with the psychological background). However, it also contained a number of expressions of opinion as to the likely damage that Cadbury would suffer as a result of Darrell Lea's conduct. In preparing their evidence, the experts had limited awareness of the way in which Darrell Lea had actually used the colour purple, and no direct awareness of the specific usages complained of during the period in contention (2000–4). As noted above, there was no evidence of any instances of actual confusion on the part of consumers, nor was there any other evidence of any actual loss or damage that might have been sustained by Cadbury.

In the light of *Red Bull*, the decision to furnish such extensive expert opinion evidence was understandable, perhaps even advisable, but its limitations should have been apparent, even at the outset and its admissibility and utility ended up becoming the principal issues in the proceeding. At first instance, following objection by Darrell Lea, Heerey J. excluded it altogether, though not on the ground urged by Darrell Lea, namely that the factual material relied upon by the witnesses was not proved and/or was inadequate (no challenge was made to the expertise of the witnesses).[26] Rather, his Honour referred to the decisions of other Federal Court judges in brand protection cases, in which there had been criticism of the utility of expert opinion evidence on matters of ordinary everyday experience.[27] Thus, in *Cat Media Pty Ltd* v. *Opti-Healthcare Pty Ltd*[28] Branson J. had said:

> It seems to me that evidence of opinions based on market research and expert appreciation of consumer behaviour will rarely be of assistance in litigation where the Court's primary concern is with the behaviour to be expected of, and the judgments likely to be made by, ordinary (even if it might be thought, somewhat

[26] *Cadbury Schweppes Pty Ltd* v. *Darrell Lea Chocolate Shops Pty Ltd* (2006) 228 ALR 719 ('*Cadbury* (*Earlier Judgment*)').
[27] *Ibid.* 722–3 [8]–[13]. [28] [2003] FCA 133 (4 March 2003) ('*Cat Media*').

credulous) members of the community intent on making a relatively modest purchase in a conventional way. I endorse the comment of Beaumont J in *Pacific Publications Pty Ltd* v. *IPC Media Pty Ltd* [2003] FCA 104 at [92] that where a claim is essentially a matter for the Court's impression, expert views which are merely 'impressionistic' can be given no more than nominal weight.[29]

Passing approval of these remarks was also to be found in the Full Federal Court in *Domain Names Australia Pty Ltd* v. *.au Domain Administration Ltd*.[30] Nonetheless, questions of admissibility were not in issue in these cases, but rather the weight to be assigned to such evidence. At common law, exclusion altogether would have been allowable, on the basis that 'the experience which a judge must be taken to possess as an ordinary shopper or consumer will enable him, just as well as any other, to assess the likelihood of confusion'.[31] Heerey J. therefore proceeded to exclude the evidence completely, on the basis that it would provide no assistance to him in the case before him above and beyond his own experience as an everyday consumer. In making his admissibility ruling, his Honour did not refer to s. 80 of the Evidence Act, which, as seen above, allows expert opinion evidence even on a matter of common knowledge. The possible relevance of this section was also not raised in submissions by the parties at the time of his ruling or later during the proceeding.[32] His Honour then went on to render a decision against Cadbury's claim on the basis of the remaining evidence.[33]

The matter was duly appealed, and Cadbury was successful,[34] solely on the ground of his Honour's failure to take account of s. 80. While the Full Court acknowledged that there might well be deficiencies in the expert evidence, it was not prepared to conclude that it was of so little weight that the trial judge would have reached the same result even had

29 *Ibid.* [55]. 30 (2004) 139 FCR 215, 221 [21].

31 *Dalgety Spillers Foods Ltd* v. *Food Brokers Ltd* [1994] FSR 504, 527 (Blackburne J.), and see also *Symonds Cider & English Wine Company Ltd* v. *Showerings (Ireland) Ltd* [1997] IEHC 1 (10 January 1997) [20]), both referred to by Heerey J. at 723 [13].

32 See the comments of the Full Court on appeal: *Cadbury (Full Court)*, 409–410 [49]. The same point was made by Heerey J in a subsequent hearing in the proceeding when he said (of his initial admissibility ruling): 'The primary judge should have been aware of s. 80(b), and counsel should have directed his attention to it' (*Cadbury Schweppes Pty Ltd* v. *Darrell Lea Chocolate Shops Pty Ltd (No. 5)* [2007] FCA 1245 [42] ('*Cadbury (No. 5)*'). It should be noted, however, that his Honour's failure to refer to s. 80 does not receive any specific comment in Dr Beaton-Wells' otherwise critical and perceptive case comment on his admissibility ruling (Beaton-Wells, 'Judges Buy Chocolate', 228).

33 *Cadbury Schweppes Pty Ltd* v. *Darrell Lea Chocolate Shops Pty Ltd (No. 4)* ('*Cadbury (No. 4)*') (2006) 69 IPR 23. For the record, it should be noted that a significant volume of other evidence was excluded on the basis of late filing, but this was not the subject of any subsequent appeal.

34 *Cadbury (Full Court)*.

it been admitted[35] (this was the argument advanced by Darrell Lea in its submission that the appeal should therefore be dismissed). The upshot was that the Full Court referred the case back to Heerey J. for further hearing, so as to allow him to reconsider the admissibility question, as well as any possible objections that might still arise under s. 135.[36] After a number of interruptions, including an unsuccessful application for special leave to appeal to the High Court against the Full Court's order of a further hearing and an application for his Honour to remove himself on the basis of apprehended bias (and several appeals back to the Full Court on this and other matters),[37] Heerey J. admitted the disputed expert evidence which was supplemented by further reports directed at explaining the foundations for the expert opinions. The expert witnesses were duly cross-examined and re-examined, and lengthy submissions were then made on the questions of admissibility (including interesting submissions by Cadbury as to the inferences to be drawn in its favour because of the alleged failure of the cross-examiner to challenge certain aspects of the experts' evidence under the rule in *Browne* v. *Dunn*).[38] After

[35] *Ibid.* 420 [111].

[36] *Ibid.* 419–20 [101]–[110]. See further the discussion of the Full Court's decision by Dr Caron Beaton-Wells entitled 'Even if Judges Do Buy Chocolate, it Should Not Matter' (2008) 16 *Trade Practices Law Journal* 55.

[37] The allegation of apprehended (not actual) bias lay in the Applicant's view that his Honour had expressed himself too strongly on the lack of utility of this kind of expert evidence and therefore that 'a fair minded lay observer might reasonably apprehend that the judge might not bring an impartial and unprejudiced mind to the resolution of the question the judge is required to decide' (the relevant test being that laid down by the High Court of Australia in *Johnson* v. *Johnson* (2000) 201 CLR 488, 492 [11]). His Honour dismissed the application for him to recuse himself in *Cadbury* (*No. 5*), saying at [42] that while he disagreed with the policy behind s. 80 (in the context of expert evidence on marketing), he would, of course, apply the law as it stood:

> The primary judge should have been aware of *s 80(b)*, and counsel should have directed his attention to it. Judges, like other citizens, do not always agree with laws. But judges have to administer the law as it stands. The observer would think, as did the Full Court, that this will happen in the present case.

His Honour's decision was upheld on appeal: *Cadbury* (*Full Court*) 174 FCR 175, but the issue of apprehended bias was reactivated after his Honour had given his further decision in the proceeding (see further n. 40 below).

[38] (1893) 6 R 67. This is a rule of 'procedural fairness' (*Raben Footwear Pty Ltd* v. *Polygram Records Inc.* (1997) 145 ALR 1, 14–15, per Tamberlin J.) which is 'designed to ensure fairness to the witness so as to enable the witness to deal with the disputed matter and perhaps to give further evidence in corroboration or to contradict any inference which may be sought to be drawn' (*Allied Pastoral Holdings Pty Ltd* v. *FCT* [1983] 1 NSWLR 1, 26–7, per Hunt J.). In the *Cadbury* case, the argument was that, as its experts had not considered many of the 'actual facts' of the case – that is, the actual usage of purple by Darrell Lea – it should have been cross-examined as to its opinions on these matters rather than the more limited scenarios that it had considered in its written evidence. To the extent that the Darrell Lea cross-examination did not seek to elicit the experts'

consideration of this further evidence, as well as reviewing the findings he had already made in relation to the remainder of the evidence (the 'factual' evidence), his Honour confirmed his previous findings that there was no passing off or contravention of the TPA provisions by Darrell Lea.[39] Although further appeals were instituted against this decision, the matter was finally settled by the parties without any appellate determination of his Honour's findings on liability.[40]

Ultimately, the issue of expert opinion evidence in the *Cadbury* litigation turned upon the weight to be attached to that evidence, rather than any question of admissibility (or even the application of the discretion to exclude under s. 135 or the application of the rule in *Browne* v. *Dunn* – both interesting questions in their own right). The second decision of Heerey J., however, indicates clearly the difficulties involved in adducing expert opinion evidence in this area. This may be illustrated by considering the 'factual' findings that he made in his initial decision, on the basis of the 'factual' evidence before him but in the absence of the expert opinion evidence. This evidence was extensive, including internal marketing reports, exhibits of various Cadbury products using the colour purple, volume of sales and market distribution, advertising campaigns, internal marketing reports and evaluations, and the like. In the words of Captain Renault in the film *Casablanca*, most of this was a rounding up of 'the usual suspects' one would expect to see in any passing off/trade practices case in Australia, although it was noteworthy that there was no evidence of any consumer confusion of any sort. As his Honour's findings on this

further opinions on these matters, Heerey J. held that this was unnecessary, as Cadbury (and its experts) were well aware throughout of the challenges being made to their evidence and there was no basis therefore for invoking the rule in *Browne* v. *Dunn*: *Cadbury (No. 8)* (2008) 75 IPR 557, 569 [32]–[37], 572 [44]–[45]. In this regard, the remarks of the Full Court in the first appeal as to the responsibilities of cross-examiners in relation to expert evidence (set out above in the principal text) are clearly pertinent: *Cadbury (Full Court)*, 420 [108].

39 *Cadbury Schweppes Pty Ltd* v. *Darrell Lea Chocolate Shops Pty Ltd (No. 8)* (2008) 75 IPR 557 ('*Cadbury (No. 8)*').

40 Although an appeal on all grounds was instituted by Cadbury, the Full Court divided this into two segments: the first related to an appeal against his Honour's refusal to recuse himself on the basis of apprehended bias, and the second dealt with all the remaining grounds, including alleged errors in his Honour's reasoning, including his treatment of the expert evidence. It was correct for the Full Court to proceed this way, in view of the High Court decision in *Concrete Pty Ltd* v. *Parramatta Design and Developments Pty Ltd* (2006) 229 CLR 577, under which the apprehended bias issue is to be dealt with first in any appeal: obviously, if a trial judge's ruling on this question is upheld, the Full Court can then proceed to determine the other appeal grounds, but if the bias ground is found to be made out this will require the case to be sent back for a new trial. In the *Cadbury* case, the Full Court dismissed (by a majority) the apprehended bias part of the appeal (*Cadbury (Full Court)*), and the parties then reached a confidential settlement on the substantive issues of liability before the second tranche of the appeal was determined).

evidence are set out in a concise list, they are worth setting out here in full, before considering how and in what way expert opinion evidence might further have assisted the court. His Honour found as follows:

1. There is wide awareness among Australian consumers of the use by Cadbury of a dark purple colour: (i) in connection with the marketing, packaging and presentation of certain chocolate products, particularly Cadbury Dairy Milk and other block milk chocolate products; and (ii) as a corporate colour.
2. Cadbury does not have an exclusive reputation in the use of this dark purple colour in connection with chocolate. Other traders have, with Cadbury's knowledge, for many years used a similar shade of purple. Cadbury has not consistently enforced its alleged exclusive reputation. In relation to its chief competitor Nestlé, Cadbury has, for its own commercial reasons, permitted a use of purple in relation to popular chocolate products.
3. Cadbury markets many chocolate products which have little or no purple in their packaging.
4. Cadbury products, regardless of the presence or absence of purple in the packaging, always bear the Cadbury name in a distinctive script.
5. Cadbury's use of purple in marketing advertising and promotion is, and is seen by consumers to be, inextricably bound up with the well-known name 'Cadbury' in its distinctive script. Cadbury never uses the colour purple in isolation as an indicium of trade.
6. Cadbury products, with insignificant exceptions, are not sold at retail level at premises owned or occupied by Cadbury.
7. Cadbury's marketing of chocolate heavily emphasises specific products and, in particular, Cadbury Dairy Milk block chocolate.
8. 'Darrell Lea' is a name well known in connection with chocolate in those parts of Australia where it operates, even though not as well known as Cadbury.
9. The names 'Darrell Lea' and 'Cadbury' are quite distinct in sound and appearance (especially with the respective scripts the parties have adopted) and not likely to be mistaken for each other.
10. Darrell Lea has, since at least Christmas 2000, used in its marketing, packaging, promotion and point of sale presentation a purple colour much like that used by Cadbury. There has been particular use at Christmas 2000 to 2004 inclusive and also uses at other times. Such usage has diminished and purple has been to a significant extent replaced by blue since 2004.
11. Darrell Lea did not adopt the colour purple with the intention of leading consumers to believe its products were Cadbury products or that it, or its products, had some kind of association with Cadbury.

12. Most of Darrell Lea's retailing occurs in premises which it owns or occupies. Other retailing occurs from separate stands or displays in retail premises, such as newsagents, pharmacies, convenience stores and video stores. Darrell Lea has only a minor presence in supermarkets and only, in the past, to a very limited and transient extent in the major chains. Its products are not presented for sale in close proximity to Cadbury's.
13. Darrell Lea's marketing gives less emphasis to particular products than does Cadbury.
14. Darrell Lea does not sell moulded block chocolate.
15. Darrell Lea uses its name in a distinctive script widely and consistently in marketing, packaging and point of sale presentation.
16. Colour recognition or attraction can play an important part in consumer decisions to purchase chocolate.
17. Consumer decisions to purchase chocolate are often made quickly and on impulse but not necessarily irrationally. Price and brand recognition can play an important part.[41]

It was on the basis of these factual findings that Heerey J. proceeded to find that there had been neither passing off nor contraventions of the TPA. Some well-recognised principles of law developed by Anglo-Australian courts can be seen at play at here, in particular the following:

- There was third-party usage of purple on chocolate products that meant that Cadbury was not the only trader using that colour – a point going to the question of its repute or marketplace recognition (which was still very extensive).
- The parties' products bore different names, were generally marketed along different trade channels, and Darrell Lea did not make or sell the particular chocolate product on which Cadbury focused most of its purple usage: the moulded chocolate bar. This was clearly a factor going to the question of confusion or likely confusion.
- Darrell Lea's adoption of a purple colour had not been done deliberately with reference to Cadbury's products – again, this is relevant to case law which suggests court will be readier to find a likelihood of confusion where the defendant has acted deliberately (*Red Bull* was such a case).[42]

[41] *Cadbury (No. 4)*, 41–2 [96]–[112]. Note that the findings have been renumbered here from 1 to 17 for ease of reference.

[42] See further *Australian Woollen Mills Limited* v. *F S Walton & Co* (1937) 58 CLR 641, 657, referred to by Heerey J. in his first judgment on liability at (2006) 69 IPR 23, 30 [43].

In his second decision,[43] Heerey J. amplified the relevant legal principles in several ways: first, so as to note that it was unnecessary for Cadbury to establish that its reputation was exclusive, and, second, that under the trade practices claims simple confusion in the sense of being caused to wonder about something was insufficient – there must be a likelihood of consumers being misled or deceived.[44] However, there was no real dispute between the parties as to the legal principles to be applied: the real issue was whether his Honour's factual findings (not challenged in themselves, so far as the non-expert evidence was concerned) should be modified, altered or even reversed, in the light of the now admitted expert opinion evidence. The issue now was one of weight, but it is important to note that none of the experts, except possibly one, had personal experience of the chocolate confectionary retailing industry, including direct knowledge of the way in which Darrell Lea marketed its products, apart from materials provided to them by Cadbury's solicitors. In a careful re-examination of his previous factual findings, his Honour therefore assessed the weight to be attached to this expert evidence in relation to each of them. On many of these, it added nothing, in the sense that the findings were not disputed by the parties, in particular by Cadbury: this was the case in relation to findings 3, 5, 6, 7, 8, 9, 12, 13, 14 and 15. The same was true in relation to the remaining findings, either in the sense that it merely confirmed what was already evident or it was irrelevant:

- Finding 1 (widespread consumer awareness): There was an implicit argument by Cadbury here that his Honour had underestimated the importance of purple to Cadbury's business, and should have taken account of statements by the experts pointing to the 'iconic' importance of this brand element, and its capacity to 'trigger the rich set of tangible and intangible but meaningful brand judgements, attitudes, concepts, and feelings that are associated with the Cadbury brand in the mind of the consumer'.[45] In Heerey J.'s view, such statements were of no legal significance, and did not alter his finding that there was 'a widespread association in consumers' minds between Cadbury's business and its chocolate products and the colour purple'.[46]
- Finding 2 (non-exclusive reputation in colour purple): Cadbury had amended its statement of claim to delete any reference to its reputation in purple being exclusive, and there was significant evidence from

[43] *Cadbury (No. 8)*.
[44] *Parkdale Custom Built Furniture* v. *Puxu Pty Ltd* (1982) 149 CLR 191, 198 (Gibbs CJ); *Taco Co. (Aust) Inc.* v. *Taco Bell Pty Ltd* (1982) 42 ALR 177, 201 (Deane and Fitzgerald JJ).
[45] *Cadbury (No. 8)*, 574–5. [46] *Ibid.*

Darrell Lea of third-party usage of purple by other traders, including Nestle and a well-known traditional product in the Australian market called Violet Crumble). Several of the experts had discounted the significance of these third-party uses in view of the dominance of the chocolate market by Cadbury and the possibility that consumers might still believe there was a connection between these products and Cadbury. Characterising some of these opinions as 'speculative and quite unrealistic', Heerey J. found no reason to vary his earlier finding here.[47]

- Finding 10 (use of purple by Darrell Lea 2000–4 particularly at Christmas): On this matter, the experts' opinions were of 'limited' value and had little relevant to say, as they had not seen the actual usage of purple made by Darrell Lea at the relevant times (in fact, it was of a combination of purple and copper colouring), but had only viewed material provided by Cadbury in late 2005 and had inspected one or two shops only at this time. In strict terms, therefore, there was no proper factual foundation for opinions as to likely confusion.[48]
- Finding 11 (Darrell Lea did not adopt purple to mislead consumers vis-à-vis Cadbury): There was no basis on which the experts could offer opinions here, particularly given his Honour's finding, after hearing the relevant Darrell Lea witnesses, that there had been no intention to copy or emulate Cadbury (the experts obviously had no information about this at the time they prepared their reports).[49]
- Finding 16 (the importance of colour recognition in consumer chocolate-purchasing decisions): This was the subject of much evidence from each of the experts, but Heerey J. felt that this added nothing to ordinary experience. At best, this opinion evidence was only confirmatory of intuitive perceptions about the significance of colours as 'powerful stimulants of memory, identification and loyalty'. Expert opinion on the concept of 'brand equity' and the value of brands was 'not particularly arcane knowledge'.[50]

Certain other findings were not disputed, and hence the expert opinion had no application, namely that Cadbury and Darrell Lea were competitors in the retail chocolate market, that they had distinctive products lines and were sold from different premises, and were sold under distinctive trade names ('Cadbury' and 'Darrell Lea'). However, there were other issues on which Heerey J. found the expert opinion evidence went beyond the legal requirements of a passing off or trade practices claim, notably where one of the witnesses had identified a taxonomy of possible consumer reactions (and possible damage to the Cadbury brand): where

[47] *Ibid.* 576. [48] *Ibid.* 577 [70]. [49] *Ibid.* 577 [71]. [50] *Ibid.* 578 [79].

there was 'misidentification', 'miscuing', 'misinference' and 'misassociation' on the part of consumers when seeing the Darrell Lea products. Of these possible consumer reactions, Heerey J. concluded that the last two (as explained by the witness) fell outside the scope of a trade practices or passing off claim, being of the 'caused to wonder' kind of reaction rather than a positive misleading or deception, and were therefore not legally relevant.[51] In any event (and his Honour did not say so directly), they fell into the realm of speculation and hypothesis, given that there was no empirical evidence of consumer reactions in the actual circumstances of the case.

V. Some comparisons and closing observations

While this chapter has been limited to a consideration of the position in Australia, the issues canvassed here are of wider application, and should have some relevance in any jurisdiction in which protection for brands is sought. In bringing this discussion to an end, the following observations may be made.

1. Unlike other areas of expertise, marketing is far from a 'hard' science: there is much that there is intuitive and qualitative about it. Most areas of expertise have a similar subjective tinge about them, but marketing more than most is a 'soft' area where the insights of an expert need to be approached cautiously and with circumspection. While it is easy to sympathise with those judges, such as Heerey and Branson JJ, who have found it to be of little or no help, there are certain areas where it is likely that expert opinion will assist the court, in the same way as Street J. identified in *Ancher Mortlock*. These may be categorised as follows:
   (i) Evidence of product promotion and distribution in the specific industry concerned, as provided by someone who has worked in that industry for a period of time and is familiar with the way products or services are dealt with in that industry. In the *Cadbury* and *Red Bull* cases, this would be someone with experience in the retailing of chocolate confectionary and energy drinks respectively.[52] In many instances, such evidence could be of considerable assistance to a court in outlining and describing the features of the relevant marketplace, noting that these are often matters that are by no

[51] *Ibid.* 579 [88].
[52] Frequently, a lot of such evidence will come from the parties' own witnesses, but the perspective of an independent outsider as to industry conditions will clearly carry greater weight.

means obvious to an outside observer. In the same way, while everything is usually there to be seen in a design or artistic copyright case, the uninstructed eye can see more readily with the benefit of expert guidance.[53]

(ii) Expert opinion expressed on the basis of properly conducted empirical investigations, such as consumer surveys of attitudes and likely reactions, will also be of assistance, particularly in relation to such matters as sampling and formulation of questions.

(iii) More 'scientific' evidence of the behaviour of consumers may also be helpful at a very general level, for example, as in *Cadbury*, to confirm that colour may be an important brand element and the potential effect that this can have on consumers. But it can rarely go beyond this, and certainly should not reach to the level of expressing conclusions about what might happen in hypothetical situations. Empirical evidence of the kind referred to in (ii) is needed for this purpose, not the general expression of an opinion that conclusion X might follow in certain assumed circumstances because theory Y indicates that this should be so.

(iv) It is difficult to see what assistance expert commentary can provide on issues of damage or likely damage. Speculation as to loss of sales or commercial opportunity or dilution or blurring goes nowhere in the absence of actual evidence of these things occurring.

2. If expert evidence in this area has only a limited role to play, it is worth considering the way in which it is best placed before the court. For those versed in the adversary system, this is quite simple: let it be tested in the usual forensic way through rigorous cross-examination and re-examination. But experts provide a different kind of evidence from ordinary witnesses of fact, and may benefit from a different kind of treatment. For a start, they are assumed to be independent of the parties, with obligations only to the court.[54] In the Australian

[53] Instances where expert evidence has been useful to courts in such cases are to be found in *Dias Aluminium Products Pty Ltd* v. *Ullrich Aluminium Pty Ltd* (2005) 66 IPR 561, 564–7 [10]–[19] (Crennan J.) (a case involving registered designs for wardrobe components); and *Barrett Property Group Pty Ltd* v. *Dennis Family Homes Pty Ltd* [2011] FCA 246 (18 March 2011) [134]–[218] (Dodds-Streeton J.) (a case involving copyright infringement with respect to architectural plans).

[54] In this regard, it is worth noting a historic judicial scepticism in the United Kingdom about the independence and objectivity of expert witnesses and their tendency to become advocates and partisans in their client's cause: see, for example, the celebrated comments of Jessel MR in *Thorn* v. *Worthing Skating Rink Company* (1876) 6 Ch D 415n, at 416 and see further the interesting discussion of this aspect of expert evidence by Rares J. in a paper entitled 'Using the "hot tub" – how concurrent expert evidence aids understanding issues' (paper presented to the New South Wales Association Continuing Professional Development seminar, Views from the Bar and the Bench, Sydney, 23 August 2010) 306 ('Rares paper').

context, this is underlined in a series of practice notes and guidelines that have been developed by the courts over the years.[55] A further step is for experts to consult before trial with a view to producing a joint report stating those matters on which they agree and disagree – this will focus any cross-examination and will clearly save time. In a brand protection case, this could be particularly valuable where there are various 'marketplace' witnesses who might well be in agreement about the characteristics of that marketplace, while differing as to the conclusions that they reach.

3. A final technique, adopted in such areas as competition law where expert economic opinion on such matters as market definition and competitive effect is often called, is the 'hot tub' or the giving of concurrent evidence – a procedure where the experts sit around a table in the courtroom, and engage in a more interactive process with both judge and counsel, and even as between themselves. The framework for this procedure is to be found in O 34A r 3 of the Federal Court Rules 1979 (Cth).[56] It appears to work well in competition law cases, and is being increasingly used by the Federal Court in other areas, such as in patent and copyright cases, cases involving valuations, and the like. It will be seen that considerable discretion is allowed to the court in determining how the 'hot tub' is to operate, and the degree of judicial direction and witness/counsel interaction may vary considerably from case to case.[57] However, anecdotal evidence suggests that this procedure becomes more useful the more it is deployed and the parties (and court) become more comfortable with a different way of eliciting and testing expert opinion. In the best of all worlds, this may end up resembling an academic seminar where the court has the real benefit of hearing expert testimony in a more detached and less contentious atmosphere. Particular advantages are that it can remove the adversary sting from the giving of expert opinion and shore up the position of the expert as an independent and non-partisan figure;

[55] The latest version used in the Federal Court of Australia is available at www.fedcourt.gov.au/how/practice_notes_cm7.html.

[56] Available at www.austlii.edu.au/au/legis/cth/consol_reg/fcr186/s34a.3.html.

[57] Rares paper, 'Using the "hot tub"', 9–19 gives a detailed and informative account of his experience as both judge and counsel in conducting and participating in this procedure. For another useful account, from the perspective of a highly experienced senior counsel, see Neil Young, QC, 'Expert witnesses: on the stand or in the hot tub – how, when and why?' (paper presented at the Commercial Court Continuing Professional Development Seminar, Victoria, 27 October 2010), available at http://commercialcourt.com.au/PDF/Speeches/Commercial%20Court%20CPD%20Seminar%20-%20Expert%20Witnesses%20-%20Paper%20by%20Neil%20Young%20QC.pdf. See also Gary Edmond, 'Merton and the Hot Tub: Scientific Conventions and Expert Evidence in Australian Civil Procedure' (2009) 72 *Law and Contemporary Problems* 159, 168–9.

it may also lead to significant savings in times and costs.[58] It might therefore provide a valuable way of maximising the utility of expert opinion evidence in brand protection cases.

[58] One celebrated instance of such savings in time is provided by a competition case heard in the late 1990s by the same judge as in the *Cadbury* litigation: see *Australian Competition and Consumer Commission* v. *Boral Ltd* [1999] FCA 1318. While the trial in this case went for four weeks, apparently only a day was needed for the giving of concurrent expert economic evidence. By contrast, in the *Cadbury* litigation, many days were spent in both challenging and testing the expert evidence in the normal adversary fashion.

Part V

New horizons

12 Geographical Indications: Europe's strange chimera or developing countries' champion?

Melissa de Zwart

> Nowhere else in Australia that I know of has such an identifiable regional food culture: the ties to the land hearkening back to European settlers of the Valley; the traditions of the seasons upheld; a 'peasant' culture in its closest possible sense. I give this last as the greatest of accolades, because it meant that the mixed farmers or vignerons were proud of their food and their culture and they worked hard yet, I suspect, effortlessly to marry their food traditions to our climate.
>
> The other truly important factor in the Barossa food culture has to be the wine industry: that connecting with the wine, the winemakers, the enjoyment of the grape – and all that flows from there.
>
> Maggie Beer[1]

On any day in the small and somewhat run-down suburban supermarket not far from my home I can purchase food items that have been imported from all over the world, such as Parma ham (prosciutto di parma), Parmesan cheese (Parmigiano-Reggiano) and Greek feta cheese. Around the corner I can then avail myself of French champagne and Spanish sherry as well as local wines from the Barossa Valley. The expansion in world trade has therefore both boosted the sale of specialist food items and apparently created the need for the protection of their domestic names

In Greek mythology, the chimera was a fire-breathing monster, which had the body of a lioness, the head of a goat and a tail with the head of a snake. As a consequence the modern use of the term chimera has come to mean an unreal creature of the imagination, a mere wild fancy; an unfounded conception. See *Oxford English Dictionary* (2nd edn, Oxford University Press, Oxford and New York, 1989), entry for 'chimera | chimaera, n'. See also the related use of the of the term 'chimera' in biology: 'An organism (commonly a plant) in which tissues of genetically different constitution co-exist as a result of grafting, mutation, or some other process'. Thus the chimera is ultimately an unhappy combination of cells, tissues and identities derived from various unrelated origins (see *ibid.*, entry for 'chimera | chimaera, n').

The author is grateful for the insights and advice provided by Andreas Clark, General Counsel, Wine Australia (with respect to GIs and the Australian wine industry), Stefen Klaebe (with respect to the Barossa Valley and its German heritage) and Francesco de Zwart. All errors remain the author's.

1 Foreword to Angela Heuzenroeder, *Barossa Food* (Wakefield Press, Kent Town, South Australia, rev. edn, 2002), viii.

and place of origin. Inherent even within this simple example is the role that Geographical Indications (GIs) play in protecting the products of Old World Europe against similar products produced in the New World, often by the descendants of the original Old World producers. Australian farmers can certainly produce a local version of ham and cheese, given that the techniques and processes used here were brought by immigrants from the 'old countries' and then, as Maggie Beer notes above, adapted to suit the local Australian conditions. However, the exclusivity applied to words such as 'champagne' by its very nature suggests that there is something special about this product that domestic producers cannot replicate. Does this mean that geography, rather than traditional techniques, is the key determinant of authenticity? If so, how are the boundaries of that geography determined when borders have moved across the centuries?[2]

I can also purchase basmati rice and Mexican tequila. Does this mean that the protection mechanism championed by Europe may now have a role in facilitating the expansion of developing country markets in defined products? Would a heightened level of GI protection facilitate and encourage the export of specialist products from developing countries or merely reinforce European rights?

Unlike other intellectual property rights, such as copyright, patents and trade marks, which have a relatively settled, albeit occasionally controversial, underlying rationale, GIs rest upon an uncertain and contested basis. None of the individual reasons advanced for GI protection provides a completely satisfactory or comprehensive explanation for GI protection. In fact, as several commentators have noted, GIs may not strictly be intellectual property rights (IPR), but rather a hybrid creature combining elements of intellectual property with agricultural policy and trade regulation.[3] Further, GIs may allow well-used terms to be clawed back from the public domain, even where there is no risk of consumer confusion.[4]

What is the purpose of GI protection? Does this purpose or nature change according to the products to which they are applied? For example,

[2] In the Barossa Valley example discussed below, the settlers are referred to as 'German' although their emigration pre-dated the formation of the modern-day single state of Germany.

[3] William van Caenegem, 'Registered Geographical Indications: Between Intellectual Property and Rural Policy – Part 1' (2003) 6(5) *Journal of World Intellectual Property* 699; Kal Raustiala and Stephen R. Munzer, 'The Global Struggle over Geographic Indications' (2007) 18(2) *European Journal of International Law* 337; and Anthony Taubman, 'Thinking Locally, Acting Globally: How Trade Negotiations over Geographical Indications Improvise "Fair Trade" Rules' (2008) 3 *Intellectual Property Quarterly* 231, 234.

[4] Taubman, 'Thinking Locally', 232–3.

does the protection of wine varieties and regions pursuant to the GI system serve a different function from GI protection of cheese or possibly traditional craftware?

Michael Handler has described GIs as 'the form of intellectual property that does not command universal respect'.[5] This is certainly true and, interestingly, debates over the justifications for GI protection fall into different alliances from those adopted in other IPR arguments. As Ruth Okediji has observed, this debate is playing out between parties who are usually united proponents of strong intellectual property protection, being the developed economies, especially the EU and the US.[6] This is due to their own self-interest in developing and protecting export markets and is traceable directly to their historical relationship as colonisers and colonies.

This chapter will consider recent developments in the legal protection of GIs with a particular focus upon the Australian context, due both to the importance of the wine industry to Australian exports and its status as a relatively young country colonised by immigrants from the Old World. These immigrants, such as the large German population which settled in the Barossa Valley in South Australia, brought with them their traditional agricultural and production expertise.[7] It was inevitable that they would apply this expertise to the new conditions of the Australian soil and climate and create new varieties of food and wine. These varieties owed their nature to their European heritage, combined with the natural and man-made environment of the new colony. To this day, the Barossa has a strong German heritage, and visitors now come from overseas to taste its unique wine styles.[8] In fact, traditional German food production

[5] Michael Handler, 'The WTO Geographical Indications Dispute' (2006) 69(1) *Modern Law Review* 70–91.

[6] Ruth L. Okediji, 'The International Intellectual Property Roots of Geographical Indications' (2007) 82(3) *Chicago-Kent Law Review* 1329, 1352.

[7] These settlers were from Silesia, part of Prussia prior to the creation of the modern state of Germany. Modern-day wineries are proud to trace their heritage back to these original growers, see for example *Our Heritage* (2011), Saltram Wines www.saltramwines.com.au/saltram/pages/our-heritage/barossa.html Saltram was established in 1859 but the website notes that some of the vines in the region date back to the 1840s.

[8] Colin Thiele, award-winning Australian author of books such as *Storm Boy*, claimed that he did not speak English until he started school (Stephany Steggall, 'Teller of tales that teach', *The Australian* (online), 15 September 2006 www.theaustralian.com.au/news/teller-of-tales-that-teach/story-e6frgcr6-1111112212866). As with the other children of German heritage born and bred in the Barossa, Thiele spoke a localised derivation of German at home, commonly called 'Barossa Deutsch', which was commonly spoken in the streets of the Barossa until the 1960s. See further, Colin Thiele, *Barossa Valley Sketchbook* (Rigby Books, Adelaide, 1968), and Heuzenroeder, *Barossa*, 3–12. It should be noted, of course, that the outbreak of the First World War generated a lot of ill-will towards German names and practices and led to many people anglicising their names and

techniques were so well preserved that visitors from Germany in the late twentieth century were impressed to rediscover recipes and products that had been lost in modern day Germany. Such 'traditions' could then be repatriated to the German homeland.

The South Australian wine industry provides a useful case study upon which to pose a number of key questions about GIs, notably an effort to understand the nature and rationale for GI protection. This will involve an examination of the rhetoric used to justify the introduction and possible expansion of these rights, and whose interests this may serve. This chapter will consider what rights and interests GIs actually protect and conclude that the uncertain and subjective nature of identification of the existence and scope of GIs means that further expansion of such rights may be contrary to the interests sought to be protected by those seeking the expansion of such rights.

This chapter will conclude that GI protection currently serves a useful marketing purpose for wines and spirits but that the expansion of the system to cover foodstuffs and other products would benefit neither consumers nor the majority of producers in former colonised countries.

I. What are GIs?

The obligation for member countries to protect GIs is created by arts. 22, 23 and 24 of the TRIPS Agreement.[9] Although GI protection in Europe pre-dates TRIPS, this will be the starting point for consideration of GIs in this chapter, given the broader scope and implication of TRIPS and its relevance for member countries in the Asia Pacific region. Article 22.1 provides the definition of 'Geographical Indications', stating:

> Geographical indications are, for the purposes of this Agreement, indications which identify a good as originating in the territory of a Member, or a region or locality in that territory, where a given quality, reputation or other characteristic of the good is essentially attributable to its geographical origin.

This definition suggests that what is being protected is a tangible quality or characteristic of a good that is attributable to geography, indicating that what is central to the identification and recognition of a GI is some aspect of geography or place. How this is to be measured or assessed is not prescribed.

language, including common names for foodstuffs. For example, the jam-filled Berliner Pfannkuchen became Kitchener buns (see Heuzenroeder, *Barossa*, 14–16).

9 Agreement on Trade-Related Aspects of Intellectual Property Rights (TRIPS), opened for signature 15 April 1994, 1869 UNTS 299 (entered into force 1 January 1996).

Article 22.2 requires Members to protect parties against:

(a) the use of any means in the designation or presentation of good that indicates or suggests that the good in question originates in a geographical area other than the true place of origin in a manner which misleads the public as to the geographical origin of the good;
(b) any use which constitutes an act of unfair competition within the meaning of Article 10*bis* of the Paris Convention (1967).

However, it does not prescribe *how* such GIs are to be protected. This may be achieved through a *sui generis* system or through existing laws, such as trade mark registration, passing off and consumer protection laws. A current issue of contention between member nations raised within the Doha Round of trade negotiations, concerns the desirability of having a GI registration system (either mandatory or optional).[10]

Neither does TRIPS prescribe exactly what may be protected by a GI system. As Kireeva and O'Connor explain: 'Traditionally, the use of GIs is linked to agricultural products due to specific geographical climatic and geological conditions.'[11] However, in some countries this also includes handcrafts and industrial products, such as glassware and ceramics. Thus, in some contexts, GIs protect a human creation, recognising something unique about the skills and traditions associated with a particular area.[12]

Article 23 provides additional protection for Geographical Indications for wines and spirits. It states:

> Each Member shall provide the legal means for interested parties to prevent use of a geographical indication identifying wines for wines not originating in the place indicated by the geographical indication in question or identifying spirits for spirits not originating in the place indicated by the geographical indication in question, even where the true origin of the goods is indicated or the geographical indication is used in translation or accompanied by expressions such as 'kind', 'type', 'style', 'imitation' or the like.

Thus art. 23 creates a two-tier system for GI protection, with the level of protection granted to wines and spirits extending to prevent even references to a varietal type or style where it is made clear that the product does not in fact originate from that area, for example, preventing the use of phrases such as 'an Australian sparkling white wine in the style of

10 Tshimanga Kongolo, 'Any New Developments with Regard to GIs Issues Debated under WTO?' (2011) 33(2) *European Intellectual Property Review* 83.

11 Irina Kireeva and Bernard O'Connor, 'Geographical Indications and the TRIPS Agreement: What Protection Is Provided to Geographical Indications in WTO Members?' (2009) 13(2) *Journal of World Intellectual Property* 275.

12 World Intellectual Property Organization (WIPO), *About Geographical Indications*, www.wipo.int/geo_indications/en/about.html See further, Raustiala and Munzer, 'Global Struggle', 342–3.

méthode champenoise'. As Broude and others have pointed out, this level of protection goes well beyond traditional levels of intellectual property and consumer protection laws which look at the question of whether a consumer would be misled by the use of the GI: 'Products in this category enjoy a near absolute degree of exclusivity, that prevents the use of the GI by others, even when measures have been taken to prevent confusion.'[13]

Interestingly and controversially, art. 24 further provides that Members agree to enter into negotiations aimed at increasing the protection of geographical indications for products other than wine and spirits to this higher level of protection. This proposed extension of the higher standard of protection was also the subject of Doha Round negotiations, the consequences of which will be discussed further below.

GI protection under TRIPS evolved from the Lisbon Agreement for the Protection of Appellations of Origin and their International Registration 1958,[14] which provides for a registration system. As at May 2011, Lisbon had only twenty-seven members. It used the concept of 'appellation of origin' defined as the 'geographical name of a country, region, or locality, which serves to designate a product originating therein, the quality and characteristics of which are due exclusively or essentially to the geographic environment, including natural and human factors'. It is not, therefore, confined to food, nor does it necessarily require the use of natural resources, meaning that it may be extended to industrial products that embody particular local skills and know-how.[15]

Therefore although the concepts are very similar, as Daniel Gervais notes, appellations of origin are confined to the geographical names of the relevant locality, whereas GIs extend to any indication of origin. Further, the definition of 'appellations of origin' specifically refers to the natural and human factors of the geographic environment, whereas TRIPS refers merely to 'geographical origin'.[16] Finally, the explicit reference to 'reputation' of the good may appear to extend the concept of GI, as opposed to the reference in Lisbon to the 'quality and characteristics' of the product. However, as Gervais has pointed out, Lisbon refers to 'reputation' as an element in the definition of 'country of origin'.[17] Again,

[13] Tomer Broude, 'Taking "Trade and Culture" Seriously: Geographical Indications and Cultural Protection in WTO Law' (1 May 2005) 17, available at Social Sciences Research Network: http://papers.ssrn.com/sol3/papers.cfm?abstract_id=714981. See also Taubman, 'Thinking Locally', 232.

[14] Opened for signature 31 October 1958, 923 UNTS 205 (entered into force 25 September 1966).

[15] Daniel Gervais, 'Traditional Knowledge: Are We Closer to the Answer(s)? The Potential Role of Geographical Indications' (2009) 15(2) *ILSA Journal of International and Comparative Law* 552, 559.

[16] *Ibid.* 560. [17] Gervais, 'Traditional Knowledge', 561.

whether anything in particular should be made of this difference remains unclear.

Lisbon also includes the higher threshold of protection created for wines and spirits in art. 23.1 of TRIPS, providing that:

> Protection shall be ensured against any usurpation or imitation, even if the true origin of the product is indicated or if the appellation is used in translated form or accompanied by terms such as 'kind', 'type', 'imitation', or the like.

At the heart of the Lisbon Agreement is the French appellation of origin (in French *appellation d'origine contrôlée*, or AoC) concept, which was established to restore public faith in the integrity and quality of French wine.[18] The French AoC system involves a rigorous set of controls over the variety of grapes that can be harvested, growing and fermentation methods, size of crop, etc and therefore straddles both an agricultural regulation role and a quality certification (trade mark) function. By contrast, the wine industry in Australia, although it has implemented a GI system, has nothing approaching this level of government intervention in farming methods employed in the relevant region. Indeed, this would be seen as counter to the innovative nature of the Australian wine industry.[19]

Importantly, the appellation-of-origin concept is built upon the notion of *terroir*.[20] As Barham observes *terroir* is 'a French word without a suitable English translation'.[21] She explains that historically *terroir* was used to refer to an area which manifests a particular climate and geography, including soil type, which imbued the produce grown in that area with 'distinctive qualities'.[22] The term has become closely associated with wine, with winegrowers matching particular grape types with

[18] For a discussion of the champagne riots of 1911 that led to the implementation of the earliest form of appellation-of-origin protection of the term 'champagne', see Bronwyn Parry, 'Geographical Indications: Not All "Champagne and Roses"', in Lionel Bently, Jennifer Davis and Jane C. Ginsburg (eds.), *Trade Marks and Brands: An Interdisciplinary Critique* (Cambridge University Press, 2008), 361, 371.

[19] Department of Foreign Affairs and Trade website provides the following:

> Australia's reputation as one of the most technologically advanced wine-producing nations owes much to the industry's emphasis on research and development. Key research and development sources include the Australian Wine Research Institute, the Commonwealth Scientific and Industrial Research Organisation, the National Wine and Grape Industry Centre, state departments of agriculture and universities. A number of Australian universities and other tertiary education institutions offer courses in viticulture and oenology.

Department of Foreign Affairs and Trade, Australian Wine Industry (April 2008) www.dfat.gov.au/facts/wine.html

[20] See Elizabeth Barham, 'Translating Terroir: The Global Challenge of French AOC Labeling' (2003) 19 *Journal of Rural Studies* 127.

[21] *Ibid.* 128. [22] *Ibid.* 131.

particular regions.[23] Barham observes that the concept of *terroir* has met with renewed interest from various actors in the context of commodification of 'authentic' heritage.[24] However, Parry has taken issue with Barham's implication that there was a time when *terroir* ever could be defined and ascertained. Rather, Parry concludes that places are not and have never been hermetically sealed.[25] *Terroir*, she claims, depends upon 'a highly constructed, deeply essentialized and static, conception of place'.[26] How relevant, therefore, is this contested concept as the centrepiece of an intellectual property regime?[27]

Thus the GI system may be perceived as a chimera, involving political, agricultural, marketing and quality control elements. As distinct from other forms of IP protection (with the possible exception of certification marks), GIs are therefore collective and potentially perpetual in nature.[28]

II. The Australian wine industry

According to the Department of Foreign Affairs and Trade: 'Australia was ranked sixth in the list of world wine producers in 2005, producing 1.4 billion litres of wine'.[29] Wine is produced throughout mainland Australia and in Tasmania, and, due to the vast geological and climate difference across this area, Australia produces every one of the major wine styles. There are several well-known wine growing regions in Australia, many of which are in south-eastern Australia. These include the regions discussed in this chapter, the Barossa and the Coonawarra in South Australia, as well as the Hunter Valley (NSW), the Yarra Valley and Rutherglen (Victoria). There are also smaller regions in Western Australia, such as Margaret River, and in Tasmania and Queensland. As indicated above, with respect to the Barossa experience, wine growing and production arrived with the first European settlers, and as early as 1822 wine was being exported to the UK.[30]

The Australian wine industry is regarded as being innovative and consumer friendly, right through from the nature of the wine itself, to its

[23] This concept has received a modern manifestation in Wine Australia's promotion of certain wines as 'Regional Heroes', being wines that foster 'a clear association between region and variety/style'. Wine Australia, Regional Heroes www.wineaustralia.com/Australia/Default.aspx?tabid=3854.

[24] Barham, 'Translating Terroir', 132.

[25] Parry, 'Geographical Indications', 376. [26] *Ibid.* 364.

[27] For a critique of Parry's view, see Dev Ganjee, '(Re)Locating Geographical Indications: A Response to Bronwyn Parry', in Bently *et al.*, *Trade Marks and Brands*, 381.

[28] Rhonda Chesmond, 'Protection or Privatisation of Culture? The Cultural Dimension of the International Intellectual Property Debate on Geographical Indications of Origin' (2007) 29(9) *European Intellectual Property Review* 379, 379.

[29] Department of Foreign Affairs and Trade website. [30] *Ibid.*

packaging and labelling.[31] In many ways this emphasis on innovation runs counter to the whole *raison d'être* of the GI system which protects tradition and continuity.[32] However, Australia has moved to identify its key wine regions, to establish them as tourist destinations, each with its own regional flavour and style. Thus the regions, plus a handful of well-known wines, such as Penfolds Grange Hermitage, serve as the focus for marketing of Australian wine.

III. GIs in Australia

In Australia, GI protection extends only to wine and spirits, under the Wine Australia Corporation Act 1980 (Cth) ('WAC Act'). Protection of any other product must be achieved under the trade marks legislation, the law of passing off or consumer protection legislation, such as s. 18 of the Australian Consumer Law (formerly s. 52 of the Trade Practices Act 1974 (Cth)).

Wine Australia (formerly the Australian Wine and Brandy Corporation (AWBC)), established by the WAC Act as a statutory marketing authority, is empowered by the Act to determine applications for GIs and to maintain a register of protected names and expressions.[33] This regime has been introduced to satisfy Australia's obligations under TRIPS and, more specifically, the Australia–European Community Agreement on Trade in Wine 2008 ('Agreement')[34] (and its predecessor signed in 1994).[35]

[31] The wine cask was invented in South Australia by William Thomas Angove of Angove's Winery in the 1960s in order to preserve bulk quantities of wine: Power House Museum, *Wine Cask: 1966* (2001) www.powerhousemuseum.com/australia_innovates/?behaviour=view_article&Section_id=1000&article_id=10021.

[32] Michael Handler, 'The EU's Geographical Indications Agenda and Its Potential Impact on Australia' (2004) 15 *Australian Intellectual Property Journal* 173, 179. See also William van Caenegem, 'Registered GIs: Intellectual Property, Agricultural Policy and International Trade' (2004) 26(4) *European Intellectual Property Review* 170.

[33] WAC Act s. 8 (formerly, the Australian Wine and Brandy Corporation Act 1980 (Cth)). See regarding change of name of the authority, Wine Australia, *Wine Australia: Looking to the Future* (9 December 2010) www.wineaustralia.com/australia/Portals/2/MediaReleases/Media%20release%20-%20Wine%20Australia%20name%20change%2009122010.pdf.

[34] Signed 1 December 2008 [2010] ATS 19 (entered into force 1 September 2010). See also Department of Agriculture, Fisheries and Forestry, Australia–European Community Agreement on Trade in Wine (3 February 2011), www.daff.gov.au/agriculture-food/wine-policy/trade-in-wine. WAC Act s. 40A provides:

> The object of this Part is to regulate the sale, export and import of wine:
> (a) for the purpose of enabling Australia to fulfil its obligations under prescribed wine-trading agreements; and
> (b) for certain other purposes for which the Parliament has power to make laws;
> and this Part is to be interpreted and administered accordingly.

[35] Agreement between Australia and the European Community on Trade in Wine, and Protocol (Brussels–Canberra, 26–31 January 1994), Entry into force: 1 March 1994,

Australia and the European Community signed the Agreement on 1 December 2008 however it did not enter into force as a treaty until 1 September 2010. That Agreement, which replaces the earlier Agreement signed in 1994, regulates the trade in wine between Australian and the European Community (EC), Australia's largest export market. The Agreement was signed in the shadow of the dispute before the WTO brought by Australia and the US against the EC – *European Communities – Protection of Trademarks and Geographical Indications for Agricultural Products and Foodstuffs* – which essentially concerned the question whether the EC's methods of protecting GIs were in compliance with TRIPS.[36]

Key aspects of that Agreement are the protection in Australia of more than 2,500 registered European GIs and eleven GIs that have been used in Australia to describe Australian wines (with a one-year phase-in period).[37] In return, novel Australian winemaking techniques that are considered unorthodox according to traditional European methods, such as the use of oak chips, spinning cone technology and reverse osmosis, will be recognised in Europe and simplified labelling requirements imposed upon Australian exports. It also provides automatic approval of new winemaking practices, with a six-month period for objection following notification. The Agreement also regulates the use of certain European traditional expressions which relate to the method of production or certain qualities of the wine in their original language, such as 'Grand Cru', with respect to Champagne.

A GI is defined in s. 4 of the WAC Act:

> geographical indication, in relation to wine goods, means an indication that identifies the goods as originating in a country, or in a region or locality in that country, where a given quality, reputation or other characteristic of the goods is essentially attributable to their geographical origin.[38]

Terminated: 1 September 2010, www.austlii.edu.au/au/other/dfat/treaties/1994/6.html. Note that the extended provisions of these Agreements relating to translated terms, terms that have become generic in a particular region and terms that 'evoke' a geographical indication would be prohibited if the Trans-Pacific Partnership Agreement IP chapter is adopted in the form put forward by the US and leaked to the public in February 2011 http://keionline.org/sites/default/files/tpp-10feb2011-us-text-ipr-chapter.pdf.

36 See Handler, 'WTO'.

37 These are Burgundy, Chablis, Champagne, Graves, Manzanilla, Marsala, Moselle, Port, Sauterne, Sherry and White Burgundy.

38 Previously, s. 4 of the WAC Act provided that 'geographical indication', in relation to wine, means:
(a) a word or expression used in the description and presentation of the wine to indicate the country, region or locality in which the wine originated; or
(b) a word or expression used in the description and presentation of the wine to suggest that a particular quality, reputation or characteristic of the wine is attributable to

Under the WAC Act, the power to determine GIs with respect to Australian regions is invested in the Geographical Indications Committee (GIC), a statutory committee of Wine Australia.[39] That power includes both the determination of the boundary of the relevant region, subregion or zone,[40] and the word or expression that is to be used as the GI

the wine having originated in the country, region or locality indicated by the word or expression.

[39] WAC Act s. 40N. See also s. 40P which sets out the functions and powers of the GIC:

(1) The functions of the Committee are:
  (a) to deal with applications for the determination of geographical indications for wine in relation to regions and localities in Australia (Australian GIs) in accordance with this Part; and
  (b) to make determinations of Australian GIs in accordance with this Part (including determining any conditions of use applicable to such GIs); and
  (c) to make determinations for the omission of Australian GIs in accordance with this Part; and
  (d) any other functions conferred on the Committee under this Part or under the regulations.

(2) The Committee has power to do all things that are necessary or convenient to be done by, or in connection with, the performance of its functions.

[40] See Australian Wine and Brandy Corporation Regulations 1981 (Cth) reg. 24:

'region' means an area of land that:
(a) may comprise one or more subregions; and
(b) is a single tract of land that is discrete and homogeneous in its grape growing attributes to a degree that:
  (i) is measurable; and
  (ii) is less substantial than in a subregion; and
(c) usually produces at least 500 tonnes of wine grapes in a year; and
(d) comprises at least 5 wine grape vineyards of at least 5 hectares each that do not have any common ownership, whether or not it also comprises 1 or more vineyards of less than 5 hectares; and
(e) may reasonably be regarded as a region.

'subregion' means an area of land that:
(a) is part of a region; and
(b) is a single tract of land that is discrete and homogeneous in its grape growing attributes to a degree that is substantial; and
(c) usually produces at least 500 tonnes of wine grapes in a year; and
(d) comprises at least 5 wine grape vineyards of at least 5 hectares each that do not have any common ownership, whether or not it also comprises 1 or more vineyards of less than 5 hectares; and
(e) may reasonably be regarded as a subregion.

'wine grape vineyard' means a single parcel of land that:
(a) is planted with wine grapes; and
(b) is operated as a single entity by:
  (i) the owner; or
  (ii) a manager on behalf of the owner or a lessee, irrespective of the number of lessees.

'zone' means an area of land that:
(a) may comprise one or more regions; or
(b) may reasonably be regarded as a zone.

applicable to that area.[41] As at January 2011, there are 112 registered Australian GIs.[42]

The criteria to be applied in determining the boundaries of a GI are prescribed in Part V of the Australian Wine and Brandy Corporation Regulations 1981 (Cth) (AWBC Regulations).[43] Regulation 24 provides the definitions of the key terms and reg. 25 sets out a list of the matters to be considered in making a determination under sub-section 40T(2) of the Act. These are:

(a) whether the area falls within the definition of a subregion, a region, a zone or any other area;
(b) the history of the founding and development of the area, ascertained from local government records, newspaper archives, books, maps or other relevant material;
(c) the existence in relation to the area of natural features, including rivers, contour lines and other topographical features;
(d) the existence in relation to the area of constructed features, including roads, railways, towns and buildings;
(e) the boundary of the area suggested in the application to the Committee under section 40R;
(f) ordinance survey map grid references in relation to the area;
(g) local government boundary maps in relation to the area;
(h) the existence in relation to the area of a word or expression to indicate that area, including:

[41] Section 40T:

(1) In determining a geographical indication, the Committee must:
  (a) identify in the determination the boundaries of the area or areas in the region or locality to which the determination relates; and
  (b) determine the word or expression to be used to indicate that area or those areas.
(2) If the regulations prescribe criteria for use by the Committee in determining a geographical indication, the Committee is to have regard to those criteria.
(3) When making a determination as a result of an application, the Committee may do either or both of the following:
  (a) determine an area or areas having boundaries different from those stated in the application;
  (b) determine a word or expression to be used to indicate the area or areas constituting the geographical indication that is different from a word or expression proposed in the application.
(4) In determining a geographical indication, the Committee must not consider any submission to the extent that the submission asserts a trade mark right in respect of the proposed geographical indication.

See also the AWBC Regulations.

[42] For a list of all of the Australian GIs included in the Register of Protected Names, see Wine Australia, Register of Protected GIs and Other Terms www.wineaustralia.com/australia/Default.aspx?tabid=834.

[43] AWBC Regulations reg. 23.

(i) any history relating to the word or expression; and
(ii) whether, and to what extent, the word or expression is known to wine retailers beyond the boundaries of the area; and
(iii) whether, and to what extent, the word or expression has been traditionally used in the area or elsewhere; and
(iv) the appropriateness of the word or expression;

(i) the degree of discreteness and homogeneity of the proposed geographical indication in respect of the following attributes:
(i) the geological formation of the area;
(ii) the degree to which the climate of the area is uniform, having regard to the temperature, atmospheric pressure, humidity, rainfall, number of hours of sunshine and any other weather conditions experienced in the area throughout the year;
(iii) whether the date on which harvesting a particular variety of wine grapes is expected to begin in the area is the same as the date on which harvesting grapes of the same variety is expected to begin in neighbouring areas;
(iv) whether part or all of the area is within a natural drainage basin;
(v) the availability of water from an irrigation scheme;
(vi) the elevation of the area;
(vii) any plans for the development of the area proposed by Commonwealth, State or municipal authorities;
(viii) any relevant traditional divisions within the area;
(ix) the history of grape and wine production in the area.

The note to this regulation provides: 'In determining a geographical indication under subsection 40Q (1) of the Act, the Committee is not prohibited under the Act from having regard to any other relevant matters.'

As the discussion above regarding the nature of *terroir* indicates, the drawing of boundaries is a difficult and often contentious exercise. The complexity of this exercise is clearly demonstrated by the Coonawarra dispute which occupied many parties over many years and resulted in a redrawing of the Coonawarra boundaries which had been set by the Australian GIC, but only in favour of those who had been a party to the Federal Court action.[44]

The Coonawarra case study has received substantial analysis elsewhere, therefore it will only be discussed briefly here to highlight the key issues that can be drawn from the outcomes.[45]

44 *Beringer Blass Wine Estates Ltd* v. *Geographical Indications Committee* (2002) 125 FCR 155 ('*Beringer Blass*').

45 For a comprehensive account of this saga, see Gary Edmond, 'Disorder with Law: Determining the Geographical Indication for the Coonawarra Wine Region' (2006) 27 *Adelaide Law Review* 59, and Matthew Rimmer, 'The Grapes of Wrath: The Coonawarra Dispute, Geographical Indications and International Trade', in Sam Ricketson, Megan Richardson and Andrew T. Kenyon (eds.), *Landmarks in Australian Intellectual Property* (Cambridge University Press, Melbourne and New York, 2009), 209.

Coonawarra, like the Barossa, is a wine-growing district in South Australia. Settled in the 1840s, it is most famous for its premium red wines. Importantly, the district contains a slightly raised strip or 'cigar' of terra rossa soil. This soil is said to favour the growth of premium-quality red wine grapes, although as wine growing increased in the area, wines were planted outside of the cigar.[46] The terra rossa soil had been used as a marketing focus for Coonawarra wines since the 1950s. However, it emerged during the course of expert evidence provided to the Court that not only does the term terra rossa have no precise meaning in soil classification, but also that soil types vary dramatically throughout the Coonawarra. Soil experts testified that they could replicate the nature of the terra rossa qualities simply through adding treatments to the soil. At issue, of course, was fundamentally where the boundaries of the Coonawarra should be drawn. Who would benefit from being counted inside the GI and therefore entitled to the market cachet and higher prices that went with being able to use the name Coonawarra and who would miss out? Being a long-established wine-growing area there were many families who had owned land and worked the vineyards for a long time. There were also corporate interests in the form of Southcorp and other large producers who owned land both in and outside the Coonawarra region.

After a protracted period of submission and consideration, the GIC had provided a Final Determination on the boundaries of the Coonawarra GI on 10 May 2000.[47] The determination was immediately appealed to the AAT by several applicants whose properties had not been included within the boundaries of the Coonawarra GI. The AAT increased the area determined by the GIC, concluding that: 'Whether one characterises it as a "marketing tool" or even challenges the homogeneity of the cigar itself, it is historically and scientifically the signature of the Coonawarra Wine Region. Proximity to this strip of arable soil would be in our view, an important factor in the determination of the boundary.'[48]

The case then went on appeal to the Federal Court, which was critical of both the GIC and the AAT, noting that they had both given undue emphasis to historical evidence.[49] They were also critical of the concept

[46] Edmond, 'Disorder', 71. [47] *Ibid.* 90.

[48] *Coonawarra Penola Wine Industry Association Inc. & Others and Geographical Indications Committee* [2001] AATA 844 [137].

[49] *Beringer Blass*, 176:

> [73] The difficulties in identifying boundaries to an area that may reasonably be regarded as the Coonawarra region within the meaning of reg 24 provides reason for a decision-maker to have regard to historical information, but only insofar as that information is

of proximity in the context of identifying the boundary of the GI.[50] The matter was to be returned to the AAT for a redetermination of the boundaries, but due to the retirement of the President of the AAT, Justice O'Connor, who had heard the matter in the AAT, the Court instead remitted the matter to the AAT to ratify an extension of the boundaries to include the five parties to the appeal. Those vineyards that had not joined the appeal, and may on objective evidence have just as strong a claim to be included, were not considered in this procedure.[51]

At issue in this case was the drawing of the boundaries of the Coonawarra region. Ultimately the boundaries of the region were determined by the Court on a pragmatic and strategic basis rather than upon the factors identified by the extensive number of wine growing or geography experts who gave evidence before the Court. Human and historical factors appeared to be as important as scientific or geological matters. The evidence before the Court seemed to conclude that the famous terra rossa soil had little to do with the ultimate quality or identity of the wine. This case therefore clearly raises the question of what in fact is being protected by the concept of GIs, and the circular reasoning that must be engaged in to determine what factors are relevant to establishing whether justification exists for recognition of a GI in any given circumstances.[52] What does this dispute tell us about the nature of GIs in Australia, and how does that translate (if at all) to other contexts?

There have been a handful of other cases involving GI boundaries, such as *Baxendale's Vineyard Pty Ltd* v. *The Geographical Indications Committee*.[53] This case, heard by the Full Federal Court on appeal from

> properly to be taken into account in light of the definitional requirements of reg 24, and the purpose of the criteria in reg 25. In the application by Petaluma Ltd the AAT relied heavily on historical information, namely the industry and market acceptance and recognition of the Coonawarra region as a descriptor of the characteristics of wine originating from the Sharefarmers' vineyard. The AAT treated that evidence as an 'overwhelming countervailing reason' to depart from the Hundred boundaries. The weight attributable to that kind of historical evidence in the case of Petaluma Ltd illustrates the importance of similar evidence in the cases of other applicants who claim to have their vineyards included within the boundaries of the Coonawarra Region.
>
> [74] For the reasons already given, we consider that the AAT fell into error of law in its construction of regs 24 and 25, and we think it is clear that the misconstruction of the regulations directly affected the outcome of the Beringer Blass application. Accordingly the application by Beringer Blass must succeed.

See also Edmond, 'Disorder', 136–7.

50 *Beringer Blass*, 176. 51 Edmond, 'Disorder', 141.

52 See further, Chesmond, 'Protection', 382–3, for a discussion of what elements of 'culture' may be protected in the recognition of a GI.

53 (2007) 160 FCR 542.

the Administrative Appeals Tribunal, concerned the issues of whether there should be a Whitlands High Plateaux GI separate from the King Valley GI (being in Victoria). The AAT had found that despite some difference between the valley and the plateaux lands, there was an overall degree of homogeneity encompassing the whole King Valley area. This decision was upheld by the Full Federal Court.

IV. GIs and developing countries

As noted above, GIs constitute a different zone from the other areas of IP negotiated during TRIPS, representing a narrow space where the developed countries lack a common cultural base upon which to base their strategic policy.[54] In fact, this represents an area in which the interests of the EU and the US are quite opposed, reflecting the fact that the New World producers had taken their products and expertise with them along with their language when they had left the Old World. The only thing that they could not take with them was the *terroir*. Does this space then provide an opportunity for the interests of developing countries to flourish or does it merely provide the Old World with the capacity to claw back long lost language with monopolistic effect?

Gervais and others have suggested that, rather than serving as the domain of the Old World, GIs could be used as a means for developing countries to protect traditional goods originating from a specific geographical origin. Thus, 'ensuring that goods that are identified as having a *specific origin and that have higher value because of that origin* may allow producers in all nations, including developing ones, to increase prices and protect markets'.[55] Certainly, GIs enable producers to take advantage of a renewed interest in 'authentic' food. As global trade has increased and resulted in the homogenisation and standardisation of food and other products, consumers have become concerned with the quality of such products. They may feel that their local food traditions are being undermined by a push towards global (largely US) food standards. Further, consumers are worried about additives and chemicals contained in foods that are grown and imported from overseas. GIs can serve a purpose as a badge of local quality and a certification that that product emanates from and is authentically part of that culture. It is also a timely marketing tool at a time of consumer interest in aiding developing countries through supporting local trade (trade-aid). Studies suggest that consumers are

[54] Okediji, 'International Intellectual Property', 1350.
[55] Gervais, 'Traditional Knowledge', 563.

willing to pay a premium for products with a guaranteed origin.[56] As Bowen notes, GIs may help to maintain a diversity of local food cultures which is counter to the globalisation of food.[57] The question is how much of this authenticity is genuine and how much of it is the fabrication of clever marketers?

For example, Bowen discusses the tequila industry, much of which is in the capture of large US-based manufacturers who have gradually eroded the restrictions upon the production of tequila which link it most directly to the relevant region.[58] This is despite or perhaps even because of the protection of the industry attributable to GI recognition. As Raustiala and Munzer observe: 'it is hard . . . to see why a perfect stranger from a far-away community can move *into* the region and thus avail him or herself of the GI. Yet this is precisely what current GI law permits.'[59]

It is also necessary to question the validity of concepts of *terroir* and matters of traditional ('unchanged') methods of production. Justin Hughes provides the example of the entire herd of cattle used to produce Parmigiano-Reggiano cheese being changed over from local cattle to the descendants of North American Holsteins and Dutch Friesians, suggesting a disconnect, at least in some places between the concept of *terroir* and the GI system.[60]

Finally, as Broude highlights, the notion of 'authentic' food artificially attempts to crystallise or capture culture at a particular moment, when in fact culture is constantly changing and evolving.[61]

So the question of authenticity depends not only upon the introduction and recognition of GIs, but also how they are administered and managed. Is the whole concept of a GI nothing more than a manufactured label intended to capture consumers' imagination?

The WIPO Committee on Development and Intellectual Property has recently developed a project entitled 'Intellectual Property and Product Branding for Business Development in Developing Countries and Least-Developed Countries'. This project, which has a three-year time-frame, is intended to help SMEs in developing countries (particularly

[56] Carsten Fink and Keith Maskus, 'The Debate on Geographical Indications in the WTO', in Richard Newfarmer (ed.), *Trade, Doha, and Development: A Window into the Issues* (World Bank, Washington, DC, 2006), 203.

[57] Sarah Bowen, 'Development from within? The Potential for Geographical Indications in the Global South' (2009) 13(2) *Journal of World Intellectual Property* 231, 234.

[58] *Ibid.* 235, concluding that 'the GI for tequila has largely failed to benefit the local population and environment in tequila's region of origin'.

[59] Raustiala and Munzer, 'Global Struggle', 359.

[60] Justin Hughes, 'Champagne, Feta, and Bourbon: The Spirited Debate about Geographical Indications' (2006–7) 58 *Hastings Law Journal* 299, 360.

[61] Broude, 'Taking "Trade and Culture" Seriously', 18–21.

local farmers and producers) to design and implement 'strategies for the appropriate use of IP in product branding', particularly GIs and trade marks.[62] The project document notes that: 'An appropriate branding strategy which makes use, for example, of a geographical indication, a trademark and a fair trade label, adds value to the product, helps raise its market demand and increase economic return for its producers.'[63] Projects will be chosen on the basis that the country already has a legal framework for the protection of GIs. Case studies will be documented and presented at a conference for the purposes of awareness raising.

Current matters under discussion in the WTO arising from the Doha Round of trade negotiations include the proposed establishment of a GI register, and the extension of the higher level of protection to products other than wine and spirits. These proposals are being supported by the so-called 'Friends of GIs' including India, Pakistan, Sri Lanka and Thailand, who perceive that such extensions may advantage these countries in marketing their products, such as basmati rice, in a global environment. On the other side are the US, Australia, Canada, Japan, Taiwan and the Philippines. China's position is unclear.

One justification for the further expansion of the GI system is the provision of better information to consumers about the origin of products. In this respect GIs act like trade marks, providing consumers with information, reducing confusion and search costs.[64] However, this justification applies only to the lower standard of protection under TRIPS, and not the extended protection applied to wine and spirits. The proliferation of labels facilitated by the GI system can in turn lead to further confusion of consumers. Just because it has a GI, does this automatically mean that it is better than one that does not? What is the relationship between a brand and a GI, and which will consumers prefer? What does it mean for producers of 'traditional' foodstuffs in the New World? Does the recognition of a GI require an unbroken tradition associating locality and practice?

Thus it is important that before the GI system is expanded, and that developing country protection is used as the basis to justify such an extension, a clearer rationale is developed for the introduction of such rights. In particular, the issues that need to be resolved include whether

[62] See WIPO, *Project on Intellectual Property and Product Branding for Business Development in Developing Countries and Least-Developed Countries (LDCs)* (2 March 2010) www.wipo.int/meetings/en/doc_details.jsp?doc_id=131716.

[63] *Ibid.* [64] Raustiala and Munzer, 'Global Struggle', 352.

Europe's claims to claw back a large number of terms and names should be permitted in the face of competing New World claims.

V. Conclusions

Emerging from these fractured foundations, do GIs have any meaningful function to serve in the twenty-first century? Evidence suggests that the introduction of GIs in the Australian wine industry prompted a useful refocusing of the wine marketing effort, with an emphasis on consumer friendly labels that told a regional story.[65]

It is possible that developing countries may be able to leverage the GI system to develop GIs that appeal to global markets. However, there is also a risk that the GI system may be hijacked by global corporate interests, who take advantage of the reputation of a particular area without representing its traditional values. As Broude has pointed out, GIs can lead to the creation of invented traditions and imagined communities.[66]

As the Coonawarra dispute, discussed above, demonstrates, the drawing of a GI boundary can unfairly discriminate against those left outside of its boundaries, and possibly, unjustly reward those found within it. Consumers looking to 'do the right thing' can be encouraged to purchase a product manufactured, not by an artisan cheese or wine maker, but by the multinational conglomerate who has purchased the farm within that zone.

Finally, as the history of the Barossa outlined above suggests, there is a danger that culture can be clawed back by Old Europe from its New World descendants. As Parry argued, there is a 'very real risk that specialized products that result from generations of development in communities that are nomadic or diasporic (in other words not rooted in or associated with a specific, bounded and named place) may find themselves ineligible for protection under the proposed new GI system'.[67]

Culture is a difficult concept to pin down, it constantly evolves and matures. The German background of the Barossa settlers has created a rich context for forging a new food culture, combining elements of German traditions and skills with the Australian *terroir*. Heuzenroeder concludes her celebration of Barossa food with a reflection upon the

65 Tony Battaglene, 'The Australian wine industry position on Geographical Indications' (paper presented at Worldwide Symposium on Geographical Indications, Parma, Italy, 27–9 June 2005) www.wipo.int/meetings/en/2005/geo_pmf/presentations/doc/wipo_geo_pmf_05_battaglene.doc.

66 Broude, 'Taking "Trade and Culture" Seriously', 33.

67 Parry, 'Geographical Indications', 378.

fact that, like most of the Western world, food traditions in the Barossa were threatened by the arrival of freezers, fast food and influences from abroad in the 1970s.[68] She asks how the Barossa food culture can survive in the face of such challenges. Would GI protection provide an answer or would it force the reconceptualisation of such foodstuffs to distinguish them from their German antecedents? The cultural and geographical elements of GI protection, presently both contested and uncertain, need to be more clearly articulated before it could be successfully argued that GI protection beyond that currently granted to wine, acts as more than the dead hand of the Old World.

68 Heuzenroeder, *Barossa*, 290–2. A group of producers have got together to create the 'Barossa Food' logo, which may be used by members under licence conditions (Food Barossa Inc., *Food Barossa* (March 2011) www.foodbarossa.com).

13 Branding indigenous peoples' traditional knowledge

Susy Frankel

I. Introduction

For many indigenous peoples, traditional knowledge either has become a tool for their development or has the potential to become such a tool. It is widely agreed that existing intellectual property laws do not protect traditional knowledge and that intellectual property laws were not designed to do so. There are a variety of suggestions about what effective legal mechanisms might be used to protect some aspects of traditional knowledge. Some suggestions have involved either accommodations within some area of intellectual property law or suggestions of changes to intellectual property law. Others propose new regimes of protection that are separate from intellectual property law and are, accordingly, *sui generis* models. The methods and proposals for protection occur in a variety of places. These places include discussions and negotiations in international settings, bilateral and regional trade agreements and protection mechanisms in national laws. One question is what are the effects, or might be the effects, of any of these legal frameworks on indigenous peoples' capacity to use their knowledge for their own development.

Traditional knowledge defies easy definition, but broadly is a term used to encapsulate the knowledge and practices that are maintained and developed by a community and that reflect the cultural heritage of that community. The World Intellectual Property Organization's (WIPO) January 2011 definition provides that traditional knowledge is:

> [I]ntellectual activity in a traditional context, and includes the know-how, skills, innovations, practices and learning that form part of traditional knowledge systems, and knowledge embodying traditional lifestyles of indigenous and local communities, or contained in codified knowledge systems passed between generations and continuously developed following any changes in the environment, geographical conditions and other factors. It is not limited to any specific

technical field, and may include agricultural, environmental and medicinal knowledge, and any traditional knowledge associated with cultural expressions and genetic resources.[1]

Traditional knowledge can relate to a variety of aspects of cultural life including the products of cultural life, such as arts and crafts (traditional cultural expressions, known as TCEs),[2] the features of the environment (biological and genetic resources)[3] and combinations of these things. These groupings reflect intellectual property law's divisions; TCEs are most closely related to copyright, design law and aspects of trade mark law, and biological and genetic resources relate to patents and plant variety rights. An important feature of traditional knowledge, however, is that the same knowledge can transcend both categories. The knowledge of a plant may include its healing properties. That plant may have become so important to a community that songs are written about it and it appears as part of the buildings or artefacts of cultural life. There are, in other words, many manifestations of traditional knowledge.

Traditional knowledge is not only information to many indigenous peoples; it is part of their identity. In a broad and non-legal sense of the concept of brand, indigenous peoples are in part identifiable and, thus, branded by association with particular manifestations of their knowledge. When others make use of that knowledge without the permission of indigenous peoples and when the outputs resulting from the use of that knowledge are severed from the indigenous people, from whom the knowledge was sourced, two kinds of complaints arise. The first is that the indigenous peoples' identity has been impacted adversely and the second is that no benefits that flow from the use are returned to the indigenous peoples. Thus, the reasons that indigenous peoples seek protection for traditional knowledge are many and varied, but broadly fall into two areas. The first is protection against offensive use of traditional knowledge, and the second is some kind of control that means indigenous peoples' consent must be obtained for uses of their traditional knowledge. Consent may be separate from any benefit sharing or could be given with the condition that some kind of benefit returns to the indigenous people from the commercial use. Through these means and indigenous

1 *The Protection of Traditional Knowledge: Revised Objectives and Principles*, WIPO Document WIPO/GRTKF/IC/18/5 (10 January 2011), annex 18.

2 For an explanation of what is meant by traditional cultural expressions, see *The Protection of Traditional Cultural Expressions: Draft Articles*, WIPO Document prepared by the Secretariat, WIPO/GRTKF/IC/18/4 REV (14 April 2011).

3 For an explanation of what is meant by genetic resources, see Draft *Objectives and Principles Relating to Intellectual Property and Genetic Resources Prepared at IWG 3*, WIPO Document prepared by the Secretariat, WIPO/GRTKF/IC/18/9 (17 March 2011).

peoples' own development of their knowledge, indigenous peoples hope to improve their economic and cultural situation.

Because indigenous peoples' own identity is marketable, it is a kind of brand. The attraction of the exotic, of the natural and previously 'undiscovered' remedy, are examples of how Western consumers are attracted to the products of traditional knowledge. Around the world there are many examples of how Westerners make use of indigenous culture. Some examples include the Fiat Motor Company using a Māori haka,[4] the Lego company using Māori names,[5] and the artwork of Aborigines in Australia featuring on tourist advertisements. But what advantages and disadvantages lie in branding traditional knowledge in this way? Could indigenous peoples extract even greater value from their traditional knowledge by using the branding tools of intellectual property law? Those tools are primarily trade mark and geographical indications. Is either of these legal regimes of any assistance to protecting traditional knowledge? Is either of these legal regimes of any assistance to indigenous peoples' development?

There are broadly two ways in which branding traditional knowledge is relevant to these wider questions. The first is what might be described as active branding and the second is defensive branding. Active branding is when indigenous peoples seek to brand aspects of their own traditional knowledge in order to exploit that knowledge. Defensive branding techniques are those that may exist to prevent others from branding indigenous peoples' traditional knowledge. This chapter discusses each of these approaches and the pros and cons of each for indigenous peoples.

II. Branding as a positive strategy

The core intellectual property rights that relate directly to branding are trade marks and geographical indications (GIs).[6]

Trade marks' primary function is to protect the trade mark, associated with a product of one trader, from those of other traders. One of the features of trade mark law is that the association is with the product sourced from a trader. Consumers do not have to know the exact details

[4] See Fiat Idea Black Label (spot) (30 March 2007) YouTube www.youtube.com/watch?v=QIgksCRFwnI.

[5] Kim Griggs, 'Lego site irks Māori sympathiser' (21 November 2002) *Wired* www.wired.com/culture/lifestyle/news/2002/11/56451.

[6] Trade marks are registered rights. Article 15 of the TRIPS Agreement requires that WTO members provide for registered trade marks. In addition countries often have protection for unregistered marks, particularly under the doctrine of passing off: Agreement on Trade-Related Aspects of Intellectual Property Rights (TRIPS), opened for signature 15 April 1994, 1869 UNTS 299 (entered into force 1 January 1996).

of who the trader is or who the trade mark owner is. Rather, what is important is the association of the trade mark with the products.[7]

There are a variety of ways in which GIs can be protected. There is much more commonality between the trade marks regimes of different countries than is found in the protection of GIs, over which there is considerable disagreement.[8] Broadly, however, the function of GIs is to identify goods that are made in a certain place. The GI indicates that the products were made to the standard associated with the type of goods coming from that place.[9]

In this part trade marks and GIs are discussed in relation to the World Intellectual Property Organization (WIPO) work on objectives and principles that relate to the protection of traditional knowledge.

WIPO undertook an extensive fact-finding mission in order to understand the issues that traditional knowledge holders[10] face. This mission developed in to a series of objectives and principles that were put together under the auspices of an intergovernmental committee (WIPO–IGC). The WIPO–IGC now has authority to negotiate a 'text-based agreement'.[11] The WIPO objectives and principles appear in related versions with subject specific differences, depending on if the document is addressing TCEs or genetic resources. The objectives are perhaps most developed, but still subject to negotiation, in relation to TCEs and so those discussed here. Also TCEs potentially include things, such as signs and symbols, that are closely analogous to the existing intellectual property rights that are of primary relevance to branding. TCEs are defined as:

> any form, tangible or intangible, or a combination thereof, in which traditional culture and knowledge are embodied and have been passed on from generation to generation, tangible or intangible forms of creativity of the beneficiaries[12] . . . but not limited to:

[7] For the international obligations to trade mark protection see TRIPS, art. 15 in particular.

[8] The TRIPS Agreement, provides some protection for GIs in arts. 22–24. Extending this protection is being negotiated, but no binding commitments to extend the protection have been entered into.

[9] For a discussion of some aspects of comparison between trade mark and GIs, see Lasse A. Sondergaard Christiensen and Janne Britt Hansen, 'A Contrast with Trade Mark Law: The Permitted Use of Geographical Indications', in Jeremy Phillips (ed.), *Trade Marks at the Limit* (Edward Elgar, Cheltenham; Northampton, MA, 2006), 34.

[10] In the WIPO documents discussed in this chapter the term 'traditional knowledge beneficiaries' is used. This term avoids the disputed concept of ownership. 'Holder' reflects the values that some indigenous people regard as important. That is that the current generation is the 'holder' (or guardian) of knowledge for future generations.

[11] See Intergovernmental Committee, WIPO www.wipo.int/tk/en/igc.

[12] The beneficiaries are defined in draft art. 2 and include indigenous peoples, communities and nations and other options shown in the draft.

(a) phonetic or verbal expressions, such as stories, epics, legends, poetry, riddles and other narratives; words, signs, names, and symbols;
(b) musical or sound expressions, such as songs, rhythms, and instrumental music, the sounds which are the expression of rituals.[13]

The objectives are several and it is useful to consider how the objectives in particular might support indigenous peoples in the branding of their traditional knowledge. The objectives include that the protection of traditional cultural expressions should aim to:

(i) Recognize value;
(ii) Promote respect;
(iii) Meet the actual needs of communities;
(iv) Prevent the misappropriation and misuse of traditional cultural expressions;
(v) Empower communities;
(vi) Support customary practices and community cooperation;
(vii) Contribute to safeguarding traditional cultures;
(viii) Encourage community innovation and creativity;
(ix) Promote intellectual and artistic freedom, research and cultural exchange on equitable terms;
(x) Contribute to cultural diversity;
(xi) Promote the [community] development of indigenous peoples and traditional and other cultural communities and legitimate trading activities;
(xii) Preclude unauthorized IP rights; and
(xiii) Enhance certainty, transparency and mutual confidence.[14]

The purpose of recognising value as an objective is aimed at ensuring that the values attached to traditional knowledge are the values of the traditional knowledge beneficiaries, which include 'social, cultural, spiritual, economic, scientific, intellectual, commercial and educational' value. Branding can be directed to many of these values. It might also undermine them.

Commercialisation does not always promote respect. However, it can do so. An international agreement cannot on its own promote respect. The underlying assumption of this objective is that the protection mechanisms must promote respect even if at a practical level the outcome of respect cannot be guaranteed. From a branding perspective this is an interesting objective because the classic legal tool of branding, the trade

[13] Protection of Traditional Cultural Expressions: Draft Articles, document prepared for the Intergovernmental Committee on Intellectual Property and Genetic Resources, Traditional Knowledge and Folklore, Eighteenth Session, WIPO Document WIPO/GRTKF/IC/18/4 (18 February 2011), draft art. 1(1) www.wipo.int/edocs/mdocs/tk/en/wipo_grtkf_ic_18/wipo_grtkf_ic_18_4.pdf.
[14] See WIPO, Protection of Traditional Cultural Expressions: Draft Articles, annex.

mark, is premised on reputation and goodwill.[15] Goodwill is not quite the same as respect. The law may recognise the goodwill in a trade mark, but the business behind it may not be respected by all.

One of the functions of geographical indications can be to add value. A cheese might be desirable because, for example, it is Roquefort, and the added value that consumers perceive in champagne is the archetype of how a GI adds value. GIs, therefore, arguably have the potential to promote respect, through added value, but unless there is a business behind a GI it will not be a success. Therefore, to promote GIs as a tool for development is not a good strategy as it will neither fulfil the objective of meeting 'the actual needs of communities', nor will it empower communities. Communities are more likely to be empowered by economic development not branding strategies alone. Successful branding strategies usually work when there are products to sell.

GIs have arguably been successful in Europe as a way of replacing subsidies and giving returns to European farming.[16] GIs can be used as a development strategy for Western farmers and rural development,[17] but this does not necessarily mean that GIs can be an effective strategy for developing country farmers or indigenous peoples. Although, the European Union, in particular, suggests that GIs could be effective for developing countries. The European Commission's website states:[18]

> Over the years European countries have taken the lead in identifying and protecting their Geographical Indications . . . However, GIs are also important for developing countries. GIs can protect and preserve intellectual property related to traditional cultures, geographical diversity and production methods. All nations have a wide range of local products that correspond to the concept of a GI – Basmati rice or Darjeeling tea – but only a few are already known as such or protected globally.

[15] Once a trade mark is registered neither reputation nor goodwill need to be established in order to enforce the right. The registration is the right. However, the rationale basis of trade mark law relates to reputation and goodwill.

[16] See European Commission, *Intellectual Property: Geographical Indications* (19 May 2011) http://ec.europa.eu/trade/creating-opportunities/trade-topics/intellectual-property/geographical-indications See also Daphne Zagrofos, 'Geographical Indications and Socio-Economic Development' (Working Paper No. 3, IQsensato, December 2008) www.iqsensato.org/wp-content/uploads/2009/02/iqsensato-wp-3-zografos-dec-2008.pdf.

[17] Daniele Giovannucci, Elizabeth Barham and Richard Pirog, 'Defining and Marketing "Local" Foods: Geographical Indications for US Products' (2009) 13 *Journal of World Intellectual Property* 94.

[18] See European Commission, *Intellectual Property*.

Better protection of GIs can be a useful contribution to increasing income, in particular in rural areas. It also encourages quality production and can promote the development of tourism. GIs grant protection to a community and not to individual right holders.

Since consumers are often ready to pay more for GI products, people from outside the region may be tempted to appropriate the GI for their own products. This not only misleads consumers, but it also dilutes the GI value as well as discourages producers from making investment decisions or launching expensive marketing campaigns.

The success stories of European GIs are often about high-end consumer products sold predominantly to wealthy consumers in developed countries. This is not yet, and may never be, a realistic target for GIs from developing countries. One or two success stories can be shown, but there are very few GIs in India, for example, when compared with the number in Europe.[19] Another issue is that GIs may not be effective tools for indigenous peoples who are not necessarily aiming to protect particular products. The needs of indigenous peoples' more localised communities are vastly different from large developing country interests.

The WIPO objectives suggest that the needs of the community are to be:

guided by the aspirations and expectations expressed directly by indigenous peoples and communities and by traditional and other cultural communities, respect their rights under national/domestic and international law, and contribute to the welfare and sustainable economic, cultural, environmental and social development of such peoples and communities.[20]

Successful GI stories seem to either be of Western businesses or large developing country interests and simply are not a realistic or effective option for many communities for whom the protection of traditional knowledge is vital for their development.

The objective of contributing to the safeguarding of traditional cultures is delicate balance. One concern of indigenous peoples is that commodification of their culture will contribute to its demise. Branding strategies, however, can contribute to supporting culture. GIs in particular, however, tend to support a static version of culture, rather than a dynamic version. A GI may be granted because of the traditional ingredient or processes lying behind products made in a particular place. Many indigenous peoples are interested in the preservation of their culture, but not in a

[19] Zagrofos, 'Geographical Indications', 8, lists that there were 268 GIs in India at 2006. Many people in developed countries could probably name that many European GIs, even if they did not know whether they were registered GIs or not.

[20] WIPO, Protection of Traditional Cultural Expressions: Draft Articles, annex (iii).

static way. Rather, they seek a way that can be used for development. That does not mean that indigenous peoples are not concerned about safeguarding tradition, but it is arguably not the same concern as European GI users.

The brand should, therefore, reflect the values of the indigenous peoples. This is where indigenous communities may find that certification marks are useful. Certification marks, are a mode of protecting standards in goods. Some geographical indications are protected by certification marks or collective marks in countries such as the United States. It is arguable that certification marks are more open to innovation because the registration authority does not police the standards behind the mark in the same way that the registration bureaucracy has quality control in relation to European GIs.[21]

The 'Fair Trade' label is an example of a successful certification mark. Whereas some indigenous peoples' authenticity labelling through certification marks have been less successful.[22] Graber and Lai have suggested that the certification mark approach is a bottom-up approach, which is more likely to assist those seeking to protect traditional knowledge than a top-down approach.[23]

In New Zealand the 'Toi Iho' mark, a certification mark applied to Māori art and craft, operated successfully for a period of time. Māori products with this mark indicated a certain quality. When government funding was withdrawn from Toi Iho it went through a period where its future was uncertain, but it is now managed and run by Māori. Many see this as preferable to how it had previously been administered by a government-funded organisation.[24]

The challenge with branding traditional knowledge as a way of protecting cultural identity is to ensure that the brand does not overtake the culture and that the brand is used to support cultural outputs, rather than become the driving force in and of itself.

[21] See Justin Hughes, 'Champagne, Feta and Bourbon: The Spirited Debate about Geographical Indications' (2006) 58 *Hastings Law Journal* 299, 340, and the discussion of how French winemakers complain about the restrictions on innovation caused by the *appellation d'origine contrôlée* (French wine form of a GI).

[22] Christoph B. Graber and Jessica Christine Lai, 'Indigenous Cultural Heritage and Fair Trade: Voluntary Certification Standards in the Light of WIPO and WTO Law and Policymaking' (Working Paper No. 11, University of Lucerne, March 2011) www.unilu.ch/files/i-call_working_paper_2011_01_graber__lai_fairtrade.pdf. See especially the discussion of the Australian Authenticity Mark for Aboriginal products and why it was not successful (8–12).

[23] *Ibid.* See also M. Chon, 'Marks of Rectitude' (2009) 77 *Fordham Law Review* 2311.

[24] DigitalMaori, 'Toi Iho in Māori control (finally!)' (22 May 2010) Tangata Whenua http://news.tangatawhenua.com/archives/5166.

Ultimately the use of trade marks or GIs should not be self-defeating. It should not confine the aspirations of indigenous peoples' use of traditional knowledge. Perhaps more importantly, however, these tools should not be held out as providing more than they can deliver.

The WIPO objective that refers to precluding unauthorised intellectual property rights covers a multitude of possible unauthorised uses. There is undoubtedly a market for products that utilise or embody traditional knowledge. If this were not so, there would be no international debate over its protection. While it is not a sufficient legal test to say that what is worth using or having is worth protecting,[25] that concept at least indicates that there are many businesses interested in using aspects of traditional knowledge. There are those who will use traditional knowledge to understand more about genetic resources, or as some kind of guide to prospect what genetic resource may be useful. However, separate from this kind of use of traditional knowledge for product development is a kind of value by association with indigenous peoples or their traditional knowledge. This can involve all kinds of uses of symbols and motifs of indigenous peoples. Countries such as Canada, Australia and New Zealand use these as part of their national identity.[26]

The uses of indigenous peoples' traditional knowledge are many. In the area of branding one particular occurrence is a third party using indigenous knowledge or symbols as their brand. Frequently this is done without permission. Often no permission was sought because as a purely legal matter no permission was needed.

The problem is that often when third parties make use of traditional knowledge they do it in a non-exact way. This non-exactness can vary from the benign to the offensive. This branding by third parties has led to a variety of difficulties, some obvious and some not so obvious. The obvious include the lack of permission and no legal basis on which the permission must be sought; the lack of sharing of any benefits with the indigenous peoples from whom the knowledge is sourced; the lack of legal redress for the misuse and offensive uses of traditional knowledge to name a few. An overarching problem with these and other difficulties is that the user of the traditional knowledge may very well end up in a better

[25] Although there are many intellectual property rights owners who often assert as much and sometimes courts appear to adopt that approach. See for example *LB (Plastics) Ltd* v. *Swish Products Ltd* [1979] RPC 623, where it was said in the context of copyright that a rough practical test is what is worth copying is worth protecting.

[26] Susy Frankel and Megan Richardson, 'Cultural Property and "the Public Domain": Case Studies from New Zealand and Australia', in Christoph Antons (ed.), *Traditional Knowledge, Traditional Cultural Expressions and Intellectual Property Law in the Asia-Pacific Region* (Kluwer Law International, Alphen aan den Rijn, 2009), 275.

position economically than those from whom they have 'appropriated' the traditional knowledge.

Some businesses are unabashed by these issues and others do not want to be seen as doing 'wrong' and regard the possibility of moral claims of misappropriation as bad corporate governance. When the Lego company, for example, found out that Māori did not like the way it was using sacred Māori words on its trade-marked 'bionicle' toys, it changed its behaviour. Lego's first reaction was that as a purely Western legal matter it could use the words, but later it seemed to adjust its policy because the incident did not sit well with its corporate image.[27]

The problems, however, can be more extreme. An example is the uses of kava. Kava is a plant that has many traditional uses associated with Pacific Island countries including Samoa, Fiji, the Solomon Islands, Tonga and Vanuatu. The roots of the plants can be made into a drink which has sedative and anaesthetic uses. Some of these countries have significant export industries of kava. Many non-traditional users of kava have sold various products allegedly associated with kava worldwide. Some of these products seem to be unsafe, resulting in the European Union banning the importation of all kava products, including the ones safely and well made by the traditional knowledge communities of the Pacific Islands.[28]

Overall the purpose of indigenous peoples' branding their knowledge would be for them to make commercial use out of their knowledge. Many of the examples of commercialised uses of traditional knowledge are uses of third parties and the third-party brand is the dominant brand. An example might be a pharmaceutical, where it is the name of the pharmaceutical that is the brand, and not the traditional knowledge that led to the development of the pharmaceutical. Although the pharmaceutical may in its packaging or marketing allude to being based on, or using, the natural healing powers of a plant or a group of people. In such situations the question might arise: for whose benefit is the branding of the traditional knowledge? It may well be more for the pharmaceutical company than the indigenous people. Branding is only useful if indigenous peoples have some kind of control over uses of their traditional knowledge and agree to the exploitation of their knowledge.

[27] In a film documentary *New Zealand up for Grabs* (directed by Toby Mills and Moana Maniapoto, 2006) a representative of Lego was interviewed indicating that after the incident Lego would set up procedures to make sure it did not occur again.

[28] See Meredith Kolsky Lewis, 'Safety Standards and Indigenous Products', in Meredith Kolsky Lewis and Susy Frankel (eds.), *International Economic Law and National Autonomy* (Cambridge University Press, Cambridge and New York, 2010), 169.

The objective of precluding unauthorised intellectual property rights raises many issues, such as what is unfair. Precluding unauthorised intellectual property rights may also be achieved through defensive strategies discussed in the next section.

III. Defensive branding

Safeguarding against third-party uses

Trade mark registration offices may refuse to register applications for trade marks for a variety of reasons, including that they do not meet the criteria for registration or they cannot be registered because they are in some way prohibited from registration. If indigenous peoples do not consider that a trade mark should be registered, they may have grounds on which to object to registration. In many jurisdictions anyone can object to the registration of a trade mark if it is likely to lead to confusion in the market. This ground is frequently not available to indigenous people because they do not trade in the relevant market.

Many national laws provide that trade marks which are immoral or contain scandalous matters are not registrable.[29] In other jurisdictions morality can be a ground for refusing registration as a trade mark. Under New Zealand law, a trade mark may not be registered if it is 'offensive to a significant section of the community, including Māori'.[30] On a comparative basis to other jurisdictions this is a strong provision.[31] However, it is limited to preventing registration and cannot function to prevent all offensive uses of traditional knowledge. However, because the registration of trade marks is desirable for many businesses, the possibility of a refusal of trade mark registration may cause businesses not to use words, signs or symbols that might not be registrable in the future.

The real difficulty arises, however, when business are not using the traditional knowledge as a trade mark, but are nevertheless using

[29] In the United States, for example, § 1052(a) of the Lanham Act 15 USC provides:

> No trademark by which the goods of the applicant may be distinguished from the goods of others shall be refused registration on the principal register on account of its nature unless it (a) consists of or comprises immoral, deceptive or scandalous matter; or matter which may disparage or falsely suggest a connection with persons, living or dead, institutions, beliefs, or national symbols, or bring them into contempt or disrepute.

[30] Trade Marks Act 2002 (NZ) s. 17.

[31] See Susy Frankel, 'Trademarks and Traditional Knowledge and Cultural Intellectual Property Rights', in Graeme B. Dinwoodie and Mark D. Janis (eds.), *Trademark Law and Theory: A Handbook of Contemporary Research* (Edward Elgar, Cheltenham; Northampton, MA, 2008), 433, where I compare the Lanham Act provisions with the New Zealand provisions.

traditional knowledge inappropriately or offensively. In the Lego example, discussed above, the way in which the Māori names were used on the toys was analogous to the use of the names as trade marks. A non- trade mark use example was McDonald's' use of a Māori symbol. McDonald's produced a paper tray mat which depicted various New Zealand 'icons': a kiwi, a native tree and a hetiki. The heitiki is a greenstone pendant personifying a human ancestor. One Māori person said:

> As a Māori I find the depiction of the hetiki in that context inappropriate. The offence felt is not easy to express, however, it could be likened to having a picture of the person on a doormat and having all manner of people scuffing and wiping their dirty shoes all over the mat. It is not obvious from the image that it is based on a reproduction of an actual hetiki, but had this been the case the offence would be even greater. It would be the equivalent of having the picture of someone dear to me or someone whom I recognise as a person of great mana (prestige) on the doormat.[32]

McDonald's was not using the Māori heitiki as a trade mark, but such a trade mark use could easily be contemplated.

Non-trade-mark uses are a good example of exactly why indigenous peoples seek a different kind of protection from that which is found in intellectual property law. That is also why some people oppose the protection of traditional knowledge. It is important, however, to recognise that there are not just two incompatible views. Protection of traditional knowledge, and the degree of protection available, have been and continue to be based on policy decisions which reflect different needs and practices in different countries. One of those factors is how the protection of traditional knowledge and the existing intellectual property system can work together for the benefit of all members of society. The challenge is how those aspirations can be met. The WIPO principles provide considerable guidance to national legislatures even if they are not, as yet, binding.

Mechanisms, such as that found in New Zealand, of allowing objection to offensive marks, can be seen not just as protecting traditional knowledge, but as a point of interface between the intellectual property system and the protection of traditional knowledge. In New Zealand there is no *sui generis* system for the protection of traditional knowledge. In a sense, the interface exists before the actual protection. Whether there should be a form of *sui generis* protection is the subject

[32] Catharine Davis, 'Te Matauranga Māori I te Taha o te Mataraunga' (LLM Research paper, Victoria University, 1997), 32.

of a claim before the Waitangi Tribunal, which was reported in July 2011.[33]

Resorting to trade marks and geographical indications as the best options available

In New Zealand there have been some instances of Māori applying for trade marks seemingly because they are the only form of protection available for names or symbols. Even if a trade mark is obtained, it might not serve to protect the Māori interest in the mātauranga Māori (traditional knowledge) behind the trade mark. Māori place names are an interesting example.

In New Zealand there is no register for GIs and so, if Māori are to seek any registration for their unique and culturally important geographical names they have to use the trade mark process. I am not suggesting that a GI register would overcome this issue because many Māori want to register geographical names for non-commercial reasons, which would not make the place names registrable as GIs. These non-commercial reasons include that Māori do not want the name traded in if it is not respectful of the mātauranga Māori that lies behind the name. The trade mark process will not help because the geographical names are not registrable because they are not distinctive. An example of this problem has arisen concerning the name known as New Zealand's longest place name. This name has considerable tourist value. The name and story is as follows:

> Near Porangahau in Hawke's Bay is an unassuming hill known as 'Taumata whakatangi hangakoauau o tamatea turi pukakapiki maunga horo nuku pokai whenua kitanatahu', which translates into English as 'the place where Tamatea, the man with the big knees, who slid, climbed and swallowed mountains, known as "landeater", played his flute to his loved one'. Locals simply call it Taumata Hill.
>
> Tamatea was a famous chief and warrior. One day, while travelling through the back of Porangahau, he encountered another tribe and had to fight them to get past. During the fight his brother was killed. Tamatea was so grieved over the

[33] A claim brought by Māori against the Crown in New Zealand, known as WAI 262. See Waitangi Tribunal, Ko Aotearoa Tēnei: A Report into Claims Concerning New Zealand Law and Policy Affecting Māori Culture and Identity (2011). The Waitangi Tribunal is a quasi-judicial body that makes recommendations to the government on claims that the Treaty of Waitangi ('Te Tiriti o Waitangi') has been breached under the Treaty of Waitangi Act 1975 (NZ). Hearings relating to the WAI 262 claim were completed in June 2007. At the time of writing the report of the Tribunal is pending. For a discussion of the Treaty of Waitangi, see Claudia Orange, *The Treaty of Waitangi* (Allen & Unwin, Wellington, 1987).

loss of his brother that he stayed at the battle site for some days. Each morning he would sit on the hill and play a lament on what is called the koauau or Māori flute.[34]

In order to gain some protection over the name, one kaitiaki (guardian) of the traditional knowledge registered the name with a slight variation.[35] This, however, from the trade mark owner's perspective is unsatisfactory. First, the registration is not the proper name and, second, it does not reflect the true aim of seeking protection, which is that the name is honoured by the present generation as respect for the past and as guardians for the future. This registration of the variation also gives no rights to control commercialisation of the name.

Another example from Māori culture related to the well-known haka, of which the first words are 'Kamate Kamate'. One of Ngati Toa's (Māori iwi) most celebrated taonga (treasures) is that haka.[36] There have been various attempts to register aspects of the lyrics as trade marks and various oppositions to those attempts a registration. There is one registration of a stylised logo incorporating the word 'Kamate'.[37] Also, the haka has been subject to at least two claims before the Waitangi Tribunal. One of those claims relates to what is known as WAI 262, the flora fauna and cultural intellectual claim.[38] The other relates specifically to the losses suffered by the Ngati Toa iwi. In the latter claim the Crown has recognised that Ngati Toa has some kind of right over the haka known as Kamate Kamate.[39] The Treaty of Waitiangi Settlement process that follows such a proceeding records the 'authorship and significance of the haka' to Ngati Toa. It is thought that this will allow Ngati Toa to 'address their concerns with the haka'. The Crown apparently does not expect Ngati Toa to receive royalties or veto a performance of the haka.[40] The exact boundaries of those rights have not been firmly set in precise legal terms. However, the Treaty of Waitangi Settlement process has resulted

34 See *History and Culture: The Longest Place Name in New Zealand* (2011), 100% Pure New Zealand, www.newzealand.com/travel/sights-activities/scenic-highlights/history-culture/sh-ThelongestplacenameinNewZealand.cfm/searchcontext/0.html.

35 New Zealand Trade Mark numbers 710608 and 732842.

36 Hēni Collins, *Ka Mate Ka Ora: The Spirit of Te Rauparaha* (Steele Roberts, Wellington, 2010).

37 Trade mark 827077 a stylised logo incorporating the word 'kamte' has been registered. See also trade mark application 814533.

38 See above n. 33.

39 NZPA and Yvonne Tahana, 'Ka Mate Haka rights part of $300m Treaty deal', 11 February 2009 www.nzherald.co.nz/nz/news/article.cfm?c_id=1&objectid=10556148.

40 *Ibid.*

in an agreement between Ngati Toa and the New Zealand Rugby Union over the use of the haka.[41]

From a branding perspective the haka is arguably recognisable as also connected to the All Blacks. Ngati Toa indicated that they are happy for the haka to be used by the All Blacks, but that commercialisation of it may be a different matter.

Outside of New Zealand it is unlikely that people seeing the haka, Kamate Kamate, would know to which Māori it is taonga treasure. From a trade mark perspective that does not matter, because as discussed above, it is the idea that there is an identifiable source that the trade mark is connected to, not the ability of consumers to legally identify the source.

From a branding perspective there is another interesting issue. The brand has multiple aspects which it can be associated with including Māori; Ngati Toa; the All Blacks and New Zealand. One thing that this example shows is that the resolution of some traditional knowledge claims simply cannot be solved through known intellectual property instruments and that creative thinking has an important role in working out how to protect traditional knowledge in particular circumstances. That intellectual property law does not provide a complete solution for the protection of traditional knowledge is a point that is generally known, but it is often thought that trade marks or GIs might provide a solution. The haka example demonstrates that this is often not necessarily true. The trade mark is secondary. It is not the solution.

IV. Conclusion

In order to protect many aspects of traditional knowledge the usual branding strategies of trade marks and GIs are a misfit because they do not achieve the goals of indigenous peoples in protecting traditional knowledge. Particularly, the goal of developing knowledge for indigenous peoples' own economic development needs. Sometimes the tools of branding can be useful, but this is only where the traditional knowledge has already been developed so there is marketable product or something well known enough, such as Kamate Kamate, that it achieves a protectable reputation of some kind. If indigenous peoples have control over their traditional knowledge, then they are free to choose whether to brand their culture or not.

[41] For many years New Zealand's national rugby team has performed Kamate Kamate, particularly before international test matches.

Index

Cambridge Intellectual Property and Information Law

Titles in the series (formerly known as *Cambridge Studies in Intellectual Property Rights*)

BRAD SHERMAN AND LIONEL BENTLY
The Making of Modern Intellectual Property Law
978-0-521-56363-5

IRINI A. STAMATOUDI
Copyright and Multimedia Products: A Comparative Analysis
978-0-521-80819-4

PASCAL KAMINA
Film Copyright in the European Union
978-0-52-77053-8

HUW BEVERLY-SMITH
The Commercial Appropriation of Personality
978-0-521-80014-3

MARK J. DAVISON
The Legal Protection of Databases
978-0-521-80257-4

ROBERT BURRELL AND ALLISON COLEMAN
Copyright Exceptions: The Digital Impact
978-0-521-84726-1

HUW BEVERLY-SMITH, ANSGAR OHLY AND AGNÈS LUCAS-SCHLOETTER
Privacy, Property and Personality: Civil Law Perspectives on Commercial Appropriation
978-0-521-82080-6

PHILIP LEITH
Software and Patents in Europe
978-0-521-86839-6

LIONEL BENTLY, JENNIFER DAVIS AND JANE C. GINSBURG
Trade Marks and Brands: An Interdisciplinary Critique
978-0-521-88965-0

GEERTRUI VAN OVERWALLE
Gene Patents and Clearing Models
978-0-521-89673-3

JONATHAN CURCI
The Protection of Biodiversity and Traditional Knowledge in International Law of Intellectual Property
978-0-521-19944-5

LIONEL BENTLY, JENNIFER DAVIS AND JANE C. GINSBURG
Copyright and Piracy: An Interdisciplinary Critique
978-0-521-19343-6

MEGAN RICHARDSON AND JULIAN THOMAS

Framing Intellectual Property: Legal Constructions of Creativity and Appropriation 1840–1940
978-0-521-76756-9

DEV GANGJEE
Relocating the Law of Geographical Indications
978-0-521-19202-6

ANDREW KENYON, NG-LOY WEE LOON AND MEGAN RICHARDSON
The Law of Reputation and Brands in the Asia Pacific
978-1-107-01772-6